Multilingual Urban Scandinavia

MULTILINGUAL MATTERS
Series Editor: John Edwards, *St. Francis Xavier University, Canada*

Multilingual Matters series publishes books on bilingualism, bilingual education, immersion education, second language learning, language policy, multiculturalism. The editor is particularly interested in 'macro' level studies of language policies, language maintenance, language shift, language revival and language planning. Books in the series discuss the relationship between language in a broad sense and larger cultural issues, particularly identity related ones.

Full details of all the books in this series and of all our other publications can be found on http://www.multilingual-matters.com, or by writing to Multilingual Matters, St Nicholas House, 31–34 High Street, Bristol BS1 2AW, UK.

MULTILINGUAL MATTERS
Series Editor: John Edwards, *St. Francis Xavier University, Canada*

Multilingual Urban Scandinavia
New Linguistic Practices

Edited by
Pia Quist and Bente A. Svendsen

MULTILINGUAL MATTERS
Bristol • Buffalo • Toronto

Library of Congress Cataloging in Publication Data
A catalog record for this book is available from the Library of Congress.
Multilingual Urban Scandinavia: New Linguistic Practices/Edited by Pia Quist and Bente A. Svendsen.
Multilingual Matters: 142
Includes bibliographical references and index.
1. Scandinavia--Languages. 2. Sociolinguistics--Scandinavia. 3. Languages in contact--Scandinavia.
I. Quist, Pia. II. Svendsen, Bente A.
P40.45.S34M85 2010
306.44'60948–dc22 2010026208

British Library Cataloguing in Publication Data
A catalogue entry for this book is available from the British Library.

ISBN-13: 978-1-84769-313-6 (hbk)
ISBN-13: 978-1-84769-312-9 (pbk)

Multilingual Matters
UK: St Nicholas House, 31–34 High Street, Bristol, BS1 2AW, UK.
USA: UTP, 2250 Military Road, Tonawanda, NY 14150, USA.
Canada: UTP, 5201 Dufferin Street, North York, Ontario M3H 5T8, Canada.

Copyright © 2010 Pia Quist, Bente A. Svendsen and the authors of individual chapters.

All rights reserved. No part of this work may be reproduced in any form or by any means without permission in writing from the publisher.

The policy of Multilingual Matters/Channel View Publications is to use papers that are natural, renewable and recyclable products, made from wood grown in sustainable forests. In the manufacturing process of our books, and to further support our policy, preference is given to printers that have FSC and PEFC Chain of Custody certification.The FSC and/or PEFC logos will appear on those books wher   e full certification has been granted to the printer concerned.

Typeset by Techset Composition Ltd., Salisbury, UK.

Contents

Contributors vii
Preface xi
Introduction xiii

Part 1: Research on Linguistic Practices in Multilingual Urban Scandinavia

1 Research on Language in Multilingual Urban Settings in Sweden 1
   S. Boyd

2 The Sociolinguistic Study of Youth and Multilingual Practices in Denmark: An Overview 6
   P. Quist

3 Linguistic Practices in Multilingual Urban Contexts in Norway: An Overview 12
   B.A. Svendsen

Part 2: Syntax, Morphology and Lexicon

4 Extended Uses of 'Sån' (Such) among Adolescents in Multilingual Malmö, Sweden 17
   L. Ekberg

5 Subject–Verb Order Variation in the Swedish of Young People in Multilingual Urban Areas 31
   N. Ganuza

6 On Some Structural Aspects of Norwegian Spoken among Adolescents in Multilingual Settings in Oslo 49
   T. Opsahl and I. Nistov

Part 3: Pronunciation

7 Pronunciation in Swedish Multiethnolect 65
   P. Bodén

8   Prosody in the Copenhagen Multiethnolect 79
     G.F. Hansen and N. Pharao

Part 4: Identity, Code and Practice

9   Transnational Identifications among Adolescents in
     Suburban Sweden 96
     C. Haglund

10   The Use of Multiethnic Youth Language in Oslo 111
     F. Aarsæther

11   Polylingualism in the Steak House: Exploring Linguistic
     Practices in Late Modern Copenhagen 127
     J.S. Møller

12   Literary Use of Multiethnic Youth Language: Noninversion
     in Swedish Fiction 142
     R. Källström

13   'Playing with Words as if it was a Rap Game': Hip-Hop Street
     Language in Oslo 156
     J.S. Knudsen

Part 5: Perceptions

14   'Rinkeby Swedish' in the Mind of the Beholder. Studying
     Listener Perceptions of Language Variation in Multilingual
     Stockholm 170
     E. Bijvoet and K. Fraurud

15   Linguistic Practice and Stereotypes among Copenhagen
     Adolescents... 189
     M. Maegaard

16   One of My Kind? Language and Ethnicity among
     Danish Adolescents 207
     M.V. Christensen

References... 225

Index 247

Contributors

Finn Aarsæther is Associate Professor in Norwegian Linguistics at Oslo University College, Faculty of Education and International Studies. He did his PhD on code-switching among Pakistani-Norwegian school children and has afterwards been doing research on multiethnic youth language in Oslo, as part of the UPUS Project that studies developmental processes in urban linguistic settings in Norway. His research interest is also directed toward education of students with minority background in Norwegian Elementary and Secondary Schools, as well as in transnational contexts.

Ellen Bijvoet has a PhD in Scandinavian Languages from Uppsala University. She has held positions as postdoctoral Fellow at Ghent University, Belgium, and as researcher at the Rinkeby Institute of Multilingual Research, Sweden. At present she is Assistant Professor of Bilingualism at Stockholm University. Her research and publications focus on bilingualism, minority languages, language attitudes, folk linguistics and young peoples' language and language use in multilingual context. She is currently involved in the project Sociolinguistic Awareness and Language Attitudes in Multilingual Contexts within the research program High-Level Proficiency in Second Language Use.

Petra Bodén has a PhD in phonetics and is currently a researcher at the Centre of Languages and Literature at Lund University in Sweden. Her dissertation from 2003 deals with prosodic grouping in spontaneous Swedish. Her current research focuses on the phonetics and phonology of children's and adolescents' spoken Swedish in multilingual urban settings. She was awarded the Swedish Academy's scholarship to young linguists in 2007 for her valuable contributions to the knowledge of the Swedish language.

Sally Boyd is Professor of general linguistics at the University of Gothenburg, Sweden. She has carried out externally funded research on a range of topics within sociolinguistics and multilingualism, including language contact, language transmission in multilingual contexts, attitudes to foreign accent in school contexts, language policy and the language of young people in multilingual urban settings. Her articles are published, among other places, in *Language Variation and Change* and the *International Journal of Bilingual Education and Bilingualism*.

Mette Vedsgaard Christensen worked at the Scandinavian Department, Århus University, Denmark, carrying out research on language variation and language attitudes in multilingual, suburban Århus. She is currently involved in school development projects aiming at qualifying minority education in schools in Silkeborg, Denmark.

Lena Ekberg is Professor of Scandinavian Languages at the Centre of Languages and Literature at Lund University in Sweden. She is also head of the Language Council in Sweden, which, besides giving advice in questions of language usage, promotes the usage of the national minority languages as well as other languages spoken in Sweden. Her main research interests are semantics and grammar, and the interface between them, as well as second language use. Several of her works are conducted within a functional-cognitive frame. She has been engaged in projects concerning second language use and multiethnic youth language.

Kari Fraurud has a PhD in General Linguistics and is Associate Professor of Bilingualism at Stockholm University. She has also held positions at Hamburg and Uppsala universities, and has been director of the Rinkeby Institute of Multilingual Research. Her research interests spans over discourse reference, language typology, minority languages, multilingualism, language attitudes and folk linguistics. Her most recent publications focus on variation in young peoples' production and perception of speech in present-day multilingual Stockholm, and she is currently directing the project Sociolinguistic Awareness and Language Attitudes in Multilingual Contexts within the research program High-Level Proficiency in Second Language Use.

Natalia Ganuza has a PhD in Bilingualism Research from Stockholm University. She is Assistant Professor of Swedish as a second language at Mälardalen University. Her research interests include language use in multilingual settings and syntactic development in early bilingual acquisition.

Charlotte Haglund has a PhD in Bilingualism from Stockholm University (2005). Haglund's research areas include multilingualism and education, interactional sociolinguistics and critical ethnography. She is currently a senior investigator at the Swedish Schools Inspectorate with responsibility of the Research and Development unit.

Gert Foget Hansen is currently a PhD student at the LANCHART Centre at the University of Copenhagen.

Roger Källström is Associate Professor in Swedish language at the Department of Swedish Language at the University of Gothenburg, Sweden, and the former Director of The Institute for Swedish as a Second Language. His PhD thesis treats grammatical agreement in Swedish, in a typological perspective. He has carried out research on bilingual education and multilingualism and also on further aspects of the grammatical structure of Swedish. Recently, he has studied the morphology of Swedish and literary representations of spoken language such as American Swedish and Multiethnic Youth Language.

Jan Sverre Knudsen is Professor at the Faculty of Education and International Studies, Oslo University College, as well as lecturer in world music at the Department of Musicology, Oslo University. His research and publications focus on the role of musical practices in immigrant communities and on issues related to multicultural music education. Knudsen's PhD thesis 'Those that fly without wings' (2004) is an ethnomusicological study based on field research among Chilean immigrants in Norway. His study on a multiethnic hip-hop group in Oslo was part of the strategic research program *CULCOM* (cultural complexity) at the Oslo University.

Marie Maegaard is a postdoctoral researcher at The LANCHART Centre, University of Copenhagen. She graduated from University of Copenhagen with a master in Danish Studies and Mathematics. She holds a PhD from the Department of Dialectology, University of Copenhagen, and works primarily with phonetic variation in spoken Danish, youth language, ethnographic methods, language attitudes and language change. She is the chief editor of the volume *Language Attitudes, Standardization and Language Change* (2009).

Janus Spindler Møller holds a PhD in polylingual language use. His main research interests are sociolinguistics, multilingualism, language attitudes and identity construction in interaction. He previously published his work in *International Journal of Multilingualism and International Journal of the Sociology of Language*. Currently, he is a postdoctoral researcher at the University of Copenhagen.

Ingvild Nistov is Associate Professor of Norwegian as a second language, University of Bergen. Prior to the current work on multiethnic youth language, her research has been concentrated on language contact and second language acquisition, including her PhD on referential management in narratives.

Toril Opsahl wrote her PhD thesis on structural characteristics associated with Norwegian spoken language among youth in multiethnic areas in Oslo. Her thesis won the Alliance Kunnskap Oslo's prize for the best research contribution on an Oslo-related topic in 2009. Opsahl is working as a member of the editorial staff of the project *Norsk Ordbok 2014* (Norwegian Dictionary 2014).

Nicolai Pharao is a postdoctoral researcher at the LANCHART Centre and the Department of Scandinavian Studies and Linguistics, University of Copenhagen. His research focuses on quantitative analysis of phonetic variation and change, particularly in modern Copenhagen Danish. His most recent research has been carried out within a usage-based framework of phonology and he plans to expand on this in future work involving perception of phonetic variation.

Pia Quist is Associate Professor at the Department of Scandinavian Research at the University of Copenhagen. She has an MA in Nordic Philology and Political Science, and a PhD in Sociolinguistics. Her research interests include urban sociolinguistics, multilingualism, gender and language, and youth and language. She has published her research on multilingual practices in national an international journals and anthologies.

Bente A. Svendsen is Associate Professor and Director of Research at the Department of Linguistics and Scandinavian Studies at the University of Oslo. She has carried out research on second language acquisition, multilingualism among migrant children and adults, and language use and identity constructions among adolescents in multilingual urban contexts. Her work has previously appeared in the *International Journal of Bilingualism*, and one of her articles on multilingualism won the Norwegian Language Award, 2009.

Preface

For more than a decade researchers in Denmark, Norway and Sweden have carried out research on the emergence of new linguistic practices among adolescents in multilingual (sub)urban Scandinavia. From early accounts of new emerging dialects in the 1980s to recent studies on linguistic performance and identity construction, Scandinavian researchers have over the years gained extensive knowledge on the subject. The most important researchers within the field met for the first time as a group at a seminar in Copenhagen in June 2007, financed by The Fund for Danish-Norwegian Cooperation and NORDPLUS Framework Programme, the Nordic Council of Ministers, and administrated by the Department of Linguistics and Scandinavian Studies, University of Oslo. This book is a result of a development of the themes presented and discussed at this seminar, and it contains a wide and representative range of researchers contributing with their latest and most interesting insights of their research on new linguistic practices in multilingual urban Scandinavia.

There are various reasons for why a monograph focusing on Scandinavia is relevant. Compared to other European countries, linguists in Scandinavia were relatively early in carrying out studies on the emergence of new linguistic practices in urban areas characterized by large amounts of migrants. Most of the Scandinavian research has so far been presented in Scandinavian books and journals in Scandinavian languages. However, we witness increasing interest in the Scandinavian studies from researchers from all over the world. This book gives scholars and students who do not speak a Scandinavian language a chance to learn about what is going on within this field of research. In addition, the Scandinavian countries are comparable with respect to urban organization and developments, and the languages are very similar in grammar and vocabulary. For the first time we are now able to present in a joint effort an overarching, trans-Scandinavian, comprehensible and comparable account of linguistic developments and practices in late modern urban contact zones.

We are grateful to Multilingual Matters, in particular to Marjukka Grover and John Edwards for accepting the book proposal right away, and to Anna Roderick for her patience and excellent practical support and guidelines through the whole process. The book depended on the contributors. We are grateful for their patience, for the discussions we have had with each and every one of them along the way, and for their thorough work. They have widened our horizons. The book is financially supported by the NORDPLUS Framework Programme and the Norwegian national project UPUS ('Utviklingsprosesser i urbane språkmiljø', *Developmental Processes in Urban Linguistic Contexts*), funded by the Research Council of Norway. We are thankful to the Department of Linguistics and Scandinavian Studies, University of Oslo, for brilliant administrative support. We would also like to thank each other for the fruitful and always cheerful collaboration as the book was formed and shaped in various places such as Paris, Amsterdam, Wassenaar, Oslo and Copenhagen.

Pia Quist and Bente Ailin Svendsen

Introduction

B.A. SVENDSEN and P. QUIST

This volume focuses on linguistic practices among adolescents in late modern Scandinavian contact zones; in urban contexts and neighborhoods with relatively high proportions of migrants. It reports from the three capitals Copenhagen, Oslo and Stockholm, from the second and third largest Swedish towns, Gothenburg and Malmö, and from Aarhus, the second largest town in Denmark (see Figure 1).[1] The language situation in Scandinavia has, at one level, become increasingly more differentiated since the 1960s as one of the consequences of the global allocation and transnational flow in the human landscape. In Norway, for instance, more than 150 languages are represented in primary and secondary schools, and more than 125 in Oslo schools (Oslo Municipality, 2009). There have never before been as many different foreign languages and speakers living side by side in Scandinavian cities as today. Interestingly, this development has taken place at the same time as Scandinavia in general, and Denmark and Sweden in particular, has experienced a general linguistic homogenization in terms of standardization of the national languages, dialect leveling and regionalization. This book focuses on the linguistic developments that follow from migration and urban multilingualism; in other words, all the processes that go against – and maybe even challenge – the processes of standardization and homogenization of the national languages: Norwegian, Swedish and Danish.

The migrant population in Denmark and Norway constitutes approximately 11% of the total population of 5.5 and 4.8 million, respectively (i.e. including children of parents who are born abroad; Statistics Denmark, 2009; Statistics Norway, 2010). In Sweden, the migrant population amounts to 17% of the total population of 9.2 million (including children of foreign-born parents) (Statistics Sweden, 2009).

We have chosen to include the term 'linguistic practices' in the title of this book because we wish to imply a broad understanding of all types of linguistic behaviors by all speakers in multilingual contexts, that is, recurring linguistic actions situated in a certain social context (cf. Maegaard,

Figure 1 Scandinavia: Research sites

this volume). The new linguistic practices can be approached and described by linguists from different perspectives ranging from descriptions of the use of slang and loan words (e.g. Kotsinas, 2002), through codeswitching and *crossing* situations where speakers employ a speech style or language '[...] which isn't generally thought to "belong to" the speaker' (Rampton, 1998: 291), to the emergence of new varieties or speech styles with a certain systematicity at different linguistic levels (e.g. Clyne, 2000; Kotsinas, 1988a,b; Quist, 2000). The chapters in this book represent, as well as discuss, a variety of such approaches.

This volume represents a coherent and multilayered approach to new linguistic practices, describing them structurally and phonologically (cf. Chapters 4 through 8), studying how these practices and their practitioners are perceived (cf. Chapters 14 through 16) and analyzing the complex sociolinguistic potentials of speakers when constructing, challenging and negotiating identities (cf. Chapters 9 through 13). Källström (Chapter 12) and Knudsen (Chapter 13), for instance, extend the traditional (socio)-linguistic domains by examining the ways new linguistic practices are represented in fiction and in music, namely in hip-hop culture and rap lyrics. The book depicts linguistic practices among adolescents who have the multilingual environment in common; it includes adolescents with and without migrant descent. One of the main purposes of this book has thus been to break the binary opposition between Majority and Minority, highlighting the cultural and linguistic differentiation, homogenization and hybridization processes that cut across such traditional dichotomies, with a view to understanding the filigree pattern of complexity that captures the linguistic realities of young people in the 21st century. This volume thus goes beyond the vast bulk of Scandinavian research on migrant-based linguistic practices and variation, namely the psycholinguistic approach to the Scandinavian languages as second languages, studying them as learner languages, their system, their use and their development (cf. Chapters 1 through 3 for a research overview).

In the 1980s, the Swedish sociolinguist Ulla-Britt Kotsinas (e.g. 1988a,b) applied a structural, variety approach to the study of linguistic practices among adolescents in linguistically and culturally diverse areas of Stockholm. Through this approach, Kotsinas made the important step away from the psycholinguistic tradition as she described the language of the Stockholm youngsters as a *variety* parallel to other Stockholm varieties (Kotsinas, 1988a,b). In a study in Copenhagen, Quist took the same kind of approach. She suggested the term *multiethnolect* as a way of describing the language practices she had observed (Quist, 2000; this volume). According to Clyne (2000: 87), multiethnolects are characterized by their use by several minority groups 'collectively to express their minority status and/or as a reaction to that status to upgrade it'. Moreover, Clyne argued by referring to other studies such as Kotsinas' (1988b) and Rampton's (1995a), that when majority speakers come to share a multiethnolect with the minorities, we see an expression of a new form of group identity (Clyne, 2000: 87). One of the most significant insights of the variety approach has been that these new linguistic practices are not results of poorly acquired skills in the majority language in question (cf. Bodén, 2004; this volume; Kotsinas, 1988a,b; Quist, 2000; Svendsen & Røyneland, 2008). Studies have demonstrated that the speakers are able to switch between language styles according to interlocutors and situations, and such switches are perceived to be arguments for the existence of a variety or a speech style in its own right, a version of the majority language. The variety approach has inspired several of the contributions in this volume, such as Opsahl and Nistov's chapter (Chapter 6) on morphosyntax, Bodén's chapter (Chapter 7) and Hansen and Pharao's chapter (Chapter 8) on prosody, in the sense that they attempt to give a formal description of a variety or speech style in relation to a standard language.

The variety approach has brought about some dispute over labelling, and some researchers have called for the 'lect' suffix to be avoided (cf. Bijvoet & Fraurud, this volume; Jaspers, 2008; Møller, this volume). The critics argue that the term implies an overly static conception of the boundaries between different sets of linguistic features: that languages are treated as fixed rather than fluid entities (cf. Møller, this volume). Moreover, it is argued that the variety approach implies a one-to-one correlation between a certain label and an imagined speech community, and therefore potentially disguises the constructed nature of labels such as (multi)ethnolect, dialect and sociolect (cf. Bijvoet & Fraurud, this volume). According to Bijvoet and Fraurud (p. 171) there is, for instance, no 'cohesive and well defined variety of Rinkeby Swedish that can be connected to a homogenous and delimited speech community'. This critique can be leveled at all terms by which we label sets of linguistic features (Jørgensen & Møller, 2008), such as 'language,' 'dialect' and 'variety'. Varieties should instead be treated as ideological constructs, as Heller (2007) argues, for example. The variety approach might obscure linguistic heterogeneity and fail to take into account the fact that migrants are neither a socioeconomic homogenous group, nor do they live in homogenous neighborhoods. There is, for instance, no empirical evidence that these new linguistic practices index ethnicity and in-group solidarity alone (cf. Aarsæther, this volume; Eckert, 2008a; Haglund, this volume; Jaspers, 2008; Quist, 2005; Rampton, 1995b). Other identity categories such as class, gender, locale, region, generation or religion might be equally as significant (cf. Rampton, 1995b). Thus, the variety approach entails a potential risk of homogenizing speakers, as well as the 'lect' in question, and of isolating the variety from the situated space in which it is used (cf. Jaspers, 2008: 87; Quist, 2008: 50).

Introduction

The criticism of the variety approach, by and large, has its origin in the social constructivist paradigm in late modern sociolinguistic theory and its emphasis on how social meaning is created in verbal and social interaction (cf. e.g. Agha, 2007; Rampton, 2006a). The ontological premises are that there are no fixed, preexisting social categories, although these do exist as sociohistorical constructs; social identities and meaning are brought along and brought about, made relevant and negotiated in interaction (Antaki & Widdicombe, 1998). The *practice* perspective is thus at the core of this paradigm. Whereas the variety approach in general examines the linguistic traits in relation to a standard language and the broader (national) speech community, the practice approach analyzes the ways speakers create and negotiate meaning in interaction. The foci of the two approaches are thus different, and the methods vary as well. Where the practice approach seems to favor talk-in-interaction, conversational analysis and ethnographic methods (cf. Aarsæther, this volume; Bijvoet & Fraurud, this volume; Fraurud & Bijvoet, 2004; Haglund, this volume; Kallmeyer & Keim, 2003; Knudsen, this volume; Maegaard, this volume; Møller, this volume; Quist, 2005; Rampton, 1995a; Svendsen & Røyneland, 2008), the variety approach tends to favor the systematic linguistic description of nonstandard features and the use of acceptability testing (Bodén, this volume; Opsahl & Nistov, this volume; Quist, 2000; Svendsen & Røyneland, 2008; Wiese, 2006, 2009).

We do not wish to argue in favor of one or the other approach or label, but merely to emphasize that there are differences and that the various approaches answer different kinds of questions. The variety approach contributes to the description of variation in the community of practice in question and it helps us to find out whether there is something systematic going on at all. The practice approach, on the other hand, is a way to examine the social meanings, functions and consequences of the speech of the adolescents (Quist, 2008: 49). A few studies try to combine the two approaches (Cornips, 2008; Maegaard, this volume; Quist, 2005; Svendsen & Røyneland, 2008), and to note, in Agha's words, that 'there is nothing wrong with paying attention to denotational segments such as phonemes and lexemes in explaining social uses of language; it is in fact impossible to imagine an approach to language study that ignores them' (2007: 136). This book is about the denotational segments of the new linguistic practices in multilingual urban Scandinavia and their connotational and social meaning in discourse.

This book is organized into five sections beginning with three short overview chapters by Sally Boyd, Pia Quist and Bente Ailin Svendsen. In each of these, a brief introduction is given to the studies of multilingual practices in Sweden, Denmark and Norway, respectively. The second section presents three contributions on morphological, syntactical and phonological features of these new linguistic practices. Lena Ekberg examines the pronoun 'sån' (such) in the language of youth in the Swedish city Malmö. The use of 'sån' has been reported to be especially frequent among adolescents in multiethnic areas of the city of Malmö, but Ekberg shows that it is a common feature among all youth in Malmö. The original function of 'sån' is comparison (such as), but the Malmö youth have extended its meaning to include a range of other functions. Ekberg analyzes these different functions, and finds that a process of grammaticalization is taking place. 'Sån' is developing into a determiner, which may replace the indefinite article 'en'/'ett' (a). Speakers who live in multiethnic communities seem to spearhead this grammaticalization process, as compared to speakers in mono-ethnic Swedish communities. However, the difference is not statistically significant.

Like Ekberg, Natalia Ganuza looks at a salient feature that is commonly thought of as typical for the speech of multiethnic youth. Ganuza analyzes in depth the grammatical feature of noninversion of subject and verb in contexts where standard Swedish normally requires inversion. She argues that it is especially interesting to look at this feature, since in Swedish and Scandinavian studies it is described as typical for multiethnic speech (for instance, Kotsinas, 1988a,b). Ganuza then uses quantitative methods to test the spread of noninversion in different grammatical, as well as, situational contexts. One of her many detailed analyses shows that noninversion seems to be more frequently used in multilingual areas of Stockholm than multilingual areas of Gothenburg and Malmö, and that speakers employ this feature actively in peer conversations, in particular as a linguistic resource that may demonstrate solidarity with peers and identification with the multilingual area.

Toril Opsahl and Ingvild Nistov examine noninversion and simplifications within the grammatical gender domain in an Oslo context. Whereas Ganuza analyzes a range of different data sets, Opsahl and Nistov limit themselves to two speech situations: (1) dyadic semistructured interviews with 22 adolescents; and (2) dyadic peer conversations with no adults present. Opsahl and Nistov find clear situational differences in terms of violations of the V2 constraint in topicalized declarative main clauses; the proportion is more than three times higher in the peer conversations than in the interviews, although the numbers of possible contexts for noninversion are higher in the interviews. Thus, violation of the V2 constraint seems to be characteristic for language use in in-group settings in general, and when the adolescents step into a high involvement speech style in particular, as pointed out by Ganuza. Opsahl and Nistov stress the linguistic contexts where these violations are found. It appears that some particular topicalized adverbs trigger noninversion such as 'egentlig' (actually). Moreover, they argue that there seems to be an interplay between syntactical and morphological features characterizing such in-group speech style; simplifications within the grammatical gender domain seem to accompany violations of the V2 constraint. Their data support Ekberg's findings, namely the grammaticalization of the Norwegian counterpart 'sån' (such) into a new determiner for introducing new referents in discourse.

The third section of this book presents two chapters on phonetic variation among youth in Sweden and Denmark, respectively. In the first chapter Petra Bodén presents the results from a study of the pronunciation of the colloquial speech styles called 'Rosengård Swedish,' 'Rinkeby Swedish' and 'Gårdstenish' (i.e. the local multiethnic speech varieties of Malmö, Stockholm and Gothenburg). Bodén bases her findings on a perceptual listener test and an acoustic–phonetic analysis of speech samples from the cities involved. In total, 246 pupils of upper secondary schools in Malmö, Gothenburg and Stockholm listened to speech samples from 62 speakers and were asked to judge whether the speakers spoke multiethnolect or not. Bodén reports that a new foreign-sounding way of speaking Swedish exists among adolescents in multiethnic areas of Malmö, Gothenburg and Stockholm. This foreign-accented Swedish is not only colored by the speaker's first languages, but seems to carry influences from a number of languages. Thus, there is good reason to regard the speech as a variety of Swedish, rather than as a learner language in which pronunciation is influenced by negative transfer from a first language. This is further substantiated by the finding that speaker background does not seem to determine a certain way of speaking. The speech of many of the speakers with parents born outside of Sweden was *not* perceived as multiethnolect. Conversely, some speakers with Swedish-born parents were perceived as speakers of multiethnolect.

Gert Foget Hansen and Nicolai Pharao present an acoustic and auditory analysis of prosodic features of Copenhagen multiethnolect in comparison with Copenhagen speech in general, as spoken by the same age group. They argue that there are systematic differences in the realization of the contrast short and long vowels in stressed and unstressed syllables. The contrast is leveled in the multiethnolect, except in words where the following syllable contains a schwa. They demonstrate that the greater similarity between long and short vowels is due to the shortening of long vowels rather than the lengthening of short vowels. Hansen and Pharao propose that the differences in vowel durations may contribute to the impression of an alternate rhythm in the multiethnolect compared to Copenhagen speech in general, and that a slightly alternate stress group pattern is a salient cue for identifying the Copenhagen multiethnolect.

The fourth section of this book comprises five chapters that – in different ways and from different perspectives – investigate discourse and processes of ethnic and social identification. Charlotte Haglund's chapter on transnational identifications among adolescents in suburban Sweden elaborates the global dimension in these adolescents' lives as illustrated in both Maegaard's and Knudsen's chapters (see below). Haglund explores the adolescents' quest for identities and building of allegiances through an in-depth ethnographic study in Durby, a Swedish suburban neighborhood with a high density of inhabitants of migrant descent (90% in 2005). She analyzes the adolescents' interactive and reflective positioning; the former referring to the process of positioning the other and the latter to positioning oneself, and the link between the adolescents' positioning and dominant societal discourses on multilingualism and ethnic diversity. Haglund demonstrates that the adolescents' individual and collective experiences of migration and minoritization are continuously made relevant in interaction. In addition, global rather than national identification is referred to; the opportunity to identify transculturally and transnationally seems to be the most rewarding factor, rather than finding and negotiating one's 'true self'.

Finn Aarsæther explores and discusses the use and functions of 'multi-ethnic youth language' in Oslo. He reports from the project UPUS (*Developmental processes in urban linguistic contexts*) where the Oslo part of the project studies linguistic practices among adolescents in multilingual contexts (cf. Svendsen, this volume). Aarsæther points out that the majority of the adolescents in question perceive the use of multiethnic youth language as an optional linguistic practice. Moreover, he emphasizes the link between the use of multiethnic youth language and ethnicity. The use of such linguistic practice, however, is by no means restricted to speakers with minority backgrounds. Aarsæther explores how girls of ethnic Norwegian descent in the inner city use multiethnic youth language to contrast with the posh West-end. He thus highlights the salience of locale and traditional socioeconomic categories as explanatory factors for the use of these new migrant-based linguistic practices.

Janus Møller examines a conversation among a group of Danish–Turkish boys who are having dinner at a restaurant. In their speech they employ linguistic features that we traditionally call, for example, Danish, Turkish or English. Møller refuses, however, the idea that linguistic features belong to separable languages. Instead he argues for a view of the linguistic practices of the boys as *polylingualism*, that is, the boys do not treat linguistic features as categorically belonging to separate languages. Rather, they use language features in combinations that dissolve language boundaries. One example, which Møller foregrounds, is the discourse particle 'lan,' when pronounced with a Danish 'stød' (glottal stop) is a hybrid – neither a Turkish nor a Danish word.

In Roger Källström's chapter the use of multiethnic speech styles in literature is examined. Källström analyzes two Swedish short stories and a novel, and looks in detail at the use of noninversion of subject and verb in sentences where the written standard requires inversion. The avoidance of inversion is a common feature in multiethnic speech, but it seems to be especially salient when employed in writing. Following Nikolas Coupland, Källström shows that noninversion is used as a performative tool when, for example, creating a deceptive literary persona.

Jan Sverre Knudsen elaborates the indigenized 'glocal' cultural effects of hip-hop culture and rap music in a Norwegian context. He explores the connections between hip-hop music culture and the development of a local language variety in central Oslo from both a sociolinguistic and a musicological perspective. Knudsen analyzes whether the codes and constructing principles underlying hip-hop style and rap music can serve as a model for the 'tactics' of linguistic development by analyzing the practices of a young hip-hop crew in Oslo, 'Minoritet1' (Minority1). He analyzes the possible connection between the stylistic and rhythmic requirements of rap music and what he calls 'multiethnolectal language features,' such as word order and alternation in prosody to satisfy the typical basis of most hip-hop beats. According to Knudsen, the hip-hop crew's 'street language' creates links to a local environment, and challenges linguistic norms for acceptable language use; they use their hybrid language variety as part of their own socially critical project, challenging everything from the parent generation to public authorities to prevailing attitudes in society. Street language works as a cultural and social act of resistance.

The fifth and last section of this volume focuses on perceptual studies of multiethnic youth language. Ellen Bijvoet and Kari Fraurud report on a perceptual study of Stockholm listeners' sociolinguistic awareness and language attitudes. Here they focus on reactions to two speech samples by the same person. In the first sample (whom they call Leo), the speaker uses a multiethnic speech style, and in the second sample (Sam), the speaker uses a speech style closer to standard Swedish. Listeners were asked to decide where the speakers live in Stockholm by marking the spot on a map of the city's underground railway system. Furthermore, listeners were asked to identify, among other things, the mother tongues of the speakers' parents and the length of time the speakers had been living in Sweden; additionally, they were asked to label the speech of the speaker. Bijvoet and Fraurud discuss the results in detail and refrain from drawing any strong conclusions as they remind us of the complex realities behind listeners' perceptions. Speech varieties are constructions that only exist in our minds. Thus, the title of their chapter is '"Rinkeby Swedish" in the Mind of the Beholder.'

Marie Maegaard applies an approach to the speech of young Copenhageners as social practice. She finds that the youngsters make an important distinction in their daily practice between using their own labels – 'foreigners' and 'Danes'. This distinction, alongside the gendered distinction between 'boys' and 'girls', is crucial in the constructions of stylistic and linguistic meanings. The speakers actively use ethnicity and linguistic variation when constructing social meaning. Maegaard (2007, this volume) combines her study with a perceptual investigation, that is, a verbal guise study, in order to test whether social meanings attached to different speech styles are the same in different communities of practice in Copenhagen. She finds that 'global' and 'local' meanings interconnect – some meanings are 'transportable' while others are specifically local. This is especially the case for meanings attached to ethnicity. Listeners attach ethnic meaning to some of the speech samples (e.g. with the labels 'foreigner' and 'immigrant') but not in the same way and to the same speakers in all the communities, that is, the social meaning of ethnicity in connection to speech styles depend on both 'global' and 'local' factors.

Mette Vedsgaard Christensen investigates how different groups of adolescents in Aarhus, the second largest town in Denmark, and in Copenhagen, recognize and perceive six different speech styles from Aarhus, addressing both ethnic and regional differences in spoken Danish. Christensen argues by analyzing quantitatively that ethnicity within the Aarhus' speech community does play an important part when adolescents perceive and evaluate the different voices. However, salience is given to regionality rather than ethnicity when respondents in Copenhagen listen to ethnically 'marked' voices from Aarhus. Although various linguistic features of 'ethnic speech forms' are alike in Copenhagen and Aarhus, Christensen argues that such linguistic practices are deeply rooted in the local speech community. Hence, she calls for caution regarding the idea of a potential 'pan-immigrant' variety.

These 16 chapters present the current state of the art of the sociolinguistic study of youth and multiethnic linguistic practices in Scandinavia. Taken together, they portray a coherent as well as a diverse image of Norway, Sweden and Denmark. Linguistically, we find striking similarities between the described practices. Historically, Norwegian, Swedish and Danish belong to the Old Norse branch of the Indo-European language families, and they are now and then described as a (dialect) continuum with no internal linguistic borders. Still today the three languages are mutually intelligible (at least with some effort). Therefore, it comes as no surprise, for instance, that alternative syntax, that is, violation of the V2 rule, is reported in all three countries, and that morphology and lexicon – slang and discourse particles – appear to be used in similar ways. Furthermore, the parallel sociodemographic developments of the three Scandinavian welfare states offer similar sociopolitical backgrounds for youngsters in the ethnically mixed areas of the larger cities. Thus, several of the chapters report on comparable identity negotiations, language attitudes and ideologies. The time is ripe for Scandinavian studies to be collected in a comprehensive volume and presented to a broader audience. We hope that this book will serve as an inspiration to others, including those outside of Scandinavia who are working in this field.

Note
1. Scandinavia is applied collectively to three countries of northern Europe – Norway and Sweden (which together form the Scandinavian Peninsula) and Denmark. Some authorities argue for the inclusion of Finland, Iceland and the Faroe Islands, but these are not within the scope of this book.

Chapter 1
Research on Language in Multilingual Urban Settings in Sweden

S. BOYD

Introduction

This chapter gives a brief overview of research on language in multilingual urban settings in Sweden. It also describes a large-scale project that was carried out in the early 2000s on the language of young people in such settings (cf. Bijvoet & Fraurud; Bodén; Ekberg; Ganuza; Källström, this volume).

Sweden has a relatively large proportion of persons born abroad among its inhabitants. Many live in the three largest cities of Sweden, where much of the research on this topic has been carried out. See Table 1.1 for a summary of the proportions of population born abroad in Sweden as a whole and in its three major cities, which are also the cities studied in the project mentioned above.

Research in Sweden on language in multilingual urban communities, in the broad sense, has been carried out since at least the 1970s including both research on Swedish and research on the languages brought to Sweden by post World War II migrants. Research whose focus is on the Swedish language in its role as a second language, target language or the like has dominated, but other research, especially on Finnish, has been pursued continuously since at least the 1980s (e.g. Huss, 1991; Lainio, 1989). Few studies have been carried out on both the majority language and the immigrant minority languages, and on the entire linguistic repertoire of the multi-ethnic community. There have also been few studies on early bilingual development in multilingual families. Research on language maintenance and shift has been carried out on the language use of multilinguals generally (Boyd, 1985) and on groups with specific origins (e.g. Bani-Shoraka, 2005; György, 2010). These and other studies have documented a language shift among the children of immigrants, and looked at different factors affecting the degree and speed of the language shift.

Table 1.1 Number and proportion of foreign-born persons in Gothenburg, Malmö, Stockholm and in Sweden as a whole

	Sweden (end of 2008)		City of Gothenburg		City of Malmö		City of Stockholm	
Foreign born persons	1,281,581	13.8%	107,130	21.4%	83,209	29.0%	172,772	21.3%
Total population	9,256,347		500,197		286,535		810,120	

Source: Statistics Sweden (2009)

Research specifically on Swedish among multilinguals can in turn be divided into two major strands. The first major strand is more psycholinguistically oriented research on the learning or acquisition of Swedish as a second language, which started at least as early as Hyltenstam (1978) and includes numerous studies not only within linguistics but also within pedagogy and other disciplines. The second is more sociolinguistically oriented research on multilingualism in Sweden, with a focus on Swedish as used by immigrants or their children. A major research project started in 2000 (SUF)[1] attempted to combine these two strands of research. The remainder of my brief overview will concern research on Swedish and research with primarily a sociolinguistic perspective, but excluding research on language maintenance and research on code-switching (e.g. Park, 2000). It will also give a brief description of the SUF project.

Sociolinguistic Research on Language in Multilingual Communities

The sociolinguistic strand of research has been devoted to several issues, including at least the following: (1) variation in the Swedish spoken by immigrants and their children and to the question of how their language use should be regarded (e.g. as a new dialect, slang, style or the like); (2) attitudes toward multilinguals' use of (primarily) Swedish; and (3) language and identity among young multilinguals.

Sociolinguistically-oriented studies of 'foreign sounding' varieties of Swedish were carried out primarily by Kotsinas at Stockholm University. In her dissertation, Kotsinas (1982) analyzes the language of *adult* immigrants and finds interesting similarities between this untutored learner language and pidgin languages. In later papers, she coins the term *Rinkeby Swedish* for the speech of young multilinguals and tries out various labels for it. As the adult language is allegedly pidgin-like, she both rejects (Kotsinas, 1988, 1998) and then accepts (Kotsinas, 2001) the label *creole* or *creoloid*, in other papers she considers it potentially as a *dialect* of Swedish (Kotsinas, 1988), and as a *youth variety* or *slang* (Kotsinas, 1994, 1998). Kotsinas documents a number of features of the Swedish of adult and younger multilinguals in the Stockholm area, documenting observations based on transcribed examples. Although she has emphasized the fact that the alleged variety is extremely variable in itself (Kotsinas, 1994: 132), her work has tended to confirm stereotypes that these features are more prevalent in the speech of multilinguals than some of them in fact turn out to be (Ganuza, 2008, this volume).

Studies have also been carried out of attitudes toward Swedish as spoken by immigrants and their children (e.g. Cunningham-Andersson, 1993; Cunningham-Andersson & Engstrand, 1988; Jahani, 1999). Bijvoet (1998) treats attitudes not only to different mono- and multilingual speakers' use of Swedish, but also to mono- and multilingual Finnish in Sweden and

Finland. Boyd (2004) studies attitudes toward accented Swedish in the context of the Swedish school. Bijvoet and Fraurud (this volume) are currently looking at the meaning of labels such as Rinkeby Swedish among different members of the speech community of Stockholm.

In recent years, a number of doctoral dissertations have been published studying the development of identity among multilingual young people. These use more ethnographic and qualitative methods rather than other sociolinguistic studies already mentioned and tend to study talk-in-interaction. Recent examples include Engblom's (2004) study of conversation and identity among young people in a multicultural environment and Haglund's (2005, this volume) study of ways in which young people's interaction reflects a larger social order in a suburban context. Otterup's (2005) study is partly quantitative and partly a grounded theory analysis of young people's identity development in relation to language. Jonsson's (2007) dissertation explores the relationship between young people's language in these settings and gender roles, particularly masculinity. Kahlin's (2008) doctoral thesis looks at video-recorded conversations to see how ethnicity, gender and generation are constituted in interaction.

The SUF Project

The overarching aim of the SUF project has been to describe, analyze and compare language and language use among young people from multilingual urban settings in Stockholm, Gothenburg and Malmö, with a focus on the majority language, Swedish. The participants in the project have been 222 young people in eight classes in eight upper secondary schools. The aim was to include schools with differing proportions of pupils with foreign background. The language of all the students in the selected classes was studied not only of the students who fulfilled one or more criteria for being multilingual. In this way, in comparison to the greater part of earlier research, comparisons were not made between multilinguals and monolinguals, rather the aim was to document and describe the language used by young people going to the selected schools, regardless of their language background or current language use.

The project team gathered data from the young people in a wide variety of settings, both in school and outside of school. The participants were first interviewed by a researcher about their backgrounds and language use and then recordings were made of semidirected and non-directed group discussions, individual presentations to the class and in a number of informal circumstances. Many informal recordings were self-recordings, where the participants borrowed the equipment and recorded themselves in various everyday situations. The individual graduate students also made more directed recordings, such as interviews, focus group discussions, film-retellings and picture series descriptions, in order to elicit speech of a specific type for their particular research questions (cf. e.g. Ganuza, this volume; Tingsell, 2007). Samples of the young people's writing, in the form of the essay, part of the national examination in Swedish, have also been collected and analyzed. The data have been collected, partially transcribed and stored in a database, which for now is available to the project coworkers collectively.

The substudies encompass analyses of phonetics and phonology (particularly prosody) (Bodén, 2007, this volume), subject–verb word order in main clauses (Ganuza, 2008, this volume), lexico-grammatical constructions (Ekberg, 2007, this volume), discourse particles and their functions (Svensson, 2007), phraseology in spoken and written language (Große, 2008; Prentice, 2010), and pragmatics (Utzén, in preparation) as well as of perceptions of varieties (Bijvoet & Fraurud, this volume), identity development (Almér, in preparation) and ethnographies of the negotiation of identity and power in the multilingual classroom (Werndin, in preparation). Boyd and Fraurud have studied the extent to which standard sociolinguistic terms such as *native speaker* (Fraurud & Boyd, 2006) and *variety* (Boyd & Fraurud, 2010) are applicable to speakers and their language use in contexts such as this one.

Conclusions

The SUF project continues in many ways the two major strands of research on Swedish in multilingual communities outlined briefly above: the psycholinguistic and the sociolinguistic. The corpus collected by the project provides an excellent base for studies of linguistic features as well as interaction, narration and pragmatic phenomena. Bodén's (e.g. this volume) study of phonetic features gives a firmer ground to Kotsinas' early observations of staccato prosody of the young peoples' language. Ekbergs (2007, this volume) and Svenssons (2007, 2009) studies of lexico-grammatical phenomena show how innovations in the language used in these contexts are complex and have no simple relation to multilingualism. Ganuza's (2008) and Tingsell's (2007) dissertations demonstrate that neither psycholinguistic (e.g. regarding age of onset) nor quantitative sociolinguistic perspectives alone (e.g. ethnicity, gender) are sufficient to account fully for variation in grammatical structures in the young people's Swedish. We look forward to further insights from the research of Almér, Utzén and Werndin regarding discourse, pragmatics and identity formation.

Note

1. SUF = Language and language use among young people in multilingual urban settings. (Swe: 'Språk och språkbruk bland ungdomar i flerspråkiga storstadsmiljöer'.) We gratefully acknowledge the support of the Bank of Sweden Tercentenary Foundation for this research.

Chapter 2
The Sociolinguistic Study of Youth and Multilingual Practices in Denmark: An Overview

P. QUIST

Introduction

This chapter gives a brief view of sociolinguistic research on multilingualism in Denmark as it has been carried out during the past approximately 20 years. The present day research in the field has roots in sociolinguistics and the study of second language acquisition. The study of Danish as a second language is an established discipline at universities in Copenhagen, Roskilde, Odense, Århus and at The Danish University of Education.[1] In 1999 the first professorship in the field was filled by Anne Holmen at The Danish University of Education, and in 2001 Jens Normann Jørgensen became professor of Danish as a second language at the University of Copenhagen. Holmen and Jørgensen were among the prime movers when the grand longitudinal study, *The Køge Project*, was launched as a pilot study in 1987 (Jørgensen *et al.*, 1991). The Køge Project's importance for and impact on the *sociolinguistic* study of bilingualism in Denmark cannot be underestimated, and since this chapter focuses on the sociolinguistic research on youth in late modern urban settings, leaving out the study of second language acquisition and language pedagogy,[2] this article will begin with a brief introduction to the Køge Project and then continue with a presentation of studies and discussions that have developed in a direct or indirect line from the Køge studies.

The Køge Project and (Some of) Its Impact

Since the 1960s, just like the other Scandinavian countries, Denmark has witnessed an increase in immigration.[3] Bilingual children with other mother tongues than Danish entered the political scene as well as the pedagogical agenda, since the new situation was regarded to be a pedagogical challenge in schools and institutions. Very little research had thus far dealt with bilingual children in Denmark. The first part of the Køge Project was therefore launched in 1987 (1987–1989: a pilot study and 1989–1998: the project proper). The research design was indeed ambitious: the researchers involved wanted to follow all bilingual children in the city of Køge (some 30 km south of Copenhagen) from the time they entered school in summer 1989. The first plan was to continue until 1992 when the children had finished third grade, but new funding was secured so that the research group could continue to collect data every year until the children left school in 1998, this time concentrating on one school and a group of Turkish-Danish bilinguals (Møller *et al.*, 1998). As a matter of fact, interviews and self-recordings with the same groups and individuals who entered school in 1989 were collected again in 2006 (Møller, 2008b) – offering the rare opportunity to study linguistic changes and developments in *real time* over a period of more than 16 years (Gregersen, 2009).[4]

The aim of the Køge Project was to conduct a multiperspective investigation of bilingualism in the school including linguistic, pedagogical and sociolinguistic aspects (Gimbel, 1994: 5). Especially interesting in the context of this article is the range of studies of code switching carried out over the years (beginning with Andersen, 1994; Jørgensen, 1993). By and large it was the studies of code switching that resulted in pragmatic analyses and sociolinguistic theory building, all of which influence the present day discussions. Jørgensen (1998) argues that bilingual children and adolescents develop code switching as a means of power wielding. At early stages the children may adopt the adult world status and social meanings of the Danish and Turkish codes. But as they grow older the use of Danish and Turkish in alternation are done for many different purposes regardless of statuses that may be connected to these languages in the surrounding world. Furthermore, the studies of code switching in combination with other studies of the same children clearly show that code switching (especially intrasentential switching) is a sophisticated linguistic competence that is used the most by those who perform well in both their first and second languages as well as in school in general (e.g. Jørgensen, 2003: 343–345; Maegaard, 1998). It was realized at an early point that the Turkish-Danish children do not code switch because they lack competence in L1 or L2. They do it for pragmatic reasons because they have the linguistic means to do so at their disposal. Switching between codes available is a practice 'which we all employ as part of our linguistic behaviour' (Jørgensen, 2004: 8). These insights beat the track for Jørgensen's development of the *languaging* approach (Jørgensen, 2004, 2010) and the notion of *polylingualism* (Jørgensen & Møller, 2008), which is further developed by Møller (2008a, this volume) and Madsen (2008a). *Languaging* denotes the universal character of speakers – 'Humankind is a languaging species. When languaging speakers employ linguistic features which are at their disposal to achieve their communicative aims as best they can'

(Jørgensen & Møller, 2008: 39). *Polylingualism* is a more specific term used to denote a different approach than the term multilingualism. The difference, according to Jørgensen and Møller (2008: 41), is that the concept of multilingualism presupposes a static view of languages as separable and countable entities, whereas polylingualism 'is based on the assumption that speakers first and foremost use features, that is they use language (and not languages)'.

Multilingualism and Dialectology: Multiethnolect

As Jørgensen and Møller point out (2008: 40) 'it is a point for sociolinguistic studies of language use that simultaneous use of features from different sets of conventions, different languages (or varieties) is *not* a deviation from typical human linguistic behaviour'. A similar point has been central to Scandinavian sociolinguists ever since Ulla-Britt Kotsinas presented her findings from a study of adolescents in Rinkeby (Boyd, this volume; Kotsinas, 1988a, 1988b). It was important to Kotsinas to show that the colloquial language of young bilinguals in Stockholm was not learner language and not incorrect or bad language. Rather their language ought to be understood by analogy with traditional Stockholm dialects. Inspired by the work of Kotsinas, Quist conducted in 1998 a study of language use in multilingual Copenhagen youth communities (Quist, 2000). This study was designed within a frame of sociolinguistic dialectology aimed at answering whether a new speech variety was emerging in multiethnic areas of Copenhagen, and whether it was possible to speak of a new Danish dialect (Quist, 2000: 145, 181). Depending on the definition of such terms as 'variety' and 'dialect' Quist argued that it was possible to describe a speech variety with morphological, syntactic and lexical features different from standard Copenhagen speech. Accordingly, she suggested labelling this as a *multiethnolect* in order to signal a parallel to other 'lects' (dialect, sociolect, cronolect, etc.) and to stress the *multi*linguality of the phenomenon as opposed to the term *ethnolect* which could imply a mono-ethnic basis. Whether or not a variety approach is compatible with an interactional and practice approach is subject to ongoing discussion (e.g. Madsen, 2008a). The obvious advantage of the dialect perspective, however, was the inclusion of bilingual speakers in the study and the description of the Copenhagen speech community in a broad sense (Quist, 2003), making it possible to talk about and treat the speech of *all* young Copenhageners as ordinary and not as deviation from general language practices in the speech community.

In Århus, the second largest city in Denmark, Mette Vedsgaard Christensen conducted a study of 'Language use and language choice among adolescents in multi-ethnic areas' (author's translation) (Christensen, forthcoming). Christensen focused on a neighborhood called Gellerupparken, where most linguistic influences come from Arabic languages. She argues that what could appear to be language mistakes are in fact signs of an emerging local ethnolect of Århus (Christensen, 2002, 2003). In a comparison of L2 (ethnolect) speakers and L1 (nonethnolect) speakers, Christensen finds that the L2 speakers – in their ethnolect – use significantly more traditional Århus dialect features than do the L1 speakers (Christensen, forthcoming, this volume). This interesting finding tells us that multiethnic language practices are locally bound and should not be treated in isolation of their local speech environments or communities.

Despite the fact that pronunciation seems to be a main characteristic of the (multi)ethnolects, very little research focuses on the description of what, in phonetic terms, distinguishes this speech from standard Danish. One important exception is the study by Gert Foget Hansen and Nicolai Pharao (2005, this volume). Hansen and Pharao compared speakers of multiethnolect to speakers of 'young standard Copenhagen' and found a systematic difference between pronunciations of the contrast between long and short vowels in stressed and unstressed syllables. Except for words with schwa in the second syllable, speakers of multiethnolect had much shorter vowels than did speakers of 'young standard Copenhagen' (Hansen & Pharao, 2005: 23, this volume).

Social and Stylistic Practices

Quist extends the dialect approach to a more practice-oriented approach in an ethnographic study of high school students in Nørrebro in Copenhagen (Quist, 2008, forthcoming). In this study she shows that the practice of including fragments of a multiethnic speech style is an integrated part of broader semiotic, stylistic practices. Those who make use of the multiethnic linguistic features (features described as characteristic of multiethnolect, Quist, 2000), and do so in a serious, nonparodic manner, also share a range of other practices such as clothing, favorite music and school orientation. The ethnic backgrounds of the speakers do not directly determine the choices of language. For instance, some speakers of Danish ethnic majority background are frequent users of multiethnolectal features, and some speakers with minority ethnic background never use these features as part of their repertoire. The stylistic practices as they are performed on a regular, daily basis also influence 'ownership' relations. Not everybody is 'allowed' to use a phrase like 'wallah jeg sværger' (wallah I swear) in a serious way. This point is further explored by Quist and Jørgensen (2007) who show that the positions of the speakers in the peer group landscape have an impact on who can and who cannot use multiethnolectal features among their peers.

Maegaard (2007, this volume) also takes an approach to the speech of young Copenhageners as stylistic practice. She finds that one important distinction made by the young people in daily practice is between – using their own labels – 'foreigners' and 'Danes'. This distinction, alongside the distinction between 'boys' and 'girls', is crucial in the construction of stylistic and linguistic meanings. The speakers actively use ethnicity and linguistic variation when constructing social meaning.

In current studies of multilingual practices it is important to stress that speech styles and ethnicity are fluent and negotiable. Madsen (2008a, 2008b) studies language practices in a multilingual sport club, and shows, among other things that competition (e.g. competition in getting the best grades in school), language play and identity negotiations often combine in unforeseen and surprising ways. A central focus in Møller's research is the construction of hybrid meanings in multi(poly)-lingual practices (2008a, this volume).

Despite the relative strong tradition of research in multilingual practices there are still unexplored areas which, in a Danish context, need further research. So far we know little about youth and multilingual practices in computer mediated communication. We also lack studies that explore the local and national similarities and differences in multiethnolectal practices, for instance by comparing the three biggest cities Copenhagen, Aarhus and Odense.

Conclusion

The sociolinguistic study of multilingual practices in Denmark draws on both national and international research with roots in sociolinguistics (including dialectology) and second language studies. The Køge Project created a vivid research environment of which the majority of present day active researchers have been a part. Fruitful discussions and research collaborations continue, and new and future projects materialize. For instance Jørgensen, Madsen and colleagues have launched an ethnographic study of linguistic practices at an urban school in Copenhagen; Maegaard and Møller are planning another school project in a multiethnic school in the suburb of Tingbjerg in connection with the LANCHART[5] studies (Gregersen, 2009); and Quist is involved in a European research collaboration that aims at comparing linguistic practices and developments in multiethnic areas of Stockholm, London, Berlin and Copenhagen. All in all, at the moment, the future looks promising for the Danish sociolinguistic study of multilingual practices.

Notes
1. For an introduction to and a critical discussion of the development of 'Danish as a Second Language' as a discipline in its own right, see Wagner (1999).
2. See e.g. Holmen and Lund (1999); Holmen, Glahn and Ruus (2003) for collections of articles on pedagogical and acquisitional aspects of 'Danish as a second language'.

3. In Denmark in 2009 the percentage of citizens of foreign decent (including second and third generation descendants) was 9.8. For the largest cities Copenhagen and Århus the numbers were 15.4% and 14.3% respectively. In Køge the number was 8.5% (cf. Statistics Denmark, 2010).
4. The set of Køge data is varied, ranging from questionnaires from teachers and parents, listening tests, interviews in Danish and Turkish, to group conversations and self recordings. Group conversations and interviews were conducted every year from 1989 until 1998 providing the possibility to trace linguistic developments from year to year in both Danish and Turkish. A large body of monographs and articles has been published during the years. For a detailed outline of data and aims, see e.g. Jørgensen, Møller, Quist and Holmen (1998) and Jørgensen (2003). Also: http://koegeprojektet.dk/publikationer/
5. The Danish National Research Council Centre for Language Change in Real Time (www.dgcss.dk).

Chapter 3
Linguistic Practices in Multilingual Urban Contexts in Norway: An Overview

B.A. SVENDSEN

Introduction

The Scandinavian research on linguistic practices in multilingual contexts, in its broad sense, has emerged during the last decades. The first Norwegian and Danish studies appeared in the 1980s, while the Swedish research dates back to the 1970s. The Swedish research has been a step ahead, and has had a broader scope than in Denmark, and in Norway in particular (cf. Boyd, this volume; Golden *et al.*, 2007; Hammarberg, 2007; Quist, this volume). However, the first professorship in second language acquisition (SLA) in the Scandinavian countries was established in Norway (in 1997).[1] One of the reasons for the later research onset in Norway and Denmark might be traced to the different migration patterns in the Scandinavian countries. Whereas the post World War II migration to Sweden was already substantial in the 1960s, only 2.6% of the Norwegian population qualified as 'migrants' (i.e. two parents born abroad) as late as 1986 (Statistics Norway, 2010). Twenty-three years later, the migration population has more than quadrupled, amounting to almost 11% of the total population of 4.8 million, and 26% of the population in Oslo, the capital (Statistics Norway, 2010). It is thus after 1995 we find the most considerable growth in studies of Norwegian as a second language (cf. Golden *et al.*, 2007).

The research on language practices and variation in multilingual contexts in Norway encompasses two main intersected disciplines: namely research on SLA and language contact research. The main foci have been, as for the Swedish research (cf. Boyd, this volume; Hammarberg, 2007), on the acquisition of Norwegian as a second language, analyzed from a psycholinguistic or cognitive perspective: studying the acquisition of Norwegian as a learner language, and its system, use and development (cf. Golden *et al.*,

2007). The latter discipline, research on language contact, includes studies on bilingualism: language socialization, language use, code switching and language maintenance, involving the indigenous Sami languages (e.g. Bull, 1996; Jernsletten, 1993), the minority language Kven (e.g. Lane, 2006; Sollid, 2005) and some migrant languages (e.g. Aarsæther, 2004; Guldal, 1997; Kulbrandstad, 1997; Lanza, 1992; Lanza & Svendsen, 2007; Skaaden, 1998; Svendsen, 2004; Turker, 2000).[2] As for the Swedish research (cf. Boyd, this volume), there is as yet a lack of studies including other languages than (variants of) Norwegian, both on an individual and on a group level, such as studies on the entire linguistic repertoire of a multiethnic community of practice. Furthermore, there are relatively few studies on early bilingualism in multilingual families (cf. Lanza, 1992), and on the simultaneous or successive acquisition of a third language (cf. Sickinghe, 2005; Svendsen, 2006). The research on language contact also encompasses a sociolinguistic dialectological approach and studies on language variation and change, such as studies on dialect leveling (cf. Røyneland, 2009, for an overview).[3] The socio-dialectological approach is, however, beside the scope of this chapter because it involves the use of traditional dialects and a (regional) standard, and has mainly been conducted in rural areas of Norway, for example, as in one of the earliest international studies on the social meaning of code switching, conducted in North-Norway (Blom & Gumperz, 1972). The socio-dialectological approach is, in addition, salient in studies on the emergence of new linguistic practices among adolescents in urban neighborhoods with a high migrant proportion (cf. Opsahl & Nistov, this volume; Svendsen & Røyneland, 2008), and in studies on dialect formation and leveling in 'new' industrial towns such as Høyanger, Odda and Tyssedal (Solheim, 2009; cf. Trudgill, 1986).

The research on Norwegian as a second language is mainly done on the basis of written data from adults (cf. Golden *et al.*, 2007). Few studies analyze *oral* language practices from a sociolinguistic and an interactional socio-pragmatic perspective, and studies on *adolescents'* language practices in multilingual urban contexts are even rarer. The interactional socio-pragmatic framework to migrant-based language practices is mainly applied within the research on language contact (e.g. Aarsæther, 2004; Guldal, 1997; Lanza, 1992; Svendsen, 2004). The socio-pragmatic framework provides the ongoing research on language practices among adolescents in multilingual urban contexts with important conversational analytic tools such as positioning (Davies & Harré, 1990), performance and other means of presentation of self (Bauman, 1986; Goffman, 1959), stylization (Coupland, 2007), and crossing (Rampton, 1995a). These analytical tools help to illuminate the complex linguistic toolkit these adolescents have at their disposal and how it is used in identity constructions (Aarsæther, this volume; Hårstad, in press; Knudsen, this volume; Røynesdal, 2007; Seim, 2006; Svendsen & Røyneland, 2008).

Linguistic Practices among Adolescents in Multilingual Urban Contexts

Whereas the Swedish researcher Kotsinas (1988a) reported on the emergence of new linguistic practices among adolescents in neighborhoods with a high proportion of migrants already in the 1980s, the first Norwegian study appeared in 1995: a study on new loanwords among adolescents in Central Oslo (Aasheim, 1995). Kotsinas' (1988a) study in Rinkeby, suburban Stockholm, and Quist's (2000) study in Nörrebro, Copenhagen, involved analyses of these new practices at different linguistic levels. Additional studies have been carried out both in Denmark (cf. Quist, this volume), and in Sweden in particular, especially under the project 'Språk och språkbruk bland ungdomar i flerspråkiga storstadsmiljöer' (*Language and language use among young people in multilingual urban settings*, cf. Boyd, this volume). In Norway, there has been a strong emphasis on the lexical level in studies of youth language in general, and in studies of linguistic practices among adolescents in multilingual neighborhoods in particular. Studies on loanwords have mainly concentrated on the import and use of English (e.g. Graedler, 1998), often subsumed under a language preservation debate (cf. Sandøy, 2006). The few studies on migrant contact-induced practices have focused, in line with Aasheim's (1995) study, on loanwords and slang from other languages than English, and on the etymological origin of those words (e.g. Drange, 2002; Drange & Hasund, 2000; Østby, 2005). Much of the research on loans and slang words have, as in the SLA research, been analyzed on the basis of written data, such as in the larger Nordic project 'Språkkontakt og ungdomsspråk i Norden' (*Language Contact and Youth Language in the Nordic Countries*) (cf. Drange *et al.*, 2002). However, this project elicited spoken data as well and thereby provided data, for instance, for Hasund's (2003) contrastive analysis on the use of *like* in English and 'liksom' (like) in Norwegian youth language. The strong emphasis on the lexical level might have contributed to reinforce the biased popular view on the linguistic practices among adolescents in multilingual urban neighborhoods; a belief that they merely consist of loanwords or slang (cf. Opsahl & Nistov, this volume; Svendsen & Røyneland, 2008: 67). Until the UPUS project (see below) commenced in the fall of 2005, there had been no Norwegian study parallel to the Scandinavian counterparts.

The UPUS Project: Quo Vadis?

The UPUS project ('Utviklingsprosesser i urbane språkmiljø', *Developmental processes in urban linguistic contexts*) is a national research project funded by the Research Council of Norway (2005–2009). Studies have been and are still carried out on language use, variation, perceptions and change in four cities in Norway: Bodø (Nesse, 2008), Tromsø (Sollid,

2008), Trondheim (Hårstad, 2008, in press) and Oslo. The Oslo part of the project is the only one under the UPUS umbrella with the main purpose of studying linguistic practices among adolescents in multilingual contexts. These practices range from insertion of loans and use of slang, through code switching and crossing, to the emergence of new varieties or styles of Norwegian with a certain degree of systematicity on different linguistic levels.

The UPUS/Oslo project has developed a corpus of spoken data elicited between 2006 and 2008 from 56 young respondents between 13 and 19 years of age from neighborhoods with a relatively high proportion of migrants ('Søndre Nordstrand', 45.6%, and 'Gamle Oslo', 34.9%, Statistics Norway, 2010). The adolescents are born and raised in Norway. The corpus consists of two types of data from the same participant, that is interviews and peer conversations. These data will be available for further research through an internet-based interface. Additionally, data from questionnaires, field observations, retrospective interviews, self-recordings and small-scale phonological perception tests have been collected.

The data provide opportunities to study different aspects of the adolescents' linguistic practices, such as loans and slang from languages other than English and Norwegian (Opsahl *et al.*, 2008), various morphosyntactic features of these practices (Opsahl & Nistov, this volume), discourse particles (Opsahl, 2009a), phonological features (Røyneland, in preparation), the pragmatics of these practices in relation to identity constructions (Aarsæther, this volume; Svendsen & Røyneland, 2008), the connection between linguistic innovation and hip hop (Brunstad *et al.*, in press; cf. Knudsen, this volume) and the adolescents' multilingual capital (Svendsen, 2009). The UPUS/Oslo data, however, do not include studies on the adolescents' entire linguistic repertoire, such as the actual conversational use of other first languages than Norwegian, a perspective often lacking in both Sweden and Norway (cf. Boyd, this volume; Golden *et al.*, 2007; Hammarberg, 2007). This perspective is, however, more frequently applied in Denmark (cf. Quist, this volume). Neither does the UPUS/Oslo project include foci on the perceptions of various migrant-based linguistic practices, as we find in the Swedish research (cf. Boyd, this volume; Bijvoet & Fraurud, this volume) for example evaluations among important gatekeepers such as teachers and employers (cf. Harnæs, 2001; Kulbrandstad, 2006a, for small-scale perceptions studies on migrant-based accents; Ims, in preparation). Norway is sometimes described as a sociolinguistic and multilingual paradise, with abundant linguistic heterogeneity, both written and spoken, and as a society 'liberal in its attitudes to languages' (Council of Europe, 2003–2004: 15; cf. Auer, 2005: 15). There are, however, ongoing processes of dialect leveling (e.g. Røyneland, 2009; Solheim, 2009), and even language shift in some villages, toward a South-Eastern standard-like variant (e.g. Papazian, 1997). Moreover, different dialects hold, as in most other countries, different prestige, and dialect *mixing* is in general looked down upon (Mæhlum & Røyneland, 2009). Dialect diversity, however, has been and still is considerable, and dialects enjoy relatively high prestige and are used in practically all social domains (cf. Røyneland, 2009). A recent study conducted by the Norwegian Broadcasting Cooperation (NRK) and the Norwegian Language Council (2009), confirms that Norwegians in general are dialect friendly; that is positive to dialect use in the society as a whole and in the national news broadcasts on radio and television. Furthermore, and in opposition to studies on language attitudes in Sweden (Boyd, 2004), Norwegians in general reveal rather positive attitudes toward the use of a foreign accent in electronic news media (taking methodological differences between the two studies in question into consideration). Larger-scale perception studies would enable us to examine the status of different migrant-based linguistic practices in various domains and; whether they will find their place within the diverse sociolinguistic landscape of Norway.

Notes

1. The professorship was held by the late Anne Hvenekilde. Always missed.
2. Golden *et al.* (2007) subsume research on bilingualism under SLA research. Although these two research areas are clearly intersected, for instance in relation to third language acquisition, they have traditionally been conceived of as being distinct; whereas studies on bilingualism have often concentrated on the differentiation of the languages and the effects of bilingualism in cognitive development, SLA research has concentrated on the 'processes involved in the acquisition of a second language and the description of the resulting proficiency' (Cenoz & Hoffmann, 2003: 3).
3. I argue, in accordance with the Council of Europe's *Language Education Policy Profile* (2003–2004: 15), that the traditional spoken dialects or regional varieties are part of the abundant linguistic heterogeneous or multilingual society in Norway, since there are no clear-cut differences between languages and dialects as such, as exemplified in the Scandinavian dialect continuum. The focus of this chapter, however, is on research of various migrant-based linguistic practices.

Chapter 4

Extended Uses of 'Sån' (Such) among Adolescents in Multilingual Malmö, Sweden

L. EKBERG

Introduction[1]

This chapter investigates the uses of the pronoun 'sån' (such) in Swedish youth language in a multilingual context. It shows that in addition to the uses in standard Swedish (Teleman *et al.*, 1999: 447–448), 'sån' is also used as a determiner and, sporadically, as a discourse marker. The analysis is based on a subset of data collected within the project *Language and language use among young people in multilingual urban settings* (referred to in the following as the SUF-project; see Boyd, this volume). The informants are female adolescents, with different linguistic backgrounds, in two upper secondary schools in Malmö, the third largest city in Sweden. Common for the informants is the multilingual school environment. The frequent use of 'sån', in a number of functions, is a characteristic feature of the local variant of multiethnic youth language, Rosengård Swedish, according to adolescents in Malmö (Bodén, 2007, this volume). As the present investigation shows, however, this use is not limited to speakers of Rosengård Swedish but is found also among other adolescents in Malmö. In contrast, 'sån' as a determiner or as a discourse marker is not found among adolescents in Stockholm.

In standard Swedish the pronoun 'sån' is typically construed as an attribute, usually preceded by the indefinite article when the head noun is singular: 'en sån klänning' (lit. a such dress). The primary meaning is to denote an entity by comparing it to another one, typically specified in an embedded clause (underlined).

(1) Jag vill ha **en sån klänning** <u>som Lisa har.</u>
     I want to-have a such dress as Lisa has.
     'I want to have a dress like Lisa's'.

Along with the primary comparative use, 'sån' may be used more or less purely deictically to refer to entities in the speech situation. This holds for standard Swedish as well as for the youth language in question. Among the adolescents in Malmö 'sån' shows further extended, and grammaticalized, uses (Ekberg, 2006, 2007, forthcoming). Most strikingly 'sån' may function as a determiner, namely in contexts where it seemingly replaces the indefinite article. In (2) one of the informants, Gordana, is telling her friends that she happened to see a cute little baby at the bank the other day. She introduces the new discourse referent (the baby) by construing it as the logical subject of a presentational construction ('var de(t) sån liten bebis', idiom. there was this little baby). (All names of the informants are pseudonyms. The transcripts are written in a modified standard orthography. See Appendix for an explanation of the symbols used.)

(2) asså när jag var i bibl+ # ee var i banken i fredags # så **var de(t) sån lite(n) bebis** # asså du vet så jag ville bara ta du vet som å # ta henne å krama henne (Gordana)
well when I was at libr+ # ee was at bank-the last Friday # so was it such little baby # well you know so I wanted just take you know like and # take her and hug her
'when I was at the libr+ # ee was at the bank last Friday # then there was this little baby # well you know I just wanted to take you know like and # take her and hug her'

In Swedish (as well as in English) the logical subject must be indefinite; in (2) the indefinite noun phrase has the form '**sån** liten bebis' (such little baby), whereas in standard Swedish it would be '**en** (sån) liten bebis', that is the logical subject would be constructed with the indefinite article 'en' (or 'ett', depending on the gender of the head noun).

Everyday language of adolescents in multilingual settings in Malmö comprises also another grammaticalized extension of 'sån', although not as apparent as the determiner function, namely the discourse function of focusing the new information in an utterance. As I will argue the two grammaticalized extensions are both motivated by the inherent deictic element of 'sån'.

Before proceeding with the extensions of the use of 'sån', I will introduce the informants and their contribution of data (section 'Informants and Data'). The bulk of the chapter (sections 'The Polyfunctional "Sån"' and 'The Meaning and Use of "Sån" as a Determiner') consists of a survey of the uses of 'sån' among the informants in Malmö, in comparison with the uses in spoken standard Swedish. I will pay particular attention to 'sån' as a determiner, arguing that the specific meaning of 'sån' in this function can be related to the comparative and deictic meaning of the pronoun.

Informants and Data

The analysis of the use of 'sån' is based on a subset of data collected in two upper secondary schools in Malmö during 2002 and 2003, henceforth referred to as the Malmö-corpus. The schools were given the code names Cypresskolan and Ekskolan. Both schools are situated in the center of Malmö and receive students from all areas of the city. The proportion of multilingual students differs between the schools, but in the groups from which our informants were selected the number of students with foreign background was fairly equal, around 65%. (i.e. either the students themselves or at least one of their parents were born abroad.) The data consist of spontaneous speech collected with no researcher or other adult present. Either the informants took part in semidirected group conversations at school, or conducted self-recordings in situations they chose themselves, interacting with peers. In both cases the recordings were carried out on mini-discs (Sharp MD MT-190H).

The informants belonged to two peer groups. The one, here referred to as the C-group, consisted of four bilingual students from Cypresskolan: Gordana, Sabaah, Jing and Duhi. The other, the E-group, consisted of three monolingual students from Ekskolan: Bodil, Märta and Aurora. Nearly six hours (357 minutes) of recorded speech were investigated. The total number of tokens is approximately 46,000. (Tokens include not only words but onomatopoetic expressions and interrupted words as well.) Of the total amount of recorded speech 193 minutes are from the C-group (the number of tokens is approximately 27,000) and 164 minutes from the E-group (approximately 19,000 tokens).

Specimens of speech from all four informants in the C-group and two of the three informants in the E-group (Märta and Aurora) were included in a perception experiment in which pupils in Malmö were asked to identify signs of Rosengård Swedish (Bodén, 2007; Hansson & Svensson, 2004). The stimuli (each approximately 30 seconds) had been extracted from the project's database. The stimuli from Sabaah and Duhi were both regarded as Rosengård Swedish of a significant majority of the listeners ($p < 0.01$), whereas the stimuli from Jing were regarded (also significant, $p < 0.05$) as not Rosengård Swedish. Concerning Gordana, the listeners did not agree; approximately half of the listeners classified her as a speaker of Rosengård Swedish. As for the two informants in the E-group, both were regarded as not speaking Rosengård Swedish by a significant majority of the listeners ($p < 0.01$). (For details of the significance test see Bodén, 2007).[2]

The result of the perception experiment supports the intuitive impression that the adolescents of the bilingual group had more traits of what we may refer to as a multiethnic youth language than the monolingual group (see Bodén, 2007, this volume for an account of phonetic characteristics of the stimuli classified as Rosengård Swedish). This result was the point of departure for a comparison of the use of 'sån' in the two peer groups, since a frequent use of this word (among other things) was reported to be characteristic of Rosengård Swedish by the adolescents taking part in the perception experiment. However, the number of the instances of 'sån'[3] in the two groups shows that there is no significant difference as regards the frequency in general; in the C-group the percentage of 'sån' is 0.74 (of approximately 27,000 tokens) whereas in the E-group the percentage is 0.72 (of approximately 19,000 tokens). However, there might still be a difference between the groups as regards the use of 'sån' as a determiner, the most obvious extension of the word. I will come back to this question in section 'The Meaning and use of "Sån" as a Determiner'.

The following section gives an overview of the meanings and functions of 'sån' in spoken standard Swedish, in comparison with the uses of 'sån' in the Malmö-corpus in general.

The Polyfunctional 'Sån'

In colloquial Swedish 'sån' is used in a number of meanings and functions. The primary meaning is to compare two referents concerning type, henceforth the *comparee* and the *comparand*. The comparand (B) serves to identify or characterize the comparee (A). The comparee is implicit, whereas the comparand is typically explicit, cf. example (1), repeated as (3a). It is however not necessary to linguistically express the comparand. In (3b) the comparand is only implied, which is fully possible for example when it is physically present in the speech act situation.

(3) a. Jag vill ha [en **sån** klänning]$_A$ [som Lisa har]$_B$
 I want to-have [a such dress]$_A$ [as Lisa has]$_B$
 'I want to have a dress like Lisa's'
 b. Jag vill ha [en **sån** klänning]$_A$
 I want to-have [a such dress]$_A$
 'I want to have a dress like that'

The meaning of comparative 'sån' is thus complex; 'sån' designates an indefinite, unspecific instance (A) by way of referring to an indefinite, specific instance (B) of the same type. In (3) however, the meaning of 'sån' is not only comparative but deictic as well; the speaker is pointing to B, linguistically and maybe also physically, in order to describe A. When B is present in the situational context, but not linguistically explicit (or specified), the deictic meaning is strengthened, cf. (3b). The speaker is either physically pointing or in another way directing the addressee's attention to B, in order to describe the relevant properties of the designated entity, A. In (4) the deictic meaning is further strengthened so that 'sån' rather functions as a demonstrative pronoun. Although bleached the meaning of comparison is however still relevant, since the implicit comparand (a 'normal' body of a 45-year-old man) plays a role in how to describe (evaluate) the comparee.

(4) tänk dej en förtifemåring ha **sån kropp** (Jing)
assume REFL a forty-five-year-old [man] have such body
'would you imagine a forty-five year old man having a body like that'

The demonstrative use in (4) is close to the purely expressive use in (5). In (5) 'sån' denotes a subjective evaluation of the propositional content of the designated entity, namely a high degree of the properties designated by the noun 'tur' (luck).

(5) **sån tur** jag hade avstängt (Sabaah)
such luck I had turned-off [said about a cell phone]
'such luck I had turned it off'

Also in (5) there is an implicit comparative meaning, since the notable properties of the designated entity can only be evaluated when compared to an imagined comparand.

Finally, 'sån' may be used deictically to refer to entities in the memory of the speech act participants. In (6)–(8), taken from the Malmö-corpus, the speaker is referring – mentally pointing – to entities that the speaker assumes the hearer can identify via shared knowledge and experience (cf. Opsahl, 2009b).[4] That is, 'sån' has a *recognitional* function in that it actualizes or introduces a referent that is construed as known to the participants. Simultaneously, the use of 'sån' may indicate that the speaker is uncertain how to denote or describe the referent. In standard Swedish 'sån' is often elaborated with the locative adverb *här* 'here' or *där* 'there' in this use (Teleman *et al.*, 1999: 447), that is *sån badplats* in (6) would optionally, and perhaps preferable, be expressed as *sån där badplats*. In the Malmö-corpus 'sån' is usually construed without *här/där*. A further difference is that the singular noun phrases with 'sån' in (6)–(7) (in bold) lack an indefinite article, which in standard Swedish would precede 'sån'. The hypothesis elaborated in the Section 'The Meaning and use of "Sån" as a Determiner' is that 'sån' itself may function as a determiner in these uses.

(6) jag var på **sån badplats** (Jing)
I was at such bathing-place
'I was at this bathing place'

(7) har du sett den filmen # om **sån chokladfabrik**? (Gordana)
have you seen that movie # about such chocolate-factory?
'have you seen that movie # about this chocolate factory?'

(8) åå vi bytte **såna kort # såna typ fotokort** (Märta)
and we exchanged such cards # such like photo-cards
'and we exchanged these cards # like photo cards'

The recognitional function has been observed cross-linguistically in the use of demonstratives in spoken language (Diessel, 1999: 105ff; Himmelmann, 1996: 230ff; Prince, 1992; for an account of the recognitional use of Swedish demonstratives 'den här'/'den där' (this/that) see Lindström, 2000). Like recognitional demonstratives, recognitional 'sån' introduces a referent that is new in the current discourse but in some sense is old to the hearer. Reflecting this, recognitional 'sån' is often accompanied by 'du vet' (you know), emphasizing the assumed shared knowledge (see further Svensson, 2007). Although the speaker assumes that the hearer is familiar with the referent, as Himmelmann (1996: 230) states: '[a] central feature of this use is that the speaker anticipates problems with respect to the information used in referring to a given referent'. That is, the speaker is uncertain whether or not the information given is sufficient in allowing the hearer to identify the referent. Consequently, it would be more appropriate to say that recognitional 'sån' (as well as a recognitional demonstrative) construes, rather than denotes, the referent as known or identifiable to the speaker (see further section 'The Meaning and Use of "Sån" as a Determiner').

The uses accounted for this far are found in colloquial Swedish in general as well as in the Malmö-corpus. However, in addition to those uses, typical of the Malmö-corpus is, primarily, the occurrence of 'sån' in noun phrases that lack an obligatory indefinite article, cf. (6) and (7). (I will come back to this use in section 'The Meaning and Use of "Sån" as a Determiner'.) There are also other deviating uses in the Malmö-corpus, compared to standard Swedish. What they have in common is that 'sån' appears not to be part of a noun phrase but syntactically independent. In (9) Bodil is telling Märta that the teacher always placed her furthest at the very front in the classroom. In a follow-up Bodil explains why, beginning with the conclusive 'asså' (thus, you know). The 'pointer' 'sån' is placed before the rhematic constituent, busfrö 'little devil', that is, before what is new and important in the utterance. In (9) 'sån' seems to have a focusing discourse function, rather than a descriptive or syntactical function.

(9) Bodil: i mellanstadiet fick jag alltid sitta längst fram alltid alltid alltid
in primary-school had I always to-sit furthest front always always always
'in primary school I was always forced to sit at the very front always always always'

Märta:	varför det? why that? 'why was that?'
Bodil:	hon ville inte ha mej där bak # asså jag var **sån** busfrö # she wanted not to-have me there back # you-know I was such little-devil 'she didn't want me to sit in the back [of the room] # because I was such a little devil'

An indication that 'sån' is a discourse marker, rather than being integrated in the noun phrase, is that it may have a deviating form or position, compared to standard Swedish. There are several examples in the Malmö-corpus that 'sån' does not agree with the following noun, although such agreement is obligatory in standard Swedish. In (9) 'sån' appears in common (nonneuter) gender although the following noun (*busfrö*) is neuter. Compare also (10) where 'sån' appears in singular whereas the following noun is plural. The uninflected form of 'sån' is used sporadically both by monolingual and bilingual speakers, which indicates that this 'deviation' is not a learner feature.

(10) byta typ **sån** två gånger (Aurora)
exchange type such two times
'exchange like two times'

In (11) 'sån' is indeed inflected ('såna') but the position is remarkable. 'Såna' is placed before the quantifier instead of after, which is the unmarked position in the noun phrase in standard Swedish. Finally, in (12) 'sån' is placed before an adjectival phrase (underlined), a position that is not possible for pronominal 'sån' in standard Swedish.[5]

(11) nej de(t) e journalfilm # dom har sån e sån färgfilm # ja # **såna** fem kakor (Gordana)
no it is newsreel # they have such e such colour film # yes # such five cookies
'no it is a newsreel # they have this e this colour film # yes # these five cookies

(12) **sån** <u>svensk och blond</u> å sånt du vet (Jing)
such Swedish and blond and such you know
'like Swedish and blond and all that you know'

In (9)–(12) 'sån' is used cataphorically to point to the rhematic element, that is the new information, in the utterance. In this function 'sån' is similar to the use of the English discourse marker *like* (cf. Dailey-O'Cain, 2000; Romaine & Lange, 1991; Underhill, 1988) as well as Swedish 'såhär'/'sär' (like), both functioning as focusing discourse markers (Öqvist, 1997). ('Sär' is usually analyzed as a contraction of 'såhär' (like this), but Öqvist mentions also 'sånhär'/'såndär' (lit. such this/that) as a possible source, where the first part of the compound is 'sån'.) There are comparatively few instances of 'såhär' in the Malmö-corpus that can be interpreted as discourse markers. In contrast, 'såhär' is frequently used in the language of adolescents in Stockholm, as indicated by data collected within the SUF-project, cf. the example in (13).

(13) vet du att jag drömde att jag hade f+ att jag köpte såna dära # du vet
såhär skor igår (Fawza)
know you that I dreamed that I had f+ that I bought such those # you know like shoes yesterday
'you know I dreamed that I had f+ that I bought these # you know like shoes yesterday'

In (13) 'såhär' is placed immediately before the object 'skor' (shoes), the new information. The pause before 'du vet såhär skor' (you know like shoes) indicates that the speaker is searching for the appropriate noun. The use of 'såhär' before 'skor' (shoes) may be seen as a means of 'pointing' to the (finally) chosen expression. In the examples below, taken from the SUF-data from Stockholm, 'såhär' is used before an adjective phrase, a noun phrase and a preposition phrase, respectively, obviously functioning as a means to emphasize the following constituent.

(14) a. jag var **såhär** tveksam (Fawza)
I was like hesitant
'I was like hesitant'
b. jag vill också ha ett vitt skärp men mitt skärp de(t) e **såhär** gult
smuts (Bushra)
I want also to-have a white belt but my belt it is like yellow dirt
'I also want to have a white belt but my belt is like yellow dirt'
c. å sen han kommer **såhär** från utomlands du vet (Fawza)
and then he comes like from abroad you know
'and then he comes like from abroad you know'

Comparing 'sån' in (9)–(12) with 'såhär' in (13) and (14) it seems plausible that the two expressions have an identical function in these contexts. While adolescents in Stockholm use *såhär* as a focalizer, adolescents in Malmö instead use 'sån' as a focalizer (see further Ekberg, forthcoming.).

In sum, for the uses of 'sån' exemplified in (3)–(8) there is a common deictic element; 'sån' is used to point to a referent present either in the narrowly defined speech situation (3), or in a wider context where the referent is known (or construed as known) to the participants. In the recognitional use in (6)–(8) the deictic meaning is thus extended beyond the immediate situation. The meaning of comparison is however, not absent in this use, since the referent designated by 'sån' functions as an explicit or implicit comparand needed to identify another referent, the comparee. Also when the deictic meaning is strengthened to a demonstrative (4) or an expressive meaning (5), comparison is relevant, since an imagined comparand functions as the implicit norm for evaluating the designated (properties of the) referent. Finally, 'sån' may also relate to elements in the information structure, in that it may cataphorically point to the rhematic element in an utterance (9)–(12).

When 'sån' has a recognitional function it may introduce a new referent in the current discourse. The function of 'sån' to introduce a new discourse referent coincides with the function of the indefinite article. As shown by the examples in (7) and (8), 'sån' also syntactically seems to replace the indefinite article. In the following section, we will take a closer look at 'sån' as a determiner.

The Meaning and Use of 'Sån' as a Determiner

In standard Swedish 'sån' is typically used as an attribute in an indefinite noun phrase, with or without an overt nominal head, cf. (15a) and (15b), respectively. The neuter singular 'sånt' may also be used in isolation with generic dividuative reference (15c).

(15) a. Jag vill ha **en sån klänning** som Lisa har.
    I want to-have a such dress as Lisa has.
    'I want to have a dress like Lisa's'.
  b. Jag vill ha **en sån**.
    I want to-have a such.
    'I want to have one like that'.
  c. **Sånt** gillar jag inte.
    such like I not.
    'I don't like that'.

In the Malmö-corpus there is a total of 338 occurrences of 'sån'. These include variant forms inflected for neuter gender ('sånt') and plural ('såna'), but not occurrences of 'sånt' in tags (see note 3). In the majority of cases, approximately 60%, 'sån' occurs as part of a noun phrase with an overt noun, either immediately preceding the head noun or followed by a descriptive attribute, '(en) sån (röd) klänning' [(a) such (red) dress]. In yet another 20%, 'sån' appears in a noun phrase without an overt nominal head (15b). A closer look at the indefinite noun phrases with 'sån' reveals differences between the Malmö-corpus and standard Swedish. In standard Swedish an indefinite noun phrase with a singular, countable head noun must be preceded by an indefinite determiner, that is the article 'en'/'ett' (a), or a quantifier for example 'någon' (someone) or 'ingen' (nobody) (optionally together with an adjectval attribute). When no quantifier is present the indefinite article is normally obligatory. In the

Malmö-corpus however, noun phrases with 'sån' often lack the indefinite article, even though there is no (other) quantifier; cf. the example in (6), repeated as (16):

(16) jag var på **sån badplats** (Jing)
 I was at such bathing place
 'I was at this bathing place'

Also when 'sån' occurs in a noun phrase without an overt nominal head the indefinite article may be omitted in the Malmö-corpus:

(17) **sån** har jag också (Duhi) [standard Swedish: 'en sån', cf. (15b)]
 such have I too
 'I have one like that too'

Of the 338 instances of 'sån' in the Malmö-corpus 156 are found in noun phrases where the indefinite article is obligatory in standard Swedish. These include contexts where 'sån' occurs in a headless noun phrase. Out of 156 noun phrases, 115 lack the indefinite article, that is the indefinite article is left out in approximately 74% of the cases. If we look separately at the two peer groups (Table 4.1), we find that the indefinite article is left out more often in the C-group (77%) than in the E-group (68.3%). However, the percentage of omission is notably high in both groups, and the difference is not significant according to the chi-square test [$p = 0.15$ (one-tailed)].

When the indefinite article is absent 'sån' is the only determiner candidate. The question is whether 'sån' also has the same function as the indefinite article, that is to introduce a new discourse referent. This proves to be the case. The typical syntactic context for introducing a new discourse referent is the presentational construction. One of the contexts where 'sån' occurs without an indefinite article is precisely a part of a noun phrase that is the logical subject of a presentational construction, for example 'de(t) e sån NP' (it is such NP, idiom. there is this NP), cf. the utterance in (18) where Duhi four times uses a presentational construction with 'sån' (in italics) to introduce the new discourse referent, a character in a movie. The indefinite article is left out in all four occurrences.

Table 4.1 'sån' construed without the indefinite article in the Malmö-corpus

Group	Article absent/obligatory contexts
C	74/96 ≈ 77%
E	41/60 ≈ 68.3%
Total	115/156 ≈ 73.7%

(18) så så **finns de(t) sån ee typ tecknad figur** nåt sånt # nej **de(t) e inte tecknad figur # de(t) e sån figur** du vet för barn # **så e de(t) sån fågel som e gul så** jag (Duhi)
så så is it such ee type cartoon character something such # no it is not cartoon character # it is such character you know for kids # so is it such bird that is yellow so I
'then there is this like cartoon character or something like that # no it is not a cartoon character # it is a character for kids you know # it is a bird that is yellow so I #'

As pointed out by Heine (1997: 72) an early developmental stage of indefinite articles is the use as a presentative marker to introduce a new discourse participant presumed to be unknown to the hearer. What we witness in the Malmö-corpus may thus be an instance of ongoing grammaticalization where the primary comparative, descriptive pronoun 'sån' is developing into a determiner. As 'sån' may replace the indefinite article, the unreflecting assumption is that 'sån' simply expresses the same meaning as the indefinite article. As we will see this is only partly true.

As a comparative pronoun, 'sån' relates the designated entity, the comparee, to another entity, the comparand, cf. (3a). Conceptually, 'sån' is pointing to the comparand in order to identify the comparee. The comparand is thus included within the scope of 'sån', that is, the context necessary for the interpretation of the designated entity. Whereas the comparand as well as the comparison are linguistically explicit in the prototypical comparative use, 'sån' lacks a linguistically expressed (or physically present) comparand in its recognitional use; cf. (2), repeated as (20).

(20) asså när jag var i bibl+ # ee var i banken i fredags # så **var de(t) sån lite(n) bebis** # (Gordana)
well when I was at libr+ # ee was at bank-the last Friday # so was it such little baby #
'when I was at the libr+ # ee was at the bank last Friday # then there was this little baby #'

However, when the speaker is using 'sån' in (20), she is referring to an imagined comparand, appealing to the common knowledge and experience of the participants. As the imagined (or construed) comparand is necessary to identify the comparee, the comparand is consequently part of the scope of 'sån' also in the recognitional use.

In examples such as (20) 'sån' fulfills the function of introducing a new discourse referent, not previously known to the hearer. Simultaneously 'sån' evokes a meaning of comparison. The speaker is construing the new referent as 'known to us' by way of the imagined comparand, which the hearer is encouraged to 'create' in the ongoing speech situation. Thus the comparee and the comparand are in fact fused in this use of 'sån'.

Consequently, the descriptive meaning of 'sån' (comparing two referents concerning type) is present, although in the background, also in the function as a determiner. In (20), 'sån lite(n) bebis' (such little baby) is construed as a type of baby known to the hearer, although the referent is not previously mentioned and presumably unknown to the hearer. In other words, 'sån' refers to an indefinite entity, belonging to a type of entity, which is construed as known to the hearer. The overall indefinite meaning thus comprises a definite element arising from the conception of (a known) type inherent in 'sån'. This layered meaning explains why 'sån' simultaneously can be used to identify (actualize) a referent that the hearer is familiar with – via the category it belongs to – and to introduce a new discourse referent. In the latter case the use of 'sån' functions as a signal to the hearer to 'seek for' properties characterizing the referent.

Conclusion

The pronoun 'sån', whose primary meaning is comparative, has a wide range of uses both in spoken standard Swedish and in the data studied in this chapter. The investigation of the language use of adolescents in Malmö has revealed two different, but related, grammaticalized extensions of 'sån'. The most striking one is the development of 'sån' into a determiner, replacing the indefinite article 'en'/'ett' (a). The other grammaticalized extension is the use of 'sån' as a focalizer that points to the rhematic element in an utterance, thus relating to the information structure and not to the propositional level. In this function 'sån' precedes but is not integrated in the syntactical structure of a noun phrase or an adjective phrase.

I have been arguing that the primary comparative meaning of 'sån' is present also in the extended meanings. What is common to the primary meaning and its extensions is the deictic, or demonstrative, element. 'sån' designates a referent A by pointing to an implicit or imagined referent B, which serves as an identifying category for A. The demonstrative element is fundamental to the discourse function of 'sån' as a focalizer as well. The act of pointing to an entity in the speech situation is extended to pointing to an entity adhering to the level of information structure.

As a determiner, 'sån' overlaps in meaning and distribution with the indefinite article. However, there are also differences between the two, which can be attributed to the semantics of 'sån'. In the function of introducing a new discourse referent this referent is construed as known to the hearer, thus appealing to the hearer's experience of the type of referent mentioned in the process of 'creating an image' of the new referent. Thus the meaning of 'sån' is obviously more complex than the indefinite article, which of course also may be due to the fact that 'sån' has not gone as far as the indefinite article in the process of grammaticalization.

The investigation of the use of 'sån' among adolescents in a multilingual context in Malmö was motivated by the high frequency of this word in spontaneous speech. In addition, the adolescents themselves reported that a frequent use of 'sån' was one of the characteristic traits of the multiethnic youth language in Malmö, the so-called Rosengård Swedish. The investigation was based on speech data from two female peer groups. One group consisted of four bilingual informants of which two were judged as speakers of Rosengård Swedish in a perception experiment. The other group consisted of three monolingual informants of which two were judged as not speakers of Rosengård Swedish in the same experiment. It thus seemed plausible that the speech style of the bilingual group contained traits of Rosengård Swedish, whereas the speech style of the monolingual group did not. Further, it seemed plausible that the use of 'sån' would be more frequent and extended in the bilingual group. As regards the general frequency and functional use of 'sån' there were however no differences between the groups. Although it seemed that the bilingual group used 'sån' as a determiner more often than the monolingual group this difference was not significant.

One might still wonder why the frequent use of 'sån' is perceived as characteristic of speakers of Rosengård Swedish, when 'sån' obviously is frequently used also among other adolescents in the same geographical area. Could it be that the foreign-sounding way of speaking Swedish that is connected to Rosengård Swedish (cf. Bodén, this volume) triggers the listener to search for (other) nonstandard traits? This question waits for an answer.

On the basis of the hitherto available data we can at least verify that adolescents in a multilingual school context in Malmö show extended uses of 'sån' compared to spoken standard Swedish. Above all, 'sån' is grammaticalizing into a new determiner, which will have consequences for the grammar of the Swedish noun phrase and the system of determiners.

Notes

1. I am grateful to Bente Ailin Svendsen, Carita Paradis, Christer Platzack, Pia Quist, and an anonymous reviewer for valuable comments on a previous version.
2. Note that in Bodén's study the informants have code numbers instead of pseudonyms. Sabaah = C32, Duhi = C41, Jing = C37, Gordana = C28; Aurora = E40, Märta = E33.
3. Instances with 'sån', or actually the neuter form 'sånt', in so-called tags, 'å sånt' (and such), are left out here. See Ekberg (2007) for an account of the use of 'å sånt' in the Malmö-corpus.
4. See Lie (2008) for an account of Norwegian 'sånn', which has several similar functions as 'sån'.

5. It is notable that the equivalents of the examples (10)–(12) are possible in colloquial Danish, as pointed out by an anonymous reviewer. In Danish 'sådan en' (such a), the equivalent to Swedish 'en sån' (a such), is often contracted to 'sånn'. Thus 'sån' used by the adolescents in Malmö would hypothetically be a contracted form of a regional construction 'sån en', influenced by Danish. Speaking against this hypothesis is the fact that there are no instances of the 'uncontracted' form 'sån en' in the Malmö-corpus.

Appendix

Transcription symbols
#	short pause
##	longer pause
+	interrupted speech
xxx	unintelligible sequence
<text>	quoted speech
(de)	standard orthographic addition

Chapter 5
Subject–Verb Order Variation in the Swedish of Young People in Multilingual Urban Areas

N. GANUZA

Introduction

This chapter discusses the use of variable subject–verb order in the Swedish of adolescents in multilingual settings in Sweden. It is based on the results of my thesis (Ganuza, 2008a), which was conducted within the realm of a larger research project entitled *Language and language use among adolescents in multilingual urban settings* (cf. Boyd, this volume).

Swedish, like the other Germanic languages except English, is often thought of as a robust V2 language, that is the most common position for the finite verb within main clauses in Swedish is the second position of the clause. Consequently, whenever a main clause begins with a nonsubject (X), subject (S) verb (V) inversion typically occurs (cf. Examples 1a and 1b).

Example 1a: SV order

Alicia	gick	till skolan
Alicia	went	to school-the
S	V	Adv

'Alicia went to school.'

Example 1b: XVS order

Sen	gick	Alicia	till skolan
Then	went	Alicia	to school-the
X	V	S	Adv

'Then Alicia went to school.'

Only a limited number of exceptions to the V2 rule are allowed in standard or regionalized varieties of Swedish. For example, subject–verb inversion is optional when the adverb 'kanske' (maybe) occurs in the clause-initial position, and if 'kanske' is inserted immediately after the clause-initial element, subject–verb inversion practically never occurs. A clause-initial 'så' (then/so) that indicates conclusion or consequence does not require subject–verb inversion either (SAG, 1999).

By contrast, in Swedish as a second language violations of the V2 rule are known to be common, and second language learners, especially at the early stages of development, often produce examples of SV order following clause-initial nonsubjects (from now on referred to as XSV, as shown in Example 2) (Bolander, 1988a, 1988b; Håkansson, 1992; Hyltenstam, 1977, 1978).

Example 2: XSV order

Sen	hon	gick	till	skolan
then	she	went	to	school-the
X	S	V		Adv

'Then she went to school.' (which is possible in English, but not in standard Swedish)

Some researchers have also claimed that XSV is frequently employed in the Swedish of adolescents in multilingual urban areas, even when they are not obvious second language speakers of Swedish (e.g. Kotsinas, 1988a, 1994, 1998), and similar observations have been made in Denmark (Quist, 2000) and Norway (Opsahl & Nistov, this volume). Judging by media and literary accounts as well as anecdotal evidence, many people today presume that XSV is typical of Swedish spoken among adolescents in highly multilingual suburbs (cf. Källström, 2005, 2006, this volume). What this tells us is that the use of XSV is a perceptually salient linguistic trait in the language of some adolescents, but as of yet, no empirical study has quantitatively or systematically investigated how frequently XSV is employed by adolescents in different situations (cf. Opsahl & Nistov, this volume for such an analysis in Oslo, Norway).

Therefore, one of the primary aims of my thesis work was to explore how (un)common the use of XSV was among adolescents in a few multilingual settings in Sweden and to provide quantitative data of their subject–verb orders. Another aim was to study how the adolescents' choice of subject–verb order might be constrained by different situational, demographic, linguistic, and socio-pragmatic variables, as well as to explore the link to learner language.

Participants and Data

The participants of the present study were 127 senior high school students who were part of the aforementioned project entitled *Language and language use among adolescents in multilingual urban settings* (cf. Boyd, this volume). For this project, the research team selected eight senior high school classes in Stockholm, Gothenburg, and Malmö, Sweden's three largest cities. In each city, at least one class was selected in a school located in a highly multilingual area and at least one class in a school in a less multilingual and often more centrally located area. In the less multilingual schools, a relatively large proportion of the students still had a multilingual background, and a relatively large number of them lived in multilingual suburbs, despite going to school elsewhere. The participants were 17–19 years of age at the time of the study, and information about each participant's linguistic and family background was gathered through structured interviews based on a questionnaire.

In order to be able to compare data from the various cities and schools, as well as explore the impact of different background variables on the use of XSV, oral and written production data was collected from each of the 127 participants. This pool of data includes retellings, in which the participants were asked to retell a movie of their own choice to one of the researchers; written essays, which were written as part of a national test in Swedish or Swedish as a second language; and a written grammaticality judgement test (GJT), in which the participants were asked to judge sentences with examples of XVS and XSV as either 'right' or 'wrong'. The main purpose of the retelling task was to elicit longer stretches of continuous speech with each participant. In the present chapter, I am referring primarily to the retellings when I speak about the results of *the large sample*.

In order to be able to make more in-depth inter- and intra-individual analyses of subject–verb order variation and to explore the adolescents' syntactic repertoires, a subsample of 20 participants from the Stockholm schools was selected. From now on, this sample will be referred to as *the focus sample*, as opposed to *the large sample*. In addition to retellings, written essays, and GJTs, data was analyzed with the focus participants from semidirected group conversations, self-recordings and classroom presentations.

The focus sample includes participants with both a multilingual and monolingual Swedish background. The intention was to include participants in the focus sample who had acquired Swedish at different ages in an attempt to explore the link to learner language and investigate the importance of age of onset of Swedish acquisition on the adolescents' use of XSV. The participants with a multilingual background were intended to represent both early and later acquirers of Swedish (i.e. participants with a multilingual background who reported that they had acquired Swedish before the age of four, and participants with a multilingual background who reported that they had acquired Swedish sometime after the age of six). The age intervals were chosen based on earlier findings of ages that have proven to be important for first and second language acquisition. A distinction between what leads to the simultaneous acquisition of two languages and the successive acquisition of two languages is sometimes drawn at the ages of 3–4 (Håkansson & Nettelbladt, 1993; McLaughlin, 1978, 1987). A language that is acquired before the age of three is then hypothesized to develop as a first language, whereas a language acquired after this age is expected to develop as a second language. Some studies of Swedish second language acquisition indicate that second language learners who begin to learn Swedish before the ages of 6–7 often develop an automatized syntax similar to those who learn Swedish as a first language, whereas those who start learning Swedish after this age often do not (Ekberg, 2004; Hyltenstam, 1992). If these criteria were to be used in the present study, only a minority of the 127 participants (39 individuals, or 31%) would be defined as second language speakers of Swedish, and even fewer would be expected to have a nonautomatized syntax in Swedish. This is true for participants from both the more and the less multilingual schools in the samples studied.

In the focus sample, the intention was also to include participants who were possible users of XSV and other linguistic traits often associated with youth language practices in multilingual settings (e.g. Kotsinas, 1988a, 1988b, 1994, 1996). This judgment was based on informal observations made in the schools during the semester prior to data collection. The selection of the focus sample was also dependent on the adolescents wanting to participate actively in the project and their willingness to record themselves together with friends in their spare time.

The final focus sample consists of four speakers with a multilingual background who reported that they started acquiring Swedish after the age of six, 11 speakers with a multilingual background who reported that they started acquiring Swedish before the age of four, and five speakers with a monolingual Swedish background. Considering how this focus sample was selected, the results from this group of participants cannot be said to be representative of all the participants studied.

In total, approximately 60 hours of recorded speech were analyzed for this study. Oral data was recorded and transcribed by the author using a modified standard orthography (see Ganuza, 2008a for more details).

Procedure of Analysis

For each transcript, all main declarative clauses were excerpted, including sentence fragments if they contained at least a subject and a finite verb. It was then specified how many of the declaratives that began with something other than a subject, that is which provided a context for subject–verb inversion (from now on referred to as X-clauses). Declarative clauses beginning with the type of clause-initial 'så' (so) that do not require subject–verb inversion in standard Swedish (see above) were not counted as X-clauses, whereas declaratives beginning with the adverb 'kanske' (maybe) were counted as X-clauses. The proportion of X-clauses was counted in relation to the total number of main declarative clauses produced in a recording. Different X-clause word order patterns were then specified, the most important being XVS (i.e. X-clauses produced with standard subject–verb inversion, see Example 1b), XSV (i.e. X-clauses produced with clear noninversion, see Example 3), and possible (p) examples of XSV (i.e. pXSV), which are open to alternative interpretation.

Relatively Infrequent Use of XSV

The overall results showed that relatively few examples of XSV were produced in the samples studied. In the large sample, only 3.5% of the X-clauses displayed clear XSV order (see Table 5.1). This figure does not include examples of XSV that are well-known exceptions to the V2 rule in standard and regionalized varieties of Swedish (e.g. SAG, 1999, see also above). As expected, almost all examples of XSV in the large sample were found in the oral context, that is in the retellings.

In the focus sample, which included more spontaneous data in which the participants were able to interact with their peers, XSV was comparatively more frequent, although the proportion of clear examples of XSV did not exceed 9.9% (see Table 5.1). These figures are lower than I had expected to find based on previous research (e.g. Kotsinas, 1994, 1998) and my own first impressions, at least in the oral production contexts and especially in the peer–peer interactions recorded.

In the large sample the general pattern was that participants employed standard subject–verb inversion after clause-initial nonsubjects almost all the time, although many participants, from the various schools produced sporadic examples of XSV in their retellings. In total, 72 of the 127 participants (i.e. 57%) produced at least one example of XSV in their retellings. The low proportion of XSV found in the large sample is likely due, at least in part, to the fact that the situations included in the sample were not favorable for the production of XSV. As demonstrated later, examples of XSV appear to be produced mainly in peer–peer interaction, which is also what Kotsinas claimed in her early studies conducted in the 1980s (e.g. 1988, 1994, 1998). However, no one has previously quantitatively demonstrated to what extent XSV is present, or absent, in the Swedish of adolescents in multilingual settings in different types of situations.

Despite the generally low numbers of XSV in the retellings, there were six participants who produced a relatively high number of XSV examples

Table 5.1 Distribution of results in the large sample and the focus sample

Sample	Declaratives		X-clauses			XVS		XSV		pXSV	
	N	%	N	% (x/d)	N	% (xvs/x)	N	% (xsv/x)	N	% (pxsv/x)
Large	126	22,647	100.0	6911	30.5	6434	93.1	241	3.5	144	2.1
Focus	20	11,228	100.0	2304	20.5	1938	84.1	229	9.9	107	4.6

Table 5.2 Distribution of results in the focus sample

Situation		Declaratives		X-clauses		XVS		XSV		pXSV	
	N	N	%	N	% (x/d)	N	% (xvs/x)	N	% (xsv/x)	N	% (pxsv/x)
Group conv.	19	1582	100.0	260	16.4	193	74.2	51	19.6	14	5.4
Self-record.	13	3068	100.0	400	13.0	322	80.5	55	13.8	18	4.5
Retellings	19	4238	100.0	1019	24.0	859	84.3	87	8.5	60	5.9
Presentations	18	1532	100.0	361	23.6	307	85.0	35	9.7	15	4.2
Written essays	20	808	100.0	264	32.7	257	97.3	1	0.4	0	0

in this context, between 5 and 53 examples each. Three of these participants had conducted their retellings in the company of one or two peers, which may be one explanation why they, unlike the other participants, were more prone to using XSV in this context. However, with the exception of one participant, Farhad (B02), these six participants also produced the majority of their X-clauses with subject–verb inversion.

In the focus sample, interesting variation was found between the different situational contexts (see Table 5.2). A larger proportion of X-clauses were produced with XSV in the group conversations and self-recordings than in the other contexts studied. All but three of the 20 focus participants produced at least a few examples each of XSV in their self-recordings and/or group conversations. In the focus sample, there were even a few occasions when participants used more XSV than subject–verb inversion, for example, during a group conversation among three boys, Ekmel (B05), Mehmet (B09), and Ismail (B16), in one of the more multilingual schools in Stockholm (see Ganuza, 2008a, 2008b, for more details). But, if all oral production data are considered together, all the focus participants produced more examples of standard XVS than of XSV.

The Importance of the Linguistic Context

Research on variable subject–verb order in Swedish as a second language has shown that the type and nature of the clause-initial element, the subject and the finite verb may influence learners' application of the verb-second rule (e.g. Bolander, 1988a, 1988b; see also Hagen, 1992 for Norwegian as a second language). Bolander (1988a, 1988b) revealed that second language learners of Swedish were more likely to produce subject–verb inversion after clause-initial objects (as in Example 3a) than they were after clause-initial short adverbs (Example 3b) or subordinate clauses (Example 3c).

Example 3a: Clause-initial object.

Det	tror	jag
that	think	I
X	V	S

'I think so.'

Example 3b: Clause-initial short adverb

Då	går	jag
then	walk	I
X	V	S

'Then I leave.'

Example 3c: Clause-initial subordinate clause

När	du	kommer	går	jag
when	you	come	walk	I
X (sub. clause)			V	S

'When you come, I leave.'

Bolander (1988a, 1988b) also found that inversion was favored by the subject of an X-clause being a lexical noun phrase (e.g. the little girl) rather than a pronoun (e.g. she) and also that first person pronouns favored inversion more than second or third person pronouns. Bolander also saw a tendency for certain verbs, for example, the verb 'komma' (to come), to favor inversion (see also Håkansson, 2004).

As one attempt in this study to explore the link to learner language, it was investigated whether these same linguistic variables were of importance for the adolescents' subject–verb placement, despite the fact the majority of them, as previously argued, would not be defined as obvious second language learners of Swedish since most of them started acquiring Swedish before the age of four.

The results of the linguistic analyses demonstrated that the only linguistic variable to consistently influence the participants' subject–verb order across different situational contexts in this study was the clause-initial element. XSV was more commonly produced after nonclausal adverbials, particularly after the connective adverbs 'sen' (then) and 'då' (then) (see Examples 4a and 4b) and after subordinate clauses (see Example 4c) than after other clause-initial nonsubjects.

Example 4a: XSV after the clause-initial connective adverb 'sen' (then). [Rana (L39), self-recording]

å	sen	jag	har	lunch
and	then	I	have	lunch
X		S	V	

'and then I have lunch.'

Example 4b: XSV after the clause-initial connective adverb 'då' (then) [Ekmel (B05), presentation]

då	landet	får	en sjukhus
then	country-the	gets	a hospital
X	S	V	

'then the country gets a hospital.'

Example 4c: XSV after a clause-initial subordinate clause [Semra (L43), retelling]

när	han	kom	tillbaka	man	trodde	han	levde
when	he	came	back	you	thought	he	lived

X (sub.clause)   S   V

'when he came back you thought he was alive.'

By contrast, XSV practically never occurred after clause-initial objects, predicative or infinitival clauses, and the so-called tag structures (e.g. 'han e bra, tycker jag', literally: he's good, think I) were always produced with subject–verb inversion. These results are similar to those found in Bolanders's (1988a, 1988b) studies of Swedish learner language.

In the data, the connective adverb 'sen' (then) tended to be the most common clause-initial element, followed by SV order. Many participants (in total, 63 of the 127 participants, or 50%) produced at least one or a few examples of XSV following a clause-initial 'sen', and examples of 'sen'-SV were found in all the oral contexts studied. Certain individuals produced many examples of 'sen'-SV. The connective adverb 'då' (then) and various types of clause-initial prepositional phrases were also often followed by XSV. The incidence of XSV following these elements was, however, more restricted to certain individuals and certain situational contexts. The use of XSV following 'då' or a prepositional phrase appeared to be connected to a high use of XSV in general, and only individuals with a comparatively high overall number of XSV produced these examples more than sporadically.

The results also showed that participants' subject–verb order was influenced by the presence or absence of a topic placeholder immediately following the clause-initial element. Clause-initial subordinate clauses that were followed by a topic placeholder 'så/då' (see Example 5) were produced less often with SV order than clause-initial subordinate clauses that were not immediately followed by a topic placeholder.

Example 5: Subject–verb inversion after a topic placeholder [Rachel (B25), retelling]

men	när	man	ser den	så	e	den	jätteläskig
but	when	you	see it	placeholder	is	it	really scary

'but when you see it it's really scary.'

Clause-initial 'sen' or 'då' that were immediately followed by a topic placeholder, that is 'sen så'/'då så', were also produced less often with following SV order than simple clause-initial 'sen' or 'då'. Thus, the presence of topic placeholders evidently favored subject–verb inversion in this study.

It was explored whether the type and nature of the subject of an X-clause determined participants' production of XSV, but no consistent patterns were found. The subject being a lexical noun phrase did not favor or disfavor inversion more than the subject being a pronoun, as discovered in studies of subject–verb inversion when Swedish is a second language (cf. Bolander, 1988a, 1988b). Nor was there any evidence of certain verb types (i.e. whether main, auxiliary or copula verbs) or certain verbs to systematically constrain participants' subject–verb order, as was also found in studies when Swedish is a second language (cf. Bolander, 1988a, 1988b; Håkansson, 2004).

Therefore, the overall results are both similar and partially different from the results found in studies of Swedish as a second language. As in learner language, the type and nature of the clause-initial element partly constrained the adolescents' choice of subject–verb order, whereas the type and nature of the subject and finite verb apparently did not. The general conclusion is that linguistic context alone cannot explain the variation produced in this study. Language-internal variables are, for example, unable to clarify why only certain individuals within the samples varied between XVS and XSV, and/or why these individuals varied in some contexts, but not in others.

The Importance of Different Background Variables

The importance of different background variables was explored, from both a quantitative and qualitative viewpoint. Statistical analyses were conducted on the oral production data from the large sample, that is the retellings, in order to be able to compare the results from the different cities and different schools.

As mentioned above, the majority of participants from all three cities produced no or only a few examples of XSV in their retellings. The overall results demonstrated, however, that the Stockholm participants used slightly more examples of XSV in their retellings compared to participants from the other two cities. In Stockholm, there were two participants who produced 53 and 35 examples each of XSV (36% and 63% of their total number of X-clauses) in their respective retelling, and there were another four participants who produced 5–11 examples of XSV per person (between 13% and 17% of their X-clauses). By contrast, none of the participants in Gothenburg and Malmo produced more than four examples of XSV per person, and only one participant reached a proportion of XSV within the limits of these Stockholm participants. These results indicate that the use of XSV could be linked in particular to Stockholm. As previously mentioned, the focus sample only included data from Stockholm, although unsystematic analyses of self-recordings and group conversations collected in Gothenburg and Malmo give the impression that there are no comparisons in these materials to the most frequent users of XSV in the Stockholm sample. Of course, these observations need to be investigated in more detail.

The results from the large sample indicated that the use of XSV might be linked in particular to the more multilingual schools in Stockholm, since all but one of the participants with more than five examples of XSV in their retellings were from the schools located in highly multilingual areas. This was contradicted, however, by the results of the focus sample, since XSV were produced by participants from all the schools studied in Stockholm, that is also by participants in the school located in the less multilingual setting.

A common factor for almost all of the most frequent users of XSV in the samples studied is that they come from a multilingual background, that is they have grown up with at least one language in addition to Swedish during childhood. Most of them also have in common that they live in multilingual settings, and/or report that most of their closest friends are from a multilingual background. A statistical analysis of the relationship between the use of XSV in the retellings and the participants' background as multi- or monolingual speakers of Swedish revealed that participants with a multilingual background produced significantly more examples of XSV in the retellings than did participants from a monolingual Swedish background ($p < 0.05$, Mann–Whitney U test). Results from both the large sample and the focus sample therefore suggest that the adolescents' background as multi- or monolingual speakers of Swedish was an important factor for their use of XSV; in fact, it was actually more important than whether or not they went to school in a more or less multilingual area. At the same time, it is important to remember that many participants from a multilingual background produced no or very few examples of XSV in this study. There were also individuals with a monolingual Swedish background who used more than sporadic examples of XSV in their self-recordings and/or group conversations, although these were predominantly produced in conversation with multilingual peers. To conclude, participants' background as multi- or monolingual speakers of Swedish appears to be of importance for their use of XSV, but it is far from the only variable in determining the adolescents' subject–verb order variation.

Because the occurrence of XSV is known to be common in learner Swedish, it would have been easy to assume that the use of XSV in the present study would have its origin in learner language. The link to learner language was explored by investigating the relationship between participants' use of XSV and their reported age of onset of Swedish acquisition. In retellings from the large sample, a positive correlation was found between the participants' use of XSV and their reported age of onset of Swedish acquisition ($r = 0.304$, $p < 0.01$, Spearman's rank-order correlation), that is a later reported age of onset was related to an increased use of

XSV. Nevertheless, the calculation of the coefficient of determination showed that the studied variables only shared approximately 9% of their variance; thus, only a small part of the variation produced could be explained by the participants' reported age of onset. Analyses of the focus sample also demonstrated that participants' age of onset of Swedish acquisition could not be the sole, or the most important, explanatory factor for the adolescents' use of XSV. For example, the two overall most frequent users of XSV in the study, female participant Bushra (K28) and male participant Ekmel (B05), both reported that they started learning Swedish at home along with Arabic and Turkish, respectively, before the age of three. The two of them produced many more examples of XSV than any of the participants who reported that they started to learn Swedish at a much later age. In fact, almost all of the most frequent users of XSV in both samples studied reported that they started acquiring Swedish at an early age.

The results presented in this section, along with the results presented in the previous section, show that the use of XSV in the current study cannot be reduced merely to a learner phenomenon. The finding that some of the participants with a monolingual Swedish background used XSV in conversation with peers further supports the conclusion that there is no direct link between the use of XSV and learner language in this study. At the same time, I think that learner language could *indirectly* be the source of the participants' use of XSV. The various ways of speaking Swedish, which are characteristic of second language learners in the adolescents' home and school environments, may have served as the inspiration for secondary representations of those ways of speaking Swedish (cf. Jaspers, 2008: 87). The adolescents' use of subject–verb order variation, along with other linguistic traits influenced by the multilingual setting, might constitute one resource that they employ as a means of showing solidarity with the various ways of speaking Swedish that surround them, as well as a means for them to express their identification with a multilingual setting (cf. Fraurud & Bijvoet, 2004; Kotsinas, 1989, 1996). If the learner language input is seen as an indirect source of the adolescents' use of XSV, this could explain why some, though not all, of the same linguistic factors that determine variable subject–verb order in learner language were found to constrain the subject–verb order variation produced in this study.

For some of the participants, of course, it is possible that their use of XSV is at least partly the result of them still being in the process of acquiring Swedish. For example, Kalifa, a female participant with one of the highest ages of onset of Swedish acquisition in this study, 9.5 years, produced a relatively large amount of examples of XSV in her retelling and self-recording. She was also one of the participants who deviated the most from standard Swedish norms in her judgment of variable subject–verb placement in the written grammaticality judgment test. In addition to examples of XSV, her oral production contained a number of features that are often taken as typical of Swedish as a second language, for example she sometimes left out obligatory subjects and articles, vacillated in her choice of prepositions and gender, produced examples of nonagreement in noun phrases and used certain nonidiomatic expressions. This suggests that Kalifa's use of XSV might have been the result of her learner status. Complicating this conclusion is the circumstance that most of the mentioned so-called typical second language features have been claimed by some researchers to be more or less conventionalized characteristics of multiethnic youth language varieties (e.g. Kotsinas, 1994, 1998). One possible scenario is that Kalifa's, and possibly some of the other participants', use of XSV and other 'typical' second language features is simultaneously the result of her being in the process of acquiring Swedish and the result of her using these features in accordance with local linguistic norms.

XSV as a Linguistic Strategy

Results from both the quantitative and qualitative analyses of the data suggest that the use of XSV is part of some of the participants' more casual language repertoires in certain contexts. First, examples of XSV occurred predominantly in peer–peer interactions and much more rarely in conversations with adults (see Ganuza, 2008a, 2008b). Second, most examples of XSV were found in conversational contexts characterized by a *high-involvement style* (Tannen, 1984). Most instances of XSV occurred when the participants spoke about something that was personally engaging, that is when they told someone about something that had happened to them or somebody they knew. A number of features typical of informal youth language (e.g. Nordberg, 1984) often occurred in the same passages in which examples of XSV were found with slang words, epistemic markers such as 'du vet' (you know), 'ba' (just) and 'såhär' (like) (cf. Svensson, 2007, 2009), discourse extenders (cf. Ekberg, this volume), fast speech rates, a lot of overlapping talk, expressive phonology and sometimes marked intonational patterns (cf. Bodén, this volume). The results thus suggest that XSV is part of some participants' high-involvement style and part of their informal youth language repertoire, as illustrated in Example 6 (a transcription key is found at the end of this chapter).

> *Example 6:* XSV as part of a high-involvement style [Parwin (K36) and Bushra (K28), self-recording]
>
> K36: […] men va heter re å sen hans mamma ba när dom han höll på äta # ha+ hon ba ah vi ska till eh Pakistan för att va heter re # mormor e sjuk [=! skratt] # ja å sen han skicka meddelande [XSV] jag hatar när han gör så han skickar meddelande å sen han säger [XSV] jag ringer dej sen å berättar # då jag sitter där å väntar han ska ringa [XSV].

K28: aha.
K36: <[>] jag ba ah fan jag visste xxx visste hundra procent.
K28: <[>] tänk om han ljuger.
K36: han ljuger inte xxx <u>om han skulle ljuga då han skulle ba ah</u> [XSV] # eh han skulle säga att han skoja sen [...].

[K36: [...] but you know and then his mom just when they he was eating # he+ she just yeah so we're going to eh Pakistan because you know # grandma is sick [=! laughs] # yeah <u>and then he sent a message</u> [XSV] I hate when does that he sends me a message <u>and then he says</u> [XSV] I'll call you later to explain # <u>then I sit there waiting for him to call</u> [XSV].
K28: yeah.
K36: <[>] I just what the hell I knew it xxx knew it hundred percent.
K28: <[>] what if he lies.
K36: he doesn't lie xxx <u>if he would lie then he would just like</u> [XSV] # eh he would tell that he was joking later [...].

In Example 6, female participant Parwin (K36) explains to Bushra (K28) that it irritates her when her boyfriend sends her text messages telling her that he is going to call her later to explain something and then he leaves her waiting by the phone for him to call. During the account Parwin produces several examples of XSV; she speaks fast, she is very engaged in what she is talking about and she adds many filler words and expressions. By quoting what the boyfriend and others said during the event, she also manages to make the story more vivid, which is another characteristic that is known to be typical of informal youth language (e.g. Eriksson, 1997).

As typified in Example 6 (see lines 3–5), instances of XSV often occurred when participants started to enumerate a number of events that had happened or were about to happen, especially if these enumerations began with the expression 'å sen' (and then).

The results presented so far indicate that variation between XVS and XSV may occur as a result of changes in the external situational context, and that XSV may be part of some participants' casual language repertoire, part of their 'vernacular language' (e.g. Labov, 1972), to use a traditional sociolinguistic term. Perhaps more importantly, the data also suggests that some participants might use XSV as part of an active linguistic resource or strategy, which they employ in certain situations in order to express their affiliation with the multilingual suburb, to show solidarity with their peers in a classroom situation, and/or as part of an act of contestation.

For example, one participant, Ekmel (B05), used a lot of XSV during a classroom presentation conducted together with two classmates on the subject of refugees and immigration (see Example 7). Interestingly, Ekmel used XSV particularly during parts of the presentation when he improvised, when he became more involved in something he was speaking about, and when he tried to include his classmates more in the presentation. In the same passages that his XSV occurred in, Ekmel also tended to use more slang, speak faster, keep better eye contact with the audience, and gesticulate more than during parts of the presentation in which he mostly reported facts and information about the subject matter.

> *Example 7:* XSV as part of a linguistic strategy [Ekmel (B05), presentation]
>
> […] om man e om man mår om man e sjuk å mår å mår dåligt du vet typ [=! harklar sig] om du ska typ operera hjärtat i Afghanistan tror du du kommer leva efter näej så liksom <u>då du kommer till Sverige</u> [XSV] å dom hjälper dej å sen typ såhär ah de e fint väder här jag # jag blev hotad där nere <u>å sen du får uppehållstillstånd här</u> [XSV] <u>å sen du får</u> [XSV] du vet ah du fifflar till det lite där sådära […].
>
> [[…] if you are if you feel if you're sick and feel and feel bad you know like [=! clears his throat] if you're supposed to operate your heart in Afghanistan do you think you're going to live after NO so like <u>then you come to Sweden</u> [XSV] and they help you and they sort of ah the weather's nice here I # I was threatened down there <u>and then you get a residence permit here</u> [XSV] <u>and then you get</u> [XSV] you know yeah you know you mess around a little like that […].

Practically none of the other participants used XSV in their classroom presentations. By changing his language use, Ekmel was able to get more attention from his classmates, who were much more alert during these parts of the presentation and asked more questions. Ekmel's use of XSV, along with several other linguistic traits, was one means by which he was able to manifest his allegiance and solidarity with his classmates, and in a way was also a means for him to contest the official school discourse surrounding the act of the presentation. Some comments from the teacher following the presentation confirmed the impression that Ekmel's presentation was understood as a form of contestation.

During a background interview conducted with Ekmel at the outset of the project, he explained to one of the researchers how 'Rinkeby Swedish' (cf. Kotsinas, 1994), or youth slang, was his everyday language and the way he spoke with his friends. The researcher did not ask him specific questions about 'Rinkeby Swedish', but despite this Ekmel kept getting back to the subject during the interview, and while speaking about this, he produced many examples of XSV, something he rarely did in other conversations with adults that we recorded.

There were instances when the participants' use of XSV appeared to be part of an act of resistance towards being recorded and researched upon.

For instance, during a conversation between Ekmel (B05), Mehmet (B09) and Murad (B18) in one of the more multilingual schools in Stockholm, the boys made some provocative remarks about one of the female researchers, whom they knew would listen to the recording at a later date (see Example 8). In Example 8, Ekmel, Mehmet and Murad discuss whether the female researcher is likely or not to have sex with any of them. Initially, Ekmel says that he does not think that she would 'give' them anything but Murad says that she definitely would, and later on in the recording he even claims to have evidence of her having done so already. The example ends with Ekmel's comment that the researcher is going to 'kill' them when she listens to the recording.

Example 8: XSV as part of an act of contestation [Mehmet (B09), Ekmel (B05) and Murad (B18), group conversation]

B09: asså de om vi baxar [slang] hennes nummer # <u>å sen vi ringer henne</u> [XSV] <u>å sen vi kanske kan g+ bazz [slang] henne</u> [XSV].
B05: vem?
B09: den hära XXX.
B05: jag tror inte hon ger [slang] len [slang].
B18: hon ger [slang] hon ger [slang].
[...]
B05: asså <u>när hon hör det här hon kommer spräckish</u> [slang] oss [XSV].

[B09: well if we [baxar] [steal] her number # <u>and then we call her</u> [XSV] <u>and then maybe we can g + [bazz] [fuck] her</u> [XSV].
B05: who?
B09: this XXX [name of project member].
B05: I don't think she gives [sex] [len] [man].
B18: she gives she gives.
[...]
B05: well # <u>when she hears this she's gonna [spräckish] [kill] us</u> [XSV]]

What is particularly interesting about these comments in the current study is that they are loaded with examples of XSV and slang words associated with multilingual youth language practices. The provocation being made is manifested as much in what the boys say as in how they say it. A similar example was found in a group conversation between two girls, Åsa (L37) and Radmila (L28), in the less multilingual school in the Stockholm material. In total, the girls produced few examples of XSV, but during a passage of the recording when the girls complained about being 'forced' to be recorded Åsa uttered one example of XSV, and shortly thereafter, when the girls spoke about trying to steal the recording equipment, Radmila uttered another example of XSV. In both of these examples, the use of XSV appeared to be used as part of an act of protest (for a more detailed discussion on this and more examples, see Ganuza, 2008a: 121–130).

Concluding Remarks

In this chapter, I have explored the adolescents' subject–verb placement in different situational contexts. It was concluded that relatively few examples of XSV were found if all data is considered, although considerable variation was found among different contexts and among different individuals. For the most part, the participants studied employed standard subject–verb inversion after clause-initial nonsubjects. At the same time, there were a few individuals who produced a relatively large number of examples of XSV in certain contexts, especially in interaction with peers.

The overall results indicated that the participants' choice of subject–verb order was constrained by the situational context, as well as by various language-internal, demographic, and socio-pragmatic factors. XSV was predominantly produced in oral production, particularly in peer–peer interactions. Concerning the influence of the linguistic context, the type and nature of the clause-initial element was found to influence participants' subject–verb placement. In all the oral contexts studied, XSV occurred most commonly after the clause-initial short adverb 'sen' (then). In terms of the impact of different demographic factors on the use of XSV, the analyses of the data suggested that the frequent use of XSV might be linked in particular to youth language practices in Stockholm, in particular to the more multilingual schools in the Stockholm sample. The overall results also revealed that the participants' background as multilingual or monolingual speakers of Swedish influenced their use of XSV. All of the most frequent users of XSV were from a multilingual background, reported that they lived in multilingual suburbs, and/or reported that most of their closest friends were from a multilingual background. In regard to the link to learner language, it was concluded that the use of XSV in this study could not be explained simply as a learner phenomenon, although the statistical analyses showed that a later reported age of onset of Swedish acquisition was related to an increased proportion of XSV in the large sample. Even so, age of onset could far from explain all the subject–verb order variation produced in the study, and the fact of the matter was also that the most frequent users of XSV in the samples studied could not unarguably be defined as second language speakers of Swedish since they had learned Swedish along with another language from a very early age. The data also revealed that some participants with a monolingual Swedish background actively used XSV. In conclusion, the data demonstrated that all of the participants in this study, irrespective of when they started learning Swedish, knew how to use standard subject–verb inversion in a number of different linguistic and situational contexts. With the exception of one individual, the participants used more standard subject–verb inversion than not after clause-initial nonsubjects, if all oral production data is considered.

Taken together, the results indicate that the use of XSV is part of some of the participants' more casual language repertoire, but also suggest that some of the participants might use XSV more actively as part of a linguistic strategy with which they may manifest their solidarity with their peers, and/or manifest their resistance toward being researched. In future studies, it would be important to further explore the possible communicative purposes behind an active use of XSV, as well as try to link the adolescents' use of XSV and other linguistic means to a wider social context.

Transcription key

K36	= participant code
[]	= comment
[XSV]	= sentence produced with XSV
[…]	= part of the utterance has been left out
#	= pause
##	= long pause
xxx	= unintelligible speech
xx +	= interrupted word
[=!]	= extralinguistic material
<[>]	= overlapping talk

Chapter 6
On Some Structural Aspects of Norwegian Spoken among Adolescents in Multilingual Settings in Oslo

T. OPSAHL and I. NISTOV

Introduction

Background: More than words?

This chapter is from the Oslo branch of the national Norwegian research project UPUS ('Utviklingsprosesser i urbane språkmiljø' – Developmental processes in urban linguistic settings) (cf. Svendsen, this volume). The findings presented in this chapter should be seen as complementary to the discussion of functions as presented by Aarsæther (this volume).

The idea that a new way of speaking Norwegian has emerged among adolescents in multiethnic settings in Oslo has already been established in the media and among people in general. However, prior to the UPUS-project there had not been any comprehensive study of this phenomenon apart from a master's thesis addressing vocabulary used by Oslo youth in multilingual settings (Aasheim, 1995), a study of lexical loans from immigrant languages (Drange, 2002) and a popularized 'Kebabnorsk' (kebab-Norwegian) dictionary (Østby, 2005). Studies of other Germanic languages show that language practices among adolescents in multilingual urban settings are also characterized by several structural features (cf. section 'Previous research addressing structural characteristics'). Our main purpose in this chapter is to investigate whether this is also the fact in Oslo; is it literally a question of more than words?

Previous research addressing structural characteristics

Already 20 years ago Kotsinas (1988a, 1988b) addressed the phenomenon 'rinkebysvenska' (Rinkeby Swedish) in a multilingual suburb of Stockholm, and her descriptions of the structural features of this variety appear to have relevance also for today's research. Kotsinas describes deviations regarding gender, agreement, prepositions and word order (Kotsinas, 1988a, 1988b). Several studies both in Scandinavia and elsewhere in Europe relate to Kotsinas' description of 'rinkebysvenska'. Two of the structural features mentioned by Kotsinas are also found in Danish for 'københavnsk multietnolekt' (Copenhagen multiethnolect) (cf. Quist, 2000: 152), namely violation of the V2 constraint (see section 'Violations of the V2 constraint') and simplification of the grammatical gender system. Wiese (2006) reports violations of the V2 constraint in German 'Kiezsprache' (Neighborhood talk), and Ganuza has addressed this phenomenon in depth in a recent Swedish study (cf. Ganuza, 2008; Ganuza, this volume). Cornips has on several occasions addressed the loss of grammatical gender in acquisition of Dutch by older Moroccan and Turkish children (cf. Cornips, 2008 with further references). Nortier (2001: 65–66) reports the use of wrong gender for both 'street language' and 'Murk', a stereotypical imitation of foreigners, used by in-group ethnic Dutch adolescents.

The purpose of this chapter

A first brief encounter with our Norwegian data reveals that the features mentioned by Kotsinas (1988a, 1988b) and in corresponding studies in other European cities may serve as a point of departure for our study: We observe, as touched upon by Svendsen and Røyneland (2008), violations of the V2 constraint; we see traces of what seems to be a simplification within the grammatical gender domain; we notice extended use of the preposition 'på' (on) as well as several instances of bare singular nouns or partially omission of definiteness marking. In this chapter we wish to take a closer look at the first two characteristics mentioned in this list: The violations of the V2 constraint and simplifications within the grammatical gender domain.

Our research question is twofold. We start by taking an emic perspective asking whether structural features are reported in the adolescents' own descriptions of their language use. Our next question is what characterizes their actual linguistic behavior regarding grammatical gender and violations of the V2 constraint. Furthermore, in order to shed light on the question of whether we are dealing with in-group linguistic practices their linguistic behavior is observed in two different speech situations with different degree of formality and colloquial character (cf. section 'Two different speech situations').

Design of the Study

Data and informants

The main body of data for the UPUS/Oslo project consist of a questionnaire, video-recorded interviews and conversations between peers (cf. Svendsen, this volume). The recordings of the interviews and peer conversations took place – with a few exceptions – at youth clubs in the young peoples' neighborhood. The informants were all born and raised in Oslo, and their parents are either Norwegian born or foreign born (cf. Table 6.1). In this chapter we report results from an analysis of a sample of 22 informants.

The sample of 22 informants represents a cross section of the youth population at the youth clubs we visited for observations and recordings: There were more boys than girls attending the clubs, and the majority had some sort of minority background, that is one or two of their parents were born abroad. At the time of the recordings two of the boys, Aswan and Anders, were attending high school (aged 16–19), while the others were pupils in secondary school (Norwegian 'ungdomsskolen', aged 13–15).

Table 6.1 Sample of informants organized by gender and parental background

	Two foreign-born parents	*One foreign-born parent*	*Two Norwegian-born parents*
Boys	Aswan	Anders	Lars
	Farid	Gabriel	Olav
	Leonel	Michael	Roger
	Lukas		
	Mike		
	Murat		
	Robert		
	Samir		
	Waqar		
	Ömer		
Girls	Aysha	Aud-Jeanette	Kine
	Kadra		Linn
	Suna		

Two different speech situations

The semistructured interview conducted by one of the researchers and the peer conversations that took place without any adult researcher present, were designed to represent two different speech situations. This makes it possible for us to compare the informants' actual linguistic behavior in different settings. Furthermore, the two speech situations give insights regarding the informants' reported speech and meta-linguistic reflections compared to their actual linguistic behavior. An interesting observation pertaining to the two speech situations is the negotiation and tension in how the young people wish to express a certain image of themselves in the interviews, and how this self portrayal gets multidimensional, so to speak, in the peer conversations. Robert's behavior may serve as an illustration: Robert is a boy with two foreign-born parents (cf. Table 6.1). The interviewer mentions several words he has picked up from some of the other adolescents, and Robert laughs and says: 'Yes, there are some people using it, but I'm not the kind of guy who uses those words' (authors' translation). In the peer conversation Robert uses exactly the same words he denies to be a user of, for instance 'sjpa' (Berber, 'good') and 'wallah' (Arabic, 'swear by Allah'), and there are no cues in the conversation that point in the direction of this use being unnatural or surprising.

Findings and Discussion

Characteristics as reported by the informants themselves

A recent survey of 39 UPUS-informants reveals that the majority of them strongly confirm that there exists a certain way of speaking Norwegian in the multiethnic environment they are a part of (cf. Aarsæther, this volume). When they are asked to characterize this form of language, most of them point to lexical items; some of them refer to special words, others mention slang words. Quite many also mention prosodic features (cf. Aarsæther *et al.*, 2007; Svendsen & Røyneland, 2008). The informants' emphasis on the use of words as the most prominent characteristic feature is in line with the results of Fraurud and Bijvoet in Sweden, who found that the speakers of what they call multiethnic youth language also define this variety in terms of lexicon and prosody (cf. e.g. Fraurud, 2004).

One reason for the young peoples' emphasis on words may be that words are probably one of the linguistic strata that are most cognitively available, and most easily describable from a folk linguistic point of view (Emanuelsson, 2005; Kulbrandstad, 2006a, 2006b; Preston, 1996). The young informants may not (yet) have acquired a meta-language that makes them able to describe grammatical features. Those who do, often make them in terms of examples, like Roger in (1) below. Their emphasis on words may also be connected to media's influence. As mentioned above the few studies that already exist on Norwegian spoken in multicultural areas are centered around lexical loans, and the media have periodically shown a rather intense interest in these 'new' words from immigrant languages. This media attention may have nourished the establishment of stereotypes that has also influenced the speakers' own perception of their language. They may, as part of an attempt to satisfy us as visiting scholars, give us what they expect us to want from them.

Our quest for descriptions of structural features did not leave us completely empty handed, though. Grammatical features are mentioned by some of the informants. The closest we get to an *explicit* syntactic characterization is from the boy Gabriel (cf. Table 6.1), who points to 'minor errors in their sentences'. The few grammatical descriptions in addition to Gabriel's are a handful of instances where the informants provide us with examples, like Roger's in (1) below:

(1) Før så oppdaget jeg dem sa 'et bil' istedenfor 'en bil'
'Earlier so discovered I they said 'a (neuter) car' instead of 'a (masculine) car"
Earlier I discovered they said 'a car' instead of 'a car'

Roger connects this deviant use of gender morphology to learner language, 'when they are starting to learn Norwegian', as he puts it. Interestingly enough, the two boys' characteristics are in perfect alignment with our observations of the adolescents' linguistic practices: There seems to be both characteristics regarding grammatical gender – as pointed out by Roger, and syntactic characteristics – as pointed out by Gabriel, at stake.

The statements we get about structural features are of course of value to us, but there are – as already stated – extremely few of them. Roger's and Gabriel's choice of third person in their description ('*their* sentences', '*they* said') indicates that this is someone else's language, not their own. When we turn to our investigation of the adolescents' actual language use in the next section, we shall see that statements like these don't automatically exclude them from being users of these features. This discrepancy raises some important methodological issues, also in relation to some previous studies, which we will return to in section 'Closing Remarks'.

Structural Characteristics Found in the Recorded Speech Data

Violations of the V2 constraint

Background and assumptions

Norwegian, like other Germanic languages (except English) is a V2 language, constraining the slot of the finite verb to the second position in declarative main clauses, giving a XVS word order, where 'X' is a topicalized element, 'V' the finite verb and 'S' the subject. Violation of the V2 constraint, resulting in XSV word order, has been documented and discussed for Norwegian L2 learner data (e.g. Brautaset, 1996; Hagen, 1992; Johansen, 2007; Nistov, 1991). All these studies are based on written data collected in an educational context. Violations of the V2 constraint are also found in other language contact scenarios giving birth to ethnolects such as Kven-Norwegian in Northern Norway (Sollid, 2005; Sollid & Eide, 2007).

As mentioned in section 'Previous research addressing structural characteristics', the violation of this V2 constraint, also referred to as noninversion (cf. Ganuza, this volume), has been observed and described as a feature of multiethnic youth varieties of Swedish, Danish and German. Based on these studies and our preliminary observations from the two different speech situations, we predict that this will be the case also for multiethnic youth language in Oslo. Moreover, we assume that we are dealing with in-group youth linguistic practices, and hence we expect a difference between the two speech situations: Violations of the V2 constraint are assumed to be a characteristic of language use in the peer conversations. Our first attempt toward confirming this prediction is a survey of the situational distribution of the XSV instances in our data.

Distribution of XSV in the two speech situations

We have analyzed all declarative main clauses introduced by a nonsubject in the interviews as well as the peer conversations. As can be seen in Table 6.2 below, we found a total number of 194 instances of the XSV-structure, constituting 22% of the total number of declarative main clauses with a nonsubject as the clause-initial element.

In the peer conversations the proportion of XSV is as high as 38%, whereas in the interviews the proportion is 12%. The fact that the proportion of XSV is higher for the peer conversations is in line with our prediction that violation of the V2 constraint would be a characteristic structural aspect of language use in youth in-group settings. But if we look at the

Table 6.2 Number of available XVS context and number and proportion for XSV

	Number of available XVS contexts	*Number of occurrences and proportion of XSV*
Interview	526	63 = 12%
Peer conversation	345	131 = 38%
Total	871	194 = 22%

Total numbers of informants ($N = 22$)

distribution of instances of XSV found for each of the informants some intra- and inter-individual variation is revealed that needs commenting.

Before looking closer at results for each individual informant, it should be noted that the total number of possible contexts, that is, the number of declarative main clauses introduced by other constituents than the subject, is considerably higher in the interviews than the peer conversations in spite of the fact that the interviews are shorter in duration. This may be due to the fact that we here are dealing with different text types: The interviews are more asymmetrical leading to differences in information structure. The adolescents are presented with questions by the interviewer establishing the topic, which will then often be referred to in initial position of the answers to follow. Questions about point of time and whereabouts will tend to require answers introduced by pro-forms like 'da' (then) or specifications of place by adverbial prepositional phrases like 'i Oslo' (in Oslo). Furthermore, the questions in the interviews permit reflection and thinking aloud. This results in longer turns than in the peer conversations which in most cases are characterized by negotiation of topic and more frequent change of turn-taking. The difference between the interviews and peer conversations in this respect is evident in Table 6.3, showing the number of possible XVS/XSV contexts for each informant. As can be seen, with the majority of the informants the peer conversation data provide fewer available contexts than the interview data.

The individual findings for many of the informants confirm our prediction that XSV mainly characterizes in-group language use, especially the results as shown for nine of the informants (Aswan, Kine, Linn, Lars, Leonel, Mike, Olav, Robert and Roger) where we find occurrences of XSV in the peer conversations, but no occurrences at all in the interviews. This finding is independent of parental background, and hence accentuates the fact that the occurrences of XSV for these informants cannot be ascribed to L2 usage. However, the pattern is not that clear with all the informants. Although the main tendency is that the number of XSV-occurrences increases in the peer conversation, the question arises whether we in our data may also have to do with V2 violation as an L2 feature. There are in all 11 informants who produce instances of XSV also in the interview situation. A closer analysis of the linguistic behavior of these informants sheds light on the fact that there may be a diverse and complex set of factors underlying the individual adolescents' linguistic practices. We will here comment on some of the informants who may be regarded as different types of speakers in our data.

Types of speakers

The finding of XSV also in the interview situation is particularly evident in the data from *Anders* (mixed parental background, cf. Table 6.1) where we find 51% XSV (29 of 57 possible contexts) in the interview,

Table 6.3 Number of available XVS contexts and occurrences of XSV for each individual informant

		Interview		Peer conversation	
		Available contexts for XVS	Instances of XSV	Available contexts for XVS	Instances of XSV
Two foreign-born parents					
Boys	Aswan	4	0	10	4
	Farid	6	2	5	2
	Leonel	9	0	6	2
	Lukas	16	2	9	3
	Mike	18	0	13	7
	Murat	52	2	4	2
	Robert	8	0	5	3
	Samir	36	3	15	10
	Waqar	33	8	19	14
	Ömer	15	0	7	0
Girls	Aysha	30	5	18	1
	Kadra	8	3	9	0
	Suna	55	6	38	4
One foreign-born parent					
Boys	Anders	57	29	79	49
	Gabriel	15	0	17	0
	Michael	42	1	7	3
Girls	Aud-Jeanette	39	2	28	6
Two Norwegian-born parents					
Boys	Lars	17	0	18	11
	Olav	14	0	11	6
	Roger	9	0	16	2
Girls	Kine	18	0	5	2
	Linn	25	0	7	1

compared to 63% (49 of 79) in the peer conversation. Noninversion often goes along with untraditional choice of gender, as illustrated in example (2) from the peer conversation:

(2) **den** tiltrekker seg oppmerksomhet (.) **den** kroppsspråk**et** der (.) fordi når
'it (m) attracts itself attention (.) that (m) body language-the (n) there (.) because when
it calls for attention (.) that kind of body language (.) because when

hvis noen står og breaker **alle stopper** opp
if someone stands and breakdances everybody stops up'
if someone is breakdancing everybody stops

However, Anders is clearly not an L2 speaker. He is very much conscious of his linguistic behavior, and he shows through extended use of stylization and code switching that he manages a vast repertoire of varieties of Norwegian (cf. also Svendsen & Røyneland, 2008). Anders speaks of the multiethnic youth style as 'his dialect' and makes use of this speech style also in the interview situation.

Waqar, like Anders, produces XSV in both speech situations. There are also some other L2-like features in his grammar and pronunciation. Since Waqar has parents with an immigrant background, we cannot exclude the possibility that we may be dealing here with a speaker of Norwegian where XSV represents an L2 feature. However, the proportion of XSV is still much higher in the peer conversation than in the interview, 74% and 24% respectively. In the peer conversation we notice that some of the instances of XSV occur in sequences where there is higher temperature and intensity, especially on one occasion when someone else from the youth club enters the room. This seems to support Ganuza's observation that the instances of XSV increased when the adolescents entered into a high involvement speech style (Ganuza, 2008: 117). Hence, there may be a complex set of underlying factors for Waqar's use of XSV. It may not be so straightforward to put a strict border line between L2 usage and a multiethnic in-group youth style (cf. Røynesdal, 2007: 95).

It calls for attention that one of the informants, *Kadra*, in fact has no occurrences of XSV at all in the peer conversation, whereas she has three occurrences in the interview. The fact that Kadra, like Waqar, has two foreign-born parents, raises the question of whether these occurrences must be understood in terms of L2 features. One argument in disfavor of this assumption is the fact that Kadra produces several utterances with complex clause initial elements followed by inversion, rendering the standard XVS structure, as shown in example (3).

(3) Når du ser en norsk gutt prate sånn så **er det** ganske rart
'When you see a Norwegian boy talk such then is it quite strange'
When you see a Norwegian boy talk like that it's pretty strange

The role of the linguistic context

A closer look at Kadra's use of XSV in the interview, reveals that the XSV structures occur with the adverbs 'egentlig' (actually) and 'uansett' (anyway, no matter what) in clause-initial position. A similar pattern is revealed with the informant *Suna*, where in fact all instances of XSV in the interview situation occur after the clause initial adverb 'egentlig' as illustrated in example (4).

(4) Egentlig **alle kan** bidra
 'Actually everyone can contribute'
 Actually everyone can contribute

This draws attention to an interesting aspect of our findings, namely the role of the linguistic context. It appears that there are some particular adverbs that seem to trigger XSV, 'egentlig' being one of them found with several informants. We may here be dealing with conversational routines more than syntactic variation (cf. Cheshire, 2005: 94). In the case of Kadra and Suna the pattern with noninversion seems to have become a common feature of their speech style regardless of situational context. Further research regarding the role of the linguistic context for XSV and the question of whether we here have to do with formulaic language use, is in progress (Nistov & Opsahl, 2009; Opsahl, 2009c). This will make it possible to compare findings in our data with Ganuza's findings in Swedish multiethnic youth language (cf. Ganuza, this volume).

Parental background

As can be seen in Table 6.3, only two of the informants, Ömer and Gabriel, have no instances of XSV at all. One would perhaps expect these boys to be adolescents with Norwegian-born parents, but they both have an immigrant family background. All of the informants with two Norwegian-born parents thus do produce instances of XSV, but it should be noted that none of them had any occurrence of XSV in the interviews. This finding, indicating that the adolescents with native Norwegian background seem to be more susceptible to the two speech situations, and may have access to a larger range of styles, suggests that it is worth doing a closer study of the socio-pragmatic factors that may be at work (cf. Aarsæther, this volume; Svendsen & Røyneland, 2008). L2 usage as well as the phenomenon of 'crossing' (Rampton, 1995a, 1995b) and stylization are relevant issues that may shed light on the variation that is revealed in how informants with and without an immigrant background perform in the two speech situations.

Summary remarks on the violations of the V2 constraint

The total proportion of 22% XSV in our data is higher than what was found in Ganuza's study of Swedish (Ganuza, 2008, this volume) where XSV constituted only 4% of possible contexts in the whole database and

10% in the sample where more informal conversational data was included. However, Ganuza has a group of 20 focus informants and if we look at the results for their linguistic behavior in group conversation, we find that the proportion is much higher, that is, 20% XSV (Ganuza, 2008: 69). This supports the findings in our data, showing that the informants' violations of the V2 constraint occur in higher proportions in the peer conversations than in the interview situation, thus confirming our assumption that we are mainly dealing with features characteristic of youth in-group communication.

As we have seen, there are a few exceptions with regard to this distributional pattern between interview and peer conversation, and it has been indicated that these may be the result of the fact that possible L2 speakers are part of the corpora, and thus also of the speech community. But as we have seen, the violations of the verb second constraint are present both with informants with Norwegian-born parents and informants with immigrant parents.

An important aspect of our findings is the difference in frequency of available contexts for XSV in the interview data and the peer conversation data. In some instances text type and the conversational style differ to such an extent that possible contexts for V2 violations are in some way marginalized. This also relates to the fact that a large proportion of the instances of violation of the V2 constraint seem to be restricted to certain linguistic contexts.

Some Notes on Grammatical Gender in our Data

A much used definition of gender is that '[g]enders are classes of nouns reflected in the behavior of associated words' [Corbett (following Hockett) 1991: 1]. Hence, the fact that Norwegian nouns are classified by gender has consequences for the declension of agreeing determiners and adjectives as well as possessives and other adnominals. According to *Norsk referansegrammatikk* (Norwegian Reference Grammar) (Faarlund *et al.*, 1997) gender determines both the form of the indefinite and definite article, and these can probably be said to be the most important cues to the gender of a noun.

In Oslo there has (in somewhat simplified terms) historically been a discrepancy between the traditional dialectal Eastern variety adhering to a three gender system (masculine, feminine, neuter) and the Western variety adhering to a two gender system, closely related to Danish (cf. Johannessen, 2008: 236; Larsen, 1907: 17). In the modern Oslo dialects there is a great deal of variation between a two- and three gender system, and thus variation in the adnominal cues to gender specification: You may for instance have a masculine indefinite article preceding a word with a feminine definite suffix on the noun ['en bok, boka' – a (m) book, book-the

(f) – a book, the book], and the masculine possessive in connection with an indefinite possible feminine noun ['min bok' – my (m) book (f)] (cf. Faarlund et al., 1997: 150). This possibility seems on the other hand to be ungrammatical when the noun precedes the possessive [*'boka min' – book-the (f) my (m)] and for some speakers it seems questionable in predicate position: [?'boka er min' – book-the (f) is mine (m)]. This last point has given rise to suggestions toward whether the definite suffix should be seen as an element expressing declension class rather than gender in some dialects (cf. Fretheim, 1985).

Not a single one of our informants uses the feminine indefinite article, 'ei' [a (f)]. If we confer other recent corpora of spoken Oslo dialect, for instance the NoTa-corpus (Norwegian spoken language corpus – the Oslo part, cf. Johannessen & Hagen, 2008), the same picture emerges: The indefinite feminine article seems to be on the edge of disappearing all over Oslo. The feminine *definite* article, the suffix '–a', is on the other hand still going strong among our informants: We find several nouns, for the most concretes [e.g. 'greia' (thingy-the), 'rumpa' (ass-the)] and words associated with natural feminine gender [e.g. 'mora' (mother-the), 'søstera' (sister-the)], which seem to reject a masculine declension. This pattern is not totally consistent though. The girl Aysha is typical in this respect in that she alternates between feminine and masculine possessives and definite suffixes connected to the same noun more or less within the same utterance:

(5) hun er også venninn**a mi** [...] hvis jeg er med venninn**en min**
'she is also girlfriend-the (f) my (f) [...] if I am with girlfriend-the (m) my (m)'
she is also my girlfriend [...] if I hang out with my girlfriend

A point to be made here, is that loan words from immigrant languages that seem to enter into an in-group repertoire, are being treated as feminine if they are words associated with natural feminine gender: We find for instance the forms 'kæba' [according to Drange (2002) originally Berber and Arabic 'prostitute', now used synonymous with 'girl'] and what seems to be a variant of 'kæba': 'mæba'. These words are combined with the feminine possessive marker, 'mi', in parallel with the pattern outlined for the word 'bok' (book) above. Samir talks about meeting his girlfriend as 'møte mæba mi' [meet girl-the (f) my (f)' – meet my girlfriend]. The means through which the informants establish a masculine–feminine distinction is object to extended variation both inter- and intraindividually, but they do not seem to involve any deviations from the variation patterns found elsewhere in Oslo (cf. Johannessen, 2008; Western, 1978).

On the other hand, we find that 2.6% (26 out of 991) of the gender-marked singular phrases in the peer conversational data deviate from traditional patterns of variation in that features expressing different genera are being combined. Gender mixture of this kind is described in Sami-Norwegian language contact scenarios in Northern Norway (cf. Bull, 1996) as well as found in Swedish, Danish and Dutch multiethnolectal speech styles (cf. section 'Previous research addressing structural characteristics'). The majority of the cases in our data are, in alignment with the findings for these other multiethnolectal speech styles, instances where neuter nouns are being marked as if they were masculine nouns. There are only two instances of the opposite pattern. Most of the cases are thus like Kine's utterance in (6) below, where she combines masculine adnominal features, in this case a masculine possessive, with a neuter noun:

(6) Er dette **min** glass?
 'Is this my (m) glass (n)'
 Is this my glass?

According to Corbett (1991: 71) the study of gender in connection with loan words and innovations can be treated as 'a continuously running experiment, which allows us to verify the assignment systems in the languages in question'. The study of gender in conversational data from a multiethnic youth group may also in a sense serve as a window into a continuously running experiment, in that young people with various backgrounds enter into consecutive negotiations on how to deal with the available cues to gender specification. One of the ideas raised in the discussions on gender assignment rules in Norwegian is that masculine should be considered as a kind of default category (Enger, 2001: 178; Trosterud, 2001: 32). The traces in our data may be said to support this idea.

The fact that Kine, who provided us with example (6) above, has two Norwegian-born parents (cf. Table 6.1) illuminates another important point: There seems to be no automatic correlation between deviations of this kind and the adolescents' language backgrounds. Eight out of the 22 informants provide us with examples related to the one in (6): Anders, Aswan, Farid, Kine, Leonel, Murat, Roger and Samir; five of them have two foreign-born parents, one has one foreign-born parent and two have two Norwegian-born parents.

These eight informants also show a relatively high rate of XSV-instances in their peer conversations (cf. Table 6.3 above). There seems in other words to exist an interplay between syntactic and morphological features characterizing their in-group speech styles. Grammatical gender seems on the other hand not to be as prominent as the syntactic XSV-pattern, but there are exceptions: Anders, who may be our closest encounter with a multiethnic in-group speech style (cf. Svendsen & Røyneland, 2008), has a rather strong tendency to choose the masculine indefinite article also in connection with neuter nouns. In the conversational data from Anders the masculine indefinite article is followed by a neuter noun in 18% of the cases, like in 'en land' [a (m) country (n)] and 'en maleri' [a (m) painting (n)] where one would expect 'et (n) land' and 'et (n) maleri'.

There are – bearing in mind that we are dealing with 22 adolescents, of whom many are quite talkative – relatively few gender-marked singular phrases in the conversational data ($N = 991$). One possible reason for this is connected to the observation mentioned in section 'The purpose of this chapter'; what seems to be extended use of bare singular nouns or partially omission of definiteness marking. This point calls for further research. There are only 164 indefinite article + noun phrases. This may be related to some circumstances regarding text type: The adolescents are free to speak about whatever they want, but they are given a list of suggestions for conversational topics. Some topics and discourse referents are therefore already established as known and therefore less likely to appear in the indefinite form.

The adolescents also seem to have alternate ways of introducing discourse referents without the use of indefinite articles; that is strategies where gender agreement is absent. One of these is pointed out by Ekberg in the multiethnolectal speech style used in Malmö, Sweden, namely the use of 'sån' (such), which seems to have grammaticalized into a new determiner (cf. Ekberg, this volume). Traces in our Norwegian data may be said to support this idea. One example is (7), where Ömer shares his cooking habits:

(7) eller så tar jeg **sånn** polarbrød og så smører **sånn** pizzasaus og så setter
'or then take I such polar bread and then spread such pizza sauce and then put
or then I take such polar bread and then spread such pizza sauce and then put

ned og så putter n i ovnen og så lager **sånn** min egen pizza eller noe **sånn**
down and then put 't in stove-the and then make such my own pizza or something such
down and then put it in the stove and then make such my own pizza or something

eller på pitabrød over pitabrød **sånn** rask pizza
or on pita bread over pita bread such fast pizza'
or on pita bread over pita bread such fast pizza

As pointed out by Lie (2008: 84), Norwegian 'sånn' is not object to agreement within the noun phrase in traditional sense, in that the element following 'sånn' in many cases is a plural or not even a noun phrase at all. There are several instances of 'sånn' preceding a plural in our data. Aud-Jeanette, for instance, utters: 'De ringer med sånn bjeller' [they ring with such (sing.) bells (plur.)]. There are some pragmatic differences between the traditional indefinite articles and 'sånn', resting both on the fact that 'sånn' has several functions in discourse and that we seem to be dealing with grammaticalization in progress (cf. Ekberg, this volume; Ekberg, 2007; Lie, 2008; Opsahl, 2009b). The main point to be made here is that what Faarlund *et al.* (1997) call one important cue to gender specification – the indefinite article – in many cases is absent when the adolescents introduce new discourse referents.

Cornips (2008) asks the interesting question of whether the loss of grammatical gender in Dutch should be seen as the result of bilingual acquisition and/or an act of identity. Based on our study of conversational data from 22 informants with various backgrounds, it is clear that we cannot explain the patterns regarding neither grammatical gender nor violations of the V2 constraint in our Norwegian data solely as a result of bilingual or second language acquisition.

Closing Remarks

We started out this chapter by asking whether language use in multilingual settings in Oslo is characterized by more than words. The analysis of our recordings revealed that multiethnic youth language in Oslo indeed has characteristics besides lexical items. We find both violations of the V2 constraint and, to some extent, simplifications within the grammatical gender domain as part of their in-group linguistic practices. This contradicts the adolescents themselves who hold that this form of speaking Norwegian mainly has to do with words. We are here facing a classical sociolinguistic opposition between reported and actual language use (cf. Labov, 2001). The discrepancy we found between reported and actual speech, sheds light on findings in some previous studies. It is worth noting that Appel and Schoonen (2005) who describe 'Straattaal' in the Netherlands as being characterized by a special vocabulary with non-Dutch or new Dutch words, in fact based their results on a questionnaire and interviews with a subsample of the informants; that is on what the informants themselves reported as characteristic for 'Straattaal'. The results of our study indicate that questionnaires and interviews alone may prove inadequate to describe the emergence of new multiethnic urban speech styles.

Having confirmed that we do find structural features characterizing Norwegian as spoken among youth in multilingual settings in Oslo, it should also be emphasized that the use of these features is not found with all our informants. We have seen that there may be different types of speakers within the speech community, and linguistic heterogeneity seems to be a fitting label for describing both the structural and functional aspects of the young people's linguistic practices.

A methodological issue which has crystallized as essential throughout our analysis is the limitations implied in the use of corpora. Actual occurrences of certain linguistic features are dependent on genre and text types (cf. Biber, 1988). In the analysis of the V2 constraint, we saw that the amount of available contexts for XVS varies according to text type. Also regarding the analysis of gender-marked singular phrases the question of text type seems relevant.

The results of our analysis point to the significance of taking context into account at all levels. The structural characteristics of Norwegian as spoken by adolescents in multilingual areas in Oslo are susceptible both to situational, textual and linguistic context for their appearance. The awareness of this context-dependency seems to be crucial for further research trying to capture structural aspects of multiethnic youth language.

Chapter 7
Pronunciation in Swedish Multiethnolect

P. BODÉN

Introduction

Listening to young people in Sweden today, especially adolescents in suburbs and urban areas, you may notice a new way of speaking Swedish that strongly resembles foreign-accented Swedish. The adolescents borrow foreign speech sounds, intonational and rhythmic patterns and incorporate them into their spoken Swedish. However, unlike foreign-accented Swedish which is colored by the speaker's first language, the speech of these adolescents reveals little about their language background. The foreign influences possibly come from a number of languages.

It is primarily in suburbs and urban areas with a high proportion of immigrant residents where this foreign-sounding way of speaking Swedish has evolved. It was first noticed in Rinkeby, Stockholm by Ulla-Britt Kotsinas (1988a, 1988b) but is now likely to be found in most large and medium-sized cities in Sweden (cf. the other Swedish contributions in this volume). Colloquially, these new ways of speaking Swedish are often named after suburbs and urban districts with large immigrant populations, for example Rosengård in Malmö ('Rosengård Swedish'), Gårdsten in Gothenburg ('Gårdstenish') and Rinkeby in Stockholm ('Rinkeby Swedish'). Despite of the different names, people acknowledge similarities between them. When having talked about Rinkeby Swedish with adolescents in Malmö, they instantly associated with Rosengård Swedish (i.e. with the corresponding Malmö variant), and when I played examples of Rosengård Swedish to teenagers in Lund, they associated with the Lund variant 'Fladden' (named after Norra Fäladen). In other words, obvious similarities are perceived between them. The question of whether or not the perceived similarities simply lay in a non-native pronunciation or if indeed actual phonetic similarities can be found is yet to be answered. In this chapter, this new foreign-sounding Swedish is termed 'Swedish on multilingual ground' or Swedish 'multiethnolect' (cf. Quist, 2000) thereby acknowledging its apparent influences from several ethnic groups and their first languages.

Despite the multiethnolect's obvious relation to the immigrant community and foreign accent, adolescents often comment that there are speakers of multiethnolect without immigrant background, that is those who have Swedish as their (only) first language. In a test designed to investigate listeners' ability to guess adolescents' mother tongue, Kotsinas (1990) was surprised to find that 98% of the listeners mistook a native Swede for a second language learner of Swedish. A foreign-sounding pronunciation and/or other non-native features had evidently been perceived in a speaker who had Swedish as mother tongue. The belief that speakers of multiethnolect do not necessarily have an immigrant background has previously been reported also by among others (Bijvoet, 2003).

It can be argued that the multiethnolect's most perceptually salient feature is its foreign-accented 'sound'. Even if a speaker uses a deviating morphology and syntax, the speaker is not likely to be perceived as speaking multiethnolect if he or she uses a strong regional accent and no foreign speech sounds or foreign-sounding prosody at all. A few of the specific slang words of the variety are possibly needed too in order to become characterized as a speaker of multiethnolect (Bijvoet, 2003). The origin of the foreign features of the pronunciation in Swedish multiethnolect, the reasons for their successful incorporation and spread among speakers, and the extent to which the same features are found in different Swedish cities are all interesting topics to investigate.

In this chapter, I will attempt to describe some of the characteristics of the pronunciation in Swedish multiethnolect(s) as spoken in Malmö, Gothenburg and Stockholm. Before that can be done, I need to determine if the variety (or varieties) indeed can be separated from foreign-accented Swedish and, if so, identify a number of speakers upon whose speech the description can be based. The chapter consists of two parts. The first part (sections 'Delimitation of the variety and selection of speakers' and 'Delimiting the variety') describes a listening test undertaken to select suitable speech data and delimit the variety, and the other part (sections 'Segmentals in Swedish multiethnolect' and 'Suprasegmentals in Swedish multiethnolect') consists of a description of phonetic similarities across the multiethnic varieties as spoken in Malmö, Gothenburg and Stockholm.

Method

Delimitation of the variety and selection of speakers

A total of 246 pupils of upper secondary school participated as listeners in a series of tests aimed to identify speakers of multiethnolect in Malmö,

Gothenburg and Stockholm. Seventy 30-second-long speech samples from 62 speakers were extracted from the speech database of the research project *Language and language use among young people in multilingual urban settings* and played once (over loudspeakers) to the listeners. The project has collected a large amount of comparable data in schools in Malmö, Gothenburg and Stockholm (cf. Boyd, this volume). The speakers are adolescents (mainly 17-year-olds) who attended the second year of the upper secondary school's educational program in social science when the recordings were made (during the academic year 2002–2003). The listeners were asked to make a decision on whether the speakers in the speech samples spoke multiethnolect or not. Instead of the term multiethnolect, the colloquial denominations mentioned above (see section 'Introduction') were used. The pupils were only asked to listen to the subset of speech samples that had been recorded in their own home town. The purpose of the listening tests was to have adolescents of the same age as the recorded speakers identify suitable speakers upon whose speech the description of the Swedish multiethnolect could be based. The listening tests were also designed to delimit the variety by investigating its relation to foreign-accented Swedish. Two assumptions were tested: (1) that there are speakers of multiethnolect who have Swedish as their (only) first language, and (2) that speakers of multiethnolect switch to a more standardized form of Swedish in certain situations. These assumptions are interesting to test because if they can be confirmed, then they provide evidence to support the idea that multiethnolect can be separated from foreign accented-Swedish. Foreign accent, simplistically defined here as the result of negative transfer from the speaker's first language (Major, 2001), cannot occur in the Swedish that is spoken by persons who have Swedish as their first language, nor can foreign accent easily be 'switched off' in certain situations. Foreign accent is a consequence of the learner transferring (parts of) the phonological system of the first language to the second. The pronunciation of a language variety, on the other hand, is learned. Kotsinas (2000) has suggested that the so-called Rinkeby Swedish is only one of several language varieties available to adolescents in Stockholm's multilingual urban areas. She considers many individuals as bidialectal and able to shift between local Stockholm dialect and multiethnolect depending on factors such as conversational partner and topic of conversation. Bijvoet (2003), in like manner, concludes that many of the adolescents in her study seem to be able to switch between multiethnic youth language and the so-called standard Swedish. The interviewed adolescents describe the multiethnolect (termed 'Rinkeby Swedish' or 'Fittja language' by themselves) primarily as a medium for peer-to-peer interactions and social functions and as inappropriate to use when addressing a teacher or another adult.

The listening tests were undertaken with the help of project members Sofia Hallin and Natalia Ganuza (Stockholm University), Julia Prentice (formerly Große, University of Gothenburg) and Gudrun Svensson (Lund University).

Auditory and acoustic analyses

The 27 speech samples classified as multiethnolect in the abovementioned listening tests form the basis of the description of the multiethnolect's pronunciation. With the classifications of the pupil listeners as guidance, limited additional data have been collected from the speech database when necessary. The speech material has been subject to both auditory and acoustic analyses. For the acoustic analysis, the speech analysis program Praat (Boersma & Weenink, 2008) was used.

Results and Discussion

Delimiting the variety

Multiethnolect and speakers' background

A total of 24 speakers of multiethnolect were identified by the listeners in the listening tests. Ten Malmö speakers, seven Gothenburg speakers and seven Stockholm speakers' speech samples were classified as multiethnolect by a statistically significant majority of the listeners ($p < 0.01$, Chi-square test). As shown in Table 7.1, the speakers who produced those samples have different backgrounds.

There is a clear relationship between immigrant background and perceived use of multiethnolect. Most speakers with Swedish-born parents were categorized as not being speakers of multiethnolect, and the majority of speakers categorized as speakers of multiethnolect have an immigrant background. However, the relationship between background and use of multiethnolect is not a one-to-one relationship. Out of the 34 speech samples produced by speakers with parents born outside Sweden in Table 7.1, 14 were perceived as something else than multiethnolect by a statistically significant majority of the listeners ($p < 0.05$). Not even a late arrival in Sweden (at 6 years of age or later) automatically resulted in a classification as a speaker of multiethnolect. Conversely, out of the 16 speakers with at least one Swedish-born parent, four were classified as speakers of multiethnolect by a statistically significant majority of the listeners. Two have both Swedish-born parents, the third has a Norwegian father and the fourth has a father from Morocco. All four report only speaking Swedish (apart from the languages learned in school). The belief that there are speakers of multiethnolect who have Swedish as their (only) first language is thus confirmed. [Speech samples that got an ambiguous classification ($p > 0.05$) in the listening tests are not given in Table 7.1, but cf. Figure 7.1 and section below]

Pronunciation in Swedish Multiethnolect

Table 7.1 Classification of the speech samples, sorted according to the speakers' background

	Speakers born in Sweden		Immigrant speakers	
Classification by the listeners in the tests	With at least one Swedish-born parent	With immigrant parents	Arrived in Sweden by 5 years of age or earlier	Arrived in Sweden by 6 years of age or later
Multiethnolect	E04a, P08, P35, P47	B05a, B12, B36a, C32, D31, K08, K28, P10	C29, C41, D49, E14a, L39, P19	D27, E06, E43, L26, P05, P11
Not multiethnolect	B01, C13, D02, D07, D09, E01, E19, E33, E40, L11, L35, S15	B30, B36b, C37, E26, E41, P25, P38, S30	E14b, L31b, S08	D40, E38, S40

The speech samples are referred to by the speakers' codes such as they appear in the project speech database

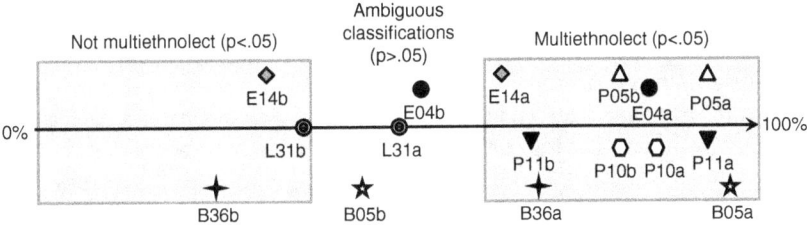

Figure 7.1 Listeners' share of multiethnolect responses (in percent) to eight speakers' speech samples. Each speaker's recording from the informal context (a) occurs to the right of his or her recording from the more formal context (b), that is was perceived as multiethnolect by a larger percentage of the listeners.

Context sensitivity

Eight speakers contributed with two speech samples each to the listening tests. The listeners heard these speakers in two different types of situations or contexts: (a) a conversation with one or several persons of the same age, for example a dialogue with a classmate, and (b) a conversation with an adult (or at least an adult present), for example an interview with a linguist or an oral presentation in class. The listeners were not informed of the fact that the same speaker could appear in more than one speech sample (and did not report having noticed it either). As mentioned above, multiethnolects such as Rinkeby Swedish have been described as a medium primarily for peer-to-peer interaction (Bijvoet, 2003). Therefore, multiethnolect is expected to be used above all in the first-mentioned types of situations.

To what extent is the recording situation and the speech used by the speaker in that situation reflected in the listeners' responses? Two speakers were clearly perceived as speaking differently depending on context (speakers with the codes E14 and B36 in Figure 7.1). These speakers were perceived as speaking multiethnolect by a statistically significant majority of the listeners in one context ($p < 0.01$), and as speaking something else than multiethnolect by a statistically significant majority of the listeners in the other ($p < 0.01$). As expected, it was in the recordings with peers that the listeners perceived them as speakers of multiethnolect. The remaining six speakers were also perceived as speaking multiethnolect by a larger number of listeners in the recordings with peers than in the recordings with adults. The perceived difference was smaller though. Several speakers were, for example, perceived as speaking multiethnolect in both contexts (see speech samples of speakers P05, P10 and P11 in Figure 7.1).

In summary, it can be concluded that some but not all speakers of multiethnolect appear to switch to a more standardized form of Swedish in interactions with adults. Whereas adolescents have been reported to feel that, for example the special vocabulary of the multiethnolect is inappropriate to use with adults (Bijvoet, 2003); the foreign-sounding pronunciation appears more difficult to turn on and off. The speech samples from context (b) are characterized by fewer slang words but in several cases an equally foreign-sounding pronunciation as that of the speech samples from context (a). It may well be that the foreign-sounding pronunciation of some speakers is the result of transfer (even if other non-native features of their speech are not transferred). Then again, the pronunciation and the prosody in particular (Gårding, 1974) is a part even of regional dialects that speakers do not give up in situations where other features of the dialect are dropped.

Segmentals in Swedish multiethnolect

When we ran the listening test in Malmö, we noticed that one of the speech samples contained one or several characteristic features of the multiethnolect at the very beginning of the recording. Instead of listening to the entire 30-second long sample, many listeners marked their answer on the answer sheet after having heard only the first two prosodic phrases. In a majority of the cases, they classified the speech sample as an example of multiethnolect. The two prosodic phrases in question are given in (1).

(A prosodic phrase is, somewhat simplistically, a stretch of speech that is set off by audible boundaries.)

(1) 'ja ska gå å plugga lite nu | asså hon checkar språket å sånt |'
    I'm gonna go and study some now | well she checks the language and such |

Apart from the phrase 'å sånt' (and such) which adolescents in Malmö perceive as particularly frequent in Rosengård Swedish (see Ekberg, this volume), the pronunciation of the word 'checkar' (checks) stands out as being nonrepresentative of the Malmö dialect as spoken by adolescents in general. The first sound in 'checkar', /ɕ/, is pronounced with the affricate [tʃ]. Although affricates are used in a few Swedish dialects, they are perceived as foreign to the Malmö dialect. They would even appear to be perceived foreign enough to constitute a fairly unambiguous marker of multiethnolect. Spelling variation in collected lists of typical Rosengård Swedish words gives further support to the idea that affricates are a feature of the multiethnolect, as discussed elsewhere (Bodén, 2007). Affricates can be heard in borrowings in the materials recorded in Gothenburg and Stockholm too. All three speech samples containing affricates in the listening tests were labeled as examples of multiethnolect by a statistically significant majority of the listeners ($p < 0.01$). They had been produced by different speakers out of whom all had immigrant background.

It is interesting to consider why the listeners in the tests perceived the affricates as such a strong marker of multiethnolect and how the affricates became incorporated into the multiethnolect. Affricates are relatively common in the languages of the world. The voiceless, sibilant affricate tʃ occurs in as many as approximately 45% of the world's languages according to estimations reported by Ladefoged and Maddieson (1996). An affricate is a stop in which the release of the constriction is modified to produce a prolonged period of frication. Whether to regard a stop and the following period of friction as a single unit (an affricate) or as two segments (stop + fricative) requires phonological considerations. A Swedish learner of English often transfer parts of his or her Swedish phonological system and substitute the English affricate with a simple fricative (Hincks, 2003).

Some speakers of multiethnolect are proficient in languages from which the affricates might have been transferred from. It is no surprise then that they know the words' pronunciation too and are in a position to mediate and spread that pronunciation to other speakers of multiethnolect. However, many of the words pronounced with affricates in our material are English borrowings. In contemporary spoken Swedish, English borrowings are quite common. Despite the fact that most Swedes know how to speak English fairly well, few choose to produce a native-like pronunciation of word initial affricates in borrowings (Lindström, 2004). How come then that the speakers of multiethnolect produce the affricates that other adolescents substitute with simple fricatives? As can be predicted by the large number of languages in which affricates occur, many bilingual Swedes with immigrant background have affricates in their first languages. They are therefore, more likely than monolingual Swedes to produce affricates in both English and other borrowings. Transfer from their first language offer a 'free ride'; a native-like pronunciation is obtained by positive transfer from their first language (Major, 2001). I believe this to be the likely explanation for the affricates' successful incorporation in the multiethnolect. The reluctance among monolingual Swedes against producing affricates (or lack of motivation to do so) gives the affricates great force as markers of multiethnolect. They have become a sufficiently strong marker of multiethnolect to motivate a spread even to speakers of multiethnolect who do not speak languages in which affricates occur. Among the three speech samples containing affricates in the listening tests, two were produced by speakers who lack the affricates in question in their respective first language.

Following Kristiansen (2006), I suggest that the speakers of multiethnolect have established a subphonemic salient contrast that from a speaker-oriented view achieves social differentiation, and that the allophone [tʃ] has been associated with a social meaning that allows the listener to categorize and characterize the speaker. This allophonic variation can be assumed to play a role in the identified functions of multiethnolect discussed by Bijvoet (2003): on the one hand it may be used as a group-identity marker, and on the other it may be used to activate dividing lines between in-group and out-group (e.g. native Swedish adolescents of the same age).

Further studies are needed in order to give a comprehensive list of segmental similarities across the multiethnic varieties in Sweden. Another speech sound with a similar potential as a marker of multiethnolect as the affricates discussed above, is the voiced fricative [z]. It is frequent in native-like pronunciations of many English borrowings but yet virtually nonexistent in native Swedes' pronunciations of English borrowings and proper names (Lindström, 2004). Typologically marked Swedish speech sounds often mispronounced by second language learners, for example the fricative /ɧ/ and vowels like /y ː/ and /ʉ ː/ (Johansson, 1973), are other sounds in the Swedish multiethnolect that merit study.

Suprasegmentals in Swedish multiethnolect

When speech is uttered, the speaker does not only articulate the sequence of speech segments that make up an utterance, but simultaneously varies vocal features such as tempo, pitch and voice quality. In this suprasegmental layer, the speaker can add elements of meaning to his or her utterance that are not contained in its lexical and syntactic make-up ('t Hart *et al.*, 1990). As in the case of the allophonic variation described above (see section 'Segmentals in Swedish Multiethnolect'), it can be argued that suprasegmental features too have the potential to add a social meaning to the utterance.

Temporal patterns

One temporal pattern in the data that occurs in all three cities is related to a clearly perceivable lengthening before breaks in the speech stream. Lengthening at the end of prosodic phrases occurs in both read and spontaneous Standard Swedish (see Hansson, 2003: 46–49 for an overview of the relevant literature). Final lengthening is defined as the effect caused to a unit of speech that 'has a longer duration when, within a larger unit, it occurs finally' (Lindblom, 1978: 85). Among other things, it functions to mark syntactic boundaries and occurs both when the boundary co-occurs with a pause and when it does not. In the multiethnolect, the final lengthening is with some frequency perceived as more pronounced than in Standard Swedish.

The duration of lengthened speech segments is acoustically measurable and thus a comparison between the amount of final lengthening in Standard Swedish and Swedish multiethnolect is possible. However, care must be taken to control a fairly large number of factors in order to obtain a meaningful comparison. In effect, the amount of extra final lengthening in multiethnolect cannot be measured reliably in the limited spontaneous material investigated here. Auditory analysis is therefore a better choice. Our perception is well equipped to determine if a given speech segment is longer than expected given, for example the number and kind of speech sounds it is comprised of. (If it was not, then final lengthening would be of little use to us as a boundary signal.)

In Figure 7.2, a perceived multiethnolectal speaker from Gothenburg utters the two prosodic phrases 'e det sant' (is it true) and 'skojar du' (are you joking). The speech wave form at the top of the figure is segmented to show the relative durations of the individual words. The lengthening of

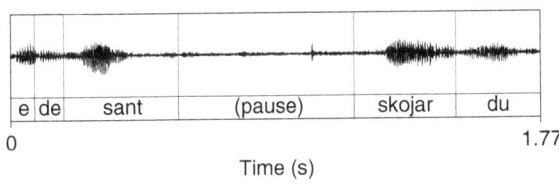

Figure 7.2 Segmented wave form of 'e de sant skojar du' (male speaker from Gothenburg, born in Sweden by parents from Syria).

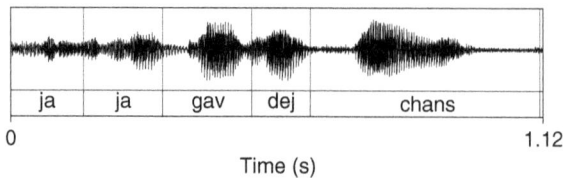

Figure 7.3 Segmented wave form of 'ja ja gav dej chans' (I I gave you opportunity) (male speaker from Malmö, born in Sweden by Swedish-born parents).

the pronoun 'du' (you) is impressionistically more substantial than expected in Gothenburg dialect. The longer duration of 'sant' (true) as compared to the durations of the other monosyllabic words in the first phrase is expected. It occurs phrase-finally and it carries a focal accent (phrasal stress). Focally accented words in Swedish are known to be produced with approximately 25% longer durations than nonfocal ones (Heldner & Strangert, 2001). The long duration of 'du' (you) in the second prosodic phrase, on the other hand, is not expected. Some lengthening is expected since it occurs phrase-finally, but the phrase's focal accent is expected on the content word 'skojar' (joking). The lengthening of 'du' (you) in Figure 7.2 is perceived as a foreign feature to a native speaker of Swedish, and examples of similar foreign-sounding lengthening can be heard also in the multiethnolectal speech data from Stockholm and Malmö (see e.g. Figure 7.3).

In Figure 7.3, a speaker of multiethnolect from Malmö utters 'jag jag gav dej chans' (I I gave you opportunity). The word 'chans' (opportunity) is perceived as longer than expected in Malmö dialect, and here the foreign-sounding impression is further strengthened by a clearly perceptible rise in pitch. In Malmö dialect, acute words such as 'chans' are normally associated with a falling word accent (Bruce & Gårding, 1978).

The main acoustic correlate of stress in Swedish is duration. Stressed syllables are longer than unstressed ones and they are often hyperarticulated (Bruce, 1998). Duration is also one of several correlates of focal accentuation (Heldner & Strangert, 2001). The lengthening at the end of prosodic phrases in Swedish multiethnolect can therefore be perceived as stress additions or shifts in the placement of focal accentuation, especially when the lengthening affects syllables that are lexically unstressed or words that are contextually 'given' (part of the utterance's theme). However, stress in Swedish is lexically determined and thematic information is often deaccented. Stress additions like the ones described above are therefore perceived as foreign or non-native to a native Swede.

Intonational patterns

The intonation of multiethnolects is often described as perceptually distinct in the literature (see e.g. Svendsen & Røyneland, 2008), and adolescents have repeatedly suggested to me that it is Arabic-sounding. Unfortunately, little has been written about colloquial Arabic intonation. The small but growing body of work on Arabic prosody nevertheless unveils significant differences between varieties; the numerous colloquial varieties of Arabic vary in their intonation. Cairene Arabic speakers, for example, have been reported to produce a rising accent on every content word and use a single level of phrasing, speakers of Emirati Arabic also use one level of prosodic phrasing but two different accents, and Lebanese Arabic speakers produce several different accents and use at least two levels of prosodic phrasing (Kulk *et al.*, 2003). If the multiethnolect has an Arabic intonation, then it is most likely influenced by one or several of the largest Arabic-speaking groups of immigrants in Sweden, that is by speakers from Iraq, Lebanon or Syria. In attempting to verify a possible Arabic influence, focus should be on these varieties' intonation.

In the following, I will describe a foreign-sounding intonation pattern that can be heard in the Swedish on multilingual ground spoken in Malmö, Gothenburg and Stockholm. The perceptual impression of speech melody correlates closely with acoustically measurable changes in fundamental frequency (hereafter abbreviated F0). The changes in F0 over the course of an utterance can be visually inspected in F0 contours. In Figures 7.4–7.6, three instances (one from each city) of the above-mentioned intonation pattern are given together with their respective F0 contour. All utterances are exclamations or rhetorical questions.

The most noticeable feature of all three F0 contours is the expanded F0 range. Male speakers' normal speaking voice varies between roughly 90 and 160 Hz and female speakers' voices between 170 and 250 Hz (Lindblad, 1992). In Figures 7.4–7.6, there are F0 peaks that reach up to 500 Hz and beyond. The expanded F0 ranges are achieved by very wide F0 excursions on the focally accented words.

Kulk *et al.* (2003: 15) describe the most striking aspect of colloquial Damascene Arabic (i.e. the Arabic variety spoken in the capital of Syria) as 'its almost singing intonation'. Damascene Arabic is reported to be spoken

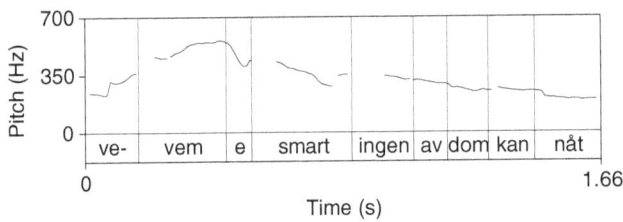

Figure 7.4 F0 contour of 've- vem e smart' (wh- who is clever) with an expanded F0 range and, for comparison, 'ingen av dom kan nåt' either of them know anything (male speaker from Gothenburg, born in Iraq).

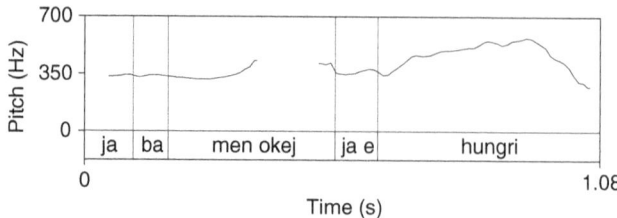

Figure 7.5 F0 contour of 'ja e hungri' (I'm hungry) with an expanded F0 range and, for comparison, 'ja ba men okej' (I just okay) (female speaker from Stockholm, born in Iran).

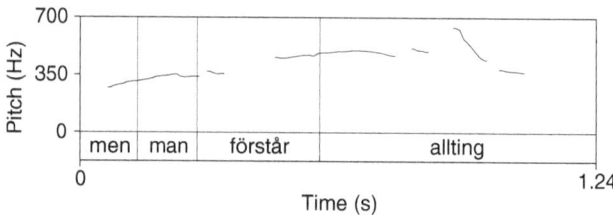

Figure 7.6 F0 contour of 'men man förstår allting' (but you understand everything) (female speaker from Malmö, born in Tunisia).

with a larger pitch range than, for example Cairene Arabic. Damascene Arabic is furthermore described as having a lengthening of the last stressed or unstressed vowel preceding pauses. The lengthening is sometimes accompanied by a rise in pitch (cf. the temporal pattern described in section 'Temporal patterns'). These are thus two aspects of Damascene Arabic prosody that have counterparts in our Swedish data. However, variation in any prosodic dimension cannot be given a label as easily as segmental contrasts. A prosodic event, for example a tonal gesture, obtains its functional meaning when it combines with the segmental string. The exact alignment with regard to the segments may change its function (as in the case of the Swedish word accents, cf. Bruce & Gårding, 1978), and an identical tonal gesture may have different functions in different languages. It is real only if the tonal gesture is used for the same purpose in both languages that one has strong evidence of transfer or another type of influence between the languages in question. In order to label a given temporal or intonational pattern as, for example Syrian Arabic, one would be helped by a similarity in its usage, but I have not been able to find such similarities. Then again, the functions may have changed as the prosodic patterns were borrowed into the multiethnolect. Regardless of their original functions, they may now serve primarily as markers of multiethnolect. Thus an Arabic influence cannot be written off, nor do I have sufficient evidence to make a strong claim of an Arabic influence. In fact, if there is such a thing as universals or unmarked patterns as far as intonation is concerned, wide pitch excursions to express emphasis would be one (see Gussenhoven, 2002 for a discussion). If indeed one of the functions of multiethnolect is to activate dividing lines between in-group and out-group (Bijvoet, 2003) or to give an impression of opposition to mainstream Swedish society (Kotsinas, 2000), then perhaps the original function and exact form of a borrowed prosodic pattern are not as important as its foreign, non-Swedish 'sound'.

Summary

Adolescents perceive Rosengård Swedish in Malmö, Gårdstenish in Gothenburg and Rinkeby Swedish in Stockholm as variations on a theme. The connection to learner language and foreign accent is obvious in all three cities. Each variety furthermore, has a set of regionally colored features (Scanian features in the Malmö variety, West Swedish features in the Gothenburg variety, and so forth). Previously, the question has not been addressed of whether the perceived similarity between the varieties arises from actual phonetic similarities or simply lay in the fact that the multiethnolect in all three cities sounds foreign-accented.

The listening tests reported on above confirm that Swedish adolescents without immigrant background are able to learn the multiethnolect sufficiently well for other adolescents to identify them as speakers of the variety. I have interpreted this as support of the claim that the multiethnolect is a foreign-sounding language variety with a pronunciation that can be learned (as opposed to the variable, idiosyncratic pronunciation of learner Swedish). The listening tests also showed that speakers of multiethnolect are perceived to vary their language use depending on situation, although perhaps to a lesser extent than expected. The foreign-sounding pronunciation is used by some speakers even in situations where multiethnolect is not expected. A few speakers of multiethnolect probably mix the variety's foreign-sounding pronunciation features with actual transfers. Determining which features are parts of the multiethnolect and which are not is thus a complicated matter. Care must be taken to control that the features believed to be typical of the multiethnolect are not solely used by speakers who use them in their first language, that is they cannot all be accounted for by transfer.

The results of the listening tests do not eliminate the possibility that the speakers of multiethnolect simply combine the variety's lexicon and grammar with an actual foreign accent (or, in the case of monolingual speakers, an imitation of any given foreign accent that happens to be known to them). In order to claim that the multiethnolect is a language variety with its own phonetics and phonology, actual similarities must be identified between speakers. Above, one segmental and two prosodic features that are foreign to Standard Swedish have been identified in the multiethnolect and discussed. They can be heard in the speech of various identified speakers of multiethnolect, and they are not only used by speakers in whose first languages the features in question occur. In other words, all occurrences cannot be accounted for by transfer. More likely, they are examples of features that have or are under way towards becoming conventionalized in the variety (see Fraurud, 2004, for a discussion of the conventionalization of multiethnic youth languages). Furthermore, these multiethnolectal features are used by speakers from all three multilingual urban areas investigated: Malmö, Gothenburg and Stockholm.

Finally, I have tried to determine the origin of some of the foreign features of the multiethnolect. Even if the search is narrowed down to the languages spoken by Sweden's largest immigrant groups, the task is still a difficult one. Very little research is available on, for example the intonation of the colloquial Arabic spoken in Iraq. To complicate matters further, several features that were identified are typologically unmarked and frequent in the world's languages. There are several immigrant groups that may have introduced them. On the other hand, the features' successful incorporation and spread among speakers of the multiethnolect may well be related to this very fact.

Chapter 8
Prosody in the Copenhagen Multiethnolect

G.F. HANSEN and N. PHARAO

Introduction

In this chapter we present results from an acoustic and auditory investigation of prosodic features of the Copenhagen Multiethnolect in comparison with Copenhagen-based speech in general, as spoken by the same age group as the one in which the Multiethnolect is most widely used. The investigation is based on elicited speech. The duration of phonologically short and long vowels in stressed and unstressed syllables have been measured and the perceived quantities have been judged. The acoustic results show systematic differences in the realization of the contrast short and long vowels, and differences in the relation between the duration of vowels in stressed and unstressed syllables. Surprisingly, our results also indicate that the duration of vowels are influenced by whether or not the following syllable contains a reducible schwa. This tendency appears to be more pronounced in the Copenhagen Multiethnolect compared to the Copenhagen-based speech. We also present examples of tonal patterns, which are particular to the Copenhagen Multiethnolect in our data.

The Copenhagen Multiethnolect

The Copenhagen Multiethnolect is a variety of Danish, which has mainly been observed to be spoken by adolescent descendants of immigrants (Quist, 2000: 174). The Multiethnolect was first described by Pia Quist (2000). It is termed a Multiethnolect since it is spoken by teenagers with a variety of ethnic and hence linguistic backgrounds. That is, it is not Danish spoken with an accent but a 'lect' or variety in its own right. Similar varieties have been described for other languages, for example Rinkeby Swedish (Kotsinas, 1996) and Dutch Straattaal (Appel, 1999), and see also the many other contributions to this volume.

Not all descendants of immigrants speak Multiethnolect. Rather, it is a variety they may choose to speak. The nature of the factors influencing the choice of variety is not well understood. One hypothesis is that the choice depends on whether the interlocutor is mono- or bilingual (Quist, 2000: 165) but this has not been fully substantiated. It is a matter of some debate whether the Multiethnolect should more appropriately be described as a register or style, but we retain the term Multiethnolect here and use it in the sense of Quist (2008) (cf. Møller, this volume; Svendsen & Quist, this volume).

Note that what we are calling simply Multiethnolect is a variety of Copenhagen-based speech, just like the Copenhagen of adolescents who do not speak Multiethnolect. We do not mean to imply that the variety we term Multiethnolect here is exclusively spoken by children of immigrants or only by adolescents. Nor do we mean to suggest that the features of Copenhagen that we find here are necessarily features of all lects spoken by adolescents in Copenhagen. That is, there may be lects within the city that are stratified according to geography or macrosocial categories like socioeconomic class or level of education. But instead of using cumbersome terms like Copenhagen Multiethnic Youth Speech and Adolescent Copenhagen Danish, we simply use the terms Multiethnolect and Copenhagen.

The pronunciation of Multiethnolect differs from that of Copenhagen in a number of ways. One prominent difference is the absence of the particular Danish syllable accent 'stød', except in a few highly frequent words, for example, 'mand' (man) used as a tag. We have noted a number of other segmental differences while listening to our material, such as devoicing of /r/ particularly after velar plosives, voicing of plosives and palatalization of /t/. However, the starting point for this investigation was some claims regarding nonsegmental characteristics of Multiethnolect. According to Quist (2000) one characteristic trait of the Multiethnolect is a different distribution of stresses; in general there are more of them and they are perceived as somewhat weaker than in Standard and Modern Copenhagen, leaving the impression that the rhythm is different from the rhythm in Copenhagen, specifically that it is more staccato-like.

Preliminaries to the Current Investigation

Taking the observations of other researchers as a starting point, we listened to some of the recordings made by Pia Quist in the late 1990s in order to narrow down some phonetic correlates of the features described (cf. Quist, 2000).

Based on our own auditory judgment of a sample of the recordings, we noted the following:

(1) The quantity difference between long and short vowels seems to be smaller – typically long vowels appear shorter than usual.

(2) It appears that stressed and unstressed syllables are less different in Multiethnolect compared to Copenhagen. In other words: It is less clear to us which syllables have main, secondary and no stress. We believe this may be due to a smaller durational difference between stressed and unstressed syllables.
(3) At least at times the pitch contour normally associated with stressed syllables in Danish differs from that found in Copenhagen. When the pitch contour differs it may affect our perception of stress.
(4) Reduction of unstressed syllables containing schwa seems to differ. We noticed cases where syllables were reduced where we would not expect it, and conversely also schwa syllables that were not reduced where that would have been the norm.

On the basis of this we came up with these specific questions that we aim to investigate:

(1) Is the difference in duration between long and short vowels smaller in Multiethnolect compared to Copenhagen?
(2) Is the difference in duration between stressed and unstressed vowels smaller in Multiethnolect compared to Copenhagen?
(3) Is the stress group pattern different in Multiethnolect compared to Copenhagen?

As mentioned these questions arise from an interest in the Multiethnolect, but in order to answer them, it is necessary to do a comparative study of Multiethnolect and its natural counterpart namely Copenhagen as spoken by adolescents of the same age.

Test Design and Implementation

In order to test these observations we needed a sufficient amount of comparable material from both Multiethnolect speakers and Copenhagen speakers. To obtain these data for the acoustic investigation, we used a modified version of the map task (Anderson *et al.*, 1991). The purpose of the modification was to ensure that the participants had a genuine task to perform, rather than asking them to act out a scenario. In our version, one map contained information about the names of roads and certain places in a fictional town. The other map was identical but contained no road or place names and the participants' task was to place stickers with road and place names accurately on this map. The subjects were seated with their backs to each other to ensure that only speech was used to carry out the task.

The names of the roads and places were designed to elicit tokens of short and long vowels, stressed as well as unstressed, of the three vowel qualities [i a u]. A total of 33 test words were included in the task. The test words all contained at least three syllables in order to reduce the effect that a difference in the number of syllables in the word would induce.

A note on the constraints on the test words

The constraints placed on the structure of the words and syllables containing the vowels to be measured were chosen for the following reasons:

(1) *Stress*: The level of stress is known to influence segmental duration in a variety of languages, including Danish. Stressed vowels are longer than the equivalent unstressed vowel, and when a stressed vowel loses its stress due to compounding or syntactic factors it is also shortened.

(2) *Vowel quality*: Danish has at least 16 surface vowel qualities, and duration is known to vary systematically with vowel height – low vowels are longer than high vowels, all other things being equal. We chose to focus on [i, a, u] because they represent extremes of the Danish vowel space with respect to placement in the dimensions front-back and high-low.

(3) *Number of syllables in the word*: Studies of vowel durations in a number of languages have shown that vowels tend to be shorter in polysyllabic words than in monosyllabic ones, and that for each extra syllable added the duration is further decreased, that is a vowel is shorter in a disyllabic word than in a monosyllabic word, and shorter still in a trisyllabic word, all other things being equal (Dauer, 1983).

(4) *Open or closed syllables*: Vowel duration is also affected by the structure of the syllable; a vowel is shorter if the syllable is closed by a consonant. We have chosen only to include words with phonetically open stressed syllables.

Thus, the basic structure of the test words, that is the words containing tokens of the vowel to be measured, was /C$\underline{V}$CVvaj/ with the underlined position containing the target vowel, for example /kiːnavaj/ or /manavaj/ (Eng.: 'China road' or 'Manna road'). Whereas, the target vowel was always either /i/, /a/ or /u/, the second position could be filled with any vowel, including schwa, /ə/. Given these constraints, we designed 33 test words given in Table 8.1. The target vowels are underlined in each test word.

Subjects

We recorded 12 13–15-year-old descendants of immigrants, who had a variety of linguistic backgrounds including western Arabic, Farsi, Turkish and Punjabi and a set of 12 age-matched speakers of Danish without immigrant background, for comparison. All subjects were recorded in matched pairs, that is, both subjects in a pair had the same type of background.

Table 8.1 Test words

Vowel quality Quantity and degree of stress	[i]/[iː]	[a]/[æː]	[u]/[uː]
Short, stressed	[ˈbibivɑjʔ]	[ˈdadɐvɑjʔ]	[ˈgubigæːðə]
	[ˈminivɑjʔ]	[ˈmanavɑjʔ]	[ˈbudavɑjʔ]
	[ˈtˢibəvɑjʔ]	[ˈmanəvɑjʔ]	[ˈkʰudɐvɑjʔ]
		[ˈlanəvɑjʔ]	
Short, unstressed (no stress)	[tˢiˈbeʔdvɑjʔ]	[baˈnaʔnvɑjʔ]	[ˈsguːdɐbutˢig]
	[miˈnisdɐvɑjʔ]	[sdaˈkʰidvɑjʔ]	[buˈtˢigsenʔtɐ]
	[miˈnudvɑjʔ]		
Long, stressed	[ˈgiːgavɑjʔ]	[ˈlæːmavɑjʔ]	([ˈsguːdɐbutˢig])
	[ˈkʰiːnavɑjʔ]	[ˈnæːbovɑjʔ]	[ˈkʰuːbavɑjʔ]
	[ˈmiːnəvɑjʔ]	[ˈdæːməvɑjʔ]	[ˈkʰuːbəvɑjʔ]
			[laˈguːnəvɑjʔ]
Long, unstressed (secondary stress)	[ˈlanmiːnɐ]	[ˈpʰlasdigkʰæːno]	[ˈvansguːdɐ]
	[ˈgulmiːnə]	[ˈfoðbʌldbæːnɐ]	[ˈbikʰuːbɐnə]
	[ˈkʰɔlmiːnɐ]	[ˈgʌlʔfbæːnɐ]	

Preliminary impression of the recordings

In most cases the task inspired a focused effort leading to a lively dialogue. Frequently mistakes and clarifications required subjects to go over details of the map numerous times, securing repetitions of the target words.

Although the task does involve reading our test words, it seems reasonable to regard the material as more spontaneous than read aloud. First, the reading was situated in a nonscripted context. Second it appeared that while the first rendition of a test word could carry traces of being read aloud, the subjects would refer to the same place names as known entities later in the conversation.

This can be inferred by the fact that the subjects sometimes negotiate the pronunciation of some of our target words and seemingly end up agreeing on a way of pronouncing them that is not fully in accord with a conventional reading. Overall, the recordings gave the impression of being spontaneous conversations, despite the fact that the subjects were participating in a test-like recording situation.

Copenhagen or multiethnolect?

As noted previously, in the section 'The Copenhagen Multiethnolect', the Multiethnolect is a variety that speakers use optionally. This means that we could not be sure that our subjects with immigrant background had in fact spoken Multiethnolect with each other while solving the map task. In order to more confidently classify the speech of the subjects as Multiethnolect we asked two colleagues at the department of Danish dialectology, Pia Quist and Marie Maegaard, to evaluate the speech of each subject on two scales: (1) Multiethnolect, (2) Copenhagen. Two scales were used, since we did not want to exclude the possibility that a prototypical speaker of Multiethnolect might also be classified as a prototypical speaker of Copenhagen. And naturally we also wanted to know whether there were speakers among our subject who could not be said to speak any of the two varieties.

The two listeners were given a sample of one minute of speech from each subject and ranked each sample on both scales from 0 to 3, where 0 indicated that the speech sample in no way resembled the variety and 3 indicated that it was a very good example of the variety. The evaluations made by the two listeners were averaged and the subjects were plotted on a graph, given in Figure 8.1.

As is apparent the two groups of subjects fall in two clearly separated clusters with a minor overlap. Only one speaker with immigrant background is classified as more of a Copenhagen speaker than a

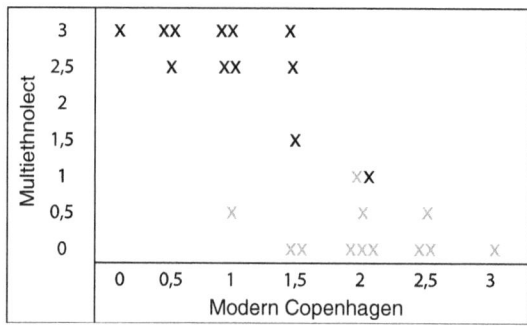

Figure 8.1 Classification of subjects. Bilingual subjects are in black and monolingual in gray

Multiethnolect speaker. We do not think that this informal test is thorough enough to validate a regrouping or exclusion of any of the subjects, however, the results are clear enough that a more thorough testing did not seem to be necessary. Therefore, we feel fairly confident in treating all the recordings of subjects with immigrant background as Multiethnolect and all the recordings of subjects without immigrant background as Copenhagen, within the scope of this investigation.

Recording process and segmentation

The audio was recorded directly on the CD using equipment of a professional standard. The acoustic analysis was done using Praat. Segmentation was done according to standard principles with one exception: According to previous research (Fischer-Jørgensen & Hutters, 1981) the most reliable starting point of vowels is found at the point where the second formant appears. Following this procedure would have resulted in an undesirably high number of the *unstressed* vowels in our material having no measurable duration, in spite of the fact that a vowel was clearly audible – notably in the case of /a/. We therefore decided to draw the first boundary of all the vowels at the point where the first formant appeared. This of course should lead to slightly longer vowel durations compared to other Danish investigations (presumably in the range 5–15 ms) and possibly slightly less precise measurements.

Phonetic properties of phonological units

In our acoustic analysis of the selected prosodic phenomena of the Multiethnolect, we classify the vowels in accordance with a canonical pronunciation in the standard norm (e.g. as described in Grønnum, 2001). We do this for three reasons:

(1) Listener's who are unfamiliar with the Multiethnolect can be assumed to compare this variety, like any other, to the standard norm. If they do, an analysis of deviations from the norm should highlight the features that are the cause of the perceived differences.
(2) It is not possible from the present material to conduct a full phonological analysis of the Multiethnolect itself.
(3) If we were to classify the acoustic data according to our own perceptions of vowel quantity and degree of stress, the analysis would amount to a description of our own perceptual categories, and would not reflect the relation between the shared system of Copenhagen youth and the usage of speakers of Multiethnolect.

For these reasons, we refer to phonemes in our analyses of the data. Obviously since phonemes are abstract units of analysis and not physically real units of speech, we are not claiming that phonemes have average durations, but rather that there is an average duration of the many different realizations of the particular phonemes. Hence, when we refer to the average duration of stressed, short /i/, we are referring to the average duration of the stressed vowel in lexemes that have a short, stressed /i/ according to the standard analysis of Modern Copenhagen Danish (e.g. Grønum, 2005), regardless of the perceived quantity and quality of the individual tokens.

Results

Duration of stressed and unstressed vowels

In Figure 8.2 we give the average durations of short stressed and unstressed vowels in the two varieties of Danish (see appendix for details on average values).

As is apparent from the graph there is a difference in the duration of short unstressed and short stressed vowels in both varieties. All differences are statistically significant (t-test, $p < 0.001$). Thus, duration can be said to correlate with stress in Multiethnolect at least when we compare short stressed and unstressed vowels, and since the pattern is much the same as in Copenhagen this result does not provide an explanation of the differences in number and manifestation of stresses between the two lects that have been mentioned in previous investigations (cf. section 'The Copenhagen Multiethnolect').

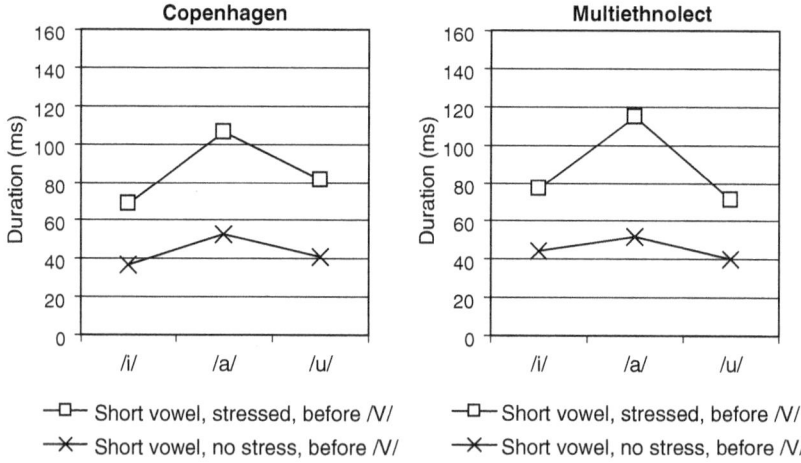

Figure 8.2 Average durations of short unstressed vowels (crosses) and short stressed vowels (squares)

Duration of phonologically short and long vowels

The comparison of the average durations of phonologically short and long vowels (given in Figure 8.3) shows an obvious difference between the two varieties.

The average durations of short vowels are indicated by empty squares and for the long vowels by filled squares. Values for Multiethnolect are shown on the right and for Copenhagen on the left.

Unsurprisingly, the short/long contrast is sustained in Copenhagen where the differences in durations are all statistically significant (t-test, $p < 0.05$ or better).

In the Multiethnolect there is hardly any difference in the average durations and *none* of the differences are statistically significant. Thus the average durations indicate that the short/long vowel contrast is not sustained in Multiethnolect.

The histograms shown in Figure 8.4 give more details of the overlap between short and long vowels in the Multiethnolect. The graphs display the distribution of tokens of short vowels (empty squares) and long vowels (filled squares) for all three vowel qualities. As can be seen from the graphs there were more test words containing long vowels than test words containing short vowels. The X-axis in each graph is divided into intervals of 20 ms and the number of tokens belonging to a particular interval may be read off the Y-axis. The middle graph displays the distribution of tokens for /a/ and it is evident that the two curves are almost identical in shape. Thus, the overlap appears to be complete in the case of /a/.

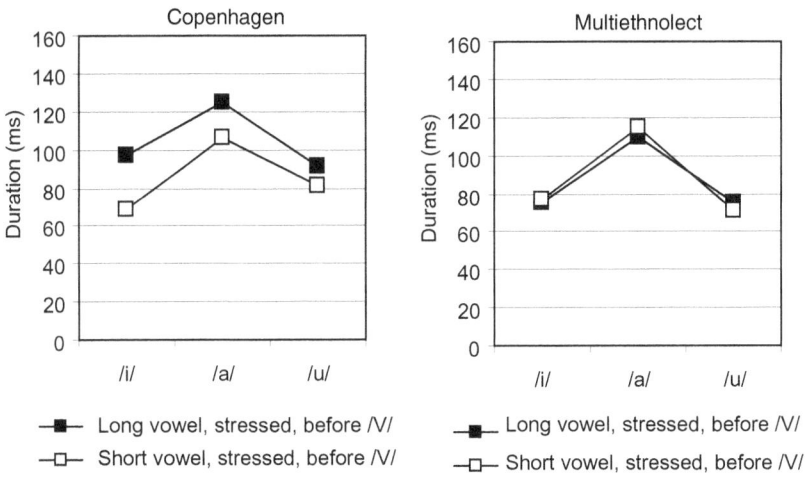

Figure 8.3 Average durations of phonologically short and long vowels (empty and filled squares, respectively)

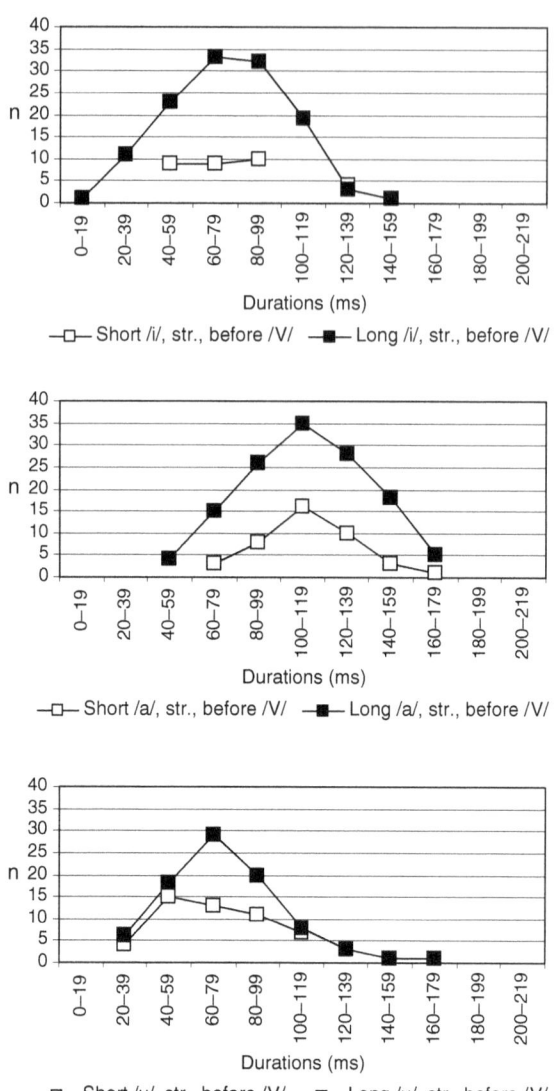

Figure 8.4 Token distributions in Multiethnolect

For /i/, shown in the top graph, the similarity in the distributions is less clear, particularly since the curve for short /i/ is almost flat. However, tokens of short vowels all fall within the range of long vowels, meaning that there is a great number of tokens of phonologically long /i/ that are as short as or shorter than tokens of phonologically short /i/.

For /u/, shown in the bottom graph, the picture is still less clear. The curve that shows the distribution of short [u]s peaks earlier than that for long [u:]s, but again all tokens of short /u/ fall within the range of tokens of long /u/.

The averages we have looked at so far are only based on tokens of vowels from test words in which the target vowel preceded a consonant + a full vowel. Since disyllabic words in which the stressed vowel is followed by a consonant + schwa are far more common in Danish, we had also included test words of this type. Initially, we did not think that this difference in the structure of the test words would exert any influence on the duration of the target vowels. However, since assimilation and elision of schwa are very common processes in Danish, and since it became apparent to us during the preliminary investigation that speakers of Multiethnolect might behave differently in this respect, we decided to see if target vowels before consonant + schwa (e.g. ['manəvɑjˀ], 'Mandevej' (Eng.: 'Man road')) exhibited different patterns than target vowels before a consonant + a full vowel (e.g. ['manavɑjˀ], 'Mannavej' (Eng.: 'Manna road')).

The average durations of phonologically short and long vowels before consonant + schwa are given in Figure 8.5. What we see in Figure 8.5 is that the difference between long and short vowels is now sustained in the Multiethnolect (except in the case of /u/, where there is still no significant difference in the average durations of short and long vowels). In Copenhagen the distance between short and long vowels is also enhanced. Thus, if we compare the average durations of short and long vowels in

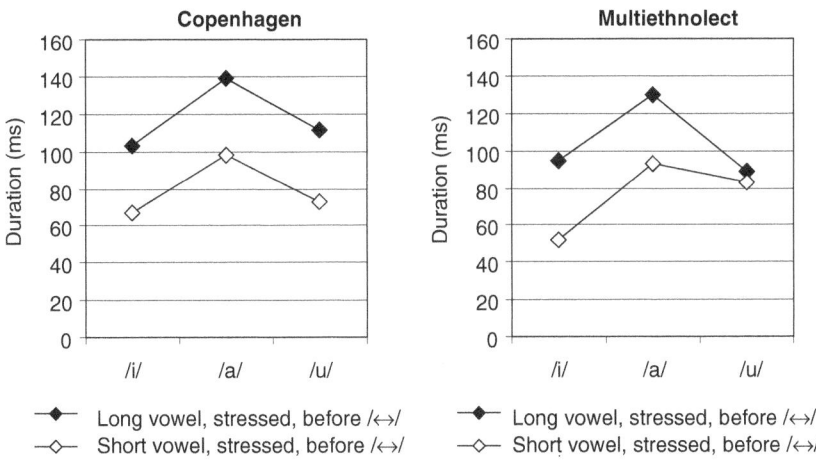

Figure 8.5 Average durations of phonologically short and long vowels followed by consonant + schwa

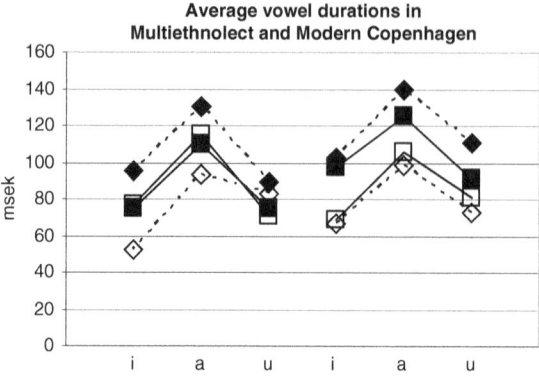

Figure 8.6 Comparison of average vowel durations for the two structures in both varieties

words of the two structures, which has been done in Figure 8.6, we see that in both varieties there is a tendency to make short vowels even shorter and long ones even longer when the immediately succeeding syllable contains a schwa – however, the difference in durations due to word structure is not statistically significant for neither short nor long /u/ in the Multiethnolect, nor for neither short nor long /i/ or indeed short /u/ in Copenhagen.

Thus, the contrast between short and long vowels can be neutralized in Multiethnolect, but when the immediately succeeding syllable contains a schwa the contrast is sustained.

Perceived vowel quantity

The results presented so far show an acoustically measurable difference in the realizations of long and short stressed vowels in Copenhagen and the Multiethnolect. In addition, we, the authors, have classified the tokens we measured auditorily, so that we can say whether the tendency for shortening of phonologically long vowels is also perceived. Tokens were classified as long, short or indeterminate, and the classifications are compared to the phonological status of the tokens in Tables 8.2 and 8.3.

Table 8.2 shows that the monolingual informants in the overwhelming majority of cases realize both short and long vowels as we would have expected, in 98% and 95% of cases, respectively. For the informants with immigrant background we see, in Table 8.3 that short vowels were most often perceived as expected, but that long vowels were only perceived as long in 72.3% of the tokens, with 24.3% being perceived as short and the last 3% as indeterminate. This auditory analysis confirms the results from the acoustic measurements, as well as our expectation that the greater

Table 8.2 Expected versus observed quantity in Copenhagen

Expected		Observed						
		Short		Long		Undecided		Sum
		n	%	n	%	n	%	n
	Short	295	98.0%	0	0%	6	2.0%	301
	Long	14	2.6%	508	95.0%	13	2.4%	535

Table 8.3 Expected versus observed quantity in Multiethnolect

Expected		Observed						
		Short		Long		Undecided		Sum
		n	%	n	%	n	%	n
	Short	451	95.2%	19	4.0%	4	0.8%	474
	Long	178	24.7%	522	72.3%	22	3.0%	722

similarity between long and short vowels in Multiethnolect was more likely to be due to shortening of long vowels rather than lengthening of short vowels. This result deserves to be tested by evaluations of both speakers of Multiethnolect and speakers of other varieties of Copenhagen Danish, in order to establish the perceptual relevance of our findings.

Fundamental frequency

During our pilot investigations we found, as noted previously in the section 'Preliminaries to the Current Investigation' that tonal movements in conjunction with stressed syllables in Multiethnolect differed characteristically from the stress group pattern described for Standard Copenhagen Danish in (Grønnum, 1992). We also found some deviations from the standard global intonation contour associated with declarative utterances, in particular a tendency for all stressed syllables to be produced on the same, fairly high-pitch level, but with a sudden drop on the very last syllable of the utterance, as shown in Figure 8.7. This high-flat patterns was, however, very rare in the material we recorded using the map task

In most cases the tonal movements associated with stressed syllables in our data are, at least as judged visually by inspecting the F_0-trackings, in accordance with the stress group pattern described by Grønnum, regardless of the speaker's linguistic background. However, we did notice tonal differences when we listened to the recordings, but not in the test words

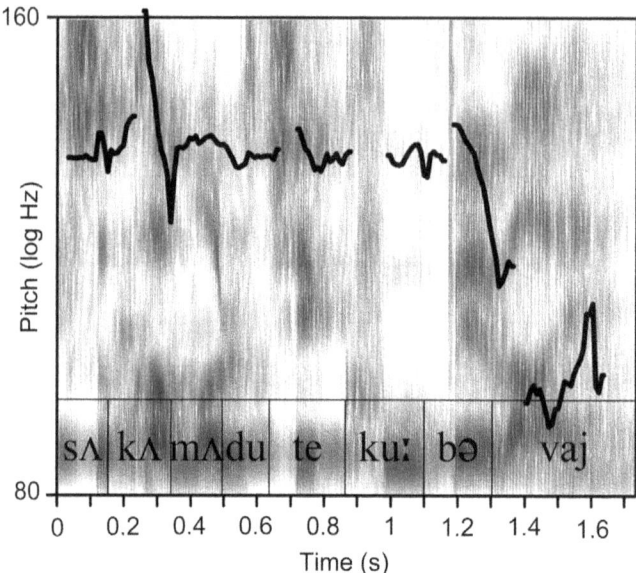

Figure 8.7 Example of tonal contour in Multiethnolect that differs from what is found in Copenhagen

themselves. And occasionally the following pattern (given in the left part of Figure 8.8) would appear and only, as far as we have been able to determine, in the speech of the subjects with immigrant background. It is to some extent like the stress group pattern in Copenhagen, having a low

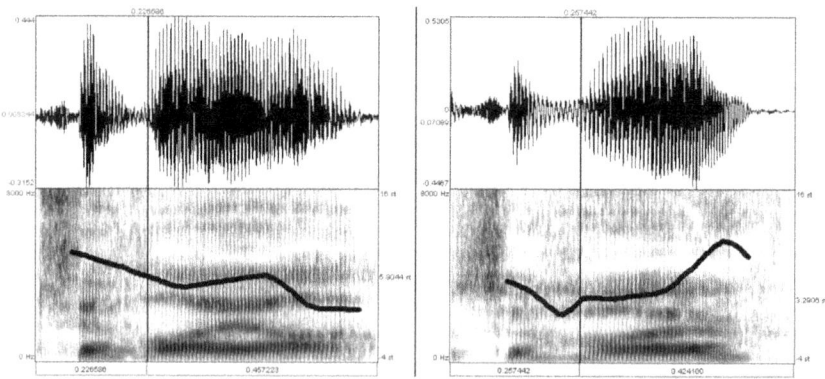

Figure 8.8 F_0-tracings of the stress group pattern in Multiethnolect on the left and Modern Copenhagen on the right. The utterance is in both cases [tˢe ˈhʌjɐ] meaning 'to the right'. The vertical line indicates the start of the stressed vowel

tone in the stressed syllable and a rise to the first post-tonic syllable. However, the peak is timed earlier, occurring in the beginning of the post-tonic, and the rise is not as steep as in Copenhagen (cf. Figure 8.8). For comparison we show the same utterance spoken by a Copenhagen speaker next to it. Here, the rise is steeper and the peak occurs later relative to the onset of the post-tonic syllable thus resembling more closely the stress group pattern seen in studies of Standard Copenhagen read speech (e.g. Grønnum, 1992).

If the patterns do look somewhat alike they certainly sound very different. A very informal perceptual experiment clearly demonstrated that we could easily trick our two expert listeners into perceiving a Copenhagen speaker as a Multiethnolect speaker by simply resynthesizing the short utterance above with the tonal pattern of the same utterance spoken by the Multiethnolect speaker. Likewise, the Multiethnolect utterance could be perceived as Copenhagen when it was resynthesized with the tonal pattern of the Copenhagen speaker. This suggests that this alternate stress group pattern is a very salient cue for identifying Multiethnolect.

This particular Multiethnolect utterance also contains an example of the so-called extra but weaker stress, namely in the last syllable. However, this impression of a weak stress vanishes completely when the Copenhagen intonation is superimposed on the utterance, thus suggesting that the cue to the (perceived) extra stress is mainly tonal. It is also possible to remove this impression of an extra stress without changing the overall impression of Multiethnolect by simply flattening out the tonal movement of the post-tonic syllable; this can be done by resynthesis in, for example Praat. Since every stressed syllable in Standard Danish initiates a certain tonal stress group pattern it is to be expected that tonal movement contributes to signaling primary stress. But, it is not generally obvious from the F_0 tracings of these syllables having extra stresses in Multiethnolect that they should be considered to be separate stress groups. In other words, it would appear that unstressed syllables in Multiethnolect *may* contain slight pitch movements that give rise to some resemblance with stressed syllables in Copenhagen. To us, the utterance still sounds like a sample of Multiethnolect when this cue to weak prominence is removed.

Summary and Suggestions for Further Work

The acoustic and auditory analyses presented here show that there is a difference in the durations of short and long vowels when we compare Multiethnolect to Copenhagen. In particular, the approximately equal duration of long and short vowels before syllables containing a full vowel must be striking to a monolingual speaker of Danish. This shortening of long vowels leads to a suspension of the phonological vowel length distinction, except in words where the following syllable contains a schwa, where the contrast is maintained, although not as clearly as in Copenhagen. It is striking that the average difference in the duration of short and long vowels is in fact greater in words of this structure in the Copenhagen speech of monolinguals. We propose that the differences in vowel durations may contribute to the impression of an alternate rhythm in Multiethnolect compared to Copenhagen. However, this suggestion ought, naturally, to be tested in perceptual experiments.

We also found that speakers of Multiethnolect occasionally employ a slightly different stress group pattern compared to Copenhagen, which in our data is peculiar to the Multiethnolect speakers, although far from common in the Multiethnolect. An informal identification task suggests that this tonal pattern is a salient marker of Multiethnolect, but naturally this also calls for a full-scale perceptual experiment.

Acknowledgments

Thanks to the Department of Danish Dialectology at the University of Copenhagen for providing us with the means to carry out the acoustic investigation reported here.

This chapter is expanded and revised relative to Hansen and Pharao (2005), but still less comprehensive than Pharao and Hansen (2005) written in the Danish language.

Appendix

Quantity	Stress	Following syllable contains	/i/ dur. (ms)	/i/ N	/i/ Std. dev.	/a/ dur. (ms)	/a/ n	/a/ Std. dev.	/u/ dur. (ms)	/u/ n	/u/ Std. dev.
Multiethnolect											
Short	No stress	Full vowel	44	56	18	52	75	15	40	52	13
Short	Stressed	Full vowel	77	33	26	115	51	25	71	52	22
Short	Stressed	schwa	52	23	16	93	58	19	83	13	41
Long	Secondary stress	Full vowel	97	39	24	130	18	37	81	49	29
Long	Secondary stress	schwa	108	11	33	126	12	25		0	
Long	Stressed	Full vowel	75	125	26	110	129	27	75	89	26
Long	Stressed	schwa	95	32	33	130	43	28	89	59	31
Copenhagen											
Short	No stress	Full vowel	37	39	11	53	41	11	41	31	12
Short	Stressed	Full vowel	69	22	19	106	36	18	81	24	21
Short	Stressed	schwa	67	17	17	98	38	14	73	15	16
Long	Secondary stress	Full vowel	90	23	16	122	35	23	100	31	20
Long	Secondary stress	schwa	121	7	11	118	8	20		0	
Long	Stressed	Full vowel	97	76	26	125	88	23	91	76	21
Long	Stressed	schwa	103	29	22	139	20	19	111	63	29

Chapter 9
Transnational Identifications among Adolescents in Suburban Sweden

C. HAGLUND

Introduction

Based on an ethnographic study that aimed to capture the daily life of adolescents in a suburban multicultural and multilingual neighborhood of Stockholm, Sweden (Haglund, 2005), this chapter explores how identities and allegiances are negotiated and constructed among the adolescents. The chapter will focus specifically on the connection between identities and allegiances and dominant discourses on multilingualism and ethnic diversity in society and school. We will also observe the role of transcultural influences and resources in the adolescents' quests for identities and building of allegiances.

Recent decades witnessed a restructuring of the key institutions of welfare as well as developments in information and communication technologies (Gee *et al.*, 1997). These changes provide a greater scope for young people to carve out more complex forms of identity and patterns of cultural association than those seen in earlier times. Young people are influenced by these changes, but also act as participants in the processes of implementing them. The changes present new challenges and opportunities for them and both support and restrain them in exercising more freedom and creativity over developing their sense of self (Beck, 1992; Cieslik & Pollock, 2002; Giddens, 1991). These circumstances also allow space for more hybrid and transgressive identification (Rampton, 1995a: 311).

The adolescents in focus in this chapter are traditionally referred to in the literature as '(linguistic) minorities', 'multilingual', 'second-language learners', and so on. Here, and throughout this chapter, they are merely referred to as 'adolescents'. This is because the adolescents themselves, as we will see, identify primarily neither as multilingual nor as minorities. In addition, not all adolescents are second-language learners or multilingual in the more traditional meanings of these terms.

The study revealed how the adolescents appear to find themselves in the midst of a vivid flow of cultures, perspectives, influences and languages. In contrast to this experience, however, the adolescents identify and associate with a striving on the part of institutions such as the school system and of society in general, to maintain traditional (mainstream Swedish) content, perspectives and language (Haglund, 2005).

This conflict appears to underpin a contradiction that permeates the adolescents' minds and influences their practices. While this contradictory situation and the adolescents' understandings and linguistic strategies in relation to it have been described and analyzed in detail elsewhere (Haglund, 2005, 2007a, 2007b, 2008), this chapter will focus specifically on the adolescents' quests for identities and building of allegiances.

Youth Identity

Identities and allegiances are understood in the present research to interact with sociocultural processes. We have seen in previous research, and will also observe in the present chapter, how identities are negotiated in relation to current societal change. Identifications among youth are understood to reflect individual and collective positionings to the social transformation and change (Giampapa, 2004; Heller, 1999; Pavlenko & Blackledge, 2004a; Rampton, 1995a, 1995b).

Culture and identity are essential concepts in research of this kind. Neither identity nor culture can be represented simply as sets of attributes or as traditions in this perspective. Instead, both are continually negotiated, created and recreated and, as a consequence, are fluid (see e.g. Butler, 2005; Gilroy, 1998; Hall, 1990).

Pavlenko and Blackledge (2004a, 2004b: 20) assert that individuals may find themselves in a 'perpetual tension between self-chosen identities and others' attempts to position them differently'. Blackledge (2005: 37) makes a distinction between interactive positioning (one individual positioning the other) and reflective positioning (the process of positioning oneself). This indicates that identity should not automatically be connected to cultural background, but should instead be seen as intimately intertwined with social relationships and power structure. Thus, much like linguistic expression, identity is observed as connected to and directed towards aspects of the sociocultural context (Heller, 2007).

The Ethnographic Fieldwork

Durby[1] is one Swedish neighborhood that must readily care for the demands of a new generation of migrants and children and/or grandchildren of migrants oriented toward the sociocultural changes of globalization and transnationalism. Measured according to socioeconomic variables, the neighborhood is poor. About 40% of the working population in Durby was unemployed or dependent on social welfare in the early 2000s. Despite a slight preponderance of people from the Middle East, and the limited representation of people of Swedish background (only 10% in 2005), Durby is a true multinational and multilingual neighborhood. The population represents more than 50 different national origins, and about 50 different languages are spoken in the neighbourhood.

Through the years of fieldwork (1999–2002), more than 100 adolescents (aged 13–16) in Durby and at Durby School regularly participated in the research activities. As a participant observer, I spent time with the adolescents in a number of different situations and contexts both in and out of school; malls, cafes, restaurants, libraries, the suburb's downtown area, street corners near the underground station, in some of the participants' homes and in various after-school activities. I maintained contact up to 2006 with a few of the adolescents through phone calls, e-mails, text messages and meetings. A number of them also participate in an on-going longitudinal research project that focuses on language and identity investments among a group of young adults (Haglund, in press).[2]

I utilized a varied set of ethnographic methods in addition to participant observation and gathered data through the ethnographic practices of taking field notes and audio-recordings, collecting subject background information through short interviews/informal interactions, semistructured or spontaneous interviews/conversations, subjects' diary notes and other correspondence, such as e-mails. As part of the ethnographic fieldwork and analysis, media accounts, including newspaper articles and television programmes were also examined.

Dominant Societal Discourses

Discourse, as it is used in this chapter, addresses 'the complex signs and practices structured through power relations to control our lives' (Roberts & Street, 1997: 184). When referring to dominant discourses in the society, the process I have in mind is that by which ideologies circulate in (spoken or written) language in order to 'enact and recognize different identities and activities, give the material world certain meanings, distribute social goods in a certain way, make meaning-full connections in our experience, and privilege certain symbol systems and ways of knowing over others' (Gee, 1999: 13).

During the nearly three years I spent among the adolescents in Durby and at Durby School, I noted that their experiences, negotiations and identifications were influenced in particular by some of the discourses of society, which were also maintained and reproduced through Durby School (see Haglund, 2008).

The media discourse in the early 2000s, where the Swedish language is predominantly thought and claimed to be the key to integration into society (Jonsson, 2007; Milani, 2007b; Runfors, 2003; Sjögren, 2001), represents one such discourse. Adapting to the mainstream, linguistically (and culturally), appears to be considered in this public discourse as the incontestable, self-evident way by which to gain status and legitimacy within general society, and consequently to escape marginalization and social exclusion (Haglund, 2005: 54ff). This discourse appears to recognize multilingualism as a set of parallel, competing monolingualisms rather than as a hybrid, integrated system (cf. Heller, 1999, 2007). There is also a tendency in the media as well as in some political and academic discourse to relate integration failures to what are identified as linguistic deficiencies in Swedish as well as in other languages, including the mother tongue (Haglund, 2005: 55).

In addition, 'insufficient education' on the part of multilingual students and their parents is referred to in the dominant public discourse as the main obstacle in the integration process (Haglund, 2005: 60ff). According to this discourse, problems arise because of children's differing cultures and ethnicities when they enter the Swedish school system, not because the school systems in both the countries of origin and in Sweden are designed to perpetuate cultural and social systems by preparing young people for roles in those systems (Spindler & Spindler, 1971: ix).

Other discourses that have a similar influence on the adolescents' negotiations of identities concern, for instance, the unpredictable ethnic and cultural identification among people who have the opportunity to negotiate membership in several ethnic or cultural communities. These discourses also concern the neighborhoods in which a large proportion of the minority members in Sweden live (Haglund, 2005: 58ff). Research has identified a process through which the stigma of certain neighborhoods is reinforced, for instance in the media, and is eventually also reflected in the understandings of minority members themselves (Pripp, 2002). This process involves not only neighborhoods but language, ethnicity and schools. The predominant majority's values, preferred languages or identities, along with their neighborhoods and schools, are commonly recognized as superior in this dominant discourse. Individuals are accordingly subjected to hegemonic practices (Gramsci, 1971), which inculcate in them the need to serve the interest of the leadership represented by the majority members. This process appears to be a consequence of an exercise in power that, in Bourdieu's terms, is meticulously 'misrecognized' (Bourdieu, 1991).

In most of the examined media accounts reflecting the dominant societal discourses, the question of how social structure partly determines and reproduces circumstances and contexts that further contribute to the maintenance of these discourses is left out. However, in cases where a more critical approach is taken (Haglund, 2005: 62ff), the accounts produce counter-discourses that we will see also play a significant role in the adolescents' identity negotiations.

Negotiations of Identities

The concept of positioning (Davies & Harré, 1990; Pavlenko and Blackledge, 2004a, 2004b) refers to all discursive practices, which position individuals or allow individuals to position themselves. The adolescents' negotiations of identities, as observed in the study, are influenced by the dominant societal discourses referred to in the previous section. We also observe how the adolescents position one other in relation to these discourses. Blackledge's distinction between reflective positioning and interactive positioning (2005: 37) is useful in examining these processes of individual and collective positionings. Initially we will look at how adolescents position themselves, and we will then turn to how they position one other.

Reflective positionings

The adolescents negotiate what it means to have left a country but still be able to refer to this country as 'my country' or not to have any home country to refer to, but rather a nation that has lived in diaspora for a long time (such as the Kurdish nation). The individual and collective experiences of migration and minoritization (diaspora) (Gilroy, 1998) are continuously negotiated as part of the adolescents' negotiations of identities. National identification does not always apply in these situations and, as we will see, the identifications of the adolescents go beyond the traditional idea that one language automatically corresponds to one culture or one (national) identity (Anderson, 1991; Heller, 1994).

The following utterances were recorded in school or after-school or were cited in the media in 2002 among adolescents residing in Durby: *'När jag blir äldre, då kanske jag vill ha, behålla traditionerna. Nu, för mig, just nu, så betyder dom inte så mycket'* (When I get older, perhaps then I'll want to have [and] keep the traditions. Now, to me, right now, they don't mean that much), *'Men jag bara bor här, nationalitet spelar egentligen ingen roll'* (This is only where I live; nationality doesn't matter really), *'Jag vill flytta till USA och där blir det fånigt att säga att jag är svensk'* (I want to move to the United States, and there it will seem silly to call myself Swedish) (the author's translations from Swedish to idiomatic English) (see Haglund, 2005: 52f).

The understandings of identity, nationality and tradition reflected in these accounts recur in the adolescents' negotiations of identities in a number of different situations and contexts. Their accounts suggest that identification to them mainly extends beyond 'traditional' national boundaries and that the role of one's cultural and ethnic background in negotiations of identities is subjected to change over time, place and, as we will see in the extract below, interlocutor. Residency in Sweden, just as in any other place, such as the United States in one of the comments above, is understood as temporary. In addition, there is a reference to global rather than national identification. Other countries, including the United States, are apparently seen as more mixed communities by some of the adolescents, and such communities perhaps seem more welcoming than Sweden.

Resources such as media, music and movies from the adolescents' countries of origin and neighboring countries come across, for some adolescents, as crucial in their attempts to evaluate, negotiate and describe themselves and their daily life. This also holds true for interactions on the internet (see section 'The internet'). Kiron, who was born in Bangladesh, is one of the adolescents whose quest for identity is influenced by the resources that provide opportunities for adolescents like her to access and negotiate both traditional and popular cultures. In Kiron's case the resources are South Asian. Kiron regularly visits a flea market in a neighboring shopping mall and a Hindi music and film stand located there. She watches Bollywood motion pictures and listens to their soundtracks and other musical productions from India and South Asia.

Given experiences of this kind, the idea of positioning oneself within one particular cultural identity hardly seems valid. As we can see in the example below, the opportunity to identify transculturally and transnationally seems to be more natural and rewarding, rather than finding and negotiating a single 'true self'. Identification, for Marcela in the following extract, seems to be about expressing and communicating oneself in a number of different ways:

Extract 1. Marcela, F (female), age 16; semistructured individual interview.

Marcela: *Jag känner inte mig som en chilenare, jag gör inte det fast jag vet inte vad jag känner mig som. Jag är, jag är, jag känner mig som jag är både och, en blandning av allt ... Jag känner mig som jag både kommer från alla möjliga länder. Fast jag är ju, ja, men det är svårt och sä-. Det är för att man bor så hära i ett ställe där det finns så många olika från många länder och dom, till sist man blir så här. Det är inte bara jag som tänker så här, min bästis Antonella, hon tänker också så här, hon 'Jag är inte chilenare, jag känner mig inte som en chilenare så att jag, om jag alltså inte känner mig som chilenare då är jag ju inte chilenare'.*

CH: *Dom andra då, hur tror du att andra ser på dig?*

Marcela: I don't feel like a Chilean, I don't, but I don't know what I feel like. I'm, I'm, I feel like I'm both, a mixture of everything ... I feel like I'm from all kinds of different countries. But I'm like, yes, it's difficult and sK That's because you live like this in a place where there are so many different people from many countries and they, in the end you turn out like this. I'm not the only one who thinks like this. My best friend Antonella, she thinks like this too, she's like, 'I'm not Chilean, I don't feel like a Chilean so I'm, if I don't feel like a Chilean then I'm not Chilean'.

CH: The others, then, what do you think they think about you?

Marcela: *Jag vet inte, som en chilenare tror jag fast ändå inte. Ibland dom säger att dom tror, dom säger 'Hon är en av oss' så dära 'Hon är som oss', fast ändå så vet dom att jag är en chilenare.*

Marcela: I don't know, Chilean I think but on the other hand no, sometimes they say they think, they say 'She's one of us', like 'She's one of us', but still they know I'm Chilean.

To Marcela, being Chilean and Swedish are not the only options, but rather a mixture of different identifications. According to her, the adolescents in Durby have a miscellany of identification options because of their everyday experiences in the multicultural and multilingual neighborhood (see also Extract 2 below). Marcela's comment indicates that she explores a transnational frame of reference rather than an ethnonational one when she positions herself.

Identifications, then, for Marcela and the other adolescents, appear to be spatially and temporally dependent rather than determined by nationality. In addition to the boundary transcendence and elusiveness, Marcela also refers to the way ethnic, cultural and linguistic boundaries are manifested among the adolescents (see Marcela's account below). Although she stresses that identity depends on space and time rather than being related to nationality, her best friend happens to be a Chilean girl.

In addition to references to the elusive character of identification along with references to how national identity may be drawn upon for specific purposes, Marcela also refers to the relationship between identification and language. Marcela and some of the other adolescents describe situations and practices that indicate how identities are linguistically mediated and produced in everyday language practices in the peer group, for instance through mocking of each others' languages and through efforts made to learn the different languages spoken among them. This practice is also frequently observed in the fieldwork (see section 'The peer group'). In the extract that follows, Marcela reveals that she believes that the rapid transformations and changes in society have implications for the role and status of multilingualism and multiculturalism as well as for the adolescents positioned at the center of these processes:

Extract 2. Marcela, F, age 16; semistructured individual interview.

Marcela: *Det är som en blandning nu, liksom hela tiden. Det är många, många fler än jag som tycker det. Dom flesta som jag umgås med tycker så ... Man kan få bra av att lära sig allt det där. Det är viktigt också om man ska, om man vill nånting så kan man allt möjligt, det är bara perfekt.* [skratt]
...

Marcela: It's like a mixture now, kind of all the time. There are lots and lots of people besides me who have this feeling. Most of the people I hang out with have this experience ... You can get something out of learning about all these things. It's important too if you're going to, if you want something, then you know about a lot of different things, it's just perfect. [laughter]
...

CH: *Men hur lär man sig allt då?*
Marcela: *Olika, från alla möjliga.* [skratt] ... *Jag känner många alla möjliga länder har jag kompisar. Man lär sig mera så här deras kultur å sen så här språket och jag älskar å lära mig språk så de är roligt dom lär mig saker på så här deras språk. De är roligt, sen några ord ... Fast, em Awista jag pratar med henne spanska också för jag har lärt henne [?], så vi blandar lite vi också [skratt] spanska. Ibland hon säger 'Va? Var det spanska?' Då förklarar jag å sen så fortsätter vi.*

CH: But how do you learn everything?
Marcela: Oh, from all sorts of people. [laughter] ... I know many, I have friends from all different countries. You learn more, like, from their cultures and then, like, with the language, and I love to learn languages, so it's fun, they teach me things in their languages. It's fun, like words ... But um, with Awista I speak to her in Spanish sometimes too because I've taught her [?], so we mix a little -Spanish, too [laughter]. Sometimes she goes 'What? Was that Spanish?' Then I explain and then we go on.

Marcela's argument in this extract recurs in much of her and the other adolescents' reasoning and positionings in negotiations with teachers and peers, spontaneous conversations and semistructured interviews. Marcela emphasizes the joy of learning a number of different languages, arguing that they are useful both on an everyday basis in the neighborhood and in a wider perspective. Marcela and the other adolescents contend that through negotiating and sharing languages and other cultural material, they learn a number of ways by which to relate to and interpret everyday life. They value these intercultural experiences and the flexibility they entail. They apparently appreciate multilingualism and the relative freedom they feel it provides for establishing different identities and for accessing different transcultural communities (cf. Extract 4 below).

As we will also see in the next section, it is primarily in social interaction and through negotiations of identifications within and across traditional cultural and national boundaries that the adolescents assign value to diversity and construct new, alternative allegiances among themselves.

Interactive positionings
The peer group

The ethnographic study shows how the adolescents collectively contest some of the dominant institutional discourses and teaching practices in the school context (Haglund, 2005, 2007a, 2007b, 2008). Their collective positionings and resistance are based in part on manifestations of solidarity in the peer group invoked through linguistic strategies such as monitoring and mocking. We will see in the following that these manifestations of solidarity and strategies of resistance in the peer group are also significant parts of the adolescents' negotiations of identities and constructions of allegiances.

The adolescents are keenly aware that discourses on ethnic diversity, exploitation of particular symbols bearing negative connotations, for example high-rise apartment buildings, concrete, women wearing veils, and so on, evoke a social order that retains social differences. In the following extract, three young women from Durby comment on the neighborhood's frequent appearance in contemporary media discourse:

Extract 3. Nadia, Rosa and Sirin, all females, aged 17–18, from Durby participate in a TV-program on the national television network SVT in 2001.

Nadia: *Nä, men när folk kommer hit då är det mer att dom vill skriva om ja, till exempel det här med Fadime då, då kom dom hit och börja intervjua några män-*

Rosa: *-som-*

Sirin: *-inte ens var kurder.*

Nadia: *Nä, precis. När det händer nåt med hundar, då ska dom alltid visa upp Durby. Det finns visst kamphundar, det gör det överallt. Alltså allt som är kopplat till nåt dåligt så dyker dom upp här. Dom pratar om ett fattigt Sverige så har dom en bild på Durby liksom, kul he he. Nä, men liksom alla som bor här är ju inte fattiga.*

Rosa: *Nä, liksom vad är kopplingen?*

Nadia: *Ja-*

Rosa: *Varför då, varför just Durby?*

Sirin: *Fattigt, vad kopplar med det till liksom?*

Rosa: *Durby-*

Sirin: *Ja-*

Nadia: *Jag ser liksom inga barn som svälter här ute direkt.*

Nadia: *Asså visst det finns ju saker som är dåligt, ju men-*

Rosa: *-det finns ju överallt ju?*

Nadia: You know, when people come here then it's more like they want to write about, you know, like this thing with Fadime,[3] they came here and started interviewing some men—

Rosa: -who-

Sirin: -weren't even Kurds.

Nadia: Yeah, exactly. When something happens with dogs, then they show Durby. There are fighting dogs, of course, but they are elsewhere, too. Like, everything that is linked to something bad, then they show up here. They talk about poverty in Sweden and then they show a picture of Durby, you know, great, huh? Well, like all people who live here are not poor.

Rosa: No, like what's the connection?

Nadia: Yes-

Rosa: Why, why Durby?

Sirin: Poverty, like what do they link that to?

Rosa: Durby-

Sirin: Yes-

Nadia: Like I don't see any kids starving out here exactly.

Nadia: All right, of course there are things that are bad, yeah, but-

Rosa: -it's like that everywhere, right?

Nadia: *Ja, det är inget perfekt ställe ... Men varför måste dom jämt komma hit och fråga om såna där grejer som man är trött på, som är riktigt uttjatat ja, kamphundar, kriminalitet och droger och så vidare? Så vi vill liksom visa upp mer än det.*

Nadia: Yes, this is not the perfect place ... But why do they always have to come here and ask about those things that you get really tired of, that have been discussed so much that you're sick and tired of it, like fighting dogs, crime and drugs and so on? So we really want to show other things than that.

Nadia, Rosa and Sirin, like many of the participants in the study, collectively argue that stigmatization is a powerful force, difficult for them to avoid. They seem to be aware of the fact that people generally tend to have strong opinions about neighborhoods such as Durby, although – or perhaps precisely because – few have actually visited them. They recognize that references to Durby occur in the media not because something has actually happened there, but simply because its image suits the purpose of much of the news reporting, which focuses on crime, drug abuse and other matters reported through contemporary media discourse related to ethnic diversity. The night after the assassination of Fadime, video coverage from Durby was broadcast on the national television network. In fact, the murder for which the woman's father was convicted and later sentenced for was entirely unrelated to Durby or the people living there, aside from the coincidence that a large number of people originating from parts of Iraq and Turkey, the majority Kurds, reside in the neighborhood.

In addition to the youths' reaction to the negative media picture, the extract illustrates how they support each other when making the point that the neighborhood does not deserve its bad reputation. The young people seem to see new hope for the future in themselves and their neighborhood. Thus, their comments also illustrate how they collectively, linguistically – through systematic turn-taking – produce a counter-discourse. In the study we identify counter-discourses of this kind as central parts of the allegiances constructed among the participants. Counter-discourses are established among the adolescents in interactions, particularly in the school context. The school does not at all times represent a positive environment but is instead a context in which the students' ethnic and linguistic backgrounds are exploited and stigmatized by teachers and other staff (Haglund, 2008).

Similar to the adolescents' reflective positionings, their interactive positionings and allegiances are in continual flux and are characterized by flexibility and unpredictability. This flexibility also has its limits. The adolescents closely monitor one another's allegiances and corresponding language practice (Haglund, 2007b). The primary purpose of the monitoring and mocking strategies seems to be to ensure solidarity within the peer group, to enhance their individual statuses within the allegiance, but also to highlight the value of the ethnic and linguistic diversity among them. The extract that follows is an example of this combination of interactional strategies:

Extract 4. Sarwat, Daniel, Faizal, all males, age 14, in the hallway next to the students' lockers at Durby school, peer-group interaction, adolescents' audio recording.

1. **Daniel** [presenterar Faizal]: *Här har vi Puttigardi.* [applåder]

   Daniel [introduces Faizal]: This is Puttigardi. [applause]

2. **Sarwat** [presenterar Daniel]: *Här är Yppalas Nikkololi Tausinkla.*

   Sarwat [introduces Daniel]: This is Yppalas Nikkololi Tausinkla.

3. **Faizal** [härmar hindi/urdu]: *Kade moni dum da da hi hi.*

   Faizal [imitates Hindi/Urdu]: Kade moni dum da da hee hee.

4. **Sarwat** [härmar finska]: *Kulu makstu kusta titati.*

   Sarwat [imitates Finnish]: Kulu makstu kusta titati.

5. **Daniel** [härmar hindi/urdu]: *Apputti dum kadi dum kadi.*

   Daniel [imitates Hindi/Urdu]: Apputti dum kadi dum kadi.

6. **Faizal** [härmar hindi/urdu]: *Dum kaddi dumi kadi kadi pubba di bud badi.* [skratt]

   Faizal [imitates Hindi/Urdu]: Dum kaddi dumi kadi kadi pubba di bud badi. [laughter]

7. **Sarwat**: *Du kan vara Finlands president.*

   Sarwat: You can be Finland's president.

8. **Daniel**: *Nej.*

   Daniel: No.

9. **Faizal** [härmar hindi/urdu]: *Meta kalika dum kadi dum mitta hattikalium hattipatti.*

   Faizal [imitates Hindi/Urdu]: Meta kalika dum kadi dum mitta hattikalium hattipatti.

10. **Sarwat**: *Hiiiiii hiiii.* [skratt]

    Sarwat: Heeeeee heeee. [laughter]

11. **Faizal**: *Jag heter Faizal, jag heter Faizal.*

    Faizal: My name is Faizal, my name is Faizal.

12. **Daniel**: *Bla bla bla did blad blblbl lalalala bla lalala lalala lalala.*

    Daniel: Bla bla bla did blad blblbl lalalala bla lalala lalala lalala.

13. **Faizal**: *Lägg av Daniel.*

    Faizal: Stop it Daniel.

14. **Daniel**: *Vänta lalalala bla la.*

    Daniel: Wait lalalala bla la.

15. **Sarwat:** *Vi skiter i det här, spela nu.*

    Sarwat: Screw this, start acting now.

16. **Faizal**: *Nej, nej, vi pratar tjing tjong.*

    Faizal: No, no, we're talking ching chong.

Daniel introduces Faizal (line 1) who in turn resists the role assigned to him. He emphasizes he is Faizal (11), not the president of Pakistan. Daniel, who is introduced as Finland's president 'Yppalas Nikkololi Tausinkla' (2, 7), is also hesitant to take on this role (8). In addition, both of them imitate each other's and their own languages in what seems to be an attempt at legitimacy and positioning against the stigma of their respective backgrounds and languages. The quest for legitimacy is perceptible in this interaction and is referred to by the adolescents themselves (cf. Extract 3).

Faizal's comment towards the end of the extract (16) is the most prevailing indication, together with Sarwat's attempt at reinforcement (15) that the activity has the character of linguistic play. Accordingly, the adolescents unintentionally, but also directly and systematically, draw on and position themselves against the negative attitudes toward their ethnic and linguistic backgrounds. In this and other peer group interactions, the adolescents also make sure to resist the attempts of their peers to position them negatively. Thereby, sometimes at the expense of their peers' status, they avoid being victimized by negative discourses.

The internet

The adolescents also collectively negotiate identities and construct allegiances on the internet. For instance Kiron's quest for identity, which, as we noticed above, was influenced to a large extent by popular culture, also involves the internet. Kiron logs on to sites such as Bengal Café, Englishtown and Global City on a nearly daily basis. Allegiances are formed and individual positioning within these allegiances is negotiated in this interactive space, which stands out as a kind of global marketplace of identity and language:

Extract 5. Kiron, F, age 15; Camar, F, age 14; 'Victor', M (male); 'Shakil', M; peer-group interaction on the internet.

One afternoon Kiron and Camar sit at a computer in the local municipal library. They are logged onto Bengal Café, chatting in English with Kiron's friend Victor. Victor lives in Sydney, Australia. Like Kiron, he was born in rural Bangladesh.

1. **Kiron**: I know Swedish and English better than Bengali.
2. **Victor**: Swedish is a crap-language. Australia is a paradise on earth, you know, no use of knowing Swedish. I know Japanese and Russian, I know Hindi and Bengali too.
   ...
3. **Victor:** Hey, Kiron, you're backdated, covering up all your body, not updated.
4. **Kiron**: I'm free to do what I want.
5. **Victor**: Ah! You're a slut.
   ...

6. **Victor**: I pray everyday five times.
7. **Kiron**: I don't know Arabic.
8. **Victor**: That's too bad, you should learn and you must pray.
9. **Kiron**: Ah, you Asian boy knows everything.
10. **Victor**: You better call me Australian boy, okay?
11. **Kiron**: So what? It's in your blood.
12. **Victor**: No. You little hard-working traditional Bangladesh gal.
13. **Kiron**: Shut up.
14. **Camar** [till Kiron, kommenterar hennes text]:
    Du borde inte använda det där ordet [shut up]. Det avslöjar din svaghet och visar att du inte har nåt bättre att säga.

    Camar [to Kiron, comments on her text]:
    You shouldn't use that word [shut up]. It reveals your vulnerability and just shows you've nothing better to say.
15. **Shakil**: O Kiron, how are u today?   What time is it where u are?

This extract is an example of how the adolescents take part in constructing and reconstructing an allegiance in a transcultural context and negotiate their own individual positionings within this allegiance. The extract indicates some of the ambivalence characteristic of this negotiation and the established community. The adolescents monitor each other's identification preferences and the identity attributes to which they refer. Victor here argues that he finds Kiron backdated and traditional (lines 3, 12), but also refers to her as 'a slut' (5). This ambiguity in Victor's positioning of Kiron (cf. also 8) might illustrate conflicting attitudes to the modernization processes taking place among young people in diaspora and especially among young women (cf. Piller & Takahashi, 2006).

In our interactions, Kiron explains that one's positioning in the interactive networks depends on what country one currently lives in, how one chooses to position oneself relative to the dominant culture of that country, and what role one's relationship with Bangladesh has played during this process. In the extract we observe this kind of negotiation. According to Kiron, most people she interacts with in the chat rooms of Bengal Café argue that Sweden (and Swedish) is a small and insignificant place compared to, for example, Australia or the United Kingdom (cf. 2). Therefore, Kiron explains that they suggest that she should make an effort to learn more about the Bangladeshi lifestyle (cf. Victor's comment, 8) and, particularly, modern forms emerging among young people there, influenced by the West.

In accordance with this suggestion, from (officially) agreeing, in the first years of junior high school, with the school's emphasis on the importance of 'Swedishness' and the Swedish language, Kiron later begins to acknowledge the value of other lifestyles and emphasizes the benefits of a multitude of experiences, knowledge and language skills. She also begins referring to her multilingualism as an asset rather than a deficit.

In addition, she refers to the United Kingdom and Australia as two plausible places where she can study, work and live in the future. As a consequence of her increasing interest in these countries, the status of knowing English becomes more valuable to her. Her conviction that Swedish must be the single most important language to her in the future is replaced later on in senior high school by an increasing devotion to improving her English skills. She often chooses to speak English when interacting with shop assistants, bus drivers, and people she meets on the streets of Durby and elsewhere. The English language to Kiron seems to represent a fairly neutral medium in contrast to the languages she speaks in school and at home, Swedish and Bengali. English appears to be linked with aspirations (cf. Piller & Takahashi, 2006) and also represents a link to her relatives living in a Bengali community in the United Kingdom.

Concluding Comment

This chapter has explored negotiations of identities and constructions of allegiances among adolescents in a multiethnic and multilingual suburb in Sweden. The multiple and relatively unpredictable directions of the identifications and allegiances seem to be consequences of a multitude of factors related to the conditions under which the adolescents live, in a hybrid and multifaceted context (cf. Extracts 1, 2).

Their abundance of competencies and transcultural learning experiences encourage them to shift among positions, identities and alignments (Extracts 1, 2, 4). Hall (1990: 234) depicts this as a boundary transcending potential, claiming that young people are the 'prototype[s] of the post-modern [...] nomad, continually moving between centre and periphery'. This position, however, is not uncomplicated. Although the adolescents, like Kiron and Marcela, experience and account for an increasing value of their languages and backgrounds, discourses that reduce the value of multiculturalism and multilingualism still dominate in society (cf. Extract 3).

In addition, as described in detail elsewhere (Haglund, 2008) attempts at accommodation, for instance, on the part of Durby School, to the social and cultural transformations and changes in society are only occasional. Therefore, other contexts and actors apparently play significant roles in the adolescents' negotiations of identities and constructions of allegiances. This chapter has shown how this endorsement of the adolescents' identity work derives from different resources, including popular culture, peer groups and young people outside of the Swedish context. It has been illustrated how the impositions from society, rather than completely obstructing the identifications, bring about development of all the more sophisticated strategies drawn upon by the adolescents, individually and collectively, in their exploitation of transcultural resources for the development and display of transnational identifications.

Notes

1. Neighborhoods, institutions and individuals have all been given fictitious names to preserve confidentiality.
2. The ongoing study is part of a research program supported by a grant from The Bank of Sweden Tercentenary Foundation (grant no. M2005-0459 to K. Hyltenstam, see www.biling.su.se/~AAA/).
3. Fadime Sahindal was a young woman of Kurdish descent who was assassinated in the city of Uppsala in 2002.

Chapter 10
The Use of Multiethnic Youth Language in Oslo

F. AARSÆTHER

Introduction

The aim of this chapter is twofold. Its first aim is to shed light upon the use of what I here, with reference to Fraurud and Bijvoet (2004) and their research from Stockholm, prefer to call multiethnic youth language. The geographical scene is Oslo, Norway, and multiethnic youth language refers to way(s) of speaking Norwegian in multicultural settings consisting of youth with minority as well as majority background. It is related to its Scandinavian 'siblings' like multiethnolect in Copenhagen (Quist, 2000) and multiethnic youth language in Swedish cities like Malmö (Bodén, 2007, this volume) and Stockholm (Fraurud & Bijvoet, 2004, this volume; Kotsinas, 1988a, 1988b) as well as several other North-West European urban areas (Auer, 2003; Cheshire *et al.*, 2008; Nortier, 2001; Rampton, 1995a, 1995b; Wiese, 2006).

Two essential questions linked to the first aim will be addressed: Is the use of multiethnic youth language the only option available to the users, or are they able to switch between this way of speaking and some kind of standard-like South-Eastern Norwegian, which is normally spoken in the Oslo area? If optional, for what purpose(s) is multiethnic youth language used?

While the first aim of the chapter is connected to linguistic practices, the second is linked more to ideology. It concerns the labeling of multiethnic youth language in Oslo, and deals with how the youth themselves name this way of speaking, as compared to the term 'Kebab Norwegian', which is frequently used in media discourse. A central question is to discuss whether 'Kebab Norwegian' is a stigmatizing label linked to an imperfect way of speaking Norwegian.

The point of departure for the work presented here is the first overview of the UPUS/Oslo project (Svendsen & Røyneland, 2008; Svendsen, this volume) as well as the chapter by Opsahl and Nistov (this volume). Svendsen and Røyneland (2008) deal with both structural and functional aspects of Norwegian spoken among youth in multicultural settings in Oslo, and below I will elaborate on how this chapter builds upon and develops their analyses.

Data and Participants

The chapter is based on data from sociolinguistic research carried out in two multiethnic parts of Oslo; a suburban area and an inner city area, in the years 2006–2008, as part of the UPUS-project (cf. Svendsen, this volume). The data referred to consist of video-recorded interviews and peer conversations. The total number of informants involved in the project is 56; these are all youth aged 13–19.[1] The majority of them have both parents born abroad, in particular in African and Asian countries (26), while seven of the informants have one Norwegian-born and one foreign-born parent. Fifteen of the informants have both parents born in Norway. A common trait is that all the informants are born and raised in Norway, except for a few with migrant background who arrived in the country as infants (before the age of three). Another characteristic is that these young people all belong to heterogeneously composed peer groups in the sense that different linguistic and cultural backgrounds are represented. From the 1970s and onwards Oslo has gradually become a multilingual city, with 26% of the population having migrant background.

Research Questions

An important research question for the UPUS/Oslo project as a whole was to decide whether it is possible to identify a certain way of speaking Norwegian among youth in multicultural Oslo, and in particular on linguistic levels in addition to the lexical (e.g. Aasheim, 1995; Østby, 2005; Opsahl et al., 2008, cf. Svendsen, this volume, for an overview). The data clearly indicate that there are grounds for assuming that youth in multiethnic groups in Oslo have at their disposal a way of speaking Norwegian that distinctly differs from standard-like South-Eastern Norwegian. Phonologically the length of vowels may differ, prosodically another 'rhythm' may occur, morphologically the gender system and the use of definiteness may be simplified, and syntactically the V2-rule may be violated. These are all linguistic features found and commented upon in earlier Scandinavian research (cf. e.g. Kotsinas, 1988a; Quist, 2000; Svendsen & Røyneland, 2008).

None of these linguistic features will be treated in detail in this chapter; however they are analyzed by other UPUS-researchers elsewhere in this book (Opsahl & Nistov, this volume). My primary purpose in this article is to analyze the use and function(s) of these linguistic practices.

Svendsen and Røyneland (2008: 66) address multiethnic youth language in Oslo focusing upon the use of what they call multiethnolectal style as 'one of several registers in language user's linguistic repertoire and in crossing situations by majority language speakers.' Further, Svendsen and Røyneland (2008) link the use of multiethnolectal style to different forms of identity constructions by youth in multicultural groups in Oslo. Their findings will no doubt be the point of departure for this chapter as well, but at the same time their results will be extended and elaborated by going into other, previously unpublished parts of the UPUS/Oslo data. For instance, this chapter will present and discuss how adolescent females from the inner city area, with Norwegian born parents, consider the use of multiethnic youth language as part of their identity construction.

The Use of Multi-Ethnic Youth Language – an Optional Linguistic Practice

The research design of the UPUS/Oslo project based upon video-recorded interviews with an adult researcher, as well as video-recorded peer conversations without the presence of an adult, has proved to be a valuable way to approach the question of switching between multiethnic youth language and more standard-like South-Eastern Norwegian. Central to this is whether the potential users change their language as the setting varies, or continue to speak the same way. As we explicitly ask about the use of multiethnic youth language in the interviews, we also get reported data on this, in addition to the observational data available from both the interviews and the peer conversations. Let us first turn to the reported data here based on responses from 27 of the informants (cf. Aarsæther et al., 2007).

As Figure 10.1 demonstrates, the large majority of the informants asked are by far of the opinion that this form of Norwegian is used for special purposes, and that users of multiethnic youth language change their linguistic behavior towards standard-like South-Eastern Norwegian in situations where they feel this is needed. Particularly they report speaking standard-like Norwegian in job interviews, in front of adults in general, and to a large extent also in the classroom. As to linguistic behavior at school, our observations from classroom activities before our recorded sessions generally confirm this picture; the informants normally choose to speak standard-like South-Eastern Norwegian in front of teachers. As far as the peer conversations are concerned, Opsahl and Nistov (this volume), show that there are several observations supporting the argument that users of multiethnic youth language change their language from standard-like South-Eastern Norwegian in the interviews to multiethnic youth language in the peer conversations.

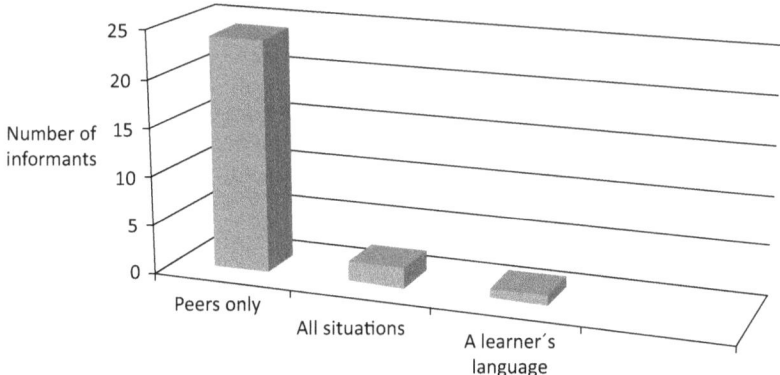

Figure 10.1 Switching between multiethnic youth language and standard-like South-Eastern Norwegian. Reported statements from 27 interviews

The overall answer to the question seems therefore to be that the use of multiethnic youth language in Oslo is perceived as an optional linguistic practice. This is similar to the conclusions drawn by Quist (2005) from her research on the use of multiethnolect in Copenhagen. Some nuances blur this picture though – one of the informants (cf. Svendsen & Røyneland, 2008) deliberately insists on speaking multiethnic youth language even in interview situations, (though he code-switches to standard-like South-Eastern Norwegian for joking purposes) and a couple of informants do not switch to standard-like South-Eastern Norwegian at all. For this latter category of speakers it may be relevant to compare their way of speaking with a learner's language, even though this would be an entirely insufficient description (cf. also discussion by Opsahl & Nistov, this volume). As mentioned earlier, the informants in this study are all born and raised in Norway, and it is therefore not appropriate to characterize these 13–19-year-olds as second language learners.

Multiethnic Youth Language: For What Purposes?

When addressing the issue of the purpose(s) for which multiethnic youth language is used, it seems reasonable to refer to similar Scandinavian research emphasizing identity construction as an overarching approach to the matter. Kotsinas (1994) describes multiethnic youth language in Stockholm as a marker of group identity and Quist (2000) points out how identity construction is a central aspect linked to the use of multiethnolect in Copenhagen. This link is likewise made by Clyne (2000) in an attempt to approach the concept of multiethnolect (cf. Svendsen & Quist, this volume), and to discuss how minority groups in a multicultural society, may speak a certain version of the majority language, '[...] collectively to express their minority status' (Clyne, 2000: 87). In the UPUS/Oslo data the link between the use of multiethnic youth language and the expression of minority status is present to some extent but is certainly not the only purpose for choosing to speak this way. However, Clyne extends his description to include members of the majority as potential speakers of this language, claiming that when '[...] members of the dominant (ethnic) group, especially young people, share it (i.e. the multiethnolect, author's comment) with the ethnic minorities in a "language crossing"-situation [...], it is the expression of a new kind of group identity.' Clyne (2000: 87). This has been shown to be a highly relevant frame for the interpretation of several bodies of data in the UPUS/Oslo project, whereby we are able to conclude that youth with minority as well as majority background make use of multiethnic youth language in different kinds of identity-work. According to Le Page and Tabouret-Keller (1985: 14) linguistic behavior is seen as 'a series of *acts of identity* in which people reveal both their personal identity and their search for social roles'. Identity is thus seen as being constructed through the use of language and according to Le Page and Tabouret-Keller (1985: 181) the '[...] individual creates for himself the patterns of his linguistic behavior so as to resemble those of the group or groups with which from time to time he wishes to be identified, or so as to be unlike those from whom he wishes to be distinguished'. What has been shown to be crucial when doing research in groups consisting of minority as well as majority youth in Oslo is that identity construction involving multiethnic youth language can be carried out in several ways and for several purposes. Sebba and Wootton (1998: 284) reflect upon this theme through the claim that 'Social identities can be seen to be flexible constructs, created, negotiated and constantly changed in the course of interaction'. They then discuss the relation between a certain part of a linguistic repertoire and identity construction and state that 'We cannot assume a fixed relationship between a social identity and the language of the utterance that evokes (or invokes) it' (Sebba & Wootton, 1998: 284). In the UPUS/Oslo data the informants show very different approaches as to the purposes for using multiethnic youth language. Whereas Anders, a male (19) of mixed parenthood from the suburban area (cf. Svendsen & Røyneland, 2008), talks about this way of speaking as 'the minority's dialect', Linn (15), from her perspective as an adolescent female from the inner city area with Norwegian parenthood, points to the use of multiethnic youth language as a way of creating a contrast to people living in the western parts of Oslo, and consequently as a way of affirming her identity as a young East-Ender. Parts of the interview with Linn below serve to illustrate this point.

Speaking 'Wollah' to create a contrast to the 'posh' West End

The extract below stems from an interview with Linn carried out by the adult researcher. As shown in Opsahl and Nistov (this volume) Linn belongs to a group of informants who adheres strictly to the V2-rule in the interview situations, whereas she is represented with one violation in the peer conversation, indicating that, in Linn's view, the use of multiethnic youth language is an in-group phenomenon. Right before this excerpt Linn had declared herself a user of 'Kebab Norwegian' (cf. discussion below), although she quickly added the terms 'Wollah' and 'Pakkis-Norsk' (a strongly derogative term meaning Pakistani-Norwegian). In the beginning of the excerpt we witness the researcher asking Linn what she thinks about speaking multiethnic youth language, or 'speaking Wollah', as Linn sometimes prefers to call it.[2]

1. **Researcher:** 'hva synes du om den språkformen i forhold til andre utgaver av norsk?'
   [what do you think about this kind of language, compared to other forms of Norwegian?]
2. **Linn:** 'jeg synes den er mye bedre enn sånn vestkant'
   [I find it much better than some kind of West-End speech]
3. **Researcher:** 'hvordan er vestkant?'
   [how is West-End speech?]
4. **Linn:** 'jålete'
   [affected]
5. **Researcher:** mm
6. **Linn:** 'sånn skikkelig sånn (knekker håndleddet) (.) homospråk'
   [really like (flips her wrist) (.) gay language]
7. **Researcher:** mm
8. **Linn:** 'selv om jeg ikke har noe imot homser altså'
   [even though I don't have anything against gay people]
9. **Researcher:** 'nei'
   [no]
10. **Linn:** 'men det blir bare litt sånn rart'
    [it's just kind of queer]
11. **Researcher:** 'mm så du kunne ikke tenke deg å (.) snakke vestkant'
    [mm so you couldn't see yourself (.) speaking West- End?]

12. **Linn:** 'nei' (rister på hodet)
    [no (shakes her head)]
13. **Researcher:** 'det sier jo litt om hvem du er også hvordan du snakker, gjør det ikke
    det?'
    [it tells something about who you are too, the way you speak, doesn't it?]
14. **Linn:** 'jo når du snakker hvis xxx snakker vestkantdialekt skjønner man du er fra vestkanten; snakker du østkant (.) dialekt så kommer du fra østkanten på en måte'
    [yes, when you speak if xxx speak West-End dialect one knows you're from the West-End, if you speak East-End (.) dialect then you come from the East-End in a way]
15. **Researcher:** 'men er du stolt av å komme fra'
    [but are you proud of coming from]
16. **Linn:** 'ja'
    [yes]
17. **Researcher:** 'østkanten?'
    [the East-End?]
18. **Linn:** 'jeg er kjempestolt'
    [I am really proud]
19. **Researcher:** 'ja nettopp'
    [yes exactly]
20. **Linn:** 'østkanten er det beste'
    [the East-End is the best]

Linn draws a distinction between the way people in the western part of Oslo speak and the variety of Norwegian used in the eastern parts of the city. Further, she links the use of multiethnic youth language to an expression of identity as a young East-Ender. At first glance this might seem a bit strange, because traditionally there are marked linguistic differences between West-End and East-End spoken Norwegian in Oslo, including, for example, different practices in the use of grammatical gender, the conjugation of certain weak verbs in the past tense, the use of diphthong versus monophthong in certain adjectives, nouns and verbs, as well as phonetic and prosodic differences (cf. Wiggen, 1990). In other words, a traditional linguistic inventory already exists that is large enough to construct a dichotomy between East-Enders and West-Enders in the city, independent of features from multiethnic youth language. How can we understand, then, Linn's claim that speaking 'Wollah' is a way of distancing herself linguistically from what she perceives as the 'posh' people living in the West-End? Linn is not quite clear on this point, for instance when she suddenly starts talking about East-End *dialect* as the opposite of West-End *dialect* (line 14), and not about speaking 'Wollah', as she initially did. This might indicate, not unexpectedly, that Linn, like most nonlinguists, is a bit uncertain in terms of defining concepts like dialects, and provides more or less precise descriptions of what characterizes a certain variety. This being so, it is nevertheless tempting to compare Linn's way of reasoning about language in the eastern and western parts of Oslo to recent research on spoken Norwegian in Oslo, addressing the traditional linguistic opposition between East-End and West-End (Johannessen & Hagen, 2008). The researchers argue that these differences are leveling out, and that the most marked features of earlier East-End and West-End dialects tend to disappear among people under the age of 50. With this in mind, one might also ask whether Linn, by characterizing the use of multiethnic youth language, is in fact exploring a new way of creating linguistic differences to reflect sociocultural differences between western and eastern parts of the city. This is slightly elaborated by Linn in the next excerpt from the same interview, during which she talks about her encounter, in the company of two adolescent female friends, with West End youth at a confirmation meeting on the western side of the city.

> **Linn (15)**: 'confirmation up at Kringsjå [West End] (.) and it was real posh and we were three (.) two others and me (.) up there (...) we spoke like really 'wollah' (.) like they had prejudice and stuff (...) they believe that (.) here (.) it is like fights and stuff all the time and that we are so much more dangerous than them and bla bla bla bla' (translation from Opsahl & Røyneland, 2008)

In the excerpt above Linn reports that she and her friends 'spoke like really wollah' as a kind of rebellious act aimed at distancing themselves from the 'posh' context they were placed in. This piece of data then demonstrates how socioeconomic differences between eastern and western parts of Oslo are perceived and 'read' into the use of multiethnic youth language by some members of the group who claim to speak it, in this case three adolescent females with Norwegian parenthood. The UPUS data collected in the central area of Oslo show that many of the informants are aware of the socio-economic differences between eastern and western parts of the city, that they are conscious of linguistic contrasts between East and West, and that they see multiethnic youth language as a linguistic marker in this context, contributing to their identity construction as young East-Enders. This finding also shows an important contrast between informants' statements from the central area and the suburban area in the UPUS data. While the East–West dichotomy is explicitly expressed by a lot of the informants from the central area, it is not presented as an important issue by the participants from the suburban area. In the latter area, the sense of community, and to some extent the opposition between minority and majority, seems to play a larger role. One might suggest that these differences are related to differences in background. There are more informants with Norwegian born parents in the central area, indicating that the well-known socio-cultural dichotomy between East and West in Oslo is also well-known among the younger generation.

The minority's language?

As mentioned above and as analyzed in Svendsen and Røyneland (2008), Anders (19), a male respondent of mixed parenthood from the suburban area, explicitly states that speaking multiethnic youth language is linked to having minority status in the Norwegian society: 'I look at it as a reflection of diversity and togetherness; it's the language of the minority youth' (author's translation). Anders is probably the most articulate person on this subject of all the informants in our data. There is only a handful (4) of similar statements from the interview data, and they are less explicit in establishing a link between language use and minority status. To some extent it is probably reasonable to ascribe Anders' attitude to his age and level of maturity; he is more than five years older than most of the other boys interviewed from the suburban area, and following this line of reasoning, one might speculate as to whether our data would have contained more explicit statements on minority–majority opposition if more of the informants were as old as Anders. Instead of emphasizing the minority–majority dimension, the other informants, interestingly enough all boys from the suburban area, refer mainly to the use of multiethnic youth language as an expression of togetherness in the local community. Michael (15), of mixed parenthood, refers to the use of multiethnic youth language in the following way: 'I think it's good, you recognize where people come from. You hear whether they are like us or not'. (author's translation). And Samir (15), who has parents with immigrant background, talks about multiethnic youth language in this way: 'I like it, I'm one of the local crowd!'. These informants all come from a township urban district in Oslo where more than 43% of the population have immigrant background, and they live in an area of the district where the sense of community tends to be considered quite strong (cf. Aguilar & Elsafadi, 2003 – a book about growing up in a multicultural suburb of Oslo). It is also interesting to note, though not surprising, that these same informants who link the use of multiethnic youth language to expression of community feeling to their area, are those who name this way of speaking after the name of their suburb (see below).

Multi-ethnic youth language and the display of toughness and aggressiveness

In the second excerpt from the interview with Linn above, she elaborates how she thinks youth from the West-End look at youth from the eastern parts of the city: 'they believe that (.) here (.) there are like fights and stuff all the time and that we are so much more dangerous than them'. Speaking 'Wollah', then, as Linn says she and her friends did in this situation, is not only linked to contrasting with the 'posh' speech of the West-End, it is also linked to a claim that people on the West-End perceive youth in the eastern parts of the city as dangerous fighters.

This is relevant to compare with recent sociological research carried out by Sandberg (2005), focusing on youth behavior in public spaces in Oslo. His research unveils that young people in contemporary, multicultural Oslo see the east–west dichotomy as the most salient contrast, and Sandberg claims that a symbolic relation between being a 'foreigner' or belonging to a minority and living in the eastern parts of the city seems to have developed in the mental representations of youth who frequently spend their spare time in public spaces in the city. Sandberg talks about a symbolic relation because statistically a lot of people living in the eastern parts of the city actually belong to the majority. Linn might well fit into this category, and the perceptions she expresses are in many ways similar to the ones Sandberg finds among his informants, namely that the East-End and the minority become one category opposed to the other category, the West-End and the majority. This becomes one possible reason why Linn sees speaking 'Wollah' as a contrast to the 'posh' speech on the West-End. According to Sandberg this development is not easily explained. One of his suggestions is that categories like East and West seem more neutral to the informants in his data, and consequently easier to handle than explicitly addressing the minority–majority dimension that is so easily associated with xenophobia and racism. Nevertheless, both dimensions seem to be present according to Sandberg, and he interestingly points to the possibility that the youth interviewed in his research consciously raise the east–west dimension in the interview situations because this is considered more politically correct, whereas outside of the interview situations, they embody the ethnicity dimension in the streets. Sandberg shows how youth from the East-End, with or without immigrant background, and boys in particular, creatively use what he labels stereotype perceptions of 'the dangerous foreigner,' (Sandberg, 2005: 40) in constructing an aggressive persona in the public space, in particular to achieve enough respect to avoid getting into trouble. And in conjunction with the aforementioned categories, East versus West, the people towards whom this aggressiveness is directed are youth from the western parts of the city, who according to these informants and Linn herself, have a prejudiced view of people from the East-End as dangerous fighters. Sandberg's point is that ethnicity thus becomes some kind of street capital in the struggle to achieve respect among youth who meet in public spaces in the city. He does not refer much to language, apart from stating that one of his core informants, having Norwegian as his first language, speaks Norwegian with 'a grammatical structure typical of a learner's language' (Sandberg, 2005: 33; Sandberg & Pedersen, 2006). This fact however, sheds light on the link between language learners and persons using multiethnic youth language in the sense that the use of elements from a learner's language might be seen as a linguistic way of playing with stereotypes that the user ascribes to members of the majority culture (Sandberg, 2005). Speaking like a 'foreigner' might function as a linguistic resource in constituting an image of dangerousness and respect.

Multi-ethnic youth language accompanying verbal excitement in in-group activities

The UPUS/Oslo data, both interviews and peer conversations, indicate that the use of multiethnic youth language is often accompanied by verbal excitement directed towards in-group members (cf. Opsahl & Nistov, this volume; Ganuza, 2008). One of the recorded peer conversations between two boys, one with two Norwegian-born parents and one with two parents born abroad, contains an interesting example of this. At some point in their conversation the two interlocutors are addressed through a window by peers (among them other boys who had participated in the project) who pretend to be intruders. The two boys respond to this interruption by speeding up their talk, by raising their voices considerably, and by using words from Arabic (the two boys have Norwegian and Norwegian-Pakistani background respectively). To the analyst, this seems like an act of 'defense' against intrusion, and that multiethnic youth language accompanies such an activity. This also resembles what Sandberg (2005) refers to as respect-related activities.

The Act of Labelling: by the Public and by the Young People Themselves

In this section I deal with the question of ascribing names to the multi-ethnic youth language in Oslo, from a position outside the multiethnic groups represented by media discourse, and from different voices within these groups. When reading Norwegian newspapers on the matter, one very often is given the impression that multiethnic youth language is a deficit phenomenon, and as stated in the introduction to this chapter, it is often characterized as 'Kebab Norwegian'. In the UPUS/Oslo research we have been interested in what our informants think about this kind of characteristic; do they identify with it, or not? I will first turn to an illustration of media attitudes towards multiethnic youth language, before moving on to an overview of the informants' opinions on the matter.

The link between 'Kebab Norwegian' and 'bad Norwegian'

In the chosen excerpt from one of the most widely read Norwegian web newspapers, 'Nettavisen' (2008-02-18), a journalist interviews a professor of Norwegian Linguistics at the University of Oslo. The title of the article is – 'They'll stop speaking "Kebab Norwegian"' and is presented as a quote from the professor. It refers to a paragraph in the interview in which the professor, in a sort of comforting way, assures the readers that the practice of speaking 'Kebab Norwegian' is a phenomenon that will end when the speakers reach their twenties. What this article tells us firstly is that the label 'Kebab Norwegian' is established in media discourse, and furthermore that it is linked to speaking 'bad Norwegian' by both journalists and some academic professionals, that is, by persons who are normally considered to be central figures in shaping public opinion. The link between 'Kebab Norwegian' and 'bad Norwegian' appears already in the introductory comment, where the journalist unveils his position:

> 'In subways and buses one hears youth of both Norwegian and foreign origin speak Norwegian so badly that one cannot help wondering what is going on. Since 'Petrine', the daughter of 'Kari' and 'Ola' at Nordstrand, sounds like she has been living for 20 years in the ghetto, it does not exactly call for celebration in the professor's chambers.' (Author's translation)

Some explanations are probably needed here in order to help readers who are not acquainted with the Norwegian sociocultural context to grasp the full meaning of this statement. The names chosen in the extract above are obviously not randomly selected; they carry heavy symbolic value in the sense that 'Kari' is the female prototype of a traditional ethnic Norwegian, while 'Ola' is the male counterpart. 'Petrine' is an old-fashioned Norwegian name for a young girl, but one with a posh flavour, and the municipality of 'Nordstrand' in Oslo, is an area where well-to-do citizens live, not people with immigrant background. On the connotative level then, it seems clear that the journalist deliberately chooses these names to emphasize that even youth with ethnic Norwegian background from socioeconomically advantaged areas of the city are influenced by 'bad language' from 'the ghetto.' As such this becomes an interesting document on how influential voices in the Norwegian majority culture perceive aspects of the multicultural society of which they are a part. Public debate on 'Kebab Norwegian' seems to be a regularly recurrent topic in media discourse; also in 2009 quite a number of articles and interviews were published (cf. e.g. http://www.dagsavisen.no/innenriks/article420802.ece).

Through this and other newspaper articles, the label 'Kebab Norwegian' is associated with speaking 'bad Norwegian', but at the same time one cannot assume that this relation is automatic or has always been present or even relevant. When the term first attracted attention (Aasheim, 1995) it was probably due more to the public interest in the contact linguistic phenomenon of lexical loans from different minority languages into Norwegian, conducted primarily by linguistic entrepreneurs in multiethnic youth groups. Kulbrandstad (2004) exemplifies how media discourse has extended the content of the concept 'Kebab Norwegian' from being the name of a slang phenomenon in the mid-1990s, to becoming a general term for an imperfect way of speaking Norwegian around 2000. This indicates that in the beginning the expression 'Kebab Norwegian' had more positive connotations in the minds of the general public than it has today, because of its association with creativity and linguistic innovation. This positive attitude is also evident in the dictionary of 'Kebab Norwegian' published 10 years later (Østby, 2005), although in a much more ambiguous way. Since a chapter on the concept of interlanguage follows the dictionary part of the book, the connection between 'Kebab Norwegian' and a learner's language or 'bad Norwegian' is, at least indirectly, assumed. And as we shall see in the data presented below, young people in multicultural groups in Oslo do not normally identify with the label (cf. Opsahl & Nistov, this volume; Svendsen & Røyneland, 2008).

In the interviews the informants are asked whether or not they can identify a certain way of speaking Norwegian in multicultural youth groups, and whether this way of speaking has a name or not. As shown in Aarsæther *et al.* (2007) almost all the informants confirm that there is a certain way of speaking Norwegian among youth in multicultural groups in Oslo.

Despite eager media pressure to call the language used in multicultural youth groups 'Kebab Norwegian', only nine out of 34 informants report using the term, while 15 said this way of speaking had no name, and four of the informants report that they prefer the name of their local community as a label for the way they speak. It is interesting to compare this with a similar trend found in multiethnic areas of, for example, Berlin, where young people living in parts of the city with high percentage of people of immigrant background prefer to talk about 'Kiez-Deutsch', a word that may be translated as 'neighbourhood-German' (Wiese, 2006) as a replacement for the strongly derogative term 'Kanak-Sprak' that has been a much

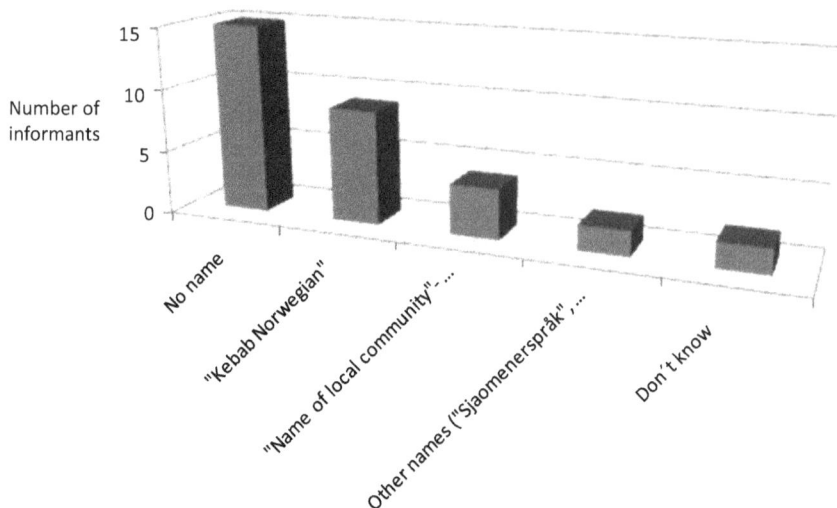

Figure 10.2 Answers to the question 'Does this language have a name?'. Statements from interview data (N = 34)

used word in German media discourse for labeling the way young people of immigrant backgrounds speak (cf. www.kiezdeutsch.de). At the same time it signals that *local identity* is relevant for the use of multiethnic youth language.

In the excerpt from the interview with Linn (section 'Speaking 'Wollah' to Create a Contrast to the 'Posh' West End') she talks about 'Wollah' and even 'Pakkis-Norwegian' as additional alternatives for the term 'Kebab-Norwegian', which is her first answer, and the one for which she is represented in Figure 10.2 above. Linn is among very few informants who offer such alternatives.[3]

A closer look at the informants' responses reveals interesting differences between the suburban and the inner city area as to whether the informants find the term 'Kebab Norwegian' acceptable or unacceptable. In the suburban area, where the majority of the informants have minority background, they do not generally identify with the term at all, in fact quite a few of the informants from this area report that they do not appreciate it; some of them say they find it overtly stigmatizing. This is a contrast to some of the speakers from the inner city area who report being comfortable with this label. Interestingly these informants have a majority background, a fact probably not irrelevant to the way they answer. It is likely to think that majority youth do not to the same extent as youth with minority backgrounds feel offended by the derogative character of the label 'Kebab Norwegian'. Kulbrandstad (2004) considers the use of 'Kebab Norwegian' as a concept mainly with pejorative value. It is furthermore interesting to note that two of the informants from the inner city area with a majority background who readily came up with 'Kebab Norwegian' as the proper label, said in the interviews that they had recently learnt about 'Kebab Norwegian' from teaching materials at school. This indicates that one source for their choice of label seems to be published material on the matter (cf. the earlier mentioned dictionary of 'Kebab Norwegian', Østby, 2005).

Concluding this point, the term 'Kebab Norwegian' does not seem to be one that youth in multiethnic groups in Oslo identify with in general, although some of them feel comfortable with the concept. In our data, the informants with minority background from the suburban area are those who resist the term above all, illustrating the fact that this is a concept imposed by the majority culture. Anders (19) puts it this way: 'Honestly 'Kebab Norwegian' is something *they* have invented'. Thus our data documents discrepancies between the way influential voices in the majority culture outside the multicultural youth groups perceive this way of speaking, as opposed to the way quite a few of the speakers themselves look at it. In addition, as already presented above, these discrepancies also create a space enabling speakers to play with these stereotypic perceptions of the linguistic behavior of people with immigrant background.

Closing Remarks

The main purpose of this chapter has been to highlight some aspects linked to the use of multiethnic youth language in contemporary Oslo. First both reported and observed data show that by far the large majority of the speakers command both standard-like South-Eastern Norwegian and multiethnic youth language (cf. Opsahl & Nistov, this volume), thus assumptions inferred from media discourse, for example, that multiethnic youth language generally represents some kind of deficit phenomenon, are wrong. The crucial question, then, has been to approach the communicative purposes for which multiethnic youth language is used. Building upon earlier work on multiethnic youth language spoken, for instance, in other Scandinavian cities such as Copenhagen and Stockholm, I place the use of multiethnic youth language in a frame of reference along with *acts of identity*. The analyses carried out show how multiethnic youth language may also be used in identity-construction related to traditional social class boundaries in Oslo. By referring to contemporary sociological research done among youth in public spaces in Oslo (Sandberg, 2005), a frame of reference is created to establish a correlation between the use of multiethnic youth language and a display of toughness on the streets. Finally the term 'Kebab-Norwegian', has been shown to have far less resonance in the multiethnic youth groups in Oslo than one might think when looking at the dominant media discourse. On this issue, interesting tendencies seem to emerge, especially among youths with immigrant backgrounds in the suburban areas, who also see their way of speaking as connected to some sort of local identity with the area in which they live, tendencies that seem to resemble the development in, for example, Berlin, where 'Kiez-Deutsch' (neighborhood German), according to Wiese (2006), may be a candidate to replace the strongly derogative label 'Kanak- sprak'.

Notes

1. These are ongoing analyses and the preliminary results may vary as to the number of informants involved. This is reflected in the figures presented, for which Figure 10.1 is based on 27 respondents, while Figure 10.2 is based on 34 respondents.
2. Transcription details: (.) = short pause, xxx = words that cannot be identified.
3. In cases where informants report or use more than one name to refer to multi-ethnic youth language, they are still represented with only one of these labels in the figure presented here. In these cases the analysts have chosen the name the informant refers to most frequently or most explicitly.

Chapter 11
Polylingualism in the Steak House: Exploring Linguistic Practices in Late Modern Copenhagen

J.S. MØLLER

Introduction

The aim of this chapter is to explore *polylingual language* use, *enregisterment*, *stylization* and the construction and negotiation of locally situated identities by speakers in informal interaction. Based on a *sequential micro-analysis*, I will show (1) how the borders between sets of linguistic features (the so-called languages, lects, etc.) are explored and negotiated by speakers in interaction, (2) how the speakers use and evaluate linguistic features in such border areas, and (3) how these features appear in the local context. Inspired by Blommaert (2005), I will argue that interactional construction of meaning by using linguistic features belonging to different sets of features is context-dependent and dialogically based.

The Concept of Polylingualism

Interactions involving more than one set of linguistic features of the kind normally referred to as a language have traditionally been described as bi- or multilingual by researchers. The point of departure for these descriptions has been that the participants possessed a number of languages (such as Danish and Turkish, for example). The *Køge Project* involves participants who traditionally would be described as bilingual speakers of Turkish and Danish (see Jørgensen, 2003). This is not wrong, but is only a part of the picture. As these speakers move from childhood to youth and adulthood, they draw upon an increasing number of different sets of linguistic features in their peer-group interaction (e.g. sets of features known as 'English' and 'German' *as well as linguistic features generally ascribed to* 'mock Chinese' etc., see Møller, 2008a). Furthermore, between participants with similar linguistic background, the sets of features called Danish and Turkish become more and more integrated over the years (Møller, 2008b). The participants sometimes treat Danish and Turkish as different sets of features and sometimes as one set of features tending towards Auer's concept of *language mixing* (Auer, 1999). This does not mean that the participants are unable to distinguish between features ascribed to Danish, features categorized as Turkish or belonging to other sets of linguistic features. It only means that they do not treat these categories as coherent and distinct 'packages' in their peer-group interaction. They combine linguistic features generally thought to belong to different 'languages' and use linguistic sets of features no matter how familiar they are with them. The boundaries between different sets of features are fuzzy and are involved in constant change. The speakers use *language* in their peer-group interaction – not *languages*, and this is the core of what we aim to describe by the term *polylingualism* (inspired by Hewitt's (1992) notion of poly-culture). Following from this, it would be misleading to describe these speakers as bi- or multilinguals and more precise to describe them as polylinguals or simply as *languagers* (Jørgensen, 2004).

A central question in the analyses to come (and a central problem for analyses dealing with polylingual interaction in general) is 'the qualitative question of where diversity lies' (Makoni & Pennycook, 2006: 16) This linguistic diversity is of course not restricted to languages, and in my analyses I will include linguistic features ascribed to different types of the set of features called 'Danish' as well. I will focus on linguistic features that are hard to categorize because they involve features normally ascribed to different sets of features or are ambiguous in other ways, and I will show how the ambiguity is sometimes explored in the participants' local identity work.

Identity Work in Interaction and *Enregisterment*

Jan Blommaert views identity as something people 'produce, enact or perform' (Blommaert, 2005: 205). He suggests that identities can be viewed as *'particular forms of semiotic potential, organised in a repertoire'* (2005: 207, italicization by Blommaert) and he stresses that every person does not have the same opportunities for identity construction, because they have different semiotic potentials and because different repertoires have different status. Speakers in interaction do not only construct and negotiate their own identity, but also the identity of the other: 'regardless of whether one wants to belong to particular groups or not one is often grouped by others in processes of – often institutionalized – social categorization called *othering*' (Blommaert, 2005: 205). As we shall see in the analyses, the process of *othering* can be directed to persons participating in the interaction as well as persons outside. The advantage of Blommaert's view on identity is that it allows an interactional and context-dependent approach in the study of identity construction and negotiation and at the same time acknowledges that people have different (linguistic) resources available. Thereby this definition makes the social (and sociolinguistic) history of the participants in an interaction relevant.

Sets of linguistic features have values ascribed to them and norms for their use that are more or less widespread. A single feature belonging to a set of linguistic features carries the ascribed values and corresponding norms as well. The boundaries of the sets of features as well as the values and norms can be negotiated and differ from situation to situation, but nevertheless these values and norms are central in order for a speaker to carry out local identity work using linguistic diversity. Speakers attach labels to sets of linguistic features, and attach (evaluating) labels to the speakers of such sets, for instance 'snobbish', 'nerdy' and 'dominant' (cf. e.g. Maegaard, this volume). 'National languages', 'lects', and other notions of sets of linguistic features are ideologically constructed focus concepts (Heller, 2007).

Agha (2007) describes the relationship between language use and social relations. A key notion for him is *registers*, which he defines as: 'cultural models of action that link diverse behavioral signs to enactable effects, including images of persona, interpersonal relationship, and type of conduct' (Agha, 2007: 145). A speaker can construct a persona and negotiate relations with the interlocutors or the frames of the situation by using a certain (linguistic) register because it is *a cultural model of action*. This presupposes that the participants have a shared knowledge of these cultural models. Agha (2007: 81) calls the process of this knowledge coming into existence *enregisterment* and defines it as:

> [K] processes and practices whereby performable signs become recognized (and regrouped) as belonging to distinct, differentially valorized semiotic registers by a population.

Some of these 'processes and practices' take place in speakers' everyday interactions. Evaluations of and boundaries between sets of linguistic features are negotiated, and sometimes new linguistic forms occur. Such phenomena are what I intend to describe in this chapter. I deal with linguistic features that occur in heterogeneous, late modern, urban environments where several different sets of features are used in the interrelated practices of identity work and enregisterment.

When speakers possess a linguistic feature, they also have knowledge of the feature's ascriptions to ideologically constructed sets of features. This knowledge can be used in code-alternation when speakers use linguistic features ascribed to different ideologically constructed sets of features in the company of speakers who share the knowledge of these ascriptions. Auer (1995: 117) includes this point in his speaker-oriented definition of *code-alternation*:

> Code alternation [K] is defined as a relationship of contiguous juxtaposition of semiotic systems, such that the appropriate recipients of the resulting complex sign are in a position to interpret this juxtaposition as such.

In analyses of code alternation (or switching between different ideologically constructed sets of linguistic features) it is not the 'languages' as countable entities that are central as widely used terms such as 'bi-lingual interaction', 'tri-lingual interaction', and so on, may suggest. The central aspect is rather how these sets of features are treated by speakers in their interactions. A specific type of code-alternation is *stylisation*. I will use the concept as defined by Rampton (2009: 2):

> Stylisation involves reflexive communicative action in which speakers produce specially marked and often exaggerated representations of languages, dialects, and styles, that lie outside their own habitual repertoire.

'Specially marked' I will understand as marked by contextualization cues (Gumperz, 1982, 1992) defined as: '[...] any feature of linguistic form that contributes to the signalling of contextual presuppositions' (Gumperz, 1982: 131). The participants use the cues to guide each other through interpretations of the interaction based on shared practices and norms. The function of these cues can only be identified in interplay with the local context. Therefore, I will analyze excerpts of interaction sequentially.

Data Analyses

The data I use in this chapter were all recorded in 2006, and they all follow a procedure in which a field worker equips the participants with microphones, starts the recording, and leaves the premises. One recording (a) involves three teenage girls: Aisha, Sümeyy, and Gülsüm. They attend the 8th grade, are class-mates, and the recording takes place at their school in Køge. They are given an assignment of making a poster about being young in Køge. Four men in their mid-twenties named Erol, Hüsseyin, Ali and Ahmet participate in recording (b). All of them have previously participated in the *Køge Project* during the 1990s when they went to school together. They still live close by one another in Køge and frequently play soccer together. They are recorded in a room in their old school. They are given a number of photos taken during their old school careers and are asked to talk about the 'good old days'. Recording (c) contains the same informants as recording (b), but this time the recording takes place in Erol's living room while the participants watch a Champions League football game. Recording (d) contains four other men in their mid-twenties recorded while having dinner at a steak house in central Copenhagen. The participants are Murat, Adnan, Ferhat and Ceyhun. Murat participated in the original *Køge Project*, Adnan and Ferhat also grew up in Køge and Ceyhun grew up in the Århus area.

All informants have a linguistic background involving Danish as well as Turkish. If they asked a field worker what language to speak, they were told that it was completely up to them. Recordings (a) and (b) were conducted on the initiative of a field worker. Recordings (c) and (d) were arranged by Erol and Murat respectively.

Polylingual interaction: The case of (Lan')

'Mand' is a feature ascribed to Danish, and 'lan' is a feature ascribed to Turkish. Both are often used as an intensifying tag placed at the end of an utterance and roughly corresponds to the English use of 'man' as a discourse marker. In our data, a form involving a linguistic feature normally ascribed to Danish and a linguistic feature normally ascribed to Turkish occurs in the same syllable – namely in [lan'] pronounced with a glottal constriction (known as 'the Danish *stød*' and marked with a raised comma, see Hansen & Pharao, this volume) as in 'mand' and an initial [l] as in 'lan'.

Excerpt 1, recording (b): You forgot nine!

1. **Ahmet:** *Ahmet bir iki üç [dört beş] altı [yedi sekiz] dokuz on*
2. **Ali:** *[kızarmış]*
3. **Erol:** *[he lan]*
4. **Field worker:** super
5. **Hüsseyin:** *dokuzu unuttun* lan
   ((lan pronounced [lan']))
   (1.0) ((everybody laughs))

Translation of excerpt 1, recording (b): You forgot nine!

1. **Ahmet:** *Ahmet one two three [four five] six [seven eight] nine ten*
2. **Ali:** *[blushing]*
3. **Erol:** *[yes man]*
4. **Field worker:** super
5. **Hüsseyin:** you forgot nine man
   (('man' pronounced [lan']))
   (1.0) ((everybody laughs))

In Excerpt 1, Ahmet counts to ten in order to test the microphones. Ali and Erol comment on Ahmet's contribution in lines 2 and 3 while he is still counting, and Hüsseyin follows up on their comments in line 5 by (wrongly) accusing Ahmet of forgetting number nine. Hüsseyin uses the form [lan'] in line 5. Besides that single utterance, all linguistic features used by Ahmet, Erol, Ali and Hüsseyin can be ascribed to Turkish. The activity in which they engage can be described as making fun of the person counting.

Excerpt 2, recording (a): Soccer fans

1. **Aisha:** jeg vil have den og den her gul *Galatasaray* ((Galatasaray, a Turkish football team, articulated with a supercilious voice))
   (1.0) ((sound of a pen knocked down in the table twice))
2. **Sümeyye:** ad hvor er du ulækker
3. **Gülsüm:** *Beşiktaş* (.) er du [også det]
4. **Sümeyye:** [*Fener*]*bahçe*
5. **Gülsüm:** æj ((Gülsüm sounds disappointed))
6. **Aisha:** pu[uuu] *kokmuş* lan ((lan pronounced [lan']))
7. **Sümeyye:** [((laughs))]
8. **Aisha:** ((laughs))
9. **Sümeyye:** *sensin kokmuş*

Translation of excerpt 2, recording (a): Soccer fans

1. **Aisha:** I want this and this one yellow *Galatasaray* ((Galatasaray articulated with a supercilious voice))
   (1.0) ((sound of a pen knocked down in the table twice))
2. **Sümeyye:** yerk you are disgusting
3. **Gülsüm:** *Beşiktaş* (.) are you [that too]
4. **Sümeyye:** [*Fener*]*bahçe*
5. **Gülsüm:** æj ((Gülsüm sounds disappointed))
6. **Aisha:** pu[uuu] *stinks* man ((man pronounced [lan']))
7. **Sümeyye:** [((laughs))]
8. **Aisha:** ((laughs))
9. **Sümeyye:** it is you who stink

In Excerpt 2, the participants are picking the colours they want to use for the assignment. Aisha picks yellow because it is the colour of the Turkish football team Galatasaray. Sümeyye reacts to this by describing her as disgusting. Gülsüm says that she supports Beşiktaş and asks if Sümeyye supports them as well. Sümeyye says she supports Fenerbahçe (another Turkish football team). Gülsüm expresses disappointment, and Aisha reacts by using a sound typical of situations where you experience something that smells unpleasant. This makes Sümeyye laugh. Aisha then elaborates on the sound made in line 6 by saying 'kokmuş' which is ambiguous. It can mean 'it stinks' as well as 'you stink'. She intensifies the expression by using the tag [lan']. Sümeyye reacts by saying that Aisha stinks.

The three girls use expressions of support for Turkish football teams in their identity work. Gülsüm wants to team up with Sümeyye, and Sümeyye and Aisha take the opportunity to mock each other in a jocular way. They both continuously laugh through the exchange. The participants use a number of contextualization cues such as exclamations ('ad', 'æj', 'puuuu') in order to show their disappointment or their disgust. Their laughter indicates that the insults should not be taken too seriously. The form [lan'] is placed next to linguistic features generally recognizable as Turkish. The girls use features generally recognizable as Danish from lines 1 to 3 except for the names of the football teams, and Turkish from lines 5 to 9 except for [lan']. The exclamations in line 5 and 6 are difficult to ascribe to a specific language.

Excerpt 3, recording (c): Of course one shouldn't generalize

1. **Erol:** de er fandme[/] (.) ja selvfølgelig skal man ikke genera-
   lisere <u>lan'</u> (.)
2. ((lan pronounced [lan'] with glottal constriction))
2. de er også men[nesker selvfølgelig
3. **Ahmet:** [*sende şey yapsaydın o zaman*
4. *onları senin odana davet etseydin* kom kom
5. ((ahmet laughs))
6. **Erol:** nej *cıvıklardı lan*
7. de var meget *cıvık* mand
8. **yani de:**

Translation of excerpt 3, recording (c), Of course one shouldn't generalize

1. **Erol:** they are so fucking[/] (.) yes of course one should not
   generalize <u>man</u> (.)
   ((lan pronounced [lan'] with glottal constriction))
2. they are also hu[man beings of course
3. **Ahmet:** [*then you could invite them to your room* come
4. come
5. ((ahmet laughs))
6. **Erol:** no *they were so clinging* man
7. they were very *clinging* man
8. *you know they*

Excerpt 3 occurs at half-time of the football game the participants are watching. Led by Erol, the participants started a discussion about Jews and Zionism. Erol tells about a Jewish family he met on vacation in Turkey and describes the persons negatively. In line 1, Erol is about to conclude, but interrupts himself and constructs a self-identity as tolerant and understanding. Ahmet does not align with this identity and asks Erol why he did not invite them in. Erol, then, returns to speaking ill of the family by saying they were clinging to him. The activity performed by Erol and Ahmet can be described as *othering*. They construct the negative identity of a different social group and possibly they create a more 'positive' self image.

None of the three speakers' turns in Excerpt 3 contain linguistic features ascribed to only one language. Erol's first turn contains Danish and the [lan'] form, Ahmet's turn is Danish and Turkish and Erol's last turn is also Danish and Turkish. Ahmet uses Turkish for his argument and Danish when he is pseudo-quoting Erol. His switch from Turkish to Danish can be viewed as a contextualization cue that underlines this change in stance. Erol alternates five times between Danish and Turkish in his second turn. Based on the frequency of the alternation, I will argue that Erol, to some degree, treats the linguistic features normally ascribed to Danish and Turkish as one set of linguistic features in this turn. This difference in how linguistic diversity is exploited in Ahmet's and Erol's contributions illustrates why it is central to apply a speaker-oriented (and not a language-oriented) approach when analyzing polylingual interaction. Sometimes, as in Ahmet's contribution, the contrast between features ascribed to Danish and Turkish are exploited to construct meaning, and sometimes these two sets of features are not contrasted. When the latter is the case, it becomes hard to maintain the idea that the speakers juxtapose two distinct sets of linguistic features (see Auer, 1999).

In opposition to the use of [lan'] in Excerpts 1 and 2, Erol uses the [lan'] form as an intensifier in a Danish-based utterance. Erol also uses both 'lan' (normally ascribed to Turkish) and 'mand' (normally ascribed to Danish). Both occur after features normally ascribed to Turkish ('cıvıklardı' and 'cıvık'). They seem to be completely interchangeable. This means that they don't primarily function as intensifiers ascribed to a certain language; just as intensifiers.

Excerpts 1, 2 and 3 illustrate how [lan'] is used in different linguistic and social contexts. There are more occurrences of the form in my material and the [lan'] form seems to appear most frequently in contexts of jocular abuse as in Excerpts 1 and 2. A more systematic investigation is needed in order to confirm this. The [lan'] form is an example of a case where the speakers do not respect boarders between languages. This [lan'] can be ascribed neither to Turkish nor Danish. The fact that it occurs as an intensifier in Danish-based as well as Turkish-based utterances strengthens this point. The three excerpts also illustrate different levels of integration between Danish and Turkish. Excerpt 1 is dominated by Turkish and Excerpt 2 contains a shift from Danish to Turkish dominance. In Excerpt 3, the alternation between Danish and Turkish is much more fluent. Sometimes Danish and Turkish are treated as two sets of linguistic features and sometimes features usually ascribed to either of these sets are used together as if they belong to the same set. The [lan'] form in Excerpts 1 to 3, as well as the use of Danish and Turkish in Excerpt 3 highlight the 'qualitative question of where diversity lies' (Makoni & Pennycook, 2006: 16) and thereby exemplify why a concept like polylingualism, addressing the use of linguistic features instead of the use of 'languages', is well suited to describe the interactional practices represented in Excerpts 1 to 3.

My next question is: Is the use of [lan'] ascribed to a certain register? This question is much harder to answer. None of my examples contain an explicit evaluation of the use of [lan'] and none of my informants ever mentioned it in interviews regarding language use. This might indicate that it is in the very early process of enregisterment. Time (and further analyses) will show how it becomes evaluated, and whether it will be ascribed to a register of forms involving linguistic features normally ascribed to Danish as well as Turkish. Also future analyses of [lan'] used in interaction will show whether the feature will indexicalize the friendly activity of jocular abuse or something completely different. The use of 'lan' (without stød) has also been described as a characteristic feature in urban youth styles in ethnically heterogeneous environments in Denmark and Germany, for example (Quist, 2000: 208; Depperman, 2007: 228). In the next examples, I will look at how linguistic features (belonging to sets of features) are used and reacted upon in local identity work.

Displays and uptakes of linguistic features and register formations

The participants in recording (d) are, as mentioned before, Murat, who has participated in the *Køge Project* previously, his older brother Adnan, and Murat's two friends Ferhat and Ceyhun. Ferhat comes from the Køge area too and has attended the same school for some of his school career. Ceyhun moved to Køge as an adult and grew up in Århus, in a neighborhood that has been stigmatized as an immigrant ghetto in the general media discourse. As my analyses will show, Ceyhun displays linguistic repertoires that differ from the repertoires displayed by the other participants. The analyses will also illustrate a practice which occurs several times during the one hour and 15-minute-long recording, namely the other participants (and especially Ferhat) assigning an identity as an (ignorant) hoodlum to Ceyhun in a jocular way (see 4b). This is an identity with which Ceyhun sometimes aligns himself; at other times, he does not.

Excerpt 4a, recording (d): The microscope

1.	**Murat:**	*fiyatını bilin*
		(1.2)
2.	**Ferhat:**	tyve [millioner
3.	**Adnan:**	[*beş milyon*
		(0.6)

4.	**Murat:**	fire komma fem millioner
5.	**Ceyhun:**	*ne lan*
6.	**Ferhat:**	ja det koster det
7.	**Murat:**	mikroskop
		(.)
8.	**Ceyhun:**	mikroskop ((*skop* said without a glottal constriction))
9.	**Murat:**	ja
10.	**Ferhat:**	*hani şu* BR'*de satılıyor ya [yüz kron şöyle ha*
11.	**Ceyhun:**	[ja ja jeg ved <u>jeg ved</u> hvad et mikroskop er
		(.) ((everybody laughs while Ceyhun is speaking))
12.		hvad fanden skal I sidde og kigge op på månen eller hvad eller
		(.)
		((Murat tells more about the microscope))

Translation of excerpt 4a, recording (d): The microscope

1.	**Murat:**	*Guess the price*
		(1.2)
2.	**Ferhat:**	twenty [millions
3.	**Adnan:**	[*five millions*
		(0.6)
4.	**Murat:**	four point five millions
5.	**Ceyhun:**	*what man*
6.	**Ferhat:**	yes it costs that
7.	**Murat:**	microscope
		(.)
8.	**Ceyhun:**	microscope ((*skop* said without a glottal constriction))
9.	**Murat:**	yes
10.	**Ferhat:**	*you know those they sell in* BR *[for a hundred kroner*
11.	**Ceyhun:**	[yes yes I know I KNOW what a microscope is
		(.) ((everybody laughs while Ceyhun is speaking))
12.		what the hell are you going to sit and watch the moon or what or
		(.)
		((Murat tells more about the microscope))

Excerpt 4a takes place between the main course and the dessert. Murat, who works at a hospital, tells the other participants about a microscope his boss recently ordered. In line 1, Murat invites the others to guess the price of the microscope, which Ferhat and Adnan do in lines 2 or 3. Murat then gives the answer in line 4. Ceyhun, who has not participated so far, asks in line 5 what they are talking about. Ferhat continues to discuss the price in line 6, and Murat answers Ceyhun in line 7. In line 8, Ceyhun repeats by saying 'microscope'. Murat confirms in line 9, and in line 10

Ferhat explains to Ceyhun what a microscope is, by saying that they can be bought in a chain of toy stores (named BR) for 100 kroner. In line 11, Ceyhun denies that he does not know what a microscope is, and everybody laughs. Then Ceyhun asks if they are going to look at the moon, and Murat elaborates on the use of the microscope.

The question here is why Ferhat in a jocular way presupposes that Ceyhun will get a better understanding of what a microscope is if he connects it to a toy store. In line 8, Ceyhun pronounces 'mikroskop' without a glottal constriction in the last syllable. Pronunciation of this word includes a glottal constriction in standard Danish. Pronunciation without the glottal constriction is a feature ascribed to a set of features that are typically ascribed to ethnically heterogeneous urban youth (Quist, 2000: 153). This and other features with a similar status have further been studied by Madsen (2008a: 211) who finds that they can be used among teenage boys to construct 'tough streetwise masculinity'. I cannot say for sure if this ascription is what Ceyhun refers to or Ferhat reacts upon, but in the conversation as well as in my general knowledge of the participants, there are some indicators that this is the case. In interviews, all of the participants express an awareness of these features and their assignment to a specific set of features. Some of the speakers label this set of features as 'gadesprog' (street language) and they heavily downgrade the speakers who produce it (Møller, 2009). Ceyhun tells in his interview that he used to talk like that, but stopped doing it, and Ferhat in his interview also tells that Ceyhun used to talk like that before. We can see from Ferhat's uptake in line 10 that he assigns an identity to Ceyhun as childish by referring to a toy store and as someone who needs explanation. Whether Ceyhun opted for 'tough streetwise masculinity' is of course an open question, but the continuation indicates that this might be the case.

Excerpt 4b, recording (d): Tax money

13.	**Ceyhun:**	*ağbi* fire komma [fem mil]lion de:t
14.	**Ferhat:**	[o:ha:]
15.	**Murat:**	[ja]
16.	**Ceyhun:**	[det] er jo vores skattepenge mand (.) [kraft]edme
17.	**Ferhat:**	[ja]
18.	**Ceyhun:**	fucking svin mand
19.	**Ferhat:**	[*oğlum sen*] *ne zaman* skattepenge *verdin*
20.	**Murat:**	[nej nej]

Translation of excerpt 4b, recording (d): Tax money

13.	**Ceyhun:**	*brother* four point [five mil]lions that is
14.	**Ferhat:**	[*o:ha:*]
15.	**Murat:**	[yes]

16.	**Ceyhun:**	[that] is our tax money man (.) [god] damnit
17.	**Ferhat:**	[yes]
18.	**Ceyhun:**	fucking swine man
19.	**Ferhat:**	[*young man*] *when did you ever pay* tax money
20.	**Murat:**	[no no]

Ceyhun expresses dissatisfaction about what he implies is a waste of money in lines 16 and 18. In doing so, he also uses a register of heavy swearing ('hvad fanden', 'kraftedme', 'fucking svin mand') and I interpret this as an(other) attempt to construct a tough masculine identity (cf. Quist, 2005). Ferhat's uptake in line 20 is ambiguous: Asking whether Ceyhun ever paid tax undermines Ceyhun's argument concerning tax money, but on the other hand assigns him an identity as a hoodlum living on the edge of the established order, which probably is more attractive for Ceyhun than an assigned identity as childish and in need of explanations.

The pronunciation without a glottal constriction in line 8 in excerpt 4a and Ferhat's uptake in line 10 can be seen as ongoing enregisterment. Ceyhun's utterance is evaluated negatively as childish. We can not know if Ceyhun has intended to signal tough masculinity but if this is the case the interaction can be viewed as part of a process in which a linguistic feature, namely the pronunciation of syllables without glottal constriction where a glottal constriction would be expected in standard Copenhagen, undergoes a change in its evaluation from masculine (Madsen, 2008) to childish among this group of peers.

Excerpt 5, recording (d): Ash tray

1.	**Ceyhun:**	hişt hallo (.) askebæger'*yi uzatsana* ((hallo pronounced with stress on the last syllable in a way I interpret as offensive))
2.	**Ferhat:**	askebæger xxx (.)
3.	**Ceyhun:**	ej slap nu af mand
4.	**Murat:**	*şuradakini al lan* (.)
5.	**Ceyhun:**	jeg ved ikke hvordan [I opfører jer xxx
6.	**Ferhat:**	[så har Ceyhun stjålet et askebæger ((Ferhat speaks directly into the microphone))
7.		(6.0) ((Ferhat and Murat laugh))
8.	**Ferhat:**	det bliver på jeres regning ((Ferhat speaks directly into the microphone))
9.		(5.0) ((Ferhat and Murat laugh))
10.	**Murat:**	o[f
11.	**Murat:**	[Ceyhun (.) tøm lommerne
12.		(1.2) ((Ferhat and Murat laugh))

13.	**Ceyhun:**	x[xx
14.	**Ferhat:**	[han har også taget bestik
15.		(2.0)
15.	**Ferhat:**	Ceyhun lad så den peberkværn være i fred
16.		(2.1) ((Ferhat and Murat laugh))
17.	**Ceyhun:**	vor er I latterlige mand
18.		(2.8) ((Ferhat and Murat laugh))

Translation of excerpt 5, recording (d), ash tray

1.	**Ceyhun:**	<u>hey</u> hallo (.) *pass me the* ash tray
		((hallo pronounced with stress on the last syllable in a way I interpret as offensive))
2.	**Ferhat:**	ash tray xxx
		(.)
3.	**Ceyhun:**	hey relax now man
4.	**Murat:**	*take that one over there man*
		(.)
5.	**Ceyhun:**	I don't know how it is [you guys behave xxx
6.	**Ferhat:**	[now Ceyhun has stolen an ashtray
		((Ferhat speaks directly into the microphone))
7.		(6.0) ((Ferhat and Murat laugh))
8.	**Ferhat:**	it's gonna be at your expence ((Ferhat speaks directly into the microphone))
9.		(5.0) ((Ferhat og Murat laugh))
10.	**Murat:**	o[h
11.	**Murat:**	[*Ceyhun* (.) empty your pockets
12.		(1.2) ((Ferhat and Murat laugh))
13.	**Ceyhun:**	x[xx
14.	**Ferhat:**	[he has also taken cutlery
		(2.0)
15.	**Ferhat:**	Ceyhun leave that pepper mill alone
16.		(2.1) ((Ferhat and Murat laugh))
17.	**Ceyhun:**	you are so ridiculous man
18.		(2.8) ((Ferhat and Murat laugh))

In line 1, Ceyhun gets the attention from the other participants in a way I interpret as rude and signalling toughness. After he has attracted attention, he demands an ash tray. Ferhat does not comply with Ceyhun's demand. Ceyhun asks him to relax in line 3 and Murat points to another ashtray in line 4. After a micro pause, Ceyhun, in a jocular way, implies that Ferhat and Murat have behaved in a criticisable way. He thereby takes a stance where he can evaluate and criticize their behavior – a cultural model of action normally linked for example, to school teachers or parents. In the middle of Ceyhun's turn, Ferhat starts speaking directly into the microphone as if he is commenting on the course of events. He uses a dramatizing voice as similar to a sports commentator. In line 6, Ferhat states that Ceyhun stole an ashtray. In line 8, he states that 'it will be on your account' speaking directly into the microphone and using the plural form 'jeres' (your) of the pronoun, which indicates that he is addressing the project workers. In line 10, Murat teams up with Ferhat and requests that Ceyhun empty his pockets. Ceyhun tries to speak in line 11, but gets interrupted in line 12 where Ferhat states that Ceyhun also took the cutlery. As in line 6, he refers to Ceyhun in the third person. In line 15, Ferhat asks Ceyhun directly to leave the pepper mill alone. Now Ferhat can hardly speak for laughter. Finally, in line 17, Ceyhun reacts by calling them ridiculous.

Ceyhun employs a cultural model of action that can be described as an 'authority' register in line 5 and Ferhat employs a 'sports commentator' register in line 6. Thereby Ferhat uses the presence of the recorder and the knowledge that somebody will listen to the recording afterwards as an opportunity to act out a performance as sports commentator, that is to construct a momentary identity. By speaking to this future audience, he also gains the advantage of being able to speak *about* Ceyhun's activities (or more likely invent them) instead of addressing him (see also Møller, 2008a: 226, for a similar activity). Ceyhun copes with this by only speaking when Murat and Ferhat address him directly during the phase including the accusations. The presence of the microphone might also be what inspires Ceyhun to perform an 'authority' role which initiates the playful activity carried out by the participants of stepping in and out of registers and ascribing each other different social identities.

In Excerpt 5, Ceyhun first performs a discourse identity I interpret as tough and dominant. When the other participants do not align with this identity, he performs a more jocular identity as someone in a position to question the behaviour of the other participants. Ferhat and Murat use Ceyhun's performance as their point of departure to describe Ceyhun's (fictive) theft of the restaurant's equipment by involving a 'commentator' register. The participants involve stylisation to create personae that are in a position to ascribe identities to other participants. Ceyhun ascribes an identity to the other participants as not behaving properly, and Ferhat and Murat react by ascribing an identity to Ceyhun as a petty thief.

Discussion and Conclusion

In Excerpts 1–3, I show how the form [lan'] involves features generally ascribed to both Danish and Turkish, which makes it difficult (and pointless) to decide where one language ends and the other one begins. As a consequence of this, I argue for a speaker-oriented, sequential approach to analyses of linguistic diversity in interaction. In Excerpt 4 and 5, I show how different registers of Danish are involved in playful negotiations of identity. In Excerpt 4, I suggest that the participants negotiate the enregistering of a single linguistic feature (pronunciation without a glottal constriction) and that this negotiation interacts with the participants' identity negotiations. Excerpt 5 exemplifies how registers can be used in the creation of momentary identities such as 'tough', 'commentator', or 'authority'.

More generally, Excerpts 1–3 illustrate how the boundaries between sets of features are fluent and how sets of features can be more or less integrated in different local contexts. Excerpt 4 exemplifies negotiation of the evaluation of a single feature and thereby provides an example of the enregistering of linguistic features on the level of interaction. Excerpt 5 exemplifies how the relationship between the speaker as a person and the cultural model of action he enacts can be questioned and rejected. In short, I dealt with the relationship between different sets of features, the relationship between a linguistic feature and its evaluation and the relationship between the speaker and the identities he constructs (partly) through the use of stylization. These different levels of speakers' relations to linguistic (sets of) features play different roles in the participants' identity work. In Excerpts 4 and 5, linguistic diversity is exploited for cheerful identity negotiations in a rather direct way. In Excerpts 1–3 the participants also negotiate local identities, but it is not clear that the [lan'] form plays a specific role in these negotiations. More likely, it mirrors a general tendency among the Turkish–Danish minority in Køge to integrate linguistic features generally ascribed to Danish or Turkish when interacting with peers with a similar linguistic background (Møller & Jørgensen, 2008). Time will show whether the [lan'] form spreads and gets enregistered among the Turkish speaking minority in Køge, the Turkish speaking minority in Denmark, young people in Denmark in general or a completely different population of speakers.

Transcription Key

[…]	: overlapping speech
(.)	: pause of less than 0.5 second
(1.5)	: approximate length of pause in seconds
CAPITALS	: loud
xxx	: inaudible word(s)
(( ))	: comments and explanations
[/]	: self interruption
recte	: Linguistic features ascribed to Danish
italics	: Linguistic features ascribed to Turkish
underlined	: Linguistic features which cannot be ascribed to a (single) national language

Chapter 12
Literary Use of Multiethnic Youth Language: Noninversion in Swedish Fiction*

R. KÄLLSTRÖM

Introduction

This chapter deals with the representation of Swedish Multiethnic Youth Language[1] in Alejandro Leiva Wenger's short stories *Elixir* ('Elixir') and *Borta i tankar* ('Lost in thoughts'), from the collection *Till vår ära* ('In our honour') (2001), and Jonas Hassen Khemiri's novel *Ett öga rött* ('An eye red') (2003). These two books caused much attention in the media immediately after they came out. New paperback editions were printed, and especially *Ett öga rött* sold very well, and a stage and a film version of this novel soon appeared. The language use in the three texts analyzed here was generally seen as representative for the way young people in multilingual suburbs speak. However, both authors rejected all claims that they represent young people in multiethnic suburbs, and Khemiri repeatedly stressed that his main character's language was representative only for the character himself. A prominent feature in the three texts is noninversion, a violation of the V2 rule in Swedish (see next section). I have chosen to analyze how noninversion is used by the authors, since it is a significant feature of Swedish learner language and Multiethnic Youth Language (Ganuza, 2008a: 141). Noninversion is a salient feature, especially when found in writing, and it is seen by many people as a sign of poorly acquired Swedish and/or bad language. I will show that noninversion is frequent in all three literary texts. The frequency of noninversion and variations in the use of noninversion in the texts are part of the literary formation of themes and characters. Noninversion is also deployed somewhat differently in each text. Some uses of noninversion will be analyzed in terms of performance, stylization and deception along the lines of Coupland (2001, 2004), and I will show that there are parallels in the literary texts to what Ganuza (2008a, this volume) found in her study of the use of noninversion by teenagers from multilingual areas in Gothenburg, Malmö and Stockholm.

Inversion and Noninversion in Standard Swedish and Learner Language

Swedish is a V2 language. Unlike English, the finite verb is always in second position in declarative main clauses, irrespective of what syntactic function occupies the first position. In (1) below the subject is in first position and the finite verb in second position, while in (2) the first position is occupied by the adverbial 'ibland' (sometimes), and the finite verb is in second position. The subject in (2) is in third position.

(1) Han såg dom komma.
    he saw them come
    'He saw them coming'

(2) Ibland såg han dom komma.
    sometimes saw he them come
    'Sometimes he saw them coming'

The word order pattern in sentences like (2) is often described in process terms: Inversion is said to have applied.

(1) and (2) illustrate the pattern of Standard Swedish. However, in learner language and Multiethnic Youth Language, clauses like (3) below, with another syntactic function than subject in first position and subject – finite verb order, are also found (cf. Ganuza, this volume; Opsahl & Nistov, this volume, for grammatical details on noninversion as a feature of Norwegian Multiethnic Youth Language).

(3) Ibland han såg dom komma.
    sometimes he saw them come
    'Sometimes he saw them coming'

The word order pattern illustrated in (3) will be called noninversion (and sometimes noninverted word order).

In Standard Swedish, inversion is also used in direct wh-questions, and noninversion in such questions occurs in learner Swedish (Philipsson, 2007), but seems to be rare in Multiethnic Youth Language (Ganuza, 2008a: 139, this volume). In this chapter, noninversion will be used with reference only to noninversion in main clause declaratives unless otherwise stated, since noninversion in wh-questions is rare in the three texts. The few instances of noninversion in wh-questions will be mentioned separately.

Although inversion in principle always applies in Standard Swedish according to the pattern just described, some phenomena in spoken language complicate the picture a little. In spoken interaction, inversion may be found in declaratives even when there is no topicalized element and the clause starts with the finite verb. Noninversion may also be found after a pause or a discourse particle, and often after the adverb 'kanske' ('perhaps') when it is in clause-initial position. Noninversion after 'kanske' is rather frequent in writing, and the other uses just mentioned can be found in written texts representing speech or in some other way influenced by spoken language. These run-of-the-mill cases of noninversion are rare in the literary texts analyzed here, and noninversion will be used in this chapter to denote cases like (3), which unlike the other types just mentioned are very conspicuous and index non-Swedish background.

Noninversion in the Language Use of Young People from Multilingual Areas

Ganuza (2008a, this volume) analyzed (non)inversion in main clause declaratives and other clause types in mainly spoken data from 127 adolescents in upper secondary schools with a substantial proportion of multilingual students in the three largest cities in Sweden. Noninversion was found only in main clause declaratives,[2] and was produced rather seldom. Ganuza's (2008a) large sample contains noninversion in 1.9% of the possible contexts in written production and in 4.6% of the contexts in oral production, while in her focus sample of 20 adolescents, noninversion was found in 1.5% and 10.2% of the possible contexts in written and oral production, respectively. Ganuza's figures include the 'kanske'-cases mentioned in the section 'Inversion and Noninversion in Standard Swedish and Learner Language'. The latter make up almost 67% of the noninversions in her written data, but only a few percent in the oral data (Ganuza, 2008a: 96).

There was great variation among participants depending on situation, interlocutor and so on. While no participant produced more than a few noninversions in the written data, some of them produced a rather substantial proportion of noninversions in the oral data. Ganuza concludes that noninversion seems to be used in situations with high involvement and by (some of) her participants as a linguistic resource for expressing solidarity with their multilingual neighborhood, for expressing opposition to demands from the school or the research team, or when acting out and playing with stereotypes of young people from multilingual neighborhoods and the way they speak (Ganuza, 2008a: 152, this volume).

Noninversion in the Literary Texts

Multiethnic language in one of the three texts discussed here has been studied by, among others, Andersson (2005), Gomér (2008), Göransson (2004), Große (2008) and Källström (2003). The main focus has generally been on a wide array of multiethnic features, which were found to be frequent in all the texts and which pertain to several linguistic levels.

A few traits distinctive for each text have been found in the studies mentioned: In the short story *Elixir* there is evidence of learner language (notably on the orthographic and morphological level), the novel *Ett öga rött* is rich in nonce lexical constructions and a few syntactic constructions that seem to have been invented by the author (in the story frame by the protagonist, see below) and in the short story *Borta i tankar* there is a rich variety of interjections and other expressive vocabulary typical of Multiethnic Youth Language. However, noninversion plays a prominent role in all three texts, and the opening sentence of each text contains a noninversion.

Leiva Wenger's *Elixir*

The short story *Elixir* is written in the first person from the point of view of a bilingual teenage boy. The ostensible author comments on his writing process a couple of times, complaining that his hand hurts from writing. The story is surrealistic: The main character and his friends start drinking an elixir that makes them look and behave more and more like cliché versions of 'Swedes'. However, the elixir turns out to be dangerous. The deeper theme of the story is the negative effects of stereotyping and categorizing people in categories such as 'immigrants' and 'Swedes', and many of the formulations about 'us' and 'the others' are quite dramatic and comical.

Although direct speech occurs, the text is a continuous flow from beginning to end, with no division into paragraphs, haphazard use of capitals and very few punctuation marks. The language is similar throughout the text, with no significant variation between, for example, representations of speech and of action. *Elixir* is dense in multiethnic features on all linguistic levels. A few phonological and morphological features are interpretable as learner language (Andersson, 2005: 29f.).

Noninversion occurs in 23% of the contexts where inversion is obligatory in Standard Swedish, and there is not much variation from page to page or between reported speech and retellings of events. The frequent and nonflexible use of noninversion fits with the theme of the story, serving as an indication of a stereotyped view of multilingual adolescents as incompetent language users along with other stereotypical attributes of the main characters such as dark hair, lack of academic success and aggressive attitude.

The beginning of the story is quoted below. In my English version, I have tried to find English equivalents to the misspellings and deviant morphology in the original. In my translations of this and the following quotations, noninversion will be rendered in English with inversion: 'idag vi lovade' has become 'today promised we'.

> *idag vi lovade vi ska sluta dricka skiten och sluta jaga katter. fetarslet Marco svärde på hans morsas grav han ska brenna reseptet...* (Leiva Wenger 2001: 29).

> today promised we we will stop drinking the shit and stop hunting cats. the fat-ass Marco sweared on his moms grave he will birn the resipe... (author's translation).

Khemiri's *Ett öga rött*

The protagonist of the novel *Ett öga rött* is Halim, an Arabic-Swedish boy in his mid-teens. After his mother's death, Halim has moved with his father from a multiethnic neighborhood to a more homogenous, 'Swedish' area. Halim tries to resist the efforts of his father, his school and Swedish society at large to make him, as he calls it, 'svennefierad' ('swedified'), that is, assimilated and mainstream Swedish. For Halim, an important way to fight 'swedification' is to write a secret diary using his own, very special variety of Swedish.

Also *Ett öga rött* is ostensibly a story told by the main character, this time in a diary, written mainly in the variety of Swedish just mentioned. This invented variety (from now on called Halim's language) is used throughout the book, with some exceptions. Several linguistic features associated with Multiethnic Youth Language, among them noninversion and lexical items, are important ingredients (Gomér, 2008: 11ff). Other traits include topicalizations of adverbs that cannot be topicalized in any variety of Swedish, and creative distortions of Swedish words and lexicalized phrases (Große, 2008: 119, 122f). There is also a certain amount of direct speech in the diary, where Halim does not use Halim's language. Standard Swedish is used in direct speech from 'monolingual Swedes', from Halim when he interacts with 'monolingual Swedes', and for ostensible direct speech in Arabic.

In *Ett öga rött*, noninversion is a main feature of Halim's language and is used in all contexts where inversion is normally used in Standard Swedish. Outside what I call Halim's language, noninversion is found in some of Halim's direct speech, but is lacking in dialogue representing Arabic or Standard Swedish, where Standard Swedish is used. The function of noninversion is connected with the theme of authenticity, which is prominent in the novel. In his diary, Halim builds a dream of himself as a 'sultan of thought' who sees through and resists all attempts to 'swedify' him. Among Halim's acts of resistance are sabotage in his school and petty theft, planting of stolen goods on a 'Swedish' middle-class man, and of course his language in the diary. However, small hints in the text make the reader doubt Halim's truthfulness and draw the conclusion that Halim is rather a normal teenager trying to find his place in life, grieving his dead mother and resenting that he had to change school and find new friends. Just like many of Halim's other acts of resistance, his invented language is known to no one but himself and this language is just as 'authentic' as his fantasies.

The following extract offers a sample of some of the syntactic peculiarities in Halim's language, including noninversion:

> *På eftermiddagen jag sa jag behövde åka till stan för köpa böcker till skolan och sen jag tog tunnelbanan ut till Skärholmen* (Khemiri, 2003: 10).
>
> In the afternoon said I I had to go to the city for buy books for school and then took I the underground out to Skärholmen (author's translation).

Leiva Wenger's *Borta i tankar*

The story line of the short story *Borta i tankar* is straightforward. The protagonist Felipe leaves his compulsory school in a multiethnic neighborhood to go to an upper secondary school dominated by middle-class students of 'Swedish' origin, while his old friends go to an upper secondary school in the old neighborhood. In his new school Felipe falls in love with Julia, a girl from a middle-class family living close to the school. In the end it turns out that his friends push Felipe into letting Julia down. The conflict in the mind of Felipe between loyalty to his old friends and the multilingual setting where he lives and loyalty to Julia and the middle class setting of his new school, is the theme of the story. The story conveys an impression of the intense working of Felipe's mind, when he is trying to sort out what has happened lately, thinking back and forth, trying to work out when, where and why things went wrong, and who he really is and where he belongs.

The story continually moves between and mixes several points in time and place, often in the same sentence. Key events and expressions of feelings (and more or less exact wordings of them) are repeated. The speech and thoughts of characters are represented directly and indirectly. The protagonist is sometimes referred to in the first and sometimes in the third person, and in the latter case with 'han' (he), his given name or a nickname, even in the same sentence: '...säger jag, säger Felipe, säger han, säger Fällan' (I say, Felipe says, he says, Fällan says) (Leiva Wenger, 2001: 10, author's translation). The narrator seems sometimes to be an external omniscient narrator, but the constant shifts (as in this example) between perspectives and the use of Multiethnic Youth Language suggest a reading where the third person narrator reporting the protagonist's actions is also really Felipe himself, remembering and visualising events, seeing himself from the outside.

The text features many lexical, morphological and syntactic traits typical of Multiethnic Youth Language (Gomér, 2008; Källström, 2003), among them a rich variety of interjections and other expressive vocabulary, expressive derivatives in '-ish' and nonstandard use of definiteness.

In *Borta i tankar*, the overall frequency of noninversion is high. It occurs in 54% of the possible contexts for inversion. But while Halim's language in *Ett öga rött* contains only noninversion and *Elixir* is characterized by a steady flow of variation between inversion and noninversion, *Borta i tankar* contains much more variation in the use of inversion and noninversion.

In two passages in *Borta i tankar*, the author has used a special typographic device that sets them apart from the rest of the text. These passages will be discussed below. As for the rest of the text, noninversion is found with varying frequencies. Standard Swedish (with inversion) is used essentially for the same functions as in *Ett öga rött*: In lines ostensibly uttered in another language (Spanish) and in utterances made by 'monolingual' Swedes. Excluding Standard Swedish speech, a systematic difference can be found. In the speech of bilinguals, reported either as direct or indirect speech, noninversion occurs in 12 out of 21 contexts for inversion (57%), while there is noninversion in only 22 out of 65 contexts (34%) when the narrator's (Felipe's) voice is heard more directly, in his representation of actions and free indirect discourse representing the narrator/protagonist's thoughts and speech. The higher frequency of noninversion when Felipe relates what was actually said between him and his friends compared to the lower frequency when he relates his own version more directly as a narrator or in an inner monologue helps shaping a contrast between what is expected from bilingual boys with Felipe's background and Felipe's 'true' attitudes and feelings. The following extract from an inner monologue shows variation between inversion and noninversion:

> *Fällan är fin nu, Fällan skäms för oss dom sa. Ibland var han trött och därför jag försökte gömma mej när han såg dom komma från andra hållet...* (Leiva Wenger, 2001: 11).
>
> Fällan is posh now, Fällan is ashamed of us said they. Sometimes he was tired and therefore tried I to hide when he saw them coming from the other direction... (author's translation)

In the two typographically deviant passages mentioned above, the text is set in two different ways, forming intertwined parallel texts. The first, third, fifth line and so on are set in small capitals, and the second, fourth, sixth and so on in lower case, each set of lines forming its own 'microtext'. The typography is shown in the following quotation:

DÄRFÖR JAG GJORDE DET DÄRA. INNERST INNE JAG VILLE INTE MEN JAG FÖRLORADE OCH

jag ska inte säga nåt, men det är bra att du byter skola, jag vill inte se dig mer, okej Julia

JAIME OCH DOM PRESSADE DU VET, DOM SA OM DU BANGAR DU ÄR TÖNT...

jag vet jag var keff, jag vet jag var falsk men du var lite också jo Julia du var (Leiva Wenger, 2001: 21)

THAT'S WHY DID I THAT. DEEP INSIDE WANTED I NOT TO BUT I LOST AND JAIME AND

I will not tell, but it is fine that you change school, I don't want to see you any more, OK

THOSE WERE PUSHING YOU KNOW, THEY SAID IF YOU DON'T DO IT YOU'RE A PRAT...

Julia I know I was bad, I know I was false but you were a little too yes Julia you were (author's translation)

The text set in small capitals differs greatly from the rest of the text in the use of inversion: The use of noninversion is taken to the extreme. There is noninversion in all the 27 possible contexts, even in wh-questions. (Note that noninversion in wh-questions does not occur in the rest of *Borta i tankar*.)

Analysis

Thematically, the three texts considered in this chapter share several similarities. The protagonists are all teenage boys from multilingual neighborhoods grappling with their identities. The tension between minority, lower class background and majority, middle-class values is a main theme in all the texts, and language plays a prominent role in forming and developing this theme. In *Elixir*, language with multiethnic features is an integral part of the stereotyped picture of the protagonist, and the contrast between his language and Standard Swedish is implicit. In *Ett öga rött* and *Borta i tankar* people of 'monolingual' Swedish background are depicted as speaking Standard Swedish. In the latter texts, the use of Arabic and Spanish by speakers of different backgrounds is rendered in Standard Swedish, which also in this case contrasts with 'impure' multiethnic Swedish. Possible variation in language use by, for example, speakers of different geographical varieties of Arabic or between young people who have grown up in Sweden and an older generation who have immigrated as adults are thereby reduced to the homogeneity of the Swedish official language norm for written language.

Several linguistic features common to all three texts are important for the identification of the language use as multiethnic. No doubt, noninversion is one of the most important of these. It is extremely salient and a strong index of 'non-Swedish' language use and background, and it seems impossible to imagine a stretch of language with much noninversion and simultaneously no other multiethnic features, except as some kind of language game. This means that the use of noninversion in the very first clause of the texts is an opening that immediately invites expectations of what kind of language the reader will meet in the text as a whole.

Inversion as stylization and deception

Literature can be understood as a kind of performance. The author performs (and lets his characters perform) in order to make an effect on the reader. The language use by characters may be crucially involved in this performance. If the objective is to achieve literary realism, the goal may be to give the reader the impression that a character uses exactly the language/s/he would use in real life in the kind of situation, context and co-text that the utterance is situated in (see Eidevall, 1974: 180). However, this is not achieved through an exact rendering of spoken language. It is done through a performance aimed at 'deceiving' the reader into a feeling of realism or authenticity. It certainly involves suppression of some features of spoken language and may involve under-representation as well as over-representation of features of spoken language (Källström, 2008). Since variation is at the heart of language use, (literary) realistic renderings of characters' language normally also involve some variation.

Coupland (2001, 2004) analyses a radio show and a TV show, respectively, in terms of performance, stylization and (in the latter case) deception. The parallels to literary representation are obvious: The radio and TV performances are mediated and more or less scripted, i.e. sifted through the norms of written language. However, the performances analyzed by Coupland represent spoken language, while two of the texts analyzed here represent the written language of the characters. Also, the radio and TV shows are of course performed in the spoken modality, not the written. Still, concepts used in Coupland's analyses are useful for my analysis of the literary texts.

While styling is treated by Coupland (2001: 348f) as a strategic response to audience characteristics and so on drawing on the speaker's primary repertoire, stylization to him involves a greater degree of conscious deployment of one's own and/or others' linguistic repertoire in order to 'challenge assumptions about the naturalness of speech (...) and about how it is owned and voiced' (Coupland, 2001: 349). Among other characteristic features, stylized utterances 'are often emphatic and hyperbolic realizations of their targeted styles and genres' (Coupland, 2001: 350), and stylization is 'strategic inauthenticity' (Coupland, 2001: 350) which evokes stereotypes and issues of identity and ideology. Stylization assumes a qualified audience that is able to interpret the semiotic value of the performance.

Deception shares most of the characteristics of stylization, while assuming an uninformed, gullible audience. In the TV show analyzed in Coupland (2004), the point is that one of the characters is such a gullible audience for the protagonist's (Sergeant Bilko) deceptions, while the TV audience sees through Bilko's performance. Thus, within the story frame, Bilko is doing deception, while in the performance frame, he is stylizing deception (Coupland, 2004: 268), letting verbal and nonverbal deception clues reveal to the audience that he is deceiving.

Stylization in Elixir

To my mind, the use of multiethnic language in the short story *Elixir* contributes significantly to the stereotyped representation of the protagonist as 'the immigrant boy from the multilingual suburb'. The language can be interpreted as a stylization addressed to the readers and allowing them to detect and re-evaluate stereotypes. The representation of multiethnic language seems emphatic and hyperbolic on at least two counts. The frequency of multiethnic features is high (Andersson, 2005). Specifically, the incidence of noninversion is high, considering that the story is ostensible *writing* by the protagonist [in writing noninversion seems much more rare than in speech, cf. e.g. Ganuza's data (2008a, this volume)]. The lack of variation in the language used by the protagonist can be seen as emphatic. Finally, the stereotyped descriptions of 'immigrant boys' and 'Swedes' and the surrealistic story line, expounding the bizarre situation and surrealistic consequences of having to choose between living up to either of those two stereotypes, strongly favour a reading of the protagonist's language as stylized.

Deception in Ett öga rött

What I dubbed Halim's language in the novel *Ett öga rött* can be analyzed in terms of stylized deception. Halim's language is not used exclusively in the diary. Halim's use of Standard Swedish for Arabic and for the speech of 'Swedes' is a case in point. There are also many instances of direct speech from Halim himself. In most of these, subject and finite verb are noninverted (but generally, the most contrived features, lexical distortions and odd topicalizations are lacking). In other cases Halim uses Standard Swedish (notably with inversion) strategically when it serves his purposes. Thus, Halim has considerable linguistic resources at his disposal and makes use of them skilfully.

The use of noninversion in Halim's language is an instance of the kind of hyperbolic representations that Coupland (2001, 2004) finds typical of stylization (and stylized deception), and the extremely high frequency of noninversion functions as a strong deception clue. Other such clues are the extensive use of odd topicalizations and distorted lexicalized expressions mentioned above. There are also a few much more infrequent and subtle linguistic cues indicating to the reader that deception is being practiced. There are in fact at least three instances of inversion in declaratives in Halim's language, and Halim uses at least one multiethnic word a few times with an unattested meaning (the opposite of the normal meaning), while he uses it with the normal meaning in other instances.

The several hints (and one outright confession) that Halim is not telling the truth all the time are also important. Halim himself often seems deceived by his own performance, and his father also seems deceived by Halim's language when he finds the diary, but the reader should not be. In the performance frame, the clues just mentioned are effective for revealing to the reader that Halim is deceiving, posing as someone he would (perhaps) like to be.[3]

The use of language is always situated, also in a literary work. Linguistic co-text and various contextual cues at different levels lead us to interpretations of the language use of the characters, as do the development of themes and the forming of characters. We have just seen this in operation in *Elixir* and *Ett öga rött*. When discussing *Borta i tankar*, this point will become even more obvious.

Styling and stylization in Borta i tankar

The story line of the short story *Borta i tankar* is straightforward and Felipe characterized as no more complicated than most people. The story and characters are most naturally interpreted in the vein of literary realism (while the structure of the story is highly modernistic). I interpret the representation of Multiethnic Youth Language in *Borta i tankar* as also realistic in this literary sense, although the overall frequency of noninversion is higher than in *Elixir*, and portions of the text contain the most consistent use of noninversion in any of the texts. However, comparisons of frequencies of linguistic features between literary works (or literary works and natural language data) should be made with caution. What counts is the internal composition and consistency of the work (Källström, 2008). And when comparisons are made, it should also be remembered that, unlike the other two texts, *Borta i tankar* mainly represents discourse (speech and thought), and noninversion seems to be considerably more frequent in speech than in writing (Ganuza, this volume).

Along with the realistic tone of characters, events and storyline, the linguistic variation between different parts of the story lends credibility to a realistic interpretation. In direct speech to Julia, Felipe uses a few multiethnic grammatical features (although not noninversion; there are no contexts for inversion), but no such vocabulary, notably no multiethnic expressive interjections, which, like noninversion, are very common in speech between the bilingual boys. In his monologic discourse (excluding the text in small capitals), Felipe uses fewer noninversions than when he is interacting with his bilingual friends. This can be interpreted as representing stylistic variation as the result of processes of accommodation or audience design.

The text in small capitals (see section 'Leiva Wenger's *Borta i tankar*' above), where the use of noninversion is extreme, can be read as stylized. This passage is construed as Felipe's turns in a fictitious telephone conversation with his now ex-girlfriend. Felipe is highly involved emotionally in what he says/thinks in this 'microtext'. He is trying out how he would tell Julia his version of what has happened between them and explain his actions. He is also defending his actions and his multiethnic background. The extreme use of noninversion can be seen as a linguistic marker of his high involvement and of identification and solidarity with his multiethnic background, and as an act of pride, defiance and contestation. What we witness is not Felipe the omniscient narrator, Felipe styling an identity as a cool bilingual young man in interaction with his friends or Felipe talking to his sweetheart at school, but Felipe, in an inner monologue, defiantly and proudly overemphasizing and stylizing his language variety, and calling alternative possibilities of identity and language into play.

The use of noninversion in the passages set in small capitals may seem extreme, but it should be assessed against the use of noninversion in other places in the text, where it is also frequent: What is relevant is that the use of noninversion differs significantly between different parts of the text (Källström, 2008). We will also see in the following section that very high frequencies of noninversion can be found in Ganuza's (2008a) data.

Stylization in actual language use and in literature

Although Ganuza's (2008a, this volume) results do not answer the question as to how noninversion is used in 'authentic' Multiethnic Youth Language (Ganuza, 2008a: 154), her findings add some credibility to the analysis of the literary functions of noninversion proposed here. The frequency of noninversion in writing was very low in Ganuza's data, while its frequency in the two texts representing the written language of the protagonists is high, in Halim's language extremely high. This indicates that the use of noninversion is exaggerated in these literary texts and in turn supports a reading of these as stylized.

Ganuza also found noninversion to be a variable phenomenon for those participants who used noninversion more often than the others. Self-recordings (most often of interaction with peers) and group conversations in school contained significantly higher frequencies of noninversion than retellings with a researcher and presentations in front of the class (and of course written essays) (Ganuza, this volume, cf. Opsahl & Nistov, this volume). The data for individual participants with a substantial number of noninversions also show that most of them vary in their use of noninversion between activity types (Ganuza, 2008a: 191). At least marginally, these findings lend support to the interpretation of Halim's language and the language of *Elixir* as stylized, since there is very little variation in the use of inversion in those texts. Also, the patterns of variation between inversion and noninversion in the speech of some of Ganuza's participants show similarities with the variation found in Felipe's language use in *Borta i tankar*.

Ganuza (2008a: 152) interprets the fact that participants tended to use noninversion more often in conversations with peers, when they were highly involved in the topic of conversation and when they were allowed to speak continuously for some time, as indicating that noninversion is part of some participants' linguistic repertoire. She finds these findings compatible with theories of involvement style, accommodation and audience design. In terms of Coupland's notion of styling mentioned above, we could say that (at least some of) these interactions triggered styling. But in some sequences in Ganuza's data, participants' language use seems to be best understood as stylization. Some participants seemed to use noninversion actively as a strategy 'to express their affiliation with the multilingual setting, show solidarity with friends, stage stereotypical images or contest official school discourses or the act of being researched' (Ganuza, 2008a: 130).

The pattern of variation in the use of noninversion in Ganuza's study seems parallel to that postulated for Felipe's use of noninversion in *Borta i tankar*. Interestingly, Ganuza (2008a: 191) also found very high frequencies of noninversion in some sequences: one participant reached a frequency of 84% noninversion in group conversations (while using almost no noninversions at all in some of the other activities). Thus, Ganuza's findings lend further support to my interpretation of the small capitals passages in *Borta i tankar* as a successful realistic representation of a character's use of language.

Conclusion

Noninversion in Swedish main declarative clauses is a powerful linguistic symbol. For mainstream Swedish society, it indexes non-Swedish background and for most people a low command of Swedish. However, many young people from multilingual neighborhoods use it as a way of expressing solidarity with a multilingual background. We have seen how noninversion is used skilfully by the two young authors, Leiva Wenger and Khemiri, in their literary composition, figuring prominently in representing themes of styling and stylizing multilingual young people's language and also in stylizing deception. We have also seen that this literary use has parallels in actual language use analyzed by Ganuza (2008a, this volume).

Notes

1. 'Multiethnic Youth Language' is an English version of Fraurud and Bijvoet's (2004) term 'multietniskt ungdomsspråk' and denotes the kind of multiethnolects found in several Swedish cities. In this chapter, 'multiethnic language' and the adjective 'multiethnic' will also be used, with more inclusive reference, including also learner Swedish.
2. There is in fact one instance of noninversion among the 693 wh-questions (Ganuza, 2008a: 62).
3. In spite of this, several literary critics accepted Halim's language as authentic (cf. Källström, 2006; forthcoming)

* Work on this study has been carried out in the project *Language and language use among young people in multilingual urban settings*, financed by the Bank of Sweden Tercentenary Foundation (cf. Boyd, this volume). I would like to thank the editors of this volume, whose comments have improved this article considerably. I would also like to thank Sally Boyd and an anonymous reviewer for their valuable comments.

Chapter 13
'Playing with Words as if it was a Rap Game': Hip-Hop Street Language in Oslo

J.S. KNUDSEN

> *The vernacular, I would argue, [...] is not a monolithic battering ram (and indeed, who would one batter) but a guerrilla incursion; it steals language, steals sounds, steals the media spotlight, then slips away, regrouping at another unpredictable cultural site.*
> Potter (1995: 76).

> *The vernacular thus stands in the place(s) of difference, articulates difference, and, indeed, actually produces difference.*
> Potter (1995: 63)

Introduction

The flow of hip-hop culture and rap music outside the United States and the indigenized result of this in countless 'glocal' cultures throughout the world, points to a trend toward the creation of urban slang, characterized by a blend of influences and rich linguistic dexterity. In Scandinavian urban settings, what may start out as the incorporation of selected words from minority languages alongside expressions from English-language hip-hop vocabulary has proven to develop over time into particular, culturally embedded language varieties, or what in recent Scandinavian studies have been labeled multiethnolects (Quist, 2000; Svendsen & Røyneland, 2008). The primary objective of this chapter is to explore connections between hip-hop music culture and the development of a local language variety in central Oslo, Norway. This is done from two different, but complementary perspectives. First, from a sociolinguistic perspective, innovation and experimentation is linked to some of the core values and discourses of hip-hop. This is exemplified by looking at the social construction of a stylized language variety as the trademark of a hip-hop crew. Second, drawing upon musicological perspectives, a close reading of selected rap lyrics points to possible connections between multiethnolectal language features and the stylistic and rhythmic requirements of rap music.

The chapter presents results from a study carried out in 2005–2007 as part of the interdisciplinary CULCOM (Cultural Complexity) research program at the Oslo University. It is based on field observations, interviews and recordings by Minoritet1, a multiethnic hip-hop crew in central Oslo. The language examples discussed are mainly lyrics selected from a total of 36 'underground' CD recordings supplied by members of the group. They are produced in various locations; in amateur home studios, in an art school studio, and at the X-ray youth center in central Oslo. This kind of music production is characterized by a great deal of spontaneity and collective improvisation in the studio as well as lively, and sometimes heated discussions (cf. Knudsen, 2008). Apart from incomplete sketches and ideas, lyrics are rarely written down in advance, hence all examples discussed are transcriptions by the author based on sound recordings.

The Hip-Hop Vernacular

In his exploration of the 'hip-hop vernacular' in the USA, Potter (1995: 64) suggests that linguistics can provide a model for the tactics and effectivity of hip-hop's cultural resistance movement. In view of the spread of hip-hop culture to multilingual environments outside the Anglophone countries, it might be relevant to raise the question whether it could not be conceptualized the other way around: That the codes and constructing principles underlying hip-hop style and rap music can serve as a model for the 'tactics' of linguistic development. Central features characterizing rap music have close parallels in the practice and development of the multiethnolectal language varieties often linked to this music: Sampling and mixing, re-appropriation, transformation and improvisation. Parallel to the practice of 'borrowing' music samples and beats from recordings by other artists, a hallmark of hip-hop lyrics is the rap artist's ability to pick up the phrases and rhymes of other performers; re-appropriating them; twisting, turning or subverting phrases through inventive poetic and linguistic variation. In hip-hop style and rap music there has always been a deep commitment to pushing, bending and breaking the limits. Hip-hop is a culture of resistance, its language a 'resistance vernacular' which 'deploys variance and improvisation in order to deform and reposition the rules of "intelligibility" set up by the dominant language' (Potter, 1995: 68). In this vocal expression of defiance and protest, language use is strategic. Rap lyrics connote defiance, and to emphasize this performers apparently set out to bend and break standard language rules in much the same way they challenge rules of society and established principles of making music.

In accordance with the terminology developed by Deleuze and Guattari (1986: 111–122), hip-hop jargon can be regarded a 'minor language'. While culturally dominant 'major languages' base their power on constants of vocabulary and grammar, the value of a minor language is based on linguistic dexterity, variance and flexibility (Potter, 1995: 68). A principal feature of a minor language is the construction, manifestation and celebration of difference versus a major language. Minor languages tend to have an 'overload of variation', an abundance of parallel forms and flexible linguistic norms (Potter: 66).

The creative use of language involves verbal strategies, which in hip-hop research have been explored in view of various 'black' American oral language practices that can be collectively characterized by the term Signifyin(g), notably following Gates' (1989) elaborations on the term with reference to African and African-American literature and oral culture. The particular orthography – capitalization and a bracketed final 'g' is used by Gates to discern the black vernacular concept Signifyin(g) from its standard English homonym, 'signifying' (Gates, 1989: 46). The act of Signifyin(g) is a rhetorical device featuring intertextuality, re-appropriation, implication, metaphorical association, double-voicing, irony, parody, puns and plays on words. It involves repetition and difference, combining words and meanings to create or associate new ones. A speaker can 'Signify upon' another person by exposing the subject to a verbal trick or double-voiced mockery, or 'Signify upon' words and expressions by repeating with a difference; appropriating them in ways that imply ironic or paradoxical connotations. Although Signifyin(g) is a trope developed in 'black' language culture, the global spread of hip-hop has led to the emergence of Signifyin(g) practices in local vernaculars worldwide (Mitchell, 2001, 2004).

Minoritet1

To illustrate some possible influences on the shaping and development of a local language variety this chapter focuses on the practices of a young hip-hop crew in the center of Oslo: Minoritet1. This pan-ethnic music collective, also known as M1, consists of around 15 young men and one woman. Apart from one Norwegian member they all have an immigrant family background: From Iraq, Morocco, Somalia, Bosnia, Pakistan, Lithuania, Uganda and Kurdistan. Their time in Norway varies from three years to their entire lives. In late 2007 the group was featured in a six-episode television documentary on the state television channel NRK, receiving considerable media attention. In early 2008 three key members left Minoritet1 to form their own group Forente Minoriteter (United Minorities), which released its first CD album, '99% ærlig' (99% honest) in September 2008.

Minoritet1 cultivated an 'underground' imagery. Their own posting on NRK's Internet page 'Urørt' (Untouched) – where young bands can promote their music – locates the underground to Grünerløkka in central Oslo: 'Undergrunn rap fra kjernen i byen Grunerløkka' [sic] (Underground rap form the core of the city Grünerløkka). The key metaphor 'underground'[1] sums up various sides of the members' self-image, norms, aesthetics, attitudes and cultural knowledge – their 'subcultural capital' (Thornton, 1995). An important aspect is that their music is created and distributed within an 'underground' network, independently of the commercial music market. In consequence, this implies a distancing toward commercial performers, especially what they call 'wacke-rap' – rap performed in English by Norwegians – which they describe as a sell-out: Unoriginal and unconvincing. The anticommercial aspect is linked to images of authenticity and honesty; an underground rapper 'keeps it real' by basing lyrics on his own life experience without bothering much about commercial success. Furthermore, 'underground' has to do with musical and poetical style. For Minoritet1, style is based on models in American gangster rap, and the underground codes of a 'gangster discourse' linked to violence, illegal drugs and sexuality (Sandberg, 2009; Sandberg & Pedersen, 2006: 238). At the same time their music is also deeply rooted in their own Norwegian street environment: 'the core of the city'. Both the key metaphor 'underground' and the group's name – Minoritet1 – connote marginalization, suggesting that there exists a contradicting 'other': An 'overground' and a 'majority', respectively. Both terms signalize opposition and resistance toward the wider Norwegian society. A striking parallel in choice of name is the Danish hip-hop group Outlandish, which also consists of young immigrants from various countries.

Street Language

Cultural and linguistic hybridity is a pervasive trait in the social interaction Minoritet1 is involved in: Music production and stage performances, lyrics and language. The local music scene in central Oslo where these young performers play a key role, affords a space for experimentation and creativity, and may arguably be regarded the primary arena for linguistic innovation in this urban setting.

The 'underground' environment Minoritet1 belongs to is characterized not only by the music they produce and perform, but also by other stylistic practices: Dress codes, body language and, of course, spoken language. Their lyrics contain excellent examples of the emerging urban language variety sometimes referred to as 'kebabnorsk' (Kebab-Norwegian), which is spoken in varying degrees among adolescents in multiethnic areas in central Oslo and the eastern suburbs (Aasheim, 1995; Østby, 2005; Svendsen & Røyneland, 2008). Since the group's start in 2001, Minoritet1 has been closely linked to the development of this novel speech style, which can be regarded as a manifestation of a hybridized identity in the field of tension between immigrant cultures, popular youth culture and 'Norwegian-ness'. Several Minoritet1 members were key informants for the noteworthy 'Kebab-Norwegian dictionary' (Østby, 2005), which includes excerpts from their lyrics used as language examples. This collaboration with a Norwegian author has apparently strengthened their image of being language innovators besides their position as role as models of localized hip-hop culture.

It could be argued that the labelling of a speech mode may have an essentialising effect and may even be regarded as stigmatizing. The term 'kebabnorsk' is by and large not appreciated by the users themselves, and may even be regarded as a pejorative (Svendsen & Røyneland, 2008: 68, 70). The young performers of Minoritet1 refer to the obvious fact that the term was launched by a Norwegian outsider, and propose their own alternative 'emic' designations such as 'asfaltspråk' and 'gatespråk' (asphalt language, street language); concepts that unmistakably evoke the 'underground' imagery of the urban hip-hop culture they are part of. However, since 'kebabnorsk' has established itself as the generally prevailing term – a fact Minoritet1 undoubtedly have contributed to themselves through their contributions to Østby's dictionary – they rarely oppose it when confronted by the media, who seem to have a particular liking for it. Despite their apparent distaste for the term, Minoritet1 have appropriated and taken advantage of it in their music, even using 'kebabnorsk' to entitle a song packed with as many of the most characteristic terms as absolutely possible.

Minoritet1 and most of the other multiethnic hip-hop groups in the Oslo area make no attempt at downplaying or hiding non-Norwegian accent and 'alternative' grammar. While the first Norwegian rappers in the early 1990s worked hard to sound like their American rap idols, Minoritet1 performers take pride in promoting their own 'street language', marking themselves as different and positioning themselves locally. Thus, they shape a stylized performance language which underscores and puts into play their identity as young immigrant rappers, emphasizing and producing the position of the ethnically defined 'other'. Through music performance, language style becomes a trademark for the hip-hop crew by affirming and celebrating ethnic otherness as well as images of social marginality.

It could almost seem natural that the majority language is unsuitable for spreading the message of the minority – Minoritet1. Through their 'street language' they create links to a particular local environment, and challenge linguistic norms, established language culture and norms for acceptable language use. Minoritet1 use their hybrid language variety as part of their own socially critical project, challenging everything from the parent generation to public authorities to prevailing attitudes in society. 'Street language' works as a cultural and social act of resistance.

Signifyin(g) in the Hip-Hop Vernacular

Besides 'kebabnorsk', another language designation that Minoritet1 pick up and Signify upon is 'Norsk 2' (Norwegian 2). This is the term used in the Norwegian school system for classes in 'Norwegian as a second language', which several Minoritet1 members report having attended with disgust, describing it as inferior to the regular Norwegian classes attended by their native Norwegian schoolmates. In the following example from their lyrics the term 'Norsk 2' is reappropriated: Inverted ironically into an alternative label for their own 'street language'.

jeg er gutten som chiller'n og alltid tar det med ro	I am the boy that chills out and always takes it easy
viser en finger og sier 'fuck you'	show one finger and say 'fuck you'
driter rett opp på norsken,	shit straight on Norwegian,
jeg rapper på Norsk 2	I rap in 'Norsk 2'
så sett deg ned og chill, kebab shit	so sit down and chill [out], kebab shit
det er jeg som får det til	I'm the one that makes it
leker med ord som om det var et rapspill	playing with words as if it was a rap game
	From 'Vi lever en gang' (We live once).

By 'playing with words as if it was a rap game', the performer is here promoting the minor language (Deleuze & Guattari, 1988) through the construction of difference against the major: Norsk 2/'street language' versus standard Norwegian. This kind of Signifyin(g) by repetition and difference, upon terms originally used in the dominant culture to oppress minorities – or in the case of Norsk 2 at least perceived as oppressive – is found in several other Minoritet1 songs. 'Svarting' (black person, literally 'nigger'), 'pakkis' (pejorative for Pakistani), 'svartskalle' (blackskull), 'utlendingjævel' (foreigner devil/bastard) and 'flyktingejævel' (refugee devil/bastard), are all originally insulting terms for non-western immigrants that Minoritet1 reappropriate and style themselves with through their lyrics. These terms can also regularly be heard in conversation within the group, with varying degrees of paradoxical irony and sarcasm; an irony which depends on, but also challenges connotations of inferiority. As in their song titled 'Velkommen til svartskalle borettslag' (Welcome to blackskull community) these terms have a double connotation, serving both as an announcement of 'this is how people of the majority label us' and as an ironical self-designation, which also includes a proclamation of the subaltern position. It must also be noted that when hip-hop performers in Scandinavia engage with 'blackness' in their lyrics and language games, it should be understood more as a key metaphor of marginalization and oppression than a category relating to their own skin color or ethnic background (cf. Cutler, 2008).

Difference and Ambiguity

As argued in research on the music of immigrant groups in Scandinavia (Hammarlund, 1990; Knudsen, 2006, 2004; Lundberg *et al.*, 2003) one of the primary functions of group specific music culture among minorities is the production of difference. This tendency toward articulating, maintaining and celebrating cultural practices that mark the particularity of the immigrant community in relation to majority culture, is often overlooked in official 'multicultural' policies, which tend to cling to images of music as a universal language with the capacity to break down cultural barriers and serve as a tool to stimulate integration.

The Signifyin(g) play of similarity and difference is a core principle of hip-hop's verbal practices. Rapping and singing in a 'different' novel language is a marker of community as well as boundaries – social belonging as well as social distancing. Using 'street language' on stage is a public expression of the group's difference and particularity. Outsiders who invariably have to struggle hard to understand just the basic vocabulary employed will often take 'street language' as a manifestation implying something like 'we have something in common that we don't share with others'. Thus, the cultural practices of Minoritet1 are, on the one hand, imbued with powerful notions of social distancing versus majority culture, but on the other hand, loudly affirm and celebrate their own hybrid community through the creative development of a cross-cultural mode of expression.

The discursive play of Signifyin(g) is a verbal performance mode confronting the listener with uncertainty and disorder. Minoritet1 lyrics reflect some of the almost genre-defining characteristics of hip-hop language: Irony, sarcasm and ambiguity; enhancing the impression of a subculture: Secretive and 'underground'. It is not supposed to be easy for outsiders to grasp all the different layers of meaning. The lyrics are loaded with ambiguity, comprising explicit warnings against drugs and crime alongside narratives of enjoying getting stoned and powerful expressions of resistance toward the police and public authorities. This can be understood in view of the different social discourses the group is involved in and the images of themselves they want to present to their audiences. On the one hand, they position themselves within the frames of a 'gangster discourse': Tough, fearless and smart; powerfully opposing law and order (Sandberg, 2009; Sandberg & Pedersen, 2006: 238). On the other hand, they operate within a conventional 'positive youth discourse': They produce their music in a studio at a public youth center where they depend on behaving reliably and responsibly, and may even play the role of ambassadors of the local community when performing at public events arranged by youth organisations. In these circumstances they will generally be understood as examples of successful integration and positive youth work. Still, performing at such events does not stop them from encouraging their young audiences to join them in the aggressive chanting of: 'fuck baosh, fuck baosh' ('baosh': 'police', from Berber), for example at a youth event arranged by the Red Cross (01.11.2005). It must also be added that as the group has developed professionally and become more exposed by the mainstream media, they have somewhat moderated their 'gangster image' by downplaying the most explicit references to illegal activities.

The elusive and ambiguous character of the lyrics will often leave both outsiders and the more initiated fans with questions regarding how seriously or literally they are to be taken. It would be a mistake to take Minoritet1 lyrics – or most any rap lyrics for that matter – entirely at face value. But still, if we were to dismiss them as only figural speech based on an indiscriminate appropriation of expressions from role models in American gangster rap, we would miss the underlying connotations of the resistance vernacular. For many Minoritet1 members their engagement in a culture of resistance is rooted in personal experiences of exclusion or harassment in school and employment situations, often with racist undertones. Ultimately, their version of hip-hop should be understood as a serious political expression of resistance promoted through a playful mode of performance with multiple layers of meaning, an 'unserious seriousness' (cf. Potter, 1995: 84).

It should be noted that although a close identification with the gangster discourse of hip-hop exerts a major influence on personal and cultural identification, the members of Minoritet1 also cultivate connections to other arenas where different social and cultural codes are valid. For example, during Ramadan two of the rappers turned up late for a scheduled recording session explaining that this was because they had attended 'iftar', the ritual evening meal ending the daily fast, with their family. The composition of the various cultural orientations of each member provides an image of cultural hybridity based on complex narratives of the self continuously negotiated in social interaction. A key part of each performer's cultural competence consists of relating in relevant ways to the diverse – sometimes seemingly contradictory – social discourses they are connected to: In musical recordings and stage performances, in lyrics and language, and in the common social interaction of daily life.

Taking part in different social settings evidently has a strong influence on the use of language varieties. Minoritet1 members practice extensive code-switching – using different levels of 'street language' according to different social situations. The impression that emerges from observations, interviews and recordings is that there is a low concentration of characteristic 'street language' features in conversations with adult outsiders (such as the inquisitive researcher), an intermediate concentration in in-group conversations, and without doubt, the highest occurrence is found in the stylized language of their lyrics. This testifies to the central position of rap performance as an arena for promoting language as the trademark of the social group.

Street Language Features in Lyrics

As Androutsopoulos (2001: 4) argues, rap lyrics developed in multilingual settings employ stylized versions of the hip-hop vernacular, characterized by the exaggeration of typical linguistic features. Minoritet1 lyrics employ and accentuate the whole gamut of characteristic lexical, grammatical and phonetic variables of the urban multiethnolectal language varieties that are described elsewhere (Aasheim, 1995; Drange, 2002; Opsahl & Nistov, this volume). Moreover, rap lyrics characteristically contain a great variety of terms related to sex, drugs and crime. Various less respectful terms for females are 'larki' (Punjabi), 'kæbe (Berber), 'puta' (Spanish), 'morta' (Punjabi) and 'bitch' (English). Hashish and marihuana may be called 'tjall' (Norwegian slang), 'kif' (Berber and Arabic), 'sortah' (Urdu), 'shit' (English), 'joint' (English) or 'pito' (Spanish). 'Baosh' (Berber) is the prevailing term for police.

There is a frequent occurrence of key terms affirming the imagery of an 'underground' urban culture, such as 'gate' (street, Norwegian), 'kempo' (neighborhood, Berber) and 'ghetto' (English). These are often used in an innovative way, as adjectives or adverbs: 'han snakker gate' (he speaks street), 'slutt å lek gate' (stop acting street), 'det låter helt ghetto' (it sounds really ghetto). Minoritet1 lyrics also contain a range of concepts from the international language of hip-hop: Battling, scratching, DJs, freestyling and dissing. Some typical rap terms appear in translated versions: 'å spytte rim' (to spit rhymes) or 'jeg spiser dere' (I'll eat you up – a common hip-hop expression for beating someone in MC-battling: the duel of rap music performance).

A common grammatical deviation in Minoritet1 lyrics is the simplification of genus (cf. Opsahl & Nistov, this volume). Typically the neuter tends to be substituted by the masculine form: 'mitt liv', 'mitt rim' (my life, my rhymes) becomes 'min liv', 'min rim', – or occasionally vice versa: 'min ære', 'min flokk' (my honor, my flock/gang) becomes 'mitt ære', 'mitt flokk'. This deviation, may even be used inconsistently within a single phrase, as in the following example, which starts out by Signifyin(g) upon the first lines of the Norwegian national anthem,[2] followed by claiming the right to stay in Norway. Here the definite article first appears correctly in the neuter ('dette', this) and just after in the grammatically deviant masculine ('den', it).

*ja, vi elsker **dette** landet*	yes, we love this country
*som **den** stiger frem*	as it rises forth
denne går til alle i landet	this goes to everyone in the country
med de tusen hjem	with the thousand homes
for det er [en] ny tid nå	for it's [a] new time now
så prøv å forstå	so try to understand
vi er kommet for å bli	we have come to stay
vi kan'ke gå	we cannot leave
	From 'Ny tid nå' (New time now)

Connections between Language and Music

The remainder of this chapter explores the use of various 'street language' features in rap lyrics in view of the stylistic requirements of hip-hop style and the overall purpose of creating powerful rap performances. The intriguing question this raises is whether the development of multiethnolectal language varieties can be linked to the rhymes and rhythms of rap and the mediation of this stylized performance speech. As argued by Androutsopoulos (2001: 21) stylized ethnolectal speech presented through the media influences and actually induces language crossing in daily speech.

Scandinavian performers of rap music have a high awareness of how language functions as a performative expression of style. A number of ethnic Norwegian rappers report that their mother tongue is unsuitable as a rap language. They experience Norwegian language as halting, jagged and difficult to adapt to the flow of the beat (Opsahl, 2000: 197–198). Likewise, several Minoritet1 members maintain in interviews that rapping in Norwegian can be problematic: 'It's difficult because there are so many words ending with "e"... It's hard to make powerful line endings' (author's translation). When they nevertheless have chosen to use Norwegian – or at least a kind of Norwegian – as their medium, it seems that their most obvious strategy for coping with the problems they experience is to adjust performance language in accordance with their own conceptions of the rhythmic, poetic and stylistic ideals of rap.

Certain alterations in prosody, which also appear in daily speech (cf. Svendsen & Røyneland, 2008) are apparently exploited consciously in order to create a 'flow' that successfully meets the requirements of the genre. One of the most salient features is the violation of the prevailing trochaic pronunciation of two-syllable words in Norwegian, a norm which implies that the second-last syllable is followed by a final unstressed syllable, often an 'e'. In Minoritet1 lyrics – especially at line endings – this is substituted by a jambic pronunciation featuring a stressed final syllable with a prolonged vowel (cf. Kotsinas & Doggelito, 2004: 145). Examples include **'mørket'** (the darkness), **'fengsel'** (prison) **'elven'** (the river) and **'solskinn'** (sunshine). A similar prosodic change is found in multi-syllable words. Dactylic pronunciation becomes anapaestic: **'hi**mmelen' (heaven) becomes 'himmel**en'** and **'na**bolag' (neighborhood) becomes 'nabol**ag'**. In some cases this deviation is consistently employed – apparently with a parodic undertone. The following excerpt from a Minoritet1 recording – an ironic/self-ironic rendition of a young man's dream of showing off in an expensive flashy car – demonstrates how the requirements of rhyming in rap are accomplished by altering standard South-East Norwegian prosody. Words that do not rhyme in standard pronunciation are 'forced' to do so by stressing and prolonging the final syllable, thereby producing more 'powerful line endings'. It can even be noticed, in line 15, that an extra stressed 'eh' with no obvious semantic meaning is added in order to accomplish this effect. (Stressed syllables violating standard trochaic/dactylic pronunciation are indicated with **bold**).

1.	*en BMW cabriolet*	a BMW cabriolet
2.	*sjof for en pakkis der, 7 ser***ie**	look ['sjof' from Berber] at the 'pakkis' there,
3.		7 series[3]
4.	*sjekk de 21 tommer felg***ene**	check those 21 inch rims
5.	*2,5 og 16V*	2,5 and 16V[4]
6.	*M1 styla og senka ned*	M1-styled and lowered
7.	*så alle kan se oss komme rullen***de**	so everyone can see us come rolling
8.	*men jeg har sota alle rut***ene**	but I have tinted all the windows
9.	*så ingen kan se oss trekke sortah ned*	so no-one can see us inhale the marihuana ['sortah', from Urdu]
10.	*ikke nok med det,*	and there is more,
11.	*bare et lite anlegg med GPS*	just a little system with GPS
12.	*og DVD*	and DVD
13.	*og alle setene*	and all the seats
14.	*har MTV*	have MTV
15.	*så det er bare å lene seg tilba***ke**	so all we've got to do is lean back
16.	*og bare slapp' av,* **eh**	and just relax, eh
17.	*puff puff, og pass den videre*	puff, puff and pass it on
		From 'Hva skjer'a?' (What's up?)

From the perspective of music analysis, the logical rationale for these violations of standard pronunciation can be linked to the typical rhythmic basis of most hip-hop beats. A defining characteristic of rock music and the many popular music styles that derive from it, is the backbeat, a sharp rhythmic accent on the second and fourth beats of a measure in 4/4 time typically marked by the snare drum.: 1–**2**–3–**4**. This rhythmic phrasing implies a strong tendency to match the rhythm by placing a stressed syllable at line endings, consequently favoring jambic and anapaestic pronunciation at line endings. In the example above, this rhythmic delivery is crucial to obtaining the desired ironic/self-ironic effect – Signifyin(g) upon young immigrants' dreams and ambitions.

Another feature which can be linked to the poetic and musical structures of rap is the tendency to concentrate the verbal message using an abbreviated 'telegram style'. Most of the music beats used by Minoritet1 favor short poetic lines with end rhymes. This encourages the tendency to pack as much essential information as possible into every line so that each line efficiently communicates a coherent statement or 'punch line'. As described in other forms of stylized ethnolectal speech (Androutsopoulos, 2001: 6) prepositions, articles and implicitly understood verbs are left out. As the following example indicates, a more conventional South-East Norwegian rendition would loose much of the desired 'flow' and rhythmic punch. Words 'left out' are placed in brackets [...].

og vis dem [at] vi kan gjøre	and show them [that] we can do
[det] bedre vi [som kommer]	[it] better, we [who come]
fra [et] fremmed land	from [a] foreign country
for Inshallah, en dag alt blir bedre, mann.	for Inshallah[5], some day everything will be better, man.
	From 'Fuck det man' (Fuck it man)

The final phrase here also includes a breach with the conventional syntax of standard Norwegian which, like other Scandinavian and most Germanic languages, follows the V2 word order rule implying that the second constituent in declarative main clauses is always a verb, giving a XVS word order, where 'X' is a topicalized element, 'V' the finite verb and 'S' the subject (cf. Ganuza; Opsahl & Nistov, this volume). Thus the standard Norwegian word order would be 'en dag **blir alt** bedre' instead of 'en dag **alt blir** bedre' (some day everything will be better). In the following example, the violation of this word order rule is apparently legitimized by the need to meet the demand for end rhymes in rap style. A South-East Norwegian word order in the last part of the first phrase would be 'nå **glemte jeg** det', which would not rhyme well with the last two words of the next phrase ('hun gjemte den').

jeg skrev det ned mann, men nå jeg glemte det	I wrote it down, man, but now I forgot it
mora mi fant rimeboka og hun gjemte den	my mother found the book of rhymes and she hid it
	From 'Tæsha unger' (Beaten kids)

A third example, in which the lyrics evoke childhood memories of the family fleeing from war in the Balkans, emphasises this point. The standard Norwegian word order 'hva Jernbanetorget var' ('what Jernbanetorget[6] was') would not rhyme with the preceding phrase.

husker lenge før, før Oslo og Norge,	remember long before, before Oslo and Norway
lenge før jeg visste hva var Jernbanetorget	long before I knew what was Jernbanetorget
da du kom inn på rommet, sa pakk alt med [det] samma	when you came into the room, said pack everything at once
gjorde alt du kunne for å få oss ut av landet	did all you could to get us out of the country
	From 'Sønn' (Son)

The Mistake Becomes a 'Take'

All the variations described so far violate standard norms of grammar and pronunciation. Accordingly, they may easily be understood as language mistakes based on lack of knowledge or training in the 'major language'. When observing a language variety with connections to hip-hop culture and rap lyrics we should pay close attention to the social and performative role of 'the mistake', and the process of incorporating 'mistakes' into spoken language. As shown in various Scandinavian studies, deviations from standard language do not necessarily mean that the speakers don't know better (Quist, 2008: 44–45; Svendsen & Røyneland, 2008: 65–66). 'Errors' that initially are committed due to lack of language proficiency may become fashionable in a language community; gradually stabilized and established as characterizing language features. This process is apparently boosted by the inclusion and exploitation of 'mistakes' in lyrics performed from a stage or mediated otherwise (cf. Androutsopoulos, 2001). For many young people with an immigrant background, the hip-hop performers of Oslo's inner east suburbs are local role models and idols; admired and looked up to. Their puns and punch-lines uttered from stage and distributed on 'underground' recordings are seen as valid interpretations of the life world of urban youth. Consequently, many of their rhymes and phrases are copied, remembered and included in the daily speech of audiences and fans. In this way, over time, mediated utterances serve to establish, maintain and celebrate 'mistakes', not only as new language indicators, but as signs of protest, opposition and resistance. As in the earlier quoted paraphrasing of the national anthem where the 'mistaken' genus supplies an additional level of ironic meaning, deviation from standard spoken language becomes a strategic move in its own right. Thus, the 'mistake' becomes a 'take': A Signifyin(g) take on the major language.

The variations, deviations and 'mistakes' discussed in this chapter suggest a reciprocal correspondence between the local multiethnolectal speech style and the rhythms and poetics of urban rap music. For the producers and performers of this music, the multifaceted linguistic setting they live in provides a much richer basis for experimentation and innovative variation than a less diverse cultural environment would. When the standard Norwegian expressions do not match their intentions – poetically, rhythmically or stylistically – there is a wide palette of alternatives within their reach. Just as the distribution of mediated music through the Internet opens up for picking and choosing beats and music samples from all over the world and using them in local music production, a multiethnic and multilingual environment affords a vast variety to choose from, appropriate, Signify upon and develop. Since hip-hop in itself is basically an art of improvisation, requiring spontaneity and reinvention from moment to moment, the performance and production of rap music must be regarded as an important empowering force in language development, stimulating the linguistic creativity of the emerging urban multiethnolectal speech styles of Scandinavia.

Notes

1. See Solomon (2005) for a discussion of the 'underground' metaphor in rap music.
2. Original version: 'Ja, vi elsker dette landet, som det stiger frem, furet, værbitt over vannet, med de tusen hjem'. English translation: 'Yes, we love this country, as it rises forth, rocky, weathered, above the sea, with those thousand homes'.
3. BMW top series.
4. BMW motor specifications.
5. Inshallah: If Allah wills; usually said when referring to a situation in the future.
6. Jernbanetorget: Square in central Oslo, part of a major drug-dealing area.

Chapter 14
'Rinkeby Swedish' in the Mind of the Beholder. Studying Listener Perceptions of Language Variation in Multilingual Stockholm

E. BIJVOET and K. FRAURUD

Introduction

Today's multilingual urban spaces in Scandinavia encompass – besides various diasporic versions of minority languages – a wide diversity of ways of speaking the majority languages, including learners' language, styles associated with multiethnic urban youth and potentially emerging local sociolects.[1] Despite sporadic studies following the pioneering work of Kotsinas (1985, 1988a) and, more recently, a number of larger research projects (e.g. Källström & Lindberg, forthcoming; Quist, 2005; Svendsen, this volume), we are only now beginning to understand the complexity of this linguistic reality. One insight gained so far, we believe, is that this object of study calls for contributions from many different theoretical and methodological approaches – several of which are represented by the other chapters of this volume.

This chapter is the first report from a perception study carried out within the project *Sociolinguistic awareness and language attitudes in multilingual contexts* (SALAM).[2] The study focuses on language variation as related to inter- and intragroup interaction (rather than, e.g. on language variation and change). The aim of the study is to explore how young people, navigating in the linguistic space of Stockholm, perceive their own and others' ways of speaking, and what kind of constructions underlie various labels attached to different ways of speaking. One notorious such label is 'rinkebysvenska' (Rinkeby Swedish), named after Stockholm's best-known multiethnic suburb Rinkeby – a place name loaded with connotations about immigration and multiethnicity.

An incentive for our research was and is the role that this notion played and still plays in discourses on multilingualism and education. In 2000, when both of us were working at the Rinkeby Institute of Multilingual Research, one of the frequently asked questions (FAQs) to the institute was 'What is Rinkeby Swedish?', uttered with worry or curiosity by parents, teachers and journalists – but also by young people who themselves were 'expected' to speak this new language. One way of answering was to return the question both to alleged speakers and to other language users. Results from an interview study (Bijvoet, 2003) as well as informal observations of media discourse suggested a wide disagreement in peoples' semantic extensions of the label Rinkeby Swedish; for some users it appeared to be a specific form of slang, while for others it covered all kinds of 'foreign sounding Swedish', and so on. More systematic knowledge was called for. The Gothenburg-Lund-Stockholm research project *Language and language use among adolescents in multilingual urban settings* (SUF),[3] that started about the same time gave us access to over 300 hours of recordings and a range of other data types (see Boyd, this volume). In the course of that project, we and other project members gradually found ourselves talking more often about language variation generally than about alleged language varieties such as Rinkeby Swedish or – after Gothenburg and Malmö suburbs – 'Gårdstenska' or 'Rosengård Swedish' (cf. Boyd & Fraurud, 2010). To us, available data and analyses suggest that there is no cohesive and well-defined variety of Rinkeby Swedish that can be connected to a homogeneous and delimited speech community (cf. Fraurud & Boyd, 2006; Ganuza, 2008; Kotsinas, 1994: 144). Moreover, there is often a considerable distance between popular beliefs about the structure of young speakers' language and their actual practices (Källström, 2006).

We believe that, in studying the complex linguistic phenomena referred to by labels such as Rinkeby Swedish, we should beware of simplistic notions of alleged varieties linked to imagined speech communities. Instead, the present study departs from a notion of varieties as abstractions or social constructions – made by lay people as well as linguists – rather than 'things' (cf. Bijvoet & Fraurud, 2008; Jaspers, 2007; Le Page, 1977). It takes as its object of study these very constructions in the way they are reflected in listeners' perceptions of language variation. Inspiration for this approach is found, in particular, in the research paradigms of folk linguistics and perceptual dialectology (cf. e.g. Kristiansen, 2006; Kulbrandstad, 2002; Niedzielski & Preston, 2003; Preston, 2010).

The main purpose of this chapter is to present the research design and the first results of the SALAM study on young peoples' different constructions of contemporary linguistic variation in Stockholm. First, we describe the methodology. Then we report some results from selected data. Finally, we briefly discuss an example of macro level influences on peoples' constructions. We hope to illustrate the potential in the present context of a systematic investigation of perceptions and, furthermore, of integrating different data types – quantitative as well as qualitative – in such an investigation.

Design of the Study

In a listener experiment, the matched/verbal guise technique (Lambert *et al.*, 1960) was used to assess listeners' perceptions of variation and varieties in the linguistic space of young Stockholm. 'Perception' is here taken to embrace both language attitudes in a traditional sense and sociolinguistic awareness, that is awareness of linguistic differences and social meanings associated with these. The design involved eliciting and combining different data types, quantitative as well as qualitative. This design was developed through a series of pilot studies, one of which is reported in Bijvoet and Fraurud (2008, forthcoming).[4]

Speech samples of 20–25 s each were elicited from a total of 48 speakers aged 17–21, all living in Stockholm.[5] The speakers differed with regard to linguistic, ethnic and social background. The stimuli were elicited by means of a method developed to produce speech stimuli that were spontaneous and peer directed at the same time as the content was controlled. The speakers were asked to make an imaginary phone call to a good friend, more or less closely following a specified structure. They were encouraged to use their own words and ways of speaking. In order to avoid verbatim repetition, no written manuscript was provided; instead the speakers listened to a couple of sample 'phone calls' recorded earlier. This procedure generated stimuli with a neutral and closely similar content. The speakers could be re-recorded until they were themselves satisfied with the recording and each speaker produced two to five 'phone calls'. Depending on the preferences of the speakers, they were sometimes recorded individually and sometimes with an 'audience' of close peers. The best recordings (with respect to spontaneity, fluency, etc.) were obtained when – as was often the case – the speakers deeply projected themselves into the envisaged situation, and when both the speaker and his/her friends were engaged in the process of evaluating and selecting samples. In all, 161 speech samples were obtained from the 48 speakers. After testing a first selection of recordings on a small listener panel, 12 samples – from six male and six female speakers – were finally selected as stimuli.

In the experiment, the stimuli were played back to 16 groups of listeners attending nine senior high schools in different areas of Stockholm ($N = 343$), each school represented by at least 30 students. The listeners had varying ethnic and social background as well as linguistic experiences. Their median age was 17.

The nine senior high schools involved in our study are indicated on the Stockholm subway map in Figure 14.1. In a very simplified way the nine schools can be characterized in terms of mono-/multilingualism and social class as follows[6]:

School(s)	Gross characterization
City East, North East	Monolingual and middle/upper class, economic capital[7]
City South	Monolingual and middle/upper class, cultural capital
South, Near South	Monolingual and working class
City West	Mixed mono-/multilingual and working/middle class
South West, North West, North	Multilingual and working /middle class

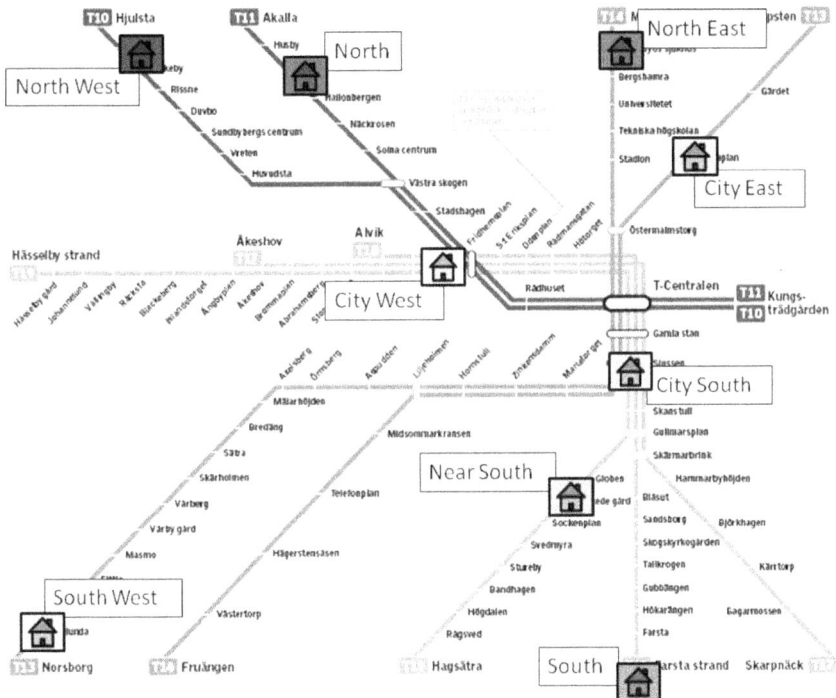

Figure 14.1 Stockholm subway map with schools participating in the study

The 343 listeners participated by filling in a questionnaire containing open as well as multiple choice questions. First, they listened to the stimuli one at a time and evaluated each speaker on semantic differential scales of the kind frequently used in language attitude studies (Garret et al., 2003: 63–66). Second, they listened again to the stimuli, now making guesses about the speakers' linguistic and social background – partly directly by appraising parents' mother tongue and speaker's length of residence in Sweden, and partly indirectly, by indicating the speaker's area of residence on a Stockholm subway map included in the questionnaire (choosing one of the altogether 100 stations). The listeners could also comment on their subway station guesses. Furthermore, they were asked, for each speaker, how they would label the kind of Swedish they were listening to.

After the whole listener group had filled in the questionnaire, three to five students selected among those volunteering to elaborate their views on language variation in Stockholm participated in a semidirected group discussion. In all, 20% of all the listeners ($N = 69$) took part in these discussions, having an average length of 40 minutes, yielding about ten hours of recordings. As a point of departure for the discussions, speech samples were played back again and the participants were asked questions about, among other things, how they would position their own way of speaking in relation to four of the samples, and how they would group these speakers with regard to likely friendships. They were also asked to associate freely about several speakers. Furthermore, they reported on their familiarity with and perceptions of different neighborhoods in Stockholm. The group discussion provided opportunities for deepened dialogue with the participants and supplied further detail on their perceptions. These data constitute an essential tool for our interpretation of the questionnaire data.

Results: Reactions to Speaker Leo alias Sam

So far only part of the extensive questionnaire and group discussion data has been analyzed. Here a selection of data will serve to illustrate the methodology developed for this study. Note that the interpretation of every instance of data is context dependent in the sense that reactions of one particular listener group (or individual listener) to one particular speech sample can only be fully interpreted in the light of data from other listeners and speech samples. Consequently, as more listeners and speech samples are included in the analysis, our understanding of data will deepen, yielding more elaborate and perhaps modified interpretations.

We will focus on the listeners' reactions to two of the twelve speech stimuli. Unlike the other ten stimuli, these two were produced by one and the same speaker (a matched guise). The speaker has Turkish parents, is born in Sweden and has lived all his life in Rinkeby. He has himself attended the school here called North West. We got to know him in the SUF project mentioned above, where he also proved to be very attentive to different ways of speaking Swedish and talented in imitating and stylizing different speakers. He produced his first speech sample (referred to as 'speaker Leo') when asked (just like all the other speakers) to imagine talking to a close friend. The second sample (referred to as 'speaker Sam') was produced when he was asked to speak the way he might when accommodating to a 'typical (monolingual) Swede'. The use of these matched guises as well as our listeners' reactions to these and other stimuli might, we believe, in interesting ways fuel the discussion on the notion of authenticity (cf. e.g. Coupland, 2003; Eckert, 2003). Space does not, however, allow a discussion on this issue here. Let us only note that, while most of our listeners did not question the authenticity of any of the speakers or speech samples, a few of them attach labels including the modifier 'fake' or 'wannabe' to Leo's and/or Sam's ways of speaking – as well as to some of the other stimuli.

Transcripts of two of the speech stimuli (with semiliteral English translation):

Leo: *ah hallå # ah shoo bror # lyssna # mina batterier e fett låga ja(g) # ah ## lyssna ja(g) träffa(de) på en snubbe på vägen han behövde pengar ## [smackljud] så vi gick förbi eh en bankautomat # den funka(de) inte vi gick ti(ll) nästa ## men ja(g) har fixat problemet ah # men lyssna ja(g) blir fett försenad ti(ll) bion # tagga du dit direkt # ja(g) kommer dit så möts vi där utanför # okej # tja*

'yea hi # yea hi brother # listen # my batteries are fat low I # yea ## listen I met a buddy on the way he needed money ## [tongue click] so we passed a cash machine # it didn't work we went to the next one ## but I have fixed the problem yea # but listen I'll be fat late to the cinema # move on there directly # I come there so we meet there outside # okay # bye'

Sam: *ah hej # du # mina batterier e jättelåga så ja(g) måste prata jättesnabbt nu # ah ja(g) blir lite försenad # # nej ja(g) träffa(de) på en kompis på vägen och eh han behövde låna lite pengar # å första bankomaten va(r) trasig så vi va(r) tvung(en) å gå vidare ti(ll) nästa # # ah # men men eh går de(t) bra om vi träffas utanför biografen # # ah va(d) bra # ah # hej*

'yea hello # you # my batteries are real low so I have to speak real fast now # yea I will be a bit late ## well I met a friend on the way and eh he needed to borrow some money # and the first cash dispenser was broken so we had to go on to the next one ## yea # but but eh is it okay if we meet outside the cinema ## yea fine # ah # goodbye'

Differences between the two samples from this speaker in his two guises are found at several linguistic and extra-linguistic levels. Judging from spontaneous comments on Leo's speech during the play back in the group discussions, the most salient features in this sample seem to be on the levels of lexicon and prosody. It contains several (comparatively) new slang words and expressions associated with the multilingual suburb, for example 'shoo bror' (hi brother), but also instances of old Stockholm slang, for example 'snubbe' (guy). Leo also uses the word 'bankautomat' (cash machine), rather than the more idiomatic 'bankomat', something which attracts the attention of many listeners. In contrast, Sam does not use any (new or old) slang words. As noted by several listeners, however, instead of 'bio', the most usual word for cinema, he chooses the almost archaic 'biograf', pronounced slowly and clearly.

The impression reported by several listeners that Sam speaks with a generally higher pitch than Leo is not supported by acoustic analysis; Sam's mean pitch is, in fact, lower (147.34 Hz)[8] than Leo's (185.31 Hz). Rather it seems to be due to Sam's considerably wider pitch range (81.86–475.42 Hz) as compared to Leo's (81.36–310.86 Hz). The two speech samples also appear to differ in speech rate. A comparison of closely parallel constructions shows that Leo speaks faster than Sam, for example:

Example 1:

Leo: *mina batterier e fett låga* 'my batteries are fat low' (1.6 s)
Sam: *mina batterier e jättelåga* 'my batteries are real low' (1.9 s)

Leo's speech sample does not contain any morphosyntactic features associated with either learner language or nonstandard varieties. Interestingly, Sam's sample contains one (albeit barely perceivable) instance of a numerous incongruent present participle:

Example 2:

vi va(r) tvung(e)n [standard Swedish: tvungna] 'we had to'.
we be-PAST obliged-SING [standard Swedish: obliged-PLUR]

None of the 343 listeners detected that the samples were produced by one and the same speaker, and many of them would hardly believe it when told afterwards.

Guesses on speakers' background

When asked to guess where in Stockholm Leo lives, there was a considerable agreement among the 343 listeners, as displayed in Figure 14.2a, where each listener's guess is represented by a star.[9] Nearly all of them

'Rinkeby Swedish' in the Mind of the Beholder   177

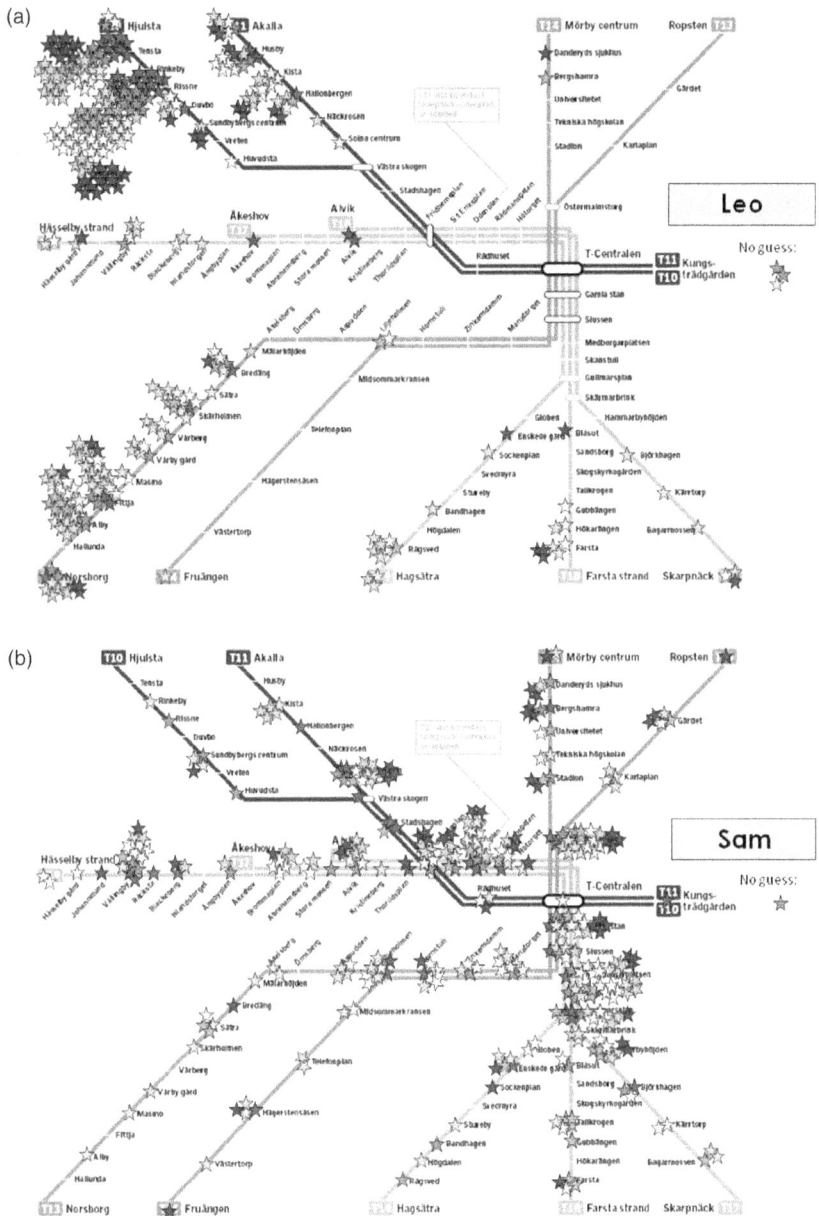

Figure 14.2 All listeners' guesses on speaker (a) Leo's place of residence and (b) Sam's place of residence

guessed that Leo lived in one of the multilingual suburbs, primarily located in the North West or South West outskirts of Stockholm. In fact, as many as one fourth of the listeners choose Rinkeby (which happens to be exactly the correct subway station). This is a higher number than for any other speaker–station combination in the whole study (the next highest was one fifth of the listeners who combined Rinkeby with Daniel, a speaker with a strong foreign accent). This clearly illustrates the emblematic character of Rinkeby in the consciousness of many people, and its association with a diversity of conceptions of 'foreign sounding Swedish', whether connected to multilingual youth, immigrants or second language users.

We can also discern some interesting differences between listeners from different schools. For example, in the City South school only one of 32 students indicate Rinkeby as Leo's subway station – in contrast to other listener groups. One possible explanation is that the students at this school tend to be highly aware of stereotypes and prejudices about immigrants and attempt to avoid such attitudes. Such an awareness surfaced during the group discussion in participants' meta-comments on their own performance and their inclination to question their spontaneous reactions. This may in turn be related to this school's possession of more cultural capital than the other schools.

For the same speaker in the guise of Sam, the guesses were much more scattered (Figure 14.2b). According to the listeners as a group he could live almost anywhere in Stockholm – *except* in the most multilingual suburbs. Most of them associate his way of speaking with either the more or less gentrified inner city (including the wealthiest neighborhoods) or the formerly monolingual suburbs now attracting socially mobile families from adjacent multilingual neighborhoods, such as, Vällingby (in the West of Stockholm). Clues for interpreting these scattered guesses are found in other data types of the study. For example, in a group discussion at City East school one participant perceived Sam's speech as 'a mixture between Söder [lit. South, that is Southern part of the city, traditionally associated with working class] and the inner city', while another listener, from the South school, said 'I wrote Stadion [subway station near the City East school] and then I wrote rich man's child'. A bilingual listener from the same school focused less on class and more on the speaker's linguistic background: 'I actually thought it sounded like an immigrant trying to speak in a very Swedish way […] 'cause he pronounced every single letter [imitating an exaggerated pronunciation] *see you at the c i n e m a'*. A listener from the multilingual North West school was even more assertive, stating with a laughter: 'trust me, he's not a Swede!'. Yet other (not necessarily incompatible!) perspectives are provided by the labeling data, where Sam's speech was characterized by a variety of labels, including 'pure Swedish' (for further examples, see section 'Labeling ways of speaking'). It seems likely that this diversity of perceptions can be related to, among other things, the listeners' own social and linguistic background.

Listeners' perceptions of Leo and Sam are also reflected in guesses about their parents' mother tongues (Figure 14.3a). For a large majority of listeners (95%) Leo has a foreign background, while Sam, for a majority of listeners (70%), passes for a Swede in the (restricted) sense of someone whose parents both have only Swedish as their mother tongue. Similar

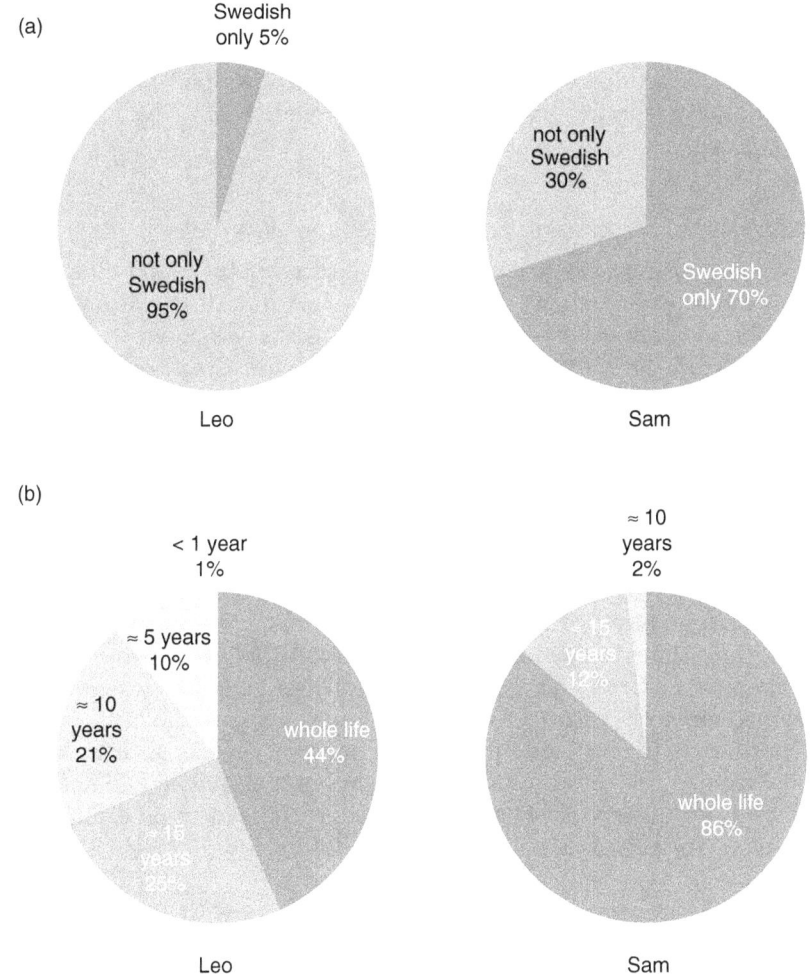

Figure 14.3 All listeners' guesses on (a) parents' mother tongues for Leo and Sam (b) Leo's and Sam's length of residence in Sweden

perceptions of the two guises are also reflected in guesses about how long the speaker has lived in Sweden (Figure 14.3b). While almost all listeners believe that Sam has lived in Sweden all his life (86%) or from an early age (12%), the guesses regarding Leo are more diverse; less than half (44%) believe that he is born in Sweden, and about a third (32%) that he has lived in Sweden for less than 10 years. It is interesting to try to relate differences in judgments between schools and/or individual listeners to their different social and linguistic experiences. Our analyses suggest that some such connections can be traced in the data, but also warns against simplifying generalizations about schools or (groups of) individuals. Let us here just mention one observation, namely that, again, the City South school (possessing cultural capital) goes against the stream, this time by showing the strongest tendency among the schools both in ascribing a foreign background to Sam (50%) and a 'Swedish only' background to Leo (13%).

Attitudes toward speakers and ways of speaking

Semantic differential scales have been employed for a long time in language attitude research with the aim to disclose attitudes toward speakers and their language in a (slightly) more indirect way than when using the kind of direct questions typical for survey studies (see above). While in fact all the different data types in the present study contribute to the analysis of listeners' language attitudes (as well as their sociolinguistic awareness), the use of semantic differential scales both provides a valuable quantitative measure for comparison between listener groups, and aids in the interpretation of the other data types.

On the basis of our pilot studies six six-graded unipolar scales were selected, involving the properties: Humorous, intelligent, well organized, self-confident, nice and tough. Through factor analysis the data from the six attitude scales were reduced to three factors that explained 79% of the variance: WELL ORGANIZED, TOUGH and HUMOROUS (with strong positive weights for well-organized–intelligent–nice, tough–self-confident and humor, respectively; Figure 14.4). The analysis reveals several evaluational differences between our speaker in his two guises, Leo and Sam, and between the schools. For sake of space, we here focus on the attitudes of four of the nine schools: The City East, City South, North West and South West.

Generally, Leo gets negative scores for the factor WELL ORGANIZED and positive for TOUGHNESS and HUMOR, while the opposite is true for Sam, in particular for the first two factors. But there are also statistically significant differences between the schools. Regarding Sam, they differ in the degree to which the factor HUMOROUS is judged to contribute to his characterization. The two monolingual schools, City South and City East, agree in

'Rinkeby Swedish' in the Mind of the Beholder 181

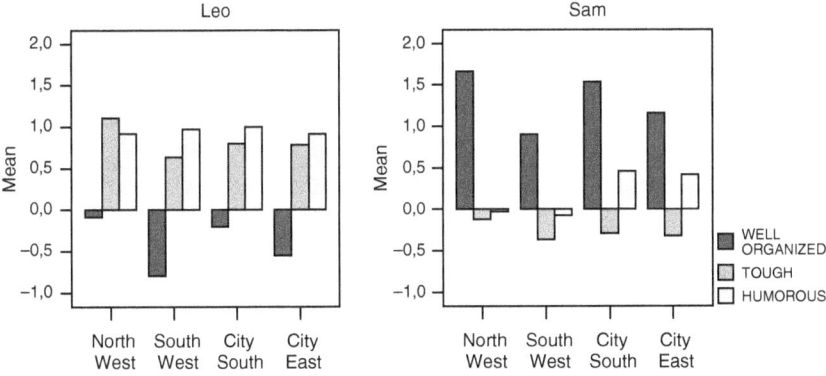

Figure 14.4 Factor analysis of attitude scales for Leo and Sam; four schools

crediting Sam with at least some degree of humor – whereas the two multilingual schools, North West and South West, do not.

Regarding Leo, there are differences in the degree to which he is judged to be 'less well organized'. At both South West (multilingual) and City East (monolingual, economic capital) this factor is negatively represented, while at North West school (multilingual) and City South (monolingual, cultural capital) listeners agree that factor WELL ORGANIZED does not contribute to the characterization of Leo.

Thus, also in semantic differential data we see that there are no *simple* relationships between listeners' perceptions and, for example, variables like mono-/multilingualism or class.

Labeling ways of speaking

The set of data in this study that in greatest detail reflects the diversity of perceptions is – together with the group discussions – generated by the labeling task, where listeners were asked to suggest labels for different ways of speaking. The use of an open question of labeling leaves maximal freedom to the listeners' own ways of describing the linguistic variation among the speakers. The decision to use an open question (rather than multiple choice) was taken after careful consideration, given that the analyses of such a large amount of qualitative data (12 speakers × 343 listeners = 4116 labels) is extremely time-demanding. Multiple choice questions on labeling were tried out in a series of minor pilot studies, but failed to capture relevant aspects of the diversity already observed in the large pilot study carried out in 2004 (Bijvoet & Fraurud, 2008, forthcoming). In this pilot study we also developed a model for classifying labels that could be taken as a basis for quantifying qualitative data in the present study. Most of this analysis remains to be done. But in order to give a first glimpse of

Table 14.1 Labels for Leo's way of speaking: Four schools, most frequent answers

Label	Translation (central element in italics)	N verbatim	Total containing central element
rinkebysvenska	*Rinkeby* Swedish	27	30
invandrarsvenska	*immigrant* Swedish	17	22
slang	*slang*	11	22
blattesvenska	*'blatte'* Swedish	8	16
förortssvenska	*suburban* Swedish	7	11
med brytning	*Broken*	2	4
ghettosvenska	*ghetto* Swedish	2	4
miljonsvenska	*million* Swedish	2	3

the diversity in labeling, we have for the purpose of this chapter made an inventory of the labels for our matched guise Leo/Sam, provided by the same four schools as in section 'Attitudes toward speakers and ways of speaking' (City East, City South, North West and South West).

The eight most frequent labels applied to Leo's speech are listed in Table 14.1, together with the numbers of verbatim occurrences as well as the total of occurrences containing the central element of these labels.[10]

Both 'blatte Swedish' and 'million Swedish' are relatively recent labels (see section 'Reflections of the Macro Level: Public Discourse and Labeling'). 'Blatte' (with unclear etymology) is – in the mouth of most outgroup speakers – a strongly derogative word for (stigmatized) immigrants (cf. Jonsson, 2007). 'Million' refers to the Swedish 'Million Program', a housing program in the 1960s and 1970s with the goal of building one million houses to meet the needs of a growing population. The labels in Table 14.1 contain elements referring to places, people and ways of speaking associated with immigrants, with one exception: 'slang', which in Sweden is neutral with regard to age and ethnicity unless further modified. It is of some interest that ten of the eleven listeners using this neutral label come from the two multilingual schools (North West and South West).

Among the 48 labels with only a single occurrence we find a variety of descriptions reflecting individual listeners' different foci of attention and sometimes completely opposite views. Some focus on correctness: 'bra svenska' (good Swedish), 'ganska bra svenska' (fairly good Swedish), 'dålig svenska' (bad Swedish), others on authenticity: 'riktig blattesvenska' (genuine blatte Swedish) vs. 'wannabe-rinkebysvenska' (wannabe Rinkeby Swedish), and for another listener this is simply 'svenska' (Swedish).

Table 14.2 Labels for Sam's way of speaking: Four schools, most frequent answers

Label	Translation (central element in italics)	N verbatim	Total containing central element
svenska	Swedish	12	[not applicable]
vanlig svenska	*ordinary* Swedish	10	19
stockholmska	*Stockholm*ian	11	17
ren svenska	*pure* Swedish	6	13
bra svenska	*good* Swedish	5	10
normal svenska	*normal* Swedish	3	3
snobbsvenska	*snobbish* Swedish	3	3
söderslang	*Söder* slang	2	8
byråkratsvenska	*bureaucrat* Swedish	2	2
innerstadssvenska	*City* Swedish	2	2
rikssvenska	*standard* Swedish	2	2
riktig svenska	*real* Swedish	2	2
överklassvenska	*upper class* Swedish	2	2

The labeling of Sam's way of speaking resulted in a disparate variety of labels (cf. the task of guessing Sam's area of residence). None of the most frequent labels, however, relate to immigrants (Table 14.2); many listeners refer to his speech as ordinary, pure, good, normal, standard or real Swedish – or simply Swedish. Others remark on class: 'snobbsvenska' (snobbish Swedish) or 'överklassvenska' (upper class Swedish).

In addition, there were altogether 63 labels with a single occurrence. Interestingly, some listeners make contrasting class associations, either explicitly, 'arbetarsvenska' (worker Swedish), or by referring to 'södersnack' (Söder talk) and similar denotations for the old Stockholm slang with roots in the former working class areas in the Southern part of the city (cf. Cockney). Some listeners sense a lack of authenticity, describing Sam as a 'fake' or 'wannabe' Swede, yet others find him effeminate: 'halvfjollig svenska' (half-effeminate Swedish) or som en 'bög' [like a gay (person)]. As many as eleven listeners detect a slight foreign accent in his speech, although describing this in different words, for example 'svenska med brytning' (Swedish with an accent), or 'vanlig svenska med italiensk brytning' (ordinary Swedish with an Italian accent).

Again we see how different listeners highlight different dimensions of language variation (e.g. social class or correctness) and value them differently (e.g. upper vs. working class), presumably depending on how they position themselves in the linguistic space of young Stockholm.

Comparing the labels of the two speech samples from this speaker (Leo/Sam), we notice a considerably higher consensus among listeners regarding Leo. Of all 12 speech stimuli Leo's is, for example, the one most frequently labeled Rinkeby Swedish. But this is not the whole story about Rinkeby Swedish; a glance at the way this label is applied to other speakers in our study reveals that this label may have very different semantic extension for different listeners at these four schools. In fact, some of them applied the label to up to eight of the 12 speakers, including speakers displaying several typical learner features but *no* suburban slang and/or speakers with a monolingual working class background.

Sam, on the other hand, was one of the speakers to whom the label never was applied. This is also one of the stimuli eliciting the most diverge reactions – something which makes it no less interesting. In fact, Sam and several other speakers in our study who do *not* easily fit into popular stereotypes but rather represent spaces in-between or 'zones of contact' (Pratt, 1987: 60) turn out to be of special importance for understanding differences in perceptions of self and others.

Navigating in the linguistic space of young Stockholm

Let us briefly consider some possible implications of perception data for preferences and choices involved in speech production, here focusing on young people with a multilingual background.

Judging from the reactions to our speaker in his two guises, a young man talking like Leo will by many people be considered tough, humorous and self-confident – but at the same time less intelligent, nice and well-organized. If he instead adjusts his speech in order to pass for a 'typical Swede', he will generally be considered more well-organized, and so on – while taking the risk to be seen as feigned or effeminate, in particular by his peers. Thus, going (too) Swedish may imply both costs and benefits.

Young language users raised in the stigmatized multilingual suburbs are particularly attentive to attitudes associated with different ways of speaking. Language is a hot topic for many of these young people; Swedishness (of course not confined to language) is continually debated and contested, and often ambivalently both strived for and challenged. During one of the group discussions two girls reflect on their own ways of speaking in different situations. On the one hand, as suggested by one of them: 'at for example a job interview you can't speak like that [referring to suburban slang words]; you must speak pure Swedish'. On the other, her classmate objects, you shouldn't go too far: 'But I feel that when you try to hide your own language [...] it's like you are trying to hide a part of yourself [...] you are not genuine. So even if I go to a job interview and I'd remove my natural way of speaking [...] I would feel more robotized, as if I just speak; no feeling, no personality. And then it seems to me that nobody would like to employ me just because I'm like a blank piece of paper' (authors' translation).

When describing the choices that people make when speaking, lay people as well as linguists often use the (railway) metaphor of *switching* – implicitly assuming the existence of clearly defined varieties. However, the complex choices engaging the two girls quoted here (as well as many other young people today) may perhaps more adequately be described as *navigating* – using a (sailing) metaphor. Navigating is a complex process involving the determination of: (1) one's own current position (self-perception), (2) the positions of alternative destinations as well as shallows and rocks (constructions of other and others' ways of speaking) and (3) the compass direction and safest course to reach the chosen destination (selection of appropriate linguistic features). This means navigating between different positions specified along dimensions of class, ethnicity, gender, authenticity, language proficiency, and so on. Without suggesting a simple causal relationship between perception and production, we may view production as a process involving a 'nautical map' of perceptions – keeping in mind that the 'nautical maps' guiding peoples' linguistic practices often are not identical.

Reflections of the Macro Level: Public Discourse and Labeling

The perceptions reflected in a study like this are products not only of local discourses and individual networks, but also of the discourses in the Swedish society at large. A macro level analysis of ideologies and discourses falls outside the scope of our own study (but see e.g. Milani, 2007a). We would here, as an example, just like to mention one macro level event, which is directly reflected in our data.

In Sweden in 2006, a language ideological debate concerning young peoples' multilingualism was initiated by the well-known literature professor Ebba Witt-Brattström, who during a panel discussion on school policy (TV24, 2006-03-26) declared: 'The government is signaling to our new Swedes that it will be good enough if they learn a bit of blatte Swedish so that they can raise a market stand and sell bananas in Rosengård' (authors' translation). The topic of the discussion was the governments' recent decision to increase the support for the use of minority languages as languages of instruction. But the following debate – which went on for weeks in daily newspapers, radio and television, as well as on the internet – came to include a number of issues related to the linguistic practices of young people with immigrant background. A wide sector of the society was engaged in the debate, ranging from the cultural elite to 'the man on the street', and a number of journalists, writers, linguists and others contributed to the heated debate.

Of particular interest for our present research is the way Witt-Brattström's deliberate use of the derogative label 'blattesvenska' seems to have legitimized its use for many speakers. This process was of course also reinforced by the subsequent use of the label in the debate [which, in fact, went under the heading 'blattedebatten' (the blatte debate)].

The blatte debate reached a wide audience, and it seems likely that this is also what is reflected in one difference that struck us between the data in our pilot study, collected in 2004, and those of the present study, collected in 2007. In the pilot study, the label 'blattesvenska' does not occur at all, while in the present study it is one of the more frequent labels. Important agents in the blatte debate were the journalists around the monthly magazine Gringo, which also published a supplement to the free daily newspaper

Äntligen har du fått ro

Rinkebysvenskan

*1981-2006

*Närmast sörjande är
kultureliten som födde dig.*

*Dina barn Blattesvenska och
Miljonsvenska kommer föra ditt
stolta arv vidare.*

*Bara de slutar bråka.
Må du vilish i fred. Jao.*

Figure 14.5 Obituary notice for the label Rinkeby Swedish (from Gringo supplement of *Metro*)

Metro. Having personal experience of growing up in the multilingual suburb, these young journalists vividly opposed the literature professor. As regards labels of new ways of speaking the majority language, they suggest that both 'rinkebysvenska' and 'blattesvenska' should be replaced by 'miljonsvenska'. They even prophesied the 'death' of 'rinkebysvenska' by formulating its obituary notice (Figure 14.5): 'At last you may rest / The Rinkeby Swedish / *1981–2006 / Chief mourners are / the cultural elite who gave birth to you. / Your children Blattesvenska and / Miljonsvenska will carry your / proud heritage. / If they only stop fighting. / May you rest*ish* in peace! *Jao*.' (Gringo supplement of *Metro*, 3rd May 2007, authors' translation, nonstandard morphemes in italics). Judging from our data, however, Rinkeby Swedish is still alive and kicking.

Rinkeby Swedish, as an object of public discourse, was 'born' about two decades ago when media reported on the research of the linguist Ulla-Britt Kotsinas, who had met young people in Rinkeby referring to their own way of speaking as Rinkeby Swedish (Kotsinas, 1989). The label apparently filled a gap and soon became a popular label for a diversity of social constructions of 'non-Swedishness' in speech (Stroud & Wingstedt, 1989). And, as the obituary also illustrates, it is still an emblematic object of debate, contestation and ambivalence.

Concluding Remarks

This chapter is the first report from the SALAM research project on young peoples' perceptions and constructions of linguistic variation and varieties in today's Stockholm, here focusing on two out of twelve speech samples and four out of nine schools in the entire database.

The main aim of the chapter has been to make a case for the systematic study of peoples' perceptions of language variation and to present a research design integrating different data types. The SALAM study combines quantitative data (semantic differential scales and guesses about speakers' area of residence, length of residence in Sweden, and mother tongue of speakers' parents), qualitative data (recordings of group discussions on language variation), and data amenable both to quantitative and qualitative analysis (labeling of ways of speaking). All data types contribute in different ways to our understanding of the listeners' sociolinguistic awareness and language attitudes. Sometimes interpretations based on different data types reinforce each other, sometimes they point in different directions or highlight different aspects of our object of study. In the latter case, we are in a fruitful way reminded of the complex realities behind individual listeners' constructions of the linguistic space and warned against simplifying generalizations.

In the data presented here, we have shown some examples of how one and the same speech sample may trigger widely differing associations for different listeners – sometimes even resulting in contradictory labels, as when, for example, Sam's speech is characterized as either 'worker Swedish' and 'upper class Swedish'. Furthermore, we showed how one and the same label may have widely differing extensions for different listeners, as when, for example, the label Rinkeby Swedish is ascribed to either just Leo or up to eight of the 12 speakers. The results of the SALAM study, as well as an earlier pilot study (Bijvoet & Fraurud, 2008, forthcoming), thus further substantiate a view of language varieties as constructions (rather than 'things'). In the words of Le Page (1994: 115), '[l]inguistic systems are in the mind of the beholder – both as speaker-listener and as descriptive and as theoretical linguist'.[11]

Notes

1. For a discussion of emerging dialects/sociolects, see Kotsinas (1988a, 1988b), Fraurud (2004), Bijvoet and Fraurud (2006).
2. This is one of nine projects within the research program *High-Level Proficiency in Second Language Use* at Stockholm University, funded by The Bank of Sweden Tercentenary Foundation (2006–2008).
3. The project was funded by The Bank of Sweden Tercentenary Foundation (2001–2006).
4. We are grateful to Tore Kristiansen, Lars-Anders Kulbrandstad, and Dennis Preston for fruitful methodological discussion in the initial phase of the SALAM project.
5. We thank Lars Sönnebo for standardizing the stimuli by means of dynamic compression and frequency correction.
6. The descriptions are based on our own ethnographic observations and on analyses of the students' resources at different schools and programs undertaken by Mikael Börjesson and Mikael Palme, SEC (Sociology of Education and Culture), Uppsala University/Stockholm University, see www.skeptron.uu.se/broady/sec/. We thank Donald Broady and his colleagues at SEC for giving us access to this material.
7. Cf. Broady's (2002) and Broady and Börjesson's (2008) application of Bourdieus' economic/cultural capital distinction in the characterization of Stockholm schools.
8. Calculations are optimized for voice analysis.
9. This form of display of the place of residence data was originally designed for giving feedback to the participants at a reunion some time after data collection, but proved useful also for the analyses, where responses from the nine schools were indicated by different colors, here partially reproduced as shades of gray. The larger white star indicates the correct answer.
10. For example, in the case of 'blattesvenska', the latter count includes labels such as 'ren blattesvenska' (pure blatte Swedish), 'blattespråk' (blatte language), and 'blatteslang' (blatte slang) – in the latter case the occurrence is included in the counts of both 'blattesvenska' and 'slang'.
11. We wish to thank Sally Boyd, Natalia Ganuza, Kenneth Hyltenstam, Marie Werndin and the editors of this volume for valuable comments on earlier versions of this chapter. We are of course solely responsible for all the remaining deficiencies.

Chapter 15
Linguistic Practice and Stereotypes among Copenhagen Adolescents

M. MAEGAARD

Introduction

In recent years, studies on relations between linguistic variation and social meaning, have had a strong focus on *local* meaning making, rather than on *global* patterns of variation connected to social meaning. This is mainly a reaction to the earlier preoccupation with large-scale quantitative studies of variation (e.g. Labov, 2006 [1966], 2001; Trudgill, 1974), which are often seen to neglect the importance of local usage of linguistic variation in constructing social meaning in interaction (see e.g. the critique in Coupland, 2007 or Eckert, 2008a, 2008b). Thus, many researchers today carry out microanalyses of interaction that bring new insights into the construction of social meaning through language, and shed new light on the complex relations between language variation and social meaning (e.g. Møller, this volume; Podesva, 2007; Rampton, 2006a, 2006b [1995]). This is indeed a very interesting and essential part of sociolinguistics, however, when it comes to understanding stereotypes, and their connection to language variation, we need to focus not only on the local dynamics of meaning making, but also on global structures of language and meaning potentials (Linell, 1998, 2001). This is the case because stereotyping (as the concept is understood in this chapter, see section 'Perceptions of Speakers') is a social psychological process that works at an intergroup level. Thus, we need to also focus on group patterns and structures at a more global level in our study of stereotypical perceptions of linguistic variation.

In the following, I will focus on stereotypes related to gender and ethnicity, using data from a project on language variation and change in Copenhagen, Denmark (Maegaard, 2007). The project combines methods from variationist sociolinguistics, ethnography, social psychology and attitudes research, and aims to shed light on relations between social categories, social practice and linguistic variation among ninth graders (around 15 years old) in a Copenhagen urban school, in the following referred to as The City School. I will introduce the study by presenting results regarding relations between phonetic variation, social categories and social practice. The focus in this chapter is also on linguistic stereotypes. Therefore, in later sections emphasis will be placed on discussions of the verbal guise studies that were carried out as part of the project. I argue that the linguistic practices of the pupils labeled 'foreign girls' are very different from those employed by the pupils labeled 'foreign boys', and that this has a major impact on perceptions of them in the verbal guise study.

Social Categories and Social Practice

The City School is a large urban school in Copenhagen with approximately 900 pupils, of different socioeconomic backgrounds, although more pupils have lower socioeconomic backgrounds. Around 30% of the pupils are multilingual, which is the average in Copenhagen public schools (according to definitions and figures from the Copenhagen City Council, www.kk.dk). Through seven months of participant observation (during 2002–03), I learned a lot about the social world of the pupils in ninth grade at The City School. I participated in classes, breaks, school parties, sports events and so on, and carried out ethnographic interviews with most of the pupils. Mainly due to cancellations and because some pupils did not want to participate in the interviews, not all the pupils were interviewed (64 out of the 83 pupils in the year group). For the entire project, the data consist of field notes, a diary written after each day I spent with the pupils, recordings of interviews, self-recordings and responses to the speech samples in the verbal guise study.

During this ethnographic field work, the focus was on social categories and social practice. Instead of deciding which social categories to focus on before entering this particular community of practice (Wenger, 1998), I selected social categories based on the ethnographic fieldwork. This resulted in analyses, which, for instance, do not distinguish between pupils from different socio-economic backgrounds, but instead distinguish between pupils belonging to the categories 'girls' or 'boys', and 'foreigners' or 'Danes', since these were the categories and the labels used by pupils and important to the social order at the school. I will not go into detail about the analyses of social categories here (see Maegaard, 2007: 127ff), but there are some important differences between the two categories.

The distinction between 'girls' and 'boys' is not negotiable in this community of practice – either you are a girl or a boy, and even though gender identities can be performed in many different ways, the gender distinction is crucial to the social order at school. There are hardly any friendship networks with both girls and boys – unless they are of a romantic character.

The distinction between 'foreigners' and 'Danes' is of a different kind. Membership in the category 'foreigners' could not have been determined on the basis of criteria such as mother tongue or ethnic background. Such criteria all play a part in the categorization but they interact with other phenomena. It is not simply a question of, for instance, bodily appearance, but also of how individuals *act* in the social field. Thus, there are pupils who under some criteria could be categorized as 'pupils with other ethnic background than Danish', 'bilinguals', 'immigrants' and so on, who are not categorized as 'foreigners' in school, because they do not participate in the same practices as the 'foreigners'. The best example of this is Saba. Her parents migrated from Eritrea to Denmark in the 1980s. Saba talks of herself as an 'Eritrean' and she is undoubtedly the darkest girl in the cohort. Nevertheless, Saba is not categorized as a 'foreigner'. One of her class mates, Samira, even states: 'I am the only foreign girl in my class'. Saba is not a 'foreigner', because she does not engage in the activities that 'foreign girls' engage in, and she does not hang out with them. Instead, she hangs out with her best friend Mira, a popular Danish girl, she straightens her curly hair, dresses just like Mira, and does not in any way take part in 'foreign-girl' activities. However, Saba is not categorized as being a 'Dane' either. This shows that the two categories are not complementary; one is not the negation of the other. It is possible to be neither 'Danish' nor 'foreign'. As seen from this example, the practices that the pupils engage in are important for the way they are categorized.

These analyses resulted in a focus on the following social practices (cf. Maegaard, 2007: 165ff): Smoking, the use of alcohol, whereabouts in the city, clothing, ways of walking, plans for the future, leisure activities, jobs, lunch habits and whereabouts during breaks in school. These practices group together in different *style clusters* (Quist, 2005: 78, 2008: 51), which are clusters of stylistic practices that contribute to a certain social meaning. The style clusters, and the labels signaling which types of personae were associated with them in school, are listed below in Table 15.1. Most of the labels were used by the pupils themselves. However, some of the clusters did not have a label attached to them, and I have given these clusters a name that would associate a persona corresponding to the persona constructions that took place every day in school. This applies to 'alternative girls' and 'tough ethnically mixed boys', since these labels were not used in school. The boys were referred to as the 'foreign boys and boys hanging out with foreigners', 'foreign boys and wannabes' and so on, and the 'alternative girls' did not have a name attached to them. Sometimes they were referred to as 'strange' or 'weird', sometimes as 'outsiders' or 'hippies' but it was not common at all to refer to the girls engaged in these specific practices (since the rest of the pupils hardly ever talked about them), and thus the term 'alternative girls' is my own, and not the pupils' invention.

The style clusters could be supplemented with numerous other practices, but the ones presented in Table 15.1 are the ones that, based on the ethnographic fieldwork, stood out as highly salient and important in the

Table 15.1 Style clusters at The City School

Style cluster	Practices
(1) Foreign girls	Plan to go to high school (*gymnasium*), take Arabic lessons in leisure time, do not do sports in leisure time, do not have jobs, do not smoke, do not drink alcohol. Clothing: Dark clothes, leather shoes or boots often with high heals, possibly scarf, long shirts or blouses that reach the thigh, gold jewellery, thin bracelets and necklaces
(2) Nice Danish girls	Plan to go to high school (*gymnasium*) or 'business' high school (*handelsgymnasium*), do fitness training in leisure time, job in shops (not in supermarkets, though), do not smoke, drink alcohol, local use of the city, stay in the central lobby during school breaks, buy lunch in the supermarket or bring rolls/fruit from home. Clothing: trainers, low waist jeans in light blue, tight T-shirts or tops, often short enough to make the belly button visible, the bra is often visible too, due to low-necked tops. Colors usually white, pink or other pastels. In the winter time over the T-shirt/top they wear a relatively short hooded sweatshirt in the same type of colors. Often jewellery and belts of different kinds
(3) Tough Danish girls	Plan to attend technical school (*teknisk skole*), do not do sports in leisure time, do not have a job, smoke, drink alcohol, local use of the city, stay in the central lobby or outside during breaks, buy lunch in the supermarket. Clothing: Very similar to the clothes described above, but colors are usually dark, black or gray. Sometimes also track suit trousers that are not part of style cluster 2 above. Over the T-shirt sometimes a sweatshirt like the ones mentioned above, or a larger fleece jumper
(4) Alternative girls	Plan to attend high school, creative leisure activities like painting, drama or music lessons, do not have jobs, do not smoke, drink alcohol, local use of the city, stay in the central lobby during breaks, bring rolls/fruit from home for lunch. Clothing: Dark clothes, but not similar to style clusters 1 or 3 above. Often black clothes, but also other colors, however never pastels. Often velvet jackets, or velour blouses, never visible belly button or bra, never tracksuit or tight clothes. Sometimes heavy necklaces or bracelets
(5) Tough ethnically mixed boys	Plan to attend high school or technical/business school, football or fitness in leisure time, job in fashion shops or no job, do not smoke, drink alcohol, global noninstitutional use of the city, stay in the central lobby or outside during breaks, buy lunch in supermarket or kebab shop, 'fidgeting' walk. Clothing: Black/gray/white pop-clothes. Jeans (blue) and pants in other fabric, usually black. Loose but not baggy. T-shirt, Jewellery, necklaces. Sometimes a cap. Labeled clothes, for example Iceman, Jack & Jones

(*Continued*)

Table 15.1 *Continued*

Style cluster	Practices
(6) Nice Danish boys	Plan to attend high school, football, tennis, piano lessons in leisure time, local use of the city, do not smoke, drink alcohol, stay in own or friends' classroom during breaks, job in supermarket or similar, buy lunch in supermarket. Clothing: Light colored pop-clothes Poloshirts, pastels. Jeans are loose but not baggy. Labeled clothes: for example Fred Perry, Lacoste, Levis
(7) Tough Danish boys	Plan to attend technical school, football in leisure time, local use of the city, drink alcohol, smoke, stay in the central lobby or outside during breaks, job in supermarket or similar, buy lunch in supermarket or at the burger shop, classical masculine walk. Clothing: Dark pop-clothes, baggy jeans or track suit trousers, often white. Sweatshirt, hooded sweatshirt, cap. Trainers. Labeled clothes: Adidas, Nike or other sport labels
(8) Nerdy boys	Plan to attend high school, do not do sports or creative leisure activities, but attend scout clubs, play computer and go to internet cafés, local use of the city, do not smoke, drink alcohol, stay in own class during breaks, do not have jobs, bring lunch packs from home. Clothing: Compared to mainstream norms, the clothes are untrendy. Trainers and jeans but the trainers are, like the jeans, often from unknown, cheap labels. Pants are neither tight nor baggy. T-shirts and sweatshirts are loose and in bright colors. No labeled clothes

community. These practices are the ones used in the systematic analysis characterizing and delimiting the different clusters. The daily practice of all pupils were analyzed according to the different clusters and on that basis, every pupil was assigned to a certain style cluster, if they were engaged in 8 out of 10 practices. The actual group of individuals assigned to a certain style cluster is later referred to as *style group*. Most of the pupils fitted in one of the clusters in Table 15.1, but of course some pupils were impossible to place in any of them. The following linguistic analyses are based on the language use of the pupils for whom it was possible to categorize in one of the eight style clusters.

Phonetic Variation

Phonetic variation is analyzed with regard to 10 variables. Nonstandard variants are shown in Table 15.2, with a few examples of words where the variant could occur. I focus on three different kinds of variables: (1) variables that have traditionally been seen to distinguish high from low

Table 15.2 Nonstandard variants of 10 phonetic variables

Traditional high/low variables	Traditional young/old variables	Nontraditional variables
'Lengthening of short vowels' (Low) 'snakke', 'gruppe', 'klasse'	Raising of (ɛ) in the æng-variable: [eŋ] (Young) 'tænke', 'engelsk', 'penge'	Devoicing of initial r: [ʁ̥] 'rimelig', 'rød', 'ryge'
Affrication of initial t: [t͡s] (Low) 'ti', 'tusind', 'teori'	Fusion of [ð] and the preceding vowel V into [ᵛð] (Young) 'tid', 'hvad', 'sidde'	Dentalization of s: [s̪] 'sidste', 'cykel', 'sejt'
Backing of the nucleus of the aj-diphthong: [ɑj] (Low) 'haj', 'lege', 'hejse'		Palatalization of initial t: [tʲ] 'ti', 'tusind', 'teori'
Fronting of the nucleus of the aj-diphthong: [aj] (High) 'haj', 'lege', 'hejse'		
Postalveolar [ʃ] for standard [ɕ] (High) 'sjov', 'speciel', 'charme'		

Copenhagen speech, (2) variables that have traditionally been seen to distinguish younger from older speech and (3) variables that have not traditionally been analyzed in Danish variation studies (see Maegaard, 2007: 81ff for a detailed description of the variables).

The linguistic analysis was an auditory analysis of the interviews with regard to the 10 variables. The interviews were semistructured, and analyses were carried out of the same phases in the interviews. If possible, at least 20 occurrences of each variable for each speaker have been analyzed, but for the æng-variable and the aj-variables this was not always possible, due to the lower frequency of these variables.

The distribution of variants in categories based on gender and ethnicity are seen in Table 15.3. As can be seen from the table, 'lengthening of short vowel' is the only variable where the 'Danes' are in the lead, and the 'foreign' girls or boys are not. With regard to all the other variables, either the 'foreign' boys or 'foreign' girls are the most extreme.

The 'foreign' girls have the highest use of [s̪], [t͡s] and [aj], while the 'foreign' boys have the highest use of [tʲ], [ʃ], [ʁ̥], fusion of [ð] and the preceding vowel, and [eŋ]. This means that they make use of the opposite variants: When the 'foreign' boys have high use of a given variant, the 'foreign' girls have a low use – and the other way around. It is worth noting

Table 15.3 Frequency of nonstandard variants according to categories based on gender and ethnicity

	Foreign Girls %	Dan. girls %	Dan. boys %	For. boys %
[s̪]	22.5	6.0	0	15.8
[t͡s]	57.5	15.2	1.0	15.8
[tʲ]	0	0.8	7.3	15.0
[ʁ̞]	16.3	4.8	4.4	23.3
Length of short V	0	21.7	21.1	11.9
[ˀð]	41.5	60.2	59.1	75.5
[ʃ]	11.8	20.7	53.6	98.1
[e̞ŋ]	0	29.5	56.3	55.6
[aj]	73.3	15.3	8.4	0

that the extreme use of variants by 'foreigners' is not restricted to the non-traditional variables, but also applies to the traditional variables. Thus, it seems that this is not merely a question of the 'foreigners' inventing new variants, but of them using existing variation in constructing social meaning through opposition. This becomes clearer when we look at the variation in relation to the style clusters.

If we see linguistic variation as social practice, we would expect the language use of pupils belonging to different style groups to be different. In Table 15.4, the pupils are categorized according to which style cluster they could be said to draw upon in their persona construction. This pattern is more fine-grained and detailed in many ways, and the pattern from Table 15.3 concerning gender and ethnicity is also found in this analysis: The 'foreign' girls in style group 1 use the opposite variants of style group 5, the 'tough ethnically mixed boys' (except regarding the use of [ʁ̞] where girls and boys have similar degree of use). It is seen that together these two groups are the most extreme language users with regard to all the variables, except for the lengthening of short vowels.

Another interesting thing to note here is how social category and practice seem to play together. In style group 5 ('the tough ethnically mixed boys') it is actually the case that the 'Danish' boys in this group use the [tʲ] and the [ʃ] variants approximately as much as the 'foreign' boys, and far more than the other groups of boys. Thus, there is a connection between language use and other social practices, in that the boys in style group 5

Table 15.4 Frequency of nonstandard variants according to style cluster

	Gr 1 Foreign girls	Gr 2 Nice Danish girls	Gr 3 Tough Danish girls	Gr 4 Alternative girls	Gr 5 Tough ethnically mixed boys	Gr 6 Nice Danish boys	Gr 7 Tough Danish boys	Gr 8 Nerdy boys
[s]	22.5	10.7	0	0	7.9	0	0	0
[ts]	57.5	27.5	6.7	8.3	8.3	1.3	0	2.5
[tɕ]	0	1.1	1.7	0	12.5	6.3	4.4	0
[ʁ̥]	16.3	5.0	15.0	8.3	12.1	6.3	4.4	0
Leng. of short V	0	22.5	26.1	2.3	11.8	3.0	38.0	40.0
[vð]	41.5	53.8	56.7	77.8	69.0	61.6	52.0	53.3
[ʃ]	11.8	15.3	40.0	33.3	95.4	48.1	34.1	60.0
[eŋ]	0	25.8	0	0	64.7	50.0	66.7	33.3
[aj]	73.3	21.2	0	0	0	27.3	3.8	0

are categorized in the same group precisely because they participate in the same practices.

On the other hand, we could consider a feature like devoiced r, [r̥]. As can be seen from Table 15.4, this feature is especially used by 'the foreign girls', 'the tough ethnically mixed boys' and 'the tough Danish girls'. But in fact the 'Danish' boys in style group 5, who participate in the same practices as the 'foreign' boys, do not use [r̥] very much. Actually, they use it even less than the 'Danish' boys who are not part of style group 5. It is possible that the 'Danish' boys in style group 5 signal by doing this that they are not 'foreigners' after all. The consequence of this interpretation is that even though it is possible to distinguish between different groups based on the practices they engage in (as in Table 15.4), abstract category membership (such as boy, girl, 'Dane', or 'foreigner') still has some importance. Thus, it seems that the style groups should not function as the only description, but that this analysis supplements the analysis based on social categories.

The linguistic analysis shows that the variation is connected both to social categories and to practices. In principle, the relations that have been found among the pupils from The City School could turn out to be entirely locally bound, which means that we could not expect to find the same relations at other places in Copenhagen. To establish whether or not this seems to be the case, a verbal guise study was carried out.

Perceptions of Speakers

In this chapter linguistic variation is regarded as social practice, and several aspects of this concept are important. Social practice is to be seen as actions, but not actions in isolation. The notion of *practice* implies that the actions are recurring, which means that they must be seen across a time span, that is in a historical context. At the same time, by using the term *social* practice, the social context is highlighted. It is the historical and social context that gives structure and meaning to the actions. Clapping ones hands as a signal of applause can only be understood as applausal if it is known in advance to have this meaning. Smoking a cigarette or wearing a cap back to front can be interpreted as oppositional acts only in so far as they have been experienced before to have relations to stances, attitudes and so on, of an oppositional character, and in social contexts where this becomes relevant. Social meaning is, in this understanding, constructed in the here and now during situated discourse, but it is to a large extent constructed by drawing on meaning potentials that have emerged through series of interactions. This means that the specific communicative event and the structure of meaning potentials like social representations (Farr & Moscovici, 1984) or stereotypes (e.g. Tajfel, 1981) constitute a dialogical relationship. Furthermore, it implies a need to study not only the dynamics of meaning making, but also the structure.

In the previous paragraphs I have reported from a study of a particular community of practice, namely a year group of pupils at The City School. However, when using the community of practice perspective, there is a risk that the researcher will overemphasize local meaning making in a specific community of practice over more global relations between clusters of resources (style clusters) and social meaning in the larger speech community. One way of introducing analyses of global meaning potentials, is by means of the verbal guise method.

The verbal guise method is a method that is meant to elicit people's *private* language attitudes (Garret *et al.*, 2003; Kristiansen *et al.*, 2005) or their *subconscious* attitudes (Kristiansen, 1991a, 1991b, 1999; Maegaard, 2001). It is claimed that this indirect technique (contrary to direct measures like interviews about attitudes) can elicit expressions of attitudes that the respondents are not aware of.

In a verbal guise experiment, respondents listen to speech samples representing language use towards which the researcher wishes to elicit attitudes. Then respondents evaluate the speakers, usually by filling out a questionnaire, and usually using scales. In the original studies by Lambert and his colleagues (Lambert *et al.*, 1960), the focus was on attitudes towards speakers of Canadian-English and Canadian-French, but the method has been modified and developed in many ways and directions since then, and has mainly been used in connection with dialect variation, not variation concerning different languages as in the original study. The verbal guise technique has been criticized and discussed continuously since the first experiment, but I will not go into these discussions here (see Garret *et al.*, 2003: 57ff for a thorough presentation of problems related to the verbal guise technique). However, in section 'The Verbal Guise Study' I will touch upon some of the methodological problems.

The verbal guise method rests upon respondents' ability to tie social meaning to the speech that they listen to. This is both related to the actual practices that speakers of certain ways of speaking engage in, and to discourses about this. The method is designed to examine stereotypes related to language use. These stereotypes are developed through repeated acts, practices that are carried out and experienced by individuals. Thus, stereotypes are based on both practice and psychology (and cognition, but this discussion is not elaborated in this chapter; see Fiske & Taylor, 1984, for a Social Cognition view on stereotypes). They are psychological phenomena, but an important aspect of the social identity approach to stereotypes is that they are also *social*, in the sense that they are shared perceptions in the community. This is what explains the consistent outcomes of most verbal guise experiments.

On the basis of language use, the respondents in a verbal guise study are assigning specific characteristics to the speaker, for example, 'interesting', 'nice', 'ambitious' and so on. This is only possible because social meaning is associated with clusters of practices, as the above analyses aims to show. This means that by isolating one part of the stereotype, such as language, the respondent will possibly associate to the rest. In line with social identity theory (Hogg & Abrams, 1988; Tajfel, 1981), *stereotypes* are here understood as generalizations about people based on category membership (Hogg & Abrams, 1988: 65). They are shared beliefs about people belonging to different social categories. An example of a stereotype is the perception of a typical 'doctor' as male, middle-aged, gray-haired, rational, serious, orderly, wearing a white coat and so on. Stereotyping is a fundamental process in human psychology, but it is at the same time potentially dangerous, because it simplifies the world and has the potential for producing social conflicts. In stereotypical perceptions, each category is treated as homogenous, and thus every member possesses the same qualities.

By use of the verbal guise technique the researcher elicits stereotypical descriptions of what is perceived to be a distinctive group associated with a particular language use. The groups need not be larger labeled categories, (like 'doctor' or 'woman'), but they might very well instead be categories of people of a certain 'type' (examples from Maegaard, 2005):

(1) 'lidt oprørsk, "rebel", egen mening, ikke påvirket af andre, selvstændig, måske flippet'
 a little rebellious, 'rebel', own opinion, is not influenced by others, independent, perhaps alternative way of clothing (response to a Copenhagen girl, modern accent)

(2) 'han er rolig, nede på jorden, lidt gammeldags, principfast og stolt'
 he is calm, down to earth, a bit old-fashioned, high-principled and proud (response to a Copenhagen boy, conservative accent)

In these examples, different characteristics are put together in clusters to construct the stereotypes. These stereotypes do not necessarily have names attached to them, but they are recognizable profiles of different types of people.

The Verbal Guise Study

Overall results

The purpose of the verbal guise study was to investigate whether other young people than the ones from the ethnographic study, tied stereotypical perceptions to the variation that corresponded to the personae constructed and reconstructed day after day by the speakers. To examine whether connections between language use, categories, and style clusters in the local community of practice could be said to exist in the broader Copenhagen speech community, the verbal guise study was carried out in two different schools. It was carried out in The City School, but in order to be certain that the respondents did not recognize the voices they heard as belonging to specific people they knew, a new year group of ninth graders had to be used. Thus, respondents at the City School attended ninth grade three years after the group of pupils from the ethnographic study. The verbal guise experiment was furthermore carried out in another school in Copenhagen, here referred to as The North School. The North School is situated in another part of the city, and has pupils from higher socioeconomic background, as well as a smaller amount of multilingual pupils. Representatives of seven of the eight style clusters were chosen (there was no obvious representative of the 'alternative girls'), and each appears in two guises in the experiment, that is with two different speech samples. The samples are extremely short, since part of the aim is also to examine if stereotypes can be invoked by only 10 s of speech. In most attitudes research using the verbal guise paradigm, the speech samples are longer, because it allows more variants to occur and it gives the respondent more time to evaluate the speakers. Judging from earlier Danish studies (e.g. Kristiansen, 2009; Maegaard, 2005), however, it seems that respondents have no problem responding to extracts 20–30 s long, which suggests that it might be possible to shorten the extracts even more. This is tested in the experiment. The shortness of the samples also minimizes the effect of semantic content, because it is more or less impossible to understand what the speaker is actually talking about based on these short extracts. (3) is an example of a speech sample from a boy, Victor, from style group 8, 'the nerdy boys':

(3) 'det er ret svært vil jeg mene \ når de ting så er opfyldt så d- det sådan nogenlunde den måde det er \ og det er også det der gør at det nærmest er umuligt at få til at \ at få arrangeret'
it is very hard I would think \ when these things are fulfilled then i- it is more or less the way it is \ and that is also what makes it almost impossible to \ to have it arranged

Here, it is not possible to interpret exactly what the content of Victor's speech is. Nevertheless, the respondents are capable of reacting to the speech sample, as the analysis will show. This means that they must be reacting, not to *what* Victor says, but to *how* it is said. Additionally, each speaker appears in two different guises. If the guises are evaluated similarly, it is a strong indication that it is the way of speaking, not the semantic content, the listeners are reacting to (for detailed transcriptions and analyses of the speech samples, see Maegaard, 2007).

The stereotypes that respondents associate with different ways of speaking were elicited using open-ended questionnaires. The use of evaluation scales in questionnaires brings along several problems, which is why they were avoided in this study. An important problem is that the use of scales presupposes the relevance of some traits over others, and it makes unexpected characterizations impossible (see Maegaard, 2005: 63ff, 2009). Thus, there were no scales in the questionnaire, which contained only one question regarding each speech sample: 'What is your immediate impression of this person? What kind of person do you think she/he is?' The samples were presented in the questionnaire using numbers from 1 to 14, so that no names were used in the questionnaire. The responses were grouped according to semantic meaning, and Table 15.5

Table 15.5 Evaluative profiles of the speakers

	The City School	*The North School*
Lykke1	Tough, dominating, confused, problem child, indifferent	Immigrant, indifferent, strange way of speaking, pop girl, suburban
Lykke5	Tough, dominating, problem child, positive	Immigrant, tough, indifferent, strange way of speaking, pop girl
Louise2	Snob, popular, self-centered, confident	Nice, snob, popular, blond, upper class, pop girl, Østerbro
Louise4	Snob, popular, self-cenetred, confident	Snob, popular, blond, bimbo/bitch, dislikeable, pop girl
Samira3	Confident, ordinary, cautious, bright, insecure, serious	Nice, ordinary, calm
Samira6	Confident, ordinary, cautious, bright	Nice, ordinary, snob, serious
Robert7	Nice, dominating, problem child	Insecure, mature, nerd, cautious
Robert12	Insecure, ordinary, dominating, problem child	Nice, nerd, boring
Victor8	Bright, indifferent, nerd	Nice, bright, confident, popular, calm, mature
Victor11	Bright, indifferent, nerd, insecure	Nice, confident, popular, calm, nerd
Rashid9	Gay, immigrant, feminine, nice, a girls friend	Gay, immigrant, feminine, confident
Rashid14	Gay, immigrant, feminine, nice, smartass	Gay, immigrant, feminine, indifferent
Gustav10	Nice, ordinary, calm, cautious, sensible	Nice, ordinary, calm, cautious, sensitive
Gustav13	Nice, ordinary, calm, sensible	Nice, ordinary, calm

Each label represents at least 14% of the total number of responses given to the specific speech sample.

shows the resulting speaker profiles (in Table 15.5, the samples are represented by the speakers' pseudonyms, whereas in the questionnaires they were presented by numbers only). In all, 101 listeners took part in the study, which amounted to 1110 responses in total, since some were blank or for other reasons were rejected from the analysis. The categorizations that appear in Table 15.5 all have a frequency of at least 6 at The City School and 5 at The North School for the specific speech sample. On average, this amounts to approximately 14% out of the total number of responses for each speech sample, which means that (on average) if a profile contains five categorizations, it will cover at least 70% of all responses given to the specific speech sample.

As can be seen from the table, the same speaker gets quite similar evaluations in different guises. However, for some of the speakers there is a difference between evaluations at the two schools. There are many interesting aspects of these evaluative profiles (see Maegaard, 2007, 2009), but in this chapter I focus on the two representatives of the 'foreigner' categories: The 'foreign' girl, Samira, and the 'foreign' boy, Rashid, and I briefly mention some results concerning the 'tough Danish girl', Lykke, who is by some respondents categorized as being an 'immigrant'.

Rashid

Rashid is in both schools evaluated as being 'gay', 'immigrant' and 'feminine'. Very interestingly, he is recognized in both schools as being an 'immigrant'.

There might be different reasons for this recognition. Regarding syntax, Rashid9 has what appears to be nonstandard word order in the utterance:

(4) 'måske **man kan** godt svinge lidt med vennerne'
maybe-you-can-well-swing-a little-with-the friends
maybe you can swing a little with the friends

instead of

(5) 'måske **kan man** godt svinge lidt med vennerne'
maybe-can-you-well-swing-a little-with-the friends
maybe you can swing a little with the friends

Danish is a V2 language, which means that the verb is commonly placed second in main declarative clauses, giving subject–verb inversion when an element is topicalized [as in (5) above, cf. Ganuza, this volume; Opsahl & Nistov, this volume]. The noninverted word order (subject–verb) as in (4) '… is a very salient feature in language use among individuals in the process of learning Danish (e.g. Quist, 2000: 152), which could indicate that this is why Rashid is recognized. On the other hand, it does not explain why he is categorized as an 'immigrant' just as often in the other guise, Rashid14, where no noninverted word order occurred. This suggests that there must be other reasons for the categorization of Rashid as 'immigrant'.

Regarding segmental features, Rashid9 and 14 has none of the typical 'foreigner' pronunciations in the speech samples – [tʲ], [ʃ] or [ʁ̥] – yet he is recognized very clearly as an 'immigrant'.

One explanation might be prosody. According to Hansen and Pharao (see Hansen & Pharao, this volume; Pharao & Hansen, 2005) there are certain prosodic features that are specific to so-called 'Copenhagen multiethnolectal' speech. Long vowels tend to be shorter than in 'standard young Copenhagen', which means that there are in general no differences between standard short and long vowels. The results from Hansen and Pharao might connect to the results from this study showing that the lengthening of short vowels is a 'Dane' variant (Table 15.3).

Furthermore, the intonation pattern in the 'multiethnolect' shows an almost leveled pitch, until the end of the utterance where it falls rapidly (in contrast to the standard Copenhagen pattern where the pitch falls steadily throughout the utterance). Rashid's intonation pattern shows a similar progress; however, the exact pattern is difficult to determine due to his creaky voice, which obscures intonation curves. Rashid also has a very abrupt delivery in both samples, which seems to be connected to his vowels being short. Thus, Rashid uses some prosodic features that have been characterized as typical of 'Copenhagen multiethnolect', and this is probably why he is recognized as being an 'immigrant'.

Rashid is also assigned the label 'gay'. This is probably a consequence of his use of [ṣ]. This variant has been referred to among Danish linguists as 'ungpigelæsp' (young girls lisp) Hutters & Bay, 2006, and in folk terminology as 'bøsse-s' (gay s). Some of the respondents even comment directly on Rashid's s-pronunciation:

(6) 'Bøsse – det kan man høre på hans s'er'
    Gay – you can tell from his s'es (response to Rashid9)

Rashid is not in any way categorized as being gay by any of his classmates, quite on the contrary. He is frequently referred to in the interviews with labels like 'tough', 'popular', 'leader of the boys', and he is dating the most popular girl in school, Louise. But when taken out of its context, his use of [ṣ] is not perceived the same way as it is when he uses it in context.

Samira

Samira is also evaluated quite similar in the two schools – for instance as 'ordinary' and 'serious', but it is noteworthy that in neither school she is evaluated as being 'immigrant' or the like. This seems odd, considering the important part the 'foreign girl' part of her persona plays in her daily life (cf. style group 1 in Table 15.1). She is undoubtedly the most stereotypical 'foreign' girl in the year group, but this is not detected in the verbal guise study. She is recognized, however, as being, for instance, 'ordinary', 'cautious', 'serious' and 'bright' that are all characteristics of the persona she constructs day after day in school. At least these are all attributes that many of her classmates ascribe to her in the interviews.

Samira's 'foreigner' position is not linguistically salient, apart from her use of devoiced r, [ʁ̥]. Apart from her use of this variant, she talks very much like a 'nice Danish girl', and shows no prosodic features characteristic of Copenhagen multiethnolect. This is actually true for the entire 'foreign' girls group. They use more or less the same variants as the 'nice Danish girls', but they use them to a higher extent (i.e. their speech has a higher frequency of the same variants typical of the 'nice Danish girls'). The other social practices employed by the 'foreign' girls are not very different from the 'nice Danish girls' either. One might say that the 'foreign' girls are 'super-nice' girls. The fact that Samira is not recognized as 'foreign' girl emphasizes that the stylistic picture of her is not complete until we look at her linguistic style in context.

Lykke

The results concerning Lykke are interesting in relation to the discussions in this chapter. At The City School Lykke is in both samples evaluated as being 'tough', 'dominating' and a 'problem child'. At the North School, however, she is among other things assigned the categorization 'immigrant' and someone who has a 'strange way of speaking'. This might be interpreted as an indication that Lykke's way of speaking is recognized at The City School to have social meaning potentials similar to the persona that Lykke constructs in school. At the North School, on the other hand, Lykke's way of speaking is not recognized as typical of a 'tough Danish girl', but as a 'pop girl' who has a 'strange way of speaking', and perhaps because of this she is perceived to be an 'immigrant'.

Lykke's way of speaking is not recognized at The North School to have the same meaning potentials as it does at the City School, and this shows that social meaning potentials are not all global, in the sense that there are ways of speaking that respondents react differently to in the two schools. The social meaning of Lykke's speech is interpreted in different ways in the two schools, and in the framework used in this chapter it is obvious to make the interpretation that this is because they are two different communities of practice, where linguistic variation is used differently, and where ways of speaking used in one community of practice are not necessarily used in the other. This makes it difficult for listeners to attach social meaning to it (as seems to be the case with the speech samples from Lykke).

Conclusions

In this chapter I have presented and discussed different approaches to the study of linguistic variation and social meaning. I have analyzed data from the same community of practice by taking a social-category perspective, a social-practice perspective, and a social-psychological perspective focussing on stereotypical perceptions of speakers.

It became clear that the linguistic analyses based on category membership (gender and ethnicity) and on practice (the style cluster analysis) supplement each other. They both gave interesting results showing the connections between language and gender, language and ethnicity and between language and style clusters. Some of the variation patterns are better explained by the category perspective (e.g. the use of *devoiced r*) whereas other patterns are better explained by the practice perspective (e.g. the use of *palatalized t*).

The third approach is the social psychological approach using the verbal guise technique to elicit stereotypical perceptions of speakers. This analysis showed that the connections between category membership, practice, and linguistic variation are not locally bound, but can be found in the larger speech community as well. Nevertheless, not all speakers are evaluated similarly in the two schools and this suggests that there are some ways of speaking that are not recognized as having the same social meaning potentials in both communities. This shows furthermore, that local and global meaning making are interrelated and that even though social meaning is experienced in the local context, it can very well draw on meaning potentials of a more global character.

The perceptions of Rashid and Samira show several things. First of all, it is seen that the local meaning making to a large extent draws on more global patterns of language variation and social meaning. Rashid is recognized as an 'immigrant' quite overwhelmingly in both schools, and this seems mainly to be due to prosodic features. However, Samira is not recognized as such, and I argued that this is because her language use is quite close to that of the 'nice Danish girls'. Her way of speaking does not index 'foreigner' but rather 'super-niceness'. That this is, in fact, in this particular community of practice, a specific 'foreign girl' characteristic does not mean that it is indexed in the next step. Thus, the results also show that it is important to see linguistic style as embedded in a broader set of stylistic practices.

Finally, the evaluations of Lykke show that there are differences between the two schools in respondents' categorizations. This is seen as an indication that Lykke's way of speaking is locally tied to certain meaning potentials, whereas in other communities of practice listeners are unfamiliar with it, and find it strange (and non-native).

The pupils at The City School use existing variation in Copenhagen to construct social meanings that are not necessarily similar to perceptions of the same variation in older generations. At the same time, they use variants that have not been noticed before in Copenhagen. However, among individuals from the same age group, it seems that their ways of speaking are to a large extent perceived as tied to meaning potentials that are also relevant in other communities of practice. Put differently, it seems that the linguistic variation among pupils in ninth grade at The City School, to a large degree resembles that among other same-age communities in Copenhagen, and that the pupils draw on meaning potentials quite similar to the stereotypical perceptions elicited in the verbal guise experiment.

Chapter 16
One of My Kind? Language and Ethnicity among Danish Adolescents

M.V. CHRISTENSEN

Introduction

Language attitude studies are of great value to sociolinguistics – they complement studies of linguistic variation and linguistic change, yielding valuable insights and explanations. Hence, understanding how language variation is perceived among the members of a speech community is an important part of the study of linguistic variation and its social meaning. Recent studies of language and ethnicity in Denmark (Christensen, 2009; Quist, 2000, 2005) show that salient linguistic traits are common to minority background speakers in both Aarhus and Copenhagen, pointing to the existence of an ethnic variety of Danish.

This chapter presents results from a language recognition study conducted in Aarhus and Copenhagen (Christensen, forthcoming). By employing the methodology from language attitude research, the study aims to investigate how different groups of adolescents recognize and perceive different speech styles. After listening to six young speakers from Aarhus, respondents are asked to identify the ethnic backgrounds of the speakers. Respondents from various social, regional and cultural backgrounds are included in the study, the aim being to understand the nature and diffusion of sociolinguistic awareness among adolescents and to understand how this relates to the background of the respondents. Are respondents from Aarhus – even though presumably unfamiliar with ethnic speech styles – able to recognize and label them as such? Are respondents from Copenhagen able to recognize a speaker with a non-Danish background when he or she is from Aarhus? Are ethnic differences in speech forms drowning regional differences on a national level? By studying speech perception and addressing both ethnic and regional differences in spoken Danish, this study aims to shed some light on how recent linguistic changes are perceived by speakers. What identificational forces are at work when different groups of speakers listen to different speech styles from Aarhus? Does Mohammed from Copenhagen perceive and label Mohammed from Aarhus as 'one of my kind' or simply as a speaker from Aarhus? As it appears from these research questions, the present study aims to investigate how ethnicity and geography intercept and influence the perception of linguistic variation in Denmark.

Studying Language Perception

Classical language attitude studies are concerned with the perceived links between speech and personality (Lambert *et al.*, 1972). Our perception of speakers based on their speech forms is a result of a cognitive and relational process based on conscious or unconscious beliefs about the relationship between language and identity. Spoken language is an identifying feature; when encountering specific language forms, listeners identify the speaker as a member of a particular national, regional, ethnic or cultural group based on presumed links between speech forms and identity. When uncovering listeners' reactions to different speech forms, both prejudices and beliefs about out-group speakers surface along with affiliative feelings toward the in-group and its speech forms (Garret *et al.*, 1999: 321). Therefore, the identification process linked to perceiving and judging speech forms works as a two-way process: when individuals identify and evaluate other people's speech forms, a basic self-identification is implied. Essentially, when listening to well-known linguistic varieties, listeners judge the speaker on the basis of whether or not he or she can be perceived as 'one of my kind'. When listening to specific speech forms and speech styles, beliefs about the speaker's identity and personality can be set off by generalizing from stereotypes about the speaker's perceived identity to the language in use. A considerable number of studies have shown that consistent and systematic patterns of evaluation emerge when listeners are asked to judge different stereotypical traits of sociolinguistic voices. The theoretical basis of language attitude studies in social psychology (Allport, 1935; Tajfel, 1981), in combination with the insights achieved from studies of sociolinguistic variation, have proved to be a valuable way of obtaining access to the ongoing construction of norms of evaluation within speech communities; thus, language attitude studies are a valuable way to access and map out identificational dynamics among speakers within a given speech community.

Methodology

Language attitude studies expose listeners to controlled linguistic stimuli; the evaluative reactions of individuals to, for example speakers of non-standard varieties can then be measured and compared. In order to uncover how adolescents in Aarhus and Copenhagen perceive various speech styles, I exposed different groups of listeners to six different voices, and by using a questionnaire, their responses and evaluations were gathered and analyzed. The respondents were 187 adolescents, aged 13–15, from different schools in Aarhus and Copenhagen. Both ethnically mixed and 'all-Danish' Aarhus schools were chosen to participate in the study, and two multiethnic schools in central Copenhagen were picked to match the globalized Aarhus classrooms. I expected respondents from ethnically mixed schools in Aarhus to be familiar with ethnic speech styles, irrespective of their own linguistic background. But what about their peers from geographically close, but socioculturally distant environments? And what happens when respondents from ethnically mixed schools in Copenhagen are exposed to ethnic speech styles from Aarhus? All the data were collected in Danish municipal schools, and the questions concerning the respondents' recognition of the voices were designed as open-ended questions in order to allow the respondents' own understanding of language and ethnicity to emerge. Open-ended questions allow for a more detailed recognition of the speakers, and – as it turned out – even unexpected regularities in the recognition patterns. The listeners were simply asked to write down the name of the town in which they thought the speaker lived and the country they thought the speaker or the speaker's parents came from. The listeners were only informed about the gender of the voices, and no other information about the voices was given to the listeners. The respondents were also asked to judge the six voices on a 5-point scale, and the scales were designed to frame and capture the identificational aspects of the perception of the speakers. The questions to be answered on these 5-point scales (1= 'not at all' and 5 = 'a lot') were:

(1) How much like you do you think this speaker looks?
(2) How much like you do you think this speaker talks?
(3) Would you like to be friends with him or her?

Classical attitude dimensions (Zahn & Hopper, 1985) such as status and social attractiveness were included in the study. Question 3 above relates to social attractiveness and two open-ended questions: 'What job do you think the speaker's parents hold?' and 'What do you think the speaker would like to be when he or she grows up'? relate to the dimension of status. In this chapter, I shall focus on language recognition and identification (for a full report on the study, cf. Christensen, forthcoming). A total of 191 respondents filled out questionnaires, and responses from 187 of them were returned to me duly filled in. Altogether, 134 respondents from Aarhus participated in the study, and 53 respondents were from Copenhagen. The respondents and their ethnic and geographical distribution are presented in Table 16.1.

Table 16.1 Respondents

	Minority background respondents	Danish background respondents	Total number of respondents
Aarhus			134
All-Danish schools	0	60	
Mixed schools	34	40	
Copenhagen			53
Mixed schools	46	7	

Due to local pupil demography, only seven respondents with a Danish background from Copenhagen participated in the study. Data from these respondents are included when the results from Copenhagen are summed up, but due to the low number of participants, no group-level analysis and comparison can include this particular group.

Before introducing and describing the six voices used in the study, a closer description of the language styles used in Aarhus is needed.

The Language of Adolescents in Aarhus

Recent sociolinguistic research in multiethnic urban Scandinavia has taken an interest in investigating how linguistic variation and ethnicity intersect. Linguistic change is powered by social change, and the increasing ethnic, cultural and linguistic diversity in Denmark has thus brought about language mix and language change (Quist, 2000, 2005). These ethnically marked and deviant speech patterns have attracted the attention of linguists and dialectologists; hence, studies of linguistic variation in multiethnic environments have mainly focussed on language change, language mix and phenomena such as language crossing (Rampton, 1995a). Having shown that ethnically marked speech seems to be systematically deviant from standard Danish, Quist (2000) names the variety 'Multiethnolect'. Characteristic of this variety is the omission of subject–verb inversion when obligatory in declaratives, use of the common gender article with words in the neuter ('en' instead of 'et' as the indefinite article), loan words from Turkish, Arabic and other minority languages, the omission of 'stød' [the Danish stød can be described as a glottal constriction resulting in a sound resembling (when distinct) a creaky voice], a distinctive tone pattern and an altered vowel lengths resulting in a staccato-like articulation (for an in-depth account of the intonation patterns and vowel lengths in Copenhagen Multiethnolect, cf. Pharao & Hansen, 2005, this volume). The above mentioned traits are by no means to be regarded as a complete and thorough description of Multiethnolect; studies have shown that speakers of Multiethnolect show a high degree of both intra- and inter-individual variation (Christensen, forthcoming; Quist, 2006), and as we will see below, that new and hitherto undescribed speech forms play an important role for the listeners in this study.

My own study of language variation among adolescents in multiethnic environments in Aarhus shows that a number of linguistic traits normally considered to be deviant from standard Danish are in use as an ethnically marked speech style primarily among speakers from a minority background (for a closer description of the traits mentioned below cf. Christensen, 2004, 2009, forthcoming). Besides using the aforementioned prosodic features and syntactic simplifications, distinct schwa-pronunciations, in which schwa assimilations or reductions would be expected and a raising of the rounded back vowels from /ʌ/ to /ɔ/ and from /ɔ/ to /o/ resulting in a generally more rounded pronunciation of the rounded back vowels, are also speech forms pointing to a speaker from a minority background (Christensen, forthcoming). Even though tone patterns of stress groups vary from region to region, intonation in standard Danish has been characterized as having a gradual, overall falling tone pattern (Grønnum, 1992). Phonetic analyses of what sounds like typical examples of deviant ethnically marked prosody show that rather than a gradually falling intonation pattern, a final and rather deep fall seems to be a distinct prosodic feature. But a quite different intonation pattern is also heard among adolescents from a non-Danish background in Aarhus. Instead of the global or final fall, a quite distinct final rise is heard. Final rises in Danish intonation are normally linked to tag questions; however, tag questions are neither phonetically nor syntactically integrated into the preceding phrases. Therefore, finding final rises in an utterance's last syllables is noticeable in spoken Danish. In contrast to syntactic and lexical traits, the final rise is not reported to be found in the Copenhagen multiethnic variety, but remarkably, the same prosodic trait is found by Bodén (this volume) in Malmoe, Sweden. To sum up, a number of speech forms related to all levels of language characterize the ethnically marked language of adolescents from West Aarhus, thus nourishing the idea of a multiethnic variety.

As a rule, former studies of language change in East Jutland have shown that local speech forms are being replaced with Copenhagen forms, and this region is no exception in this ongoing language standardization process (Brink & Lund, 1975; Pedersen, 2003). As a consequence, Danes mainly have to rely on tone patterns in order to identify regional differences in daily speech styles. Still, a number of nonstandard and regional speech forms are in use among young speakers in Eastern Jutland. In a handful of words, standard Danish reproduces /or/-constructions in written language as [oɹ], whereas the local form features a more open vowel: [ɔɹ]. The Danish –et and –ede suffixes are pronounced [əð] (the –ede suffix also [əðð]) in standard Danish, the local forms include stops: [əd] or [ət]. The discourse marker 'sådan' (like this) is normally pronounced [sʌdn] or [sʌnn] in its standard form; the local variant features a longer and altered vowel: [sɔːn], and in some cases, also a glottal stop: [sɔʔn]. The pronunciation of the adverb 'også' ('too'), which is frequently used in the discourse marker 'ikke også'? ('not also' meaning 'isn't it'?), alternates between the standard form [ʌs], or [ʌsə], and the local nonstandard form [ʌ]. (For an in-depth account of the linguistic variables cf. Nielsen, 1998; Nielsen & Nyberg, 1992). These nonstandard regional forms are mostly found among speakers positioned in the lower places in the social hierarchy, and have been interpreted by researchers as a sign of '... a local, self-assured identity' in linguistic opposition to standardized Danish (Nielsen & Nyberg, 1992: 186, author's translation). My own study of language variation in Aarhus has revealed that immigrant-background adolescents use more nonstandard local speech forms than their Danish peers (Christensen, 2009, forthcoming). Therefore, when studying the perception of Aarhus adolescents' ethnic speech styles, the regional question is raised: Just how ethnic and how regional is it perceived to be, for example by Copenhagen speakers? Below, a characterization of the six voices chosen for this study as being representative of speech styles in use among adolescents in Aarhus is presented and with all due respect to the outline of the local speech community reported above, the focus is on multiethnic speech forms and local speech forms.

The Voices

The six voices represent three male voices (Saad, Orhan and Christian) and three female voices (Samira, Trine and Maja) (the names are pseudonyms). Four are more or less ethnically marked voices (Saad, Orhan, Samira and Trine), and the latter two (Christian and Maja) represent Danish voices, meaning voices that lack ethnically marked speech forms. The actual ethnic backgrounds of the speakers behind the voices do not necessarily reflect the characteristics of the voice. In fact, the Danish voice of Maja is delivered by a girl of mixed Danish-Vietnamese origin, and the ethnically marked Trine is in real life a Danish speaking girl with a Danish mother and a Moroccan father. Even though unable to speak Arabic herself, her ethnically marked speech is typical of that of her girlfriends, all of whom have Arab backgrounds. The stimulus recordings used in this study to elicit evaluative data were recorded during sociolinguistic fieldwork in multiethnic schools and youth clubs in Aarhus. The voices were not elicited as a result of the fieldworker encouraging the interviewees to use a specific speech style. Compared to scripted or mimicked versions of speech styles, they are '...ecologically more valid source material...' (Garret *et al.*, 1999: 322). All six personal narratives are unscripted, and because they originate from sociolinguistic interviews, they are a result of the speakers' participation in that particular speech event.

Since all six speakers were born and raised in Aarhus, all six voices feature East Jutland tone patterns. In detail, the voices can be described as follows:

As shown in Table 16.2, the four ethnically marked voices are quite different. Orhan features both syntactical and phonological features, although in order to recognize Saad as an ethnically marked speaker, listeners have to rely on prosodic and phonological features only. Samira stands out as the less fluent voice; she pauses to search for words more than once. Trine represents the distinctive final rise tone pattern. Even though quite different, the four ethnic voices were not chosen because they are distinct examples of ethnic speech styles, but instead because in total, they represent the various linguistic practices found among adolescents in the multiethnic environments of Aarhus.

The data collection procedure was the same in every classroom, as respondents were only introduced to the task in very general terms. They were informed about the gender of each voice prior to listening to it, but nothing else, and no names or pseudonyms were revealed. Respondents listened to each voice twice before filling out the questionnaire (for an in-depth account of the methodology and data collection procedure cf. Christensen, forthcoming).

Table 16.2 Voices

Voice pseudonym	Multiethnic speech forms	Local speech forms
Orhan	Distinct pronunciation of schwa; omission of glottal stop; lack of inversion in declaratives	Local form of discourse marker 'sådan' ('like this')
Saad	Tonal pattern featuring deep, final fall in intonation; distinct pronunciation of schwa; rounded back vowels	
Christian		Local form of preterit suffix
Maja		Local form of /or/; local form of preterit suffix
Samira	Tonal pattern featuring deep, final fall in intonation; deviant use of gender	Local form of the –et suffix
Trine	Tonal pattern featuring final tonal rise	

Recognition of Voices

When summing up the results, the first question to answer is: How did the respondents react to the voices overall? Figure 16.1 shows how the six voices were labeled by the respondents.

As it appears, I adopt the notions used by the respondents. In most cases, the listeners labeled the voices either as 'Danish' or 'foreigner' or 'immigrant', or they wrote down 'nationalities' such as 'Turkish' or 'Arab', which are normally associated with immigrant groups in Denmark. As predicted, more respondents attributed the 'foreigner' label to Orhan: Almost 60% of all respondents wrote that Orhan was 'foreign' 'Turkish' or 'from the Middle East'. Only 40% of the respondents heard ethnically marked speech forms when listening to Saad. Samira – the voice featuring both prosodic and syntactical multiethnic forms – was recognized by less than 40% of all respondents. The Danish voices, Christian and Maja, received quite clear responses – between 60% and 80% of all respondents labeled them as Danish, and the share of 'wrong' answers is low. Less than half of all respondents identified Saad, Samira and Trine as ethnically marked speakers. Figure 16.2 shows how each of the six voices was treated by different groups of respondents.

Orhan featured both prosodic and syntactic speech forms, pointing to a minority background speaker. Sixty-six percent of the respondents from Aarhus wrote that Orhan was 'Turkish' or a 'foreigner'. The share of respondents from Copenhagen who heard ethnic speech forms when listening to Orhan (38%) was significantly lower ($p < 0.001$). Twenty-three percent of the respondents from Copenhagen wrote that Orhan must have a Danish background, which was the highest share of 'Danish' labels attributed to a voice. When comparing the share of minority labels from

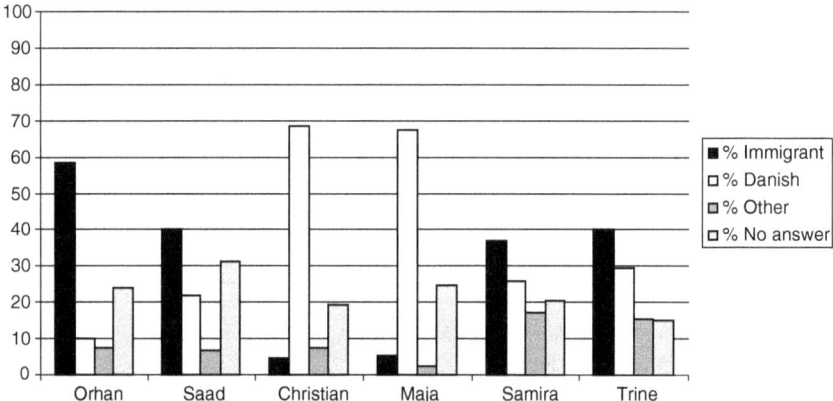

Figure 16.1 Recognition of voices

Language and Ethnicity among Danish Adolescents 215

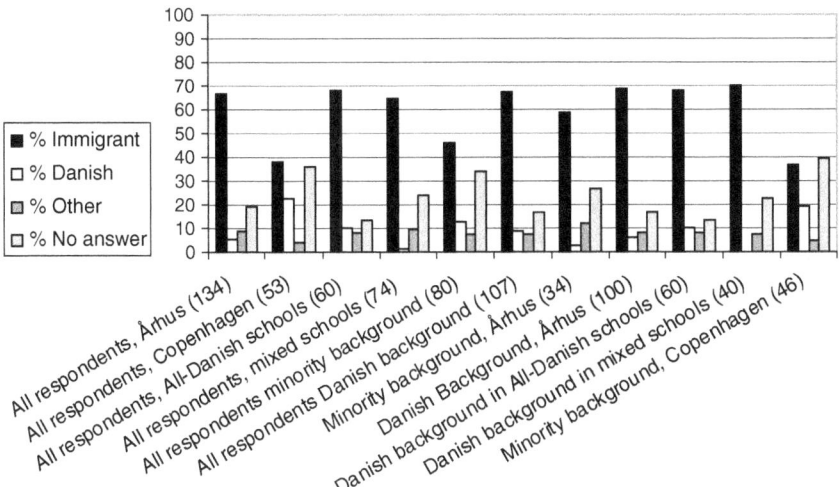

Figure 16.2 Recognition of Orhan

respondents with minority background from Aarhus (59%) to their Copenhagen counterparts (37%), the difference seems clear; the statistical tests performed confirm this ($p = 0.05$).

In the case of Orhan, it seems as if geography plays an important role in the respondents' ability to recognize and label the variety. Respondents from Aarhus, both from ethnically mixed schools where speech forms such as the ones used by Orhan are expected to be in use, as well as from all-Danish schools are familiar with the ethnically marked variety. Respondents from Copenhagen seem to be less familiar with the variety represented by the voice of Orhan. It is worth emphasizing that all Copenhagen respondents were from mixed schools, schools and environments where I would expect ethnic speech forms to be in use. Nevertheless, Orhan was more difficult to recognize for these listeners.

In the case of Orhan, respondents could rely on both syntactic and prosodic features, whereas, Saad, the voice featuring only prosodic features pointing to a speaker with a minority background, was harder to label for the respondents (see Figure 16.3).

Overall, respondents from Aarhus were less sure of Saad's origins; however, 59% of respondents from Aarhus with a minority background labeled Saad as a speaker with an immigrant background, with the highest share of ethnic labels. Again, respondents from Copenhagen figure as the group of respondents with the lowest share of ethnic answers (33%). They are closely followed by the respondents from all-white schools (35% ethnic answers): 32% of the respondents from all-white schools write that Saad must have Danish parents. The statistical tests reveal that while the

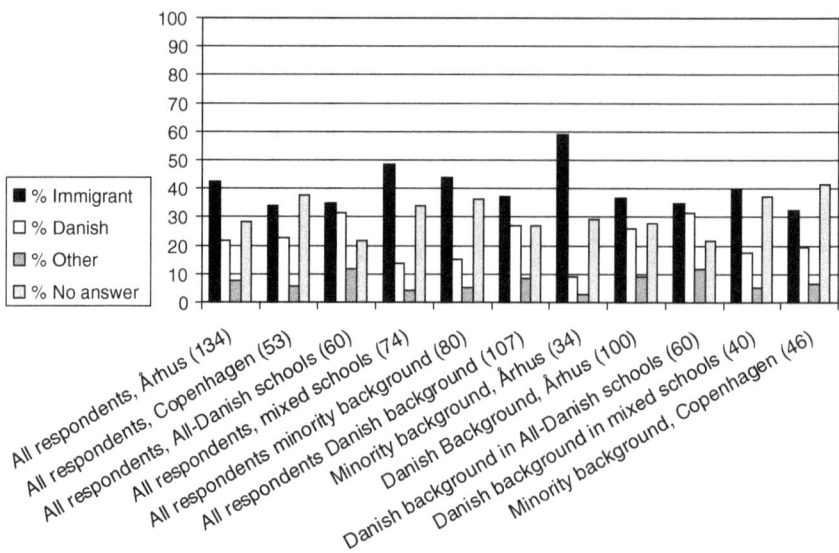

Figure 16.3 Recognition of Saad

difference between the share of correct answers from minority background respondents from Aarhus (59%) and their Danish peers (37%) is significant ($p = <0.025$), the difference between minority background respondents from Aarhus and their Copenhagen counterparts (33%) can only be classified as tendential ($p = <0.1$).

All respondent groups were less inclined to attribute an ethnic label to the voice of Saad, minority background respondents from Aarhus being the only exception. It is noteworthy that the share of ethnic labels attributed to Saad and Orhan are equally large (59%). To this specific group of respondents, prosodic features alone do the trick. Other groups of respondents are not on secure ground here, and geography does not seem to matter much. The Aarhus respondents from nonmixed schools in this study do not label an ethnically marked variety solely on the basis of prosodic features, and the fact that the share of ethnic answers from majority respondents from mixed schools is quite low as well (40%) shows that familiarity with the speech form is not enough (see Figure 16.4).

The voice of Christian lacks ethnic speech forms, but contains local forms and thus points to an Aarhusian speaker. Yet again, respondents from Aarhus are better at recognizing the voice than respondents from Copenhagen, who again have a higher number of incorrect or lacking answers. However, when listening to the Danish voice of Christian, respondents from Copenhagen seem on more secure ground: The majority (54.7%) of all Copenhagen respondents identify Christian's voice as Danish (see Figure 16.5).

Language and Ethnicity among Danish Adolescents 217

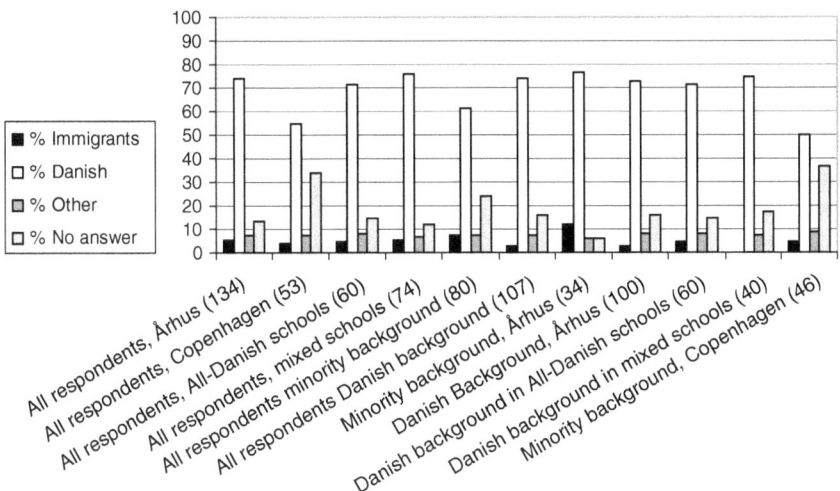

Figure 16.4 Recognition of Christian

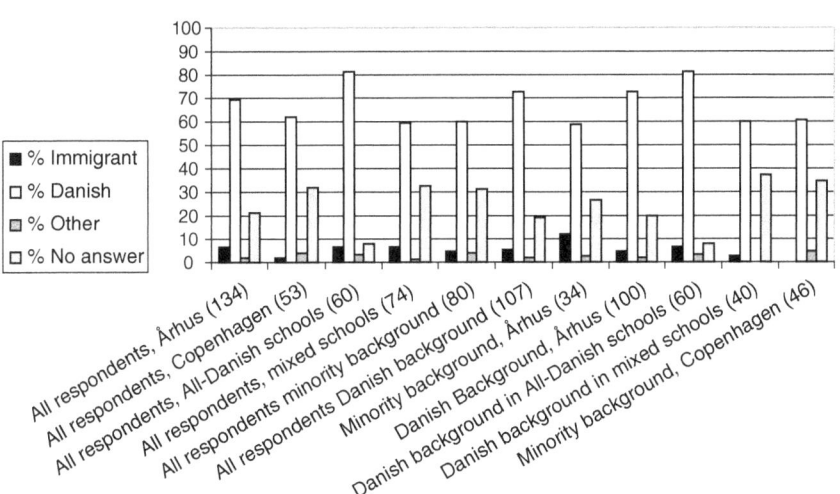

Figure 16.5 Recognition of Maja

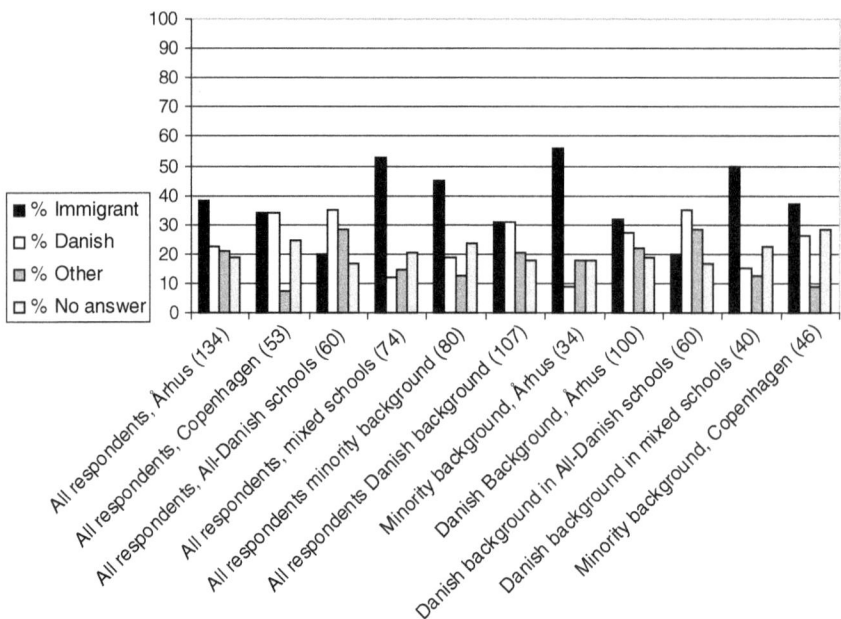

Figure 16.6 Recognition of Samira

The Danish-Vietnamese voice of Maja is Christian's female counterpart; the voice contains local speech forms, but no ethnic forms. Maja elicits a high share of Danish identifications. As in the case of Christian, a majority of respondents from Copenhagen hear a Danish speaker. Again, respondents from Copenhagen are more successful at labeling a Danish voice than labeling an immigrant voice.

In the case of Samira, respondents disagree on how to identify the voice (see Figure 16.6). Fifty-six percent of listeners from Aarhus with a minority background label Samira a speaker with an immigrant background. Only 9% of this group of respondents think they are listening to a speaker with Danish parents when they are listening to Samira. But contrary to the cases of Saad and Orhan, the results do not show differences in degrees of recognition; instead, the respondents from white schools hear something quite different. Thirty-five percent label Samira as Danish, and only 20% perceive her as a minority background speaker. The ability of the respondents to recognize Samira seems linked to their familiarity with ethnic speech forms; the majority (55.9%) of the respondents from mixed schools, irrespective of their own ethnic origin, labels Samira as an ethnically marked speaker, and 50% of Danish respondents from mixed schools in Aarhus label her as an 'immigrant' as well. It is remarkable that different groups of respondents attribute different labels

Language and Ethnicity among Danish Adolescents 219

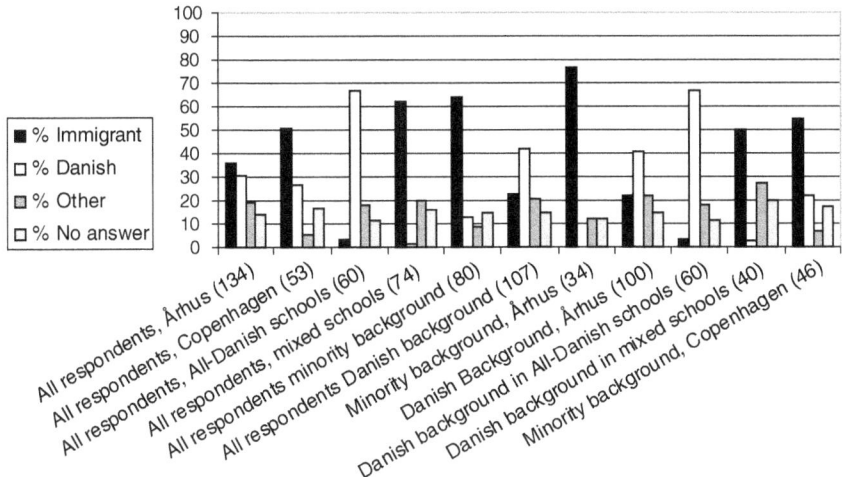

Figure 16.7 Recognition of Trine

to Samira. Why is Samira not recognizable to respondents from all-Danish schools? Can differences in linguistic traits featured in the voices explain the results? Above, I judged Samira as the less fluent voice; Samira featured distinct prosodic traits and deviant use of gender. This linguistic explanation does not seem plausible. How can it be explained then that Danish respondents in a white school misjudge her? Maybe the content (Samira talks about the car breaking down during a family vacation, making it difficult to make it back home before the re-opening of school) is not likely to evoke a picture of a minority background girl in their minds, or maybe the simple fact that Samira is a girl influenced their answers? Maybe the prevailing stereotypes among respondents unfamiliar with ethnic speech forms are mainly male?

Figure 16.7 clearly shows that the various groups of respondents strongly disagree when it comes to labeling Trine, the voice featuring the prosodic feature of the final rise. Respondents from all-Danish schools think they are listening to a Danish speaker: 66.7% of the respondents in all-Danish schools label her as Danish. In comparison, only 3% perceive the variety as being ethnically marked. On the other hand, the majority (62%) of respondents from mixed schools is quite sure of her minority background, and only 1.3% write that she must be Danish. It is worth noting that for the first time the respondents from Copenhagen (50.9% ethnic labels) are better at recognizing a voice than the respondents from Aarhus (35.8% ethnic labels). When looking closer at the answers written in response to the open-ended questions in the case of Trine, a pattern emerges. The voice is labeled not just as being 'immigrant' or 'foreigner' by respondents, as 12 out of the 18 minority background respondents from Copenhagen write that Trine is Arab, and 34 of the 60 respondents from all-white schools write that Trine must be from Bornholm, a Danish island situated in the Baltic. It is indeed possible that the final rise makes respondents think of the Bornholm variety of Danish, as the Bornholm intonation pattern is associated with a post-tonic rise (Grønnum, 1991). The majority of respondents from white schools place Trine on the 'Danish' side of the Danish–foreigner dichotomy, yet she is placed on the outskirts of the Danish speech community, probably due to the remarkable final rise featured in her voice. The speech forms represented by Trine are both very local, as only respondents from mixed schools are able to recognize the voice and label it correctly, although the speech forms must also be in use in Copenhagen, as just above half of the Copenhagen respondents recognize the voice as ethnically marked, and some are even able to assign the label 'Arab' to her, evidence of quite a fine-meshed and sophisticated sociolinguistic awareness.

Preliminary Conclusions

What do the results reported above reveal about the role of ethnicity and regionality in the speech evaluation process among different groups of respondents? The results show that the relationship between language, ethnicity and geography is a complex one. On the one hand, regionality seems to play an important role in respondents' ability to recognize ethnic speech forms. Orhan will pass as an ethnically marked speaker in Aarhus, but not in Copenhagen and neither will Saad, but then again Saad is best identified by ears very familiar with the prosodic features of ethnically marked speech forms in Aarhus. Even though ethnic speech styles in Copenhagen and Aarhus are characterized as featuring a number of identical linguistic traits, the recognition results reported above show that the two varieties must carry evidence of linguistic differences of quite a substantial nature. However, particularly in the case of Trine, the results show that familiarity with a specific speech form does not depend on geographical proximity. Trine's tonal patterns are recognized by her peers in Copenhagen, but not by respondents from all-Danish schools in Aarhus. Interestingly, Trine's tone patterns have not yet – to the best of my knowledge – been reported in Copenhagen studies of ethnic speech forms. In general, respondents at all-Danish schools in Aarhus are less able to recognize, and in the case of Trine completely unfamiliar with, ethnic speech forms, even though minority background peers from a different part of town perceive the same speech forms as having an unmistakeable ethnic color to them. Such discrepancies elucidate the level of ethnic and social segregation in the speech community.

Identification: Who is One of My Kind?

What identificational and relational processes are at work when respondents from Aarhus and Copenhagen listen to young speakers from Aarhus? As stated in the theoretical paragraphs prefacing this chapter, evaluating other people's speech forms implies relational reactions toward the perceived speaker, and the social stereotype associated with him or her. Hence, the identification process linked to perceiving and judging speech forms implies a self-identification as well. This study takes a particular interest in this aspect of speech evaluation, as identification is addressed directly in the questionnaire. Respondents were asked to judge on a 5-point scale (1= 'not at all' and 5 = 'a lot') how much they thought the six speakers behind the voices looked like and talked like themselves. Below, the results from respondents from Aarhus are presented in tabular form.

Even though almost all values reported in Tables 16.3 through 16.6 show various degrees of disaffiliation with the voices in the study, interesting

Table 16.3 Who looks like boys from Aarhus?

Respondents/voices	Saad	Samira	Christian	Orhan	Maja	Trine
Boys, minority background, Aarhus	2.05	1.68	1.79	2.16	1.74	1.42
Boys, Danish background, Aarhus	1.57	1.55	1.57	1.39	2.00	1.29
(p-value)	0.0668	(–)	(–)	0.0466	(–)	(–)

Table 16.4 Who talks like boys from Aarhus?

Respondents/voices	Saad	Samira	Christian	Orhan	Maja	Trine
Boys, minority background, Aarhus	2.16	1.89	1.89	2.37	2.00	1.63
Boys, Danish background, Aarhus	1.28	1.8	1.7	1.42	2.68	1.36
(p-value)	0.0005	(–)	(–)	0.0184	0.0509	0.0965

Table 16.5 Who looks like girls from Aarhus?

Respondents/voices	Saad	Samira	Christian	Orhan	Maja	Trine
Girls, minority background, Aarhus	1.59	1.88	1.19	1.50	2.19	1.63
Girls, Danish background, Aarhus	1.33	1.98	1.48	1.46	2.80	2.13
(p-value)	(–)	(–)	0.0338	(–)	0.0848	0.0385

Table 16.6 Who talks like girls from Aarhus?

Respondents/voices	Saad	Samira	Christian	Orhan	Maja	Trine
Girls, minority background, Aarhus	1.88	2.13	1.88	2.06	2.56	1.50
Girls, Danish background, Aarhus	1.28	1.93	1.93	1.61	3.26	1.30
(p-value)	0.0114	(–)	(–)	(–)	0.0479	(–)

patterns appear. Ethnicity seems to be an important parameter when boys from Aarhus identify themselves with Orhan. In the case of Saad, the difference is only tendential. The difference in linguistic identification is clearer; minority background boys evaluate Saad and Orhan as significantly more like their own linguistic practices. When it comes to the girls, the Danish respondents' wrong identification of Trine probably influences the results. Having established that Trine must be from Bornholm, the Danish girls look like her, but do not talk like her. But what happens when Orhan, Saad, Samira and Trine appear in a Copenhagen classroom among minority background peers? In Tables 16.7 through 16.10 the results from minority background respondents from Aarhus are compared with the results from their Copenhagen counterparts.

Table 16.7 Who looks like minority background boys?

Respondents/Voices	Saad	Samira	Christian	Orhan	Maja	Trine
Boys, minority background, Aarhus	2.05	1.68	1.79	2.16	1.74	1.42
Boys, minority background, Copenhagen	1.00	1.00	1.29	1.00	1.00	1.14
(p-value)	0.0004	0.0124	(–)	0.0034	0.0066	(–)

Table 16.8 Who talks like minority background boys?

Respondents/Voices	Saad	Samira	Christian	Orhan	Maja	Trine
Boys, minority background, Aarhus	2.16	1.89	1.89	2.37	2.00	1.63
Boys, minority background, Copenhagen	1.07	1.14	1.14	1.21	1.36	1.21
(p-value)	0.0012	0.0536	0.107	0.0096	0.0377	0.0629

Table 16.9 Who looks like minority background girls?

Respondents/Voices	Saad	Samira	Christian	Orhan	Maja	Trine
Girls, minority background, Aarhus	1.59	1.88	1.19	1.50	2.19	1.63
Girls, minority background, Copenhagen	1.21	1.28	1.14	1.31	1.83	1.90
(p-value)	0.262	0.0353	(–)	(–)	(–)	(–)

Table 16.10 Who talks like minority background girls?

Respondents/Voices	Saad	Samira	Christian	Orhan	Maja	Trine
Girls, minority background, Aarhus	1.88	2.13	1.88	2.06	2.56	1.50
Girls, minority background, Copenhagen	1.31	1.69	1.24	1.59	1.93	1.76
(p-value)	0.0305	(–)	0.0433	(–)	0.0821	(–)

Interestingly, the Copenhagen male respondents evaluate the Aarhus voices very negatively in general. Table 16.6 shows that regional differences are important when minority background boys are asked to identify themselves with Aarhus speech forms. Boys from Copenhagen with a minority background do not think they look or talk like Saad, Orhan and Maja from Aarhus; hence, salience is given to regionality and not ethnicity when evaluating the six voices in the study. Results are less clear when it comes to the girls. Even though the statistical tests cannot confirm the differences as being significant, it is worth noting that minority background girls from Aarhus generally identify more with the voices in the study, with Trine as an important exception. To a certain extent, Trine's tone patterns have triggered identification among minority respondents in Copenhagen, which is possibly a sign that Trine's tone patterns need more investigation and attention in the study of ethnic speech forms in Denmark.

Summing up, within the Aarhus speech community ethnicity seems to play an important part when adolescents perceive and evaluate linguistic practices. Nevertheless, especially in the case of the male respondents, ethnic differences are drowned by regional differences when respondents from Copenhagen listen to the ethnically marked voices from Aarhus. Trine's tone patterns have not previously been reported and described as ethnically marked speech forms, whereas the linguistic traits that have did not – interestingly enough – trigger identification across the Great Belt in this study.

Conclusions

In public discourse culture, ethnicity and nationality seem to have taken over old narratives about class. In the United Kingdom, Rampton (1995a, 1995b) and Gilroy (1987) and in Germany, Dirim and Auer (2004), note such a change in public discourse. Thus, the idea of a '... potential, imagined, "pan-immigrant" variety' (Stroud, 2004: 201) spoken by '...the ethnic "Other" in our midst' (Stroud, 2004: 197) might unintentionally, even though the aim is to promote and emphasize linguistic relativity and heterogeneity, end up reproducing and reinforcing the cultural and ethnic discourses, with further marginalization as a result. Common salient linguistic traits seem to confirm the assumption that ethnic speech forms in Aarhus and Copenhagen are alike; in addition, establishing and reproducing notions such as 'ethnolect' or 'multiethnolect' unintentionally adds to the construction of linguistic borders along ethnic and cultural differences at the risk of giving prominence to just these differences at the expense of, for example gender, age, social class or geography. The results reported above show that ethnic speech styles are deeply rooted in the local speech community. The young speakers in multiethnic suburban Aarhus find themselves in a local linguistic ecology characterized by a change from above (Maegaard, 2005) – the ongoing standardization process – and resistance from below (Nielsen & Nyberg, 1992: 186, 1989: 147). Their linguistic practices should be studied as both departing from and contributing to these processes. Speakers from linguistic and ethnic minority backgrounds are embedded in the local speech community, be it Aarhus, Copenhagen or any other locality, and should therefore be considered as such, both in sociolinguistics and in public discourse. Mohammed from Copenhagen does not consider Mohammed from Aarhus 'one of his kind'. Take his word for it – and listen.

References

Aarsæther, F. (2004) To språk i en tekst. Kodeveksling i samtaler mellom pakistansk-norske tiåringer [Two languages in one text. Code switching in conversations among ten years old Pakistani-Norwegian speakers]. PhD thesis, Oslo: Unipub.

Aarsæther, F., Nistov, I. and Opsahl, T. (2007) Youth in multiethnic Oslo: Their language and practices and their sense of belonging. Paper presented at ISB6, *The 6th International Symposium on Bilingualism*, 30.05.2007-02.06.2007, Hamburg.

Aarsæther, F., Nistov, I., Opsahl, T. and Svendsen, B.A. (2008) Negotiation of social categories through the use of multiethnolect. Paper presented at *International Sociolinguistics Symposium*, 17, 3.-5. April, 2008, Amsterdam.

Aasheim, S. (1995) "Kebab-norsk": Framandspråkleg påverknad på ungdomsspråket i Oslo ["Kebab-Norwegian": foreign language influence on youth language in Oslo]. MA thesis, University of Oslo.

Agha, A. (2007) *Language and Social Relations*. Cambridge: Cambridge University Press.

Aguilar, I. and Elsafadi, M. (eds) (2003) *Hør'a! Tekster om vennskap, tilhørighet, savn og kjærlighet [Listen up! Stories about friendship, belonging, longing and love]*. Oslo: Damm.

Allport, G.W. (1935) Attitudes. In C. Murchinson (ed.) *A Handbook of Social Psychology* (pp. 798–844). Worcester, MA: Clark University Press.

Almér, E. (in prep.) The verbal realisation of experience. A study of ideational meaning in narratives told by young people attending school in multilingual urban settings [preliminary title]. PhD thesis, University of Gothenburg.

Andersen, S. (1994) *Pragmatiske aspekter af kodeskift hos tosprogede børn [Pragmatic aspects of code switching among bilingual children]*. Københavnerstudier i tosprogethed, Køgeserien bind K2. Emdrup: Danmarks Lærerhøjskole.

Anderson, B. (1991) *Imagined Communities*. London: Verso.

Andersson, M. (2005) Språkliga medel – litterära möjligheter. En jämförelse mellan två noveller av A. Leiva Wenger [Linguistic means – literary possibilities. A comparison of two short stories by A. Leiva Wenger] (BA thesis). Göteborg: Institutionen för svenska språket, Göteborgs universitet.

Anderson, A.H., Bader, M., Bard, E.G., Boyle, E.H., Doherty, G.M., Garrod, S.C., Isard, S.D., Kowtko, J.C., McAllister, J.M., Miller, J., Sotillo, C.F., Thompson, R. and Weinert, H.S. (1991) The HCRC map task corpus. *Language and Speech* 34 (4), 351–366.

Androutsopoulos, J. (2001) From the streets to the screens and back again: On the mediated diffusion of ethnolectal patterns in contemporary German. *LAUD Linguistic Agencey* (A 522), 1–24.

Antaki, C. and Widdicombe, S. (eds) (1998) *Identities in Talk*. London: Sage.
Appel, R. (1999) Straattaal. De mengtaal van jongeren in Amsterdam [Streetspeech. The mixed speech of youths in Amsterdam]. *Toegepaste Taalwetenschap in Artikelen*, 62 (2), 39–57.
Appel, R. and Schoonen, R. (2005) Street language: A multicultural youth register in the Netherlands. *Journal of Multilingual and Multicultural Development* 26 (2), 85–117.
Auer, P. (1995) The pragmatics of code-switching: A sequential approach. In L. Milroy and P. Myusken (eds) *One Speaker, Two Languages* (pp. 115–136). Cambridge: Cambridge University Press.
Auer, P. (1999) From code-switching via language mixing to fused lects: Toward a dynamic typology of bilingual speech. *International Journal of Bilingualism* 3, 309–332.
Auer, P. (2003) Türkenslang – ein jugendsprachlicher Ethnolekt des Deutschen und seine Transformationen. In A. Häcki Buhofer (ed.) *Spracherwerb und Lebensalter* (pp. 255–264). Tübingen/Basel: Francke.
Auer, P. (2005) Europe's sociolinguistic unity, or: A typology of European dialect/ standard constellations. In N. Delbecque, J. van der Auwera and D. Geeraerts (eds) *Perspectives on Variation. Sociolinguistic, Historical, Comparative* (pp. 7–42). Berlin: Mouton de Gruyter.
Auer, P. (ed.) (2007) *Style and Social Identities. Alternative Approaches to Linguistic Heterogeneity*. Berlin: Mouton De Gruyter.
Bani-Shoraka, H. (2005) Language choice and code-switching in the Azerbaijani community in Tehran: A conversation analytic approach to bilingual practices. PhD thesis, Uppsala University.
Bauman, R. (1986) *Story, Performance and Event. Contextual Studies of Oral Narrative*. New York: Cambridge University Press.
Beck, U. (1992) *Risk Society: Towards a New Modernity*. London: SAGE.
Biber, D. (1988) *Variation across Speech and Writing*. Cambridge: Cambridge University Press.
Bijvoet, E. (1998) Sverigefinnar tycker och talar: om språkattityder och stilistisk känslighet hos två generationer sverigefinnar [Swedish-Finnish think and talk: On language attitudes and stilistic sensitivity in two generations]. PhD thesis, Uppsala University.
Bijvoet, E. (2003) Attitudes towards "Rinkeby Swedish", a group variety among adolescents in multilingual suburbs. In K. Fraurud and K. Hyltenstam (eds) *Multilingualism in Global and Local Perspectives. Selected Papers from the 8th Nordic Conference on Bilingualism, November 1–3, 2001, Stockholm-Rinkeby* (pp. 307–318). Stockholm: Centre for Research on Bilingualism, Stockholm University, and Rinkeby Institute of Multilingual Research.
Bijvoet, E. and Fraurud, K. (2006) "Svenska med något utländskt" ["Swedish with some foreign"]. *Språkvård* 2006/3, 4–10.
Bijvoet, E. and Fraurud, K. (2008) Svenskan i dagens flerspråkiga storstadsmiljöer: en explorativ studie av unga stockholmares perceptioner av variation och varieteter [Swedish in today's multilingual urban settings: an exploratory pilot study of young Stockholmers' perception of variation and varieties]. *Nordand* 3 (2), 7–38.
Bijvoet, E. and Fraurud, K. (forthcoming) Language variation and varieties in contemporary multilingual Stockholm: an exploratory pilot study of young peoples' perceptions. In R. Källström and I. Lindberg (eds) *Language and Language Use among Adolescents in Multilingual Urban Settings* [preliminary title]. ROSA (Rapporter om svenska som andraspråk). Institutet för svenska som andraspråk, Göteborgs universitet.

Blackledge, A. (2005) *Discourse and Power in a Multilingual World*. Amsterdam: John Benjamins.
Blom, J-P. and Gumperz, J.J. (1972) Social meaning in linguistic structures: Code-switching in Norway. In J.J. Gumperz and D. Hymes (eds) *Directions in Sociolinguistics* (pp. 407–434). New York: Holt, Rinehart and Winston.
Blommaert, J. (2005) *Discourse. A Critical Introduction*. Cambridge: Cambridge University Press.
Bodén, P. (2004) A new variety of Swedish? In S. Cassidy, F. Cox, R. Mannell and S. Palethorpe (eds) *Proceedings of the Tenth Australian International Conference on Speech Science and Technology*. Macquarie University, Sydney, 8th–10th December (pp. 475–480). Sydney: Australian Speech Science and Technology Association.
Bodén, P. (2007) "Rosengårdssvensk" fonetik och fonologi [Rosengård-Swedish phonetics and phonology]. In L. Ekberg (ed.) *Språket hos ungdomar i en flerspråkig miljö i Malmö. Nordlund 27. Småskrifter från Nordiska språk vid Lunds universitet* (pp. 1–47). Lund: Centre for languages and literature, Lund University.
Boersma, P. and Weenink, D. (2008) *Praat: Doing phonetics by computer*. Institute of Phonetic Sciences, University of Amsterdam. Online: http://www.praat.org (Accessed 2010-04-02)
Bolander, M. (1988a) Is there any order? On word order in Swedish learner language. *Journal of Multilingual and Multicultural Development* 9, 97–113.
Bolander, M. (1988b) Nu ja hoppas inte så mycke. Om inversion och placering av negation och adverb i svenska som andraspråk [Now I hope not so much. On inversion and placement of negations and adverbs in Swedish as a second language]. In K. Hyltenstam and I. Lindberg (eds) *Första Symposiet om Svenska som Andraspråk* (Vol. 1). Föredrag om Språk, Språkinlärning och Interaktion (pp. 203–214). Stockholm: Centre for Research on Bilingualism, Stockholm University.
Bourdieu, P. (1991) *Language and Symbolic Power*. Cambridge, MA: Harvard University Press.
Boyd, S. (1985) Language survival. A study of language contact, language shift, and language choice in Sweden. PhD thesis, Gothenburg monographs in linguistics 6. Gothenburg: University of Gothenburg.
Boyd, S. (2004) Utländska lärare i Sverige: Attityder till brytning [Foreign teachers in Sweden: Attitudes towards accents]. In K. Hyltenstam and I. Lindberg (eds) *Svenska som andraspråk – forskning, undervisning och samhälle*. Lund: Studentlitteratur.
Boyd, S. and Fraurud, K. (2010) Challenging the homogeneity assumption in language variation analysis. Findings from a study of multilingual urban spaces. In P. Auer and M. Schmidt (eds) *Language and Space – an International Handbook of Language Variation. Volume 1: Theories and Methods* (Ch. 38, pp. 686–706). Berlin/New York: Mouton de Gruyter.
Brautaset, A. (1996) *Inversjon i norsk mellomspråk. En undersøkelse av inversjon i stiler skrevet av innlærere med norsk som andrespråk. [Inversion in Norwegian interlanguage. A study of inversion in essays written by learners of Norwegian as a second language]* Oslo: Novus.
Brink, L. and Lund, J. (1975) *Dansk rigsmål [Standard Danish]* København: Gyldendal.
Broady, D. (2002) En social karta över gymnasieskolan i Stockholm i slutet av 1990-talet [A social map of high schools in Stockholm at the end of 1990s]. *Studies in Educational Policy and Educational Philosophy*, 2002:1. On WWW at http://www.upi.artisan.se/publish/docs/Doc161.pdf Accessed 07.08.2008.

Broady, D. and Börjesson, M. (2008) En social karta över gymnasieskolan [A social map of the high school]. In U.P. Lundgren (ed.) *Individ - samhälle - lärande. Åtta exempel på utbildningsvetenskaplig forskning* (pp. 24–35). Vetenskapsrådets rapportserie 2008: 2. On WWW at http://www.skeptron.uu.se/broady/sec/p-broady-borjesson-080520-social-karta-gyskolan-uvk-rapport-2008-2.pdf Accessed 07.08.2008.

Bruce, G. (1998) *Allmän och svensk prosodi. Praktisk lingvistik 16 [General and Swedish prosody. Applied linguistics 16]*. Lund: Department of Linguistics and Phonetics, Lund University.

Bruce, G. and Gårding, E. (1978) A prosodic typology for Swedish dialects. In E. Gårding, G. Bruce and R. Bannert (eds) *Nordic Prosody: Papers from a Symposium* (pp. 219–228). Malmö: Department of Linguistics and Phonetics, Lund University.

Brunstad, E., Røyneland, U. and Opsahl, T. (in press) Hip-hop, ethnicity and linguistic practice in rural and urban Norway. In M. Terkourafi (ed.) *The Languages of Global Hip-Hop*. London: Continuum.

Bull, T. (1996) Språkskifte hos kvinner og menn i ei nordnorsk fjordsamebygd [Language shift in a Northern-Norwegian fjord Sami village]. In E. Jahr and O. Skare (eds) *Nordnorske dialektar* (pp. 185–200). Oslo: Novus.

Butler, J. (2005) *Giving An Account of Oneself*. New York: Fordham University.

Cenoz, J. and Hoffmann, C. (2003) Acquiring a third language: What role does bilingualism play? *International Journal of Bilingualism* 7 (1), 1–5.

Cieslik, M. and Pollock, G. (2002) Introduction: Studying young people in late modernity. In M. Cieslik and G. Pollock (eds) *Young People in Risk Society. The Restructuring of Youth Identities and Transitions in Late Modernity* (pp. 1–21). Aldershot: Ashgate.

Cheshire, J. (2005) Syntactic variation and spoken language. In L. Cornips and K.P. Corrigan (eds) *Syntax and Variation. Reconciling the Biological and the Social* (pp. 81–106). Amsterdam: John Benjamins.

Cheshire, J., Fox, S., Kerswill, P. and Torgersen, E. (2008) Ethnicity, friendship network and social practices as the motor of dialect change: Linguistic innovation in London. *Sociolinguistica* 22, 1–23.

Christensen, M.V. (2002) Wallah det er fucked up det her [Wallah this is fucked up]. *Magasinet Humaniora* 4, 14–17.

Christensen, M.V. (2003) Etnolekt i Århus vest [Ethnolect in Aahus West]. In M. Kunøe og and P. Widell (eds) *Rapport fra 9. møde om Udforskningen af Dansk Sprog* (pp. 141–151). Århus: Århus Universitet.

Christensen, M.V. (2004) Arabiske ord i dansk hos unge i multietniske områder i Århus [Arabic words in Danish among adolescents in multiethnic areas in Aarhus, Denmark]. In C. Dabelsteen and J. Arnfast (eds) *Taler de dansk? Aktuel forskning i dansk som andetsprog* (pp. 33–52). Københavnerstudier i tosprogethed, 37, University of Copenhagen.

Christensen, M.V. (2009) Taler de århusiansk i Gellerup? [Do they speak Aarhus dialect in the Gellerup-suburb?] In S. Borchmann, Iversen, M. Kunøe and P. Sounberg (eds) *Århushistorier. Fra Bjerget til Byen 4* (pp. 130–140). Århus Universitetsforlag.

Christensen, M.V. (forthcoming) 8220, 8210 – Sproglig variation blandt unge i multietniske områder i Århus. [Zip-code 8220, 8210 – Language variation among adolescents in multiethnic areas in Aarhus]. PhD thesis, University of Aarhus.

Clyne, M. (2000) Lingua franca and ethnolects in Europe and beyond. *Sociolinguistica* 14, 83–89.

Corbett, G.G. (1991) *Gender*. Cambridge: Cambridge University Press.

Cornips, L. (2008) Loosing grammatical gender in Dutch: The result of bilingual acquisition and/or an act of identity? *International Journal of Bilingualism* 12 (1 & 2), 105–124.
Council of Europe and Norwegian Ministry of Education and Research (2003–2004) Language Education Policy Profile. Norway. On WWW at http://www.coe.int/T/DG4/Linguistic/Source/Profile_Norway_EN.pdf Accessed 11.02.09.
Coupland, N. (2001) Dialect stylization in radio talk. *Language in Society* 30, 345–375.
Coupland, N. (2003) Sociolinguistic authenticities. *Journal of Sociolinguistics* 7/3, 417–431.
Coupland, N. (2004) Stylised deception. In A. Jaworski, N. Coupland and D. Galasinski (eds) *Metalanguage. Social and Ideological Perspectives* (pp. 249–274). Berlin: Mouton de Gruyter.
Coupland, N. (2007) *Style. Language Variation and Identity*. Cambridge: Cambridge University Press.
Cunningham-Andersson, U. (1993) *Stigmatized Pronunciations in Non-native Swedish. PERILUS 17* (pp. 81–106). Stockholm: Department of Linguistics, Stockholm University.
Cunningham-Andersson, U. and Engstrand, O. (1988) *Attitudes to Immigrant Swedish – A Literature Review and Preparatory Experiments. PERILUS 8*. Stockholm: Department of Linguistics, Stockholm University.
Cutler, C. (2008) Brooklyn style: Hip-hop markers and racial affiliation among European immigrants in New York City. *International Journal of Bilingualism* 12 (1 & 2), 7–24.
Dailey-O'Cain, J. (2000) The sociolinguistic distribution of and attitudes toward focuser like and quotative like. *Journal of Sociolinguistics* 4 (1), 60–80.
Dauer, R.M. (1983) Stress-timing and syllable-timing reanalyzed. *Journal of Phonetics* 11, 51–62.
Davies, B. and Harré, R. (1990/2001) Positioning: The discursive production of selves. In M. Wetherell, S. Taylor and S.J. Yates (eds) *Discourse Theory and Practice. A Reader* (pp. 261–271). London: Sage Publications.
Deleuze, G. and Guattari, F. (1986) *Kafka: Toward a Minor Literature*. Minneapolis: University of Minnesota Press.
Deleuze, G. and Guattari, F. (1988) *A Thousand Plateaus: Capitalism and Schizophrenia*. London: Athlone Press.
Deppermann, A. (2007) Playing with the voice of the other: Stylized Kanaksprak in conversations among German adolescents. In P. Auer (ed.) *Style and Social Identities. Alternative Approaches to Linguistic Heterogeneity* (pp. 325–361). Berlin: Mouton de Gruyter.
Dirim, I. and Auer, P. (2004) *Türkisch sprechen nicht nur die Türken. Über die Unschärfbeziehung zwischen Sprache und Ethnie in Deutschland*. Berlin: de Gruyter
Diessel, H. (1999) *Demonstratives: Form, Function and Grammaticalization*. Amsterdam/Philadelphia: John Benjamins Publishing Co.
Drange, E-M. (2002) Fremmedspråklige slangord i norsk [Foreign slang words in Norwegian youth language]. In E-M. Drange, U-B. Kotsinas and A-B. Stenström (eds) *Jallaspråk, slanguage og annet ungdomsspråk i Norden* (pp. 9–18). Kristiansand: Norwegian Academic Press/HøyskoleForlaget.
Drange, E-M. and Hasund, I.K. (2000) Ungdomsspråk i Norden – en rapport om den norske UNO-forskningen [Youth language in Scandinavia – a report on the Norwegian UNO research]. In A-B. Stenström, U-B. Kotsinas, and E-M. Drange (eds) *Ungdommers språkmøter* (pp. 195–207). Nord 2000:6. København: Nordisk Ministerråd.

Drange, E-M., Kotsinas, U-B. and Stenström, A-B. (eds) (2002) *Jallaspråk, slanguage og annet ungdomsspråk i Norden* [Jalla language, slanguage and other youth languages in Scandinavia]. Kristiansand: Norwegian Academic Press/ HøyskoleForlaget.
Eckert, P. (2000) *Linguistic Variation as Social Practice*. Oxford: Blackwell.
Eckert, P. (2003) Elephants in the room. *Journal of Sociolinguistics* 7/3, 392–397.
Eckert, P. (2008a) Where do ethnolects stop? *In International Journal of Bilingualism* 12 (1 & 2), 25–42.
Eckert, P. (2008b) Variation and the indexical field. *Journal of Sociolinguistics* 12 (4), 453–476.
Eidevall, G. (1974) *Vilhelm Mobergs emigrantepos* [Vilhelm Moberg's emigrant epos]. Stockholm: P.A. Norstedt & Söner.
Ein Infoportal zu Jugendsprache in Wohngebieten mit hohen Migrantenanteil. On WWW at www.kiezdeutsch.de. Accessed 10.01.10.
Ekberg, L. (2004) Grammatik och lexikon i svenska som andraspråk på nästan infödd nivå [Grammar and lexicon in Swedish as a second language at near native level]. In K. Hyltenstam and I. Lindberg (eds) *Svenska som andraspråk: i forskning, undervisning och samhälle* (pp. 259-276). Lund: Studentlitteratur.
Ekberg, L. (2006) Bruket av sån i ungdomsspråk på mångspråkig grund [The use of *sån* (such) in the language of adolescents on a multilingual basis]. In S. Ask, G. Byrman, S. Hammarbäck, M. Lindgren and P. Stille (eds) *Lekt och lärt. Vänskrift till Jan Einarsson 2006* (pp. 65–73). Växjö: Växjö University Press.
Ekberg, L. (2007) "sån svensk å blond å sånt du vet" Lexiko-grammatiska drag i Malmöungdomars talspråk ["like Swedish and blond and such you know". Lexico-grammatical features in the spoken language of adolescents in Malmö]. In L. Ekberg (ed.) *Språket hos ungdomar i en flerspråkig miljö i Malmö* (pp. 48–77). Nordlund 27. Lund: Lund University.
Ekberg, L. (forthcoming) Joint attention and cooperation in the Swedish of adolescents in multilingual settings: The use of sån 'such' and såhär 'like'. In P. Auer, F. Hinskens and P. Kerswill (eds) *Pan-ethnic Styles of Speaking in European Metropolitan Cities. Studies in Language Variation (SiLV)*. Amsterdam: Benjamin.
Emanuelsson, B. (2005) *Gatus – ett multietniskt ungdomsspråk i Uppsala* [Gatus – a multethnic youth language in Uppsala]. *FUMS rapport 214*. Uppsala.
Engblom, C. (2004) *Samtal, identiteter och positionering: ungdomars interaktion i en mångkulturell miljö* [*Conversations, identities and positioning: Youth interactions in a multicultural environment*]. Stockholm: Almqvist and Wiksell international.
Enger, H-O. (2001) Genus i norsk bør granskes grundigere [Gender in Norwegian deserves a more careful investigation]. *Norsk Lingvistisk Tidsskrift* 19 (2), 163–183.
Enger, H-O. (2004) On the relation between gender and declension. *Studies in Language* 28 (1), 51–82.
Eriksson, M. (1997) Ungdomars berättande. En studie i struktur och interaktion [Storytelling in adolescence. A study of structure and interaction]. PhD thesis, Uppsala: Department of Scandinavian Languages, Uppsala University.
Faarlund, J.T., Lie, S. and Vannebo, K.I. (1997) *Norsk referansegrammatikk* [*Norwegian reference grammar*]. Oslo: Universitetsforlaget.
Farr, R.M. and Moscovici, S. (eds) (1984) *Social Representations*. Cambridge: Cambridge University Press.
Fischer-Jørgensen, E. and Hutters, B. (1981) Aspirated stop consonants before low vowels, a problem of delimitation, its causes and consequences. *ARIPUC 15*, 77-102.

Fiske, S.T. and Taylor, S.E. (1984) *Social Cognition*. Reading, MA: Addison-Wesley.
Fraurud, K. (2004) Några sociolingvistiska förutsättningar för språklig variation och mångfald i Rinkeby [Some sociolinguistic prerequisites for language variation and diversity in Rinkeby]. In B. Melander, U. Melander Marttala, C. Nyström, M. Thelander and C. Östman (eds) *Svenskans beskrivning 26* (pp. 25–47). Uppsala: Hallgren & Fallgren.
Fraurud, K. and Bijvoet, E. (2004) Multietniskt ungdomsspråk och andra varieteter av svenska i flerspråkiga miljöer [Multiethnic youth language and other varities of Swedish in multilingual contexts]. In K. Hyltenstam and I. Lindberg (eds) *Svenska som andraspråk: i forskning, undervisning och samhälle* (pp. 389–417). Lund: Studentlitteratur.
Fraurud, K. and Boyd, S. (2006) The native–non-native speaker distinction and the diversity of linguistic profiles of young people in Swedish multilingual urban contexts. In F. Hinskens (ed.) *Language Variation – European Perspectives*. Selected papers from the Third International Conference on Language Variation in Europe (ICLaVE 3), Amsterdam, June 2005 (pp. 53–69). Amsterdam: John Benjamins.
Fretheim, T. (1985) Er bokmålet tvekjønnet eller trekjønnet? [Does Norwegian Bokmål have two or three genders?] In E.H. Jahr and O. Lorentz (eds) *Morfologi. Studier i norsk språkvitenskap 3* (pp. 99–101). Oslo: Novus.
Ganuza, N. (2008a) Syntactic variation in the Swedish of adolescents in multilingual urban settings. Subject–verb order in declaratives, questions and subordinate clauses. PhD thesis, Stockholm University.
Ganuza, N. (2008b) Ordföljdsvariation som språklig strategi bland ungdomar i flerspråkiga storstadsmiljöer [Word order variation as a linguistic strategy among adolescents in multilingual urban settings]. *Nordand* 2 (3), 57–81.
Gardner, R.C. and Lambert W.E. (1969) *Attitudes and Motivation in Second-Language Learning*. Rowley, MA: Newbury House Publishers.
Garret, P., Coupland, N. and Williams, A. (1999) Evaluating dialect in discourse: teachers' and teenagers' responses to young English speakers in Wales. *Language in Society* 28, 321–354.
Garret, P., Coupland, N. and Williams, A. (2003) *Investigating Language Attitudes. Social Meanings of Dialect, Ethnicity and Performance*. Cardiff: University of Wales Press.
Gates, H.L. (1989) *The Signifying Monkey: A Theory of Afro-American Literary Criticism*. New York: Oxford University Press.
Gee, J.P. (1999) *An Introduction to Discourse Analysis. Theory and Method*. London: Routledge.
Gee, J.P., Hull, G. and Lankshear, C. (1997) *The New Work Order: Behind the Language of the New Capitalism*. St. Leonards, N.S.W.: Allen & Unwin.
Giampapa, F. (2004) The politics of identity, representation and the discourse of self-identification: Negotiating the periphery and the center. In A. Pavlenko and A. Blackledge (eds) *Negotiation of Identities in Multilingual Contexts* (pp. 192-218). Clevedon: Multilingual Matters.
Giddens, A. (1991) *Modernity and Self-Identity: Self and Society in the Late Modern Age*. Stanford: Stanford University Press.
Gilroy, P. (1987) *There Ain't no Black in the Union Jack. The Cultural Politics of Race and Nation*. London: Routledge.
Gilroy, P. (1998) Diasporan och identitetens omvägar [The diaspora and the long way round identity]. In T. Johansson, O. Sernhede and M. Trondman (eds) *Samtidskultur. Karaoke, karnevaler och kulturella koder* (pp. 180–203). Nora: Nya Doxa.
Goffman, E. (1959) *The Presentation of Self in Everyday Life*. London: Penguin Books.

Golden, A., Kulbrandstad, L.I. and Tenfjord, K. (2007) Norsk andrespråksforskning – utviklingslinjer fra 1980–2005 [Norwegian second language research – developments from 1980-2005]. *Nordand* 1, 5–41.
Gomér, M. (2008) "Shu len, vad händish". En analys av multietniskt ungdomsspråk i Alejandro Leiva Wengers novell Borta i tankar [Shu len, vad händish.' An analysis of Mulitethnic Youth Language in Alejandro Leiva Wenger's short story 'Borta i tankar] (BA thesis). Göteborg: Institutionen för svenska språket, Göteborgs universitet.
Graedler, A-L. (1998) Morphological, semantic and functional aspects of English lexical borrowings in Norwegian. PhD thesis, Oslo: Universitetsforlaget/ Scandinavian University Press.
Gramsci, A. (1971) *Selections From the Prison Notebooks* (Q. Hoare and G. Nowell-Smith, eds and trans.). London: Lawrence & Wishart.
Gregersen, F. (2009) The data and design of the LANCHART study. *Acta Linguistica Hafniensia* 41/1, 3–29.
Große, J. (2008) Fraseologiska enheter på flerspråkig grund. En jämförelse mellan verklighet och fiktion. *Nordisk tidsskrift for andrespråksforskning* 3 (2), 103–132.
Grønnum, N. (1991) Prosodic parameters in a variety of regional Danish standard languages, with a view towards Swedish and German. *Phonetica* 47, 188–214.
Grønnum, N. (1992) *The Groundworks of Danish Intonation. An Introduction*. København: Museum Tusculanum Press.
Grønnum, N. (2001) *Fonetik og fonologi – Almen og dansk. [Phonetics and phonology, general and Danish]* København: Akademisk.
Guldal, T.M. (1997) Three children, two languages. The role of code selection in organizing conversation. PhD thesis, Trondheim: Norges teknisk-naturvitenskapelige universitet.
Gumperz, J.J. (1982) *Discourse Strategies*. Cambridge: Cambridge University Press.
Gumperz, J.J. (1992) Contextualization revisited. In P. Auer and A. Di Luzio (eds) *The Contextualization of Language* (pp. 39–54). Amsterdam: John Benjamins.
Gussenhoven, C. (2002) Intonation and interpretation: Phonetics and phonology. In B. Bel and I. Marlien (eds) *Speech Prosody 2002*. (pp. 47–57). France: Laboratoire Parole et Langage, Université de Provence and SProSIG, ISCA.
György, K. (2010) Same mother tongue – Different origins. A study on language shift and language maintenance amongst Hungarian immigrants in Sweden. PhD thesis, Stockholm University.
Göransson, E. (2004) Khemiriska. En beskrivning av språket i romanen Ett öga rött av Jonas Hassen Khemiri [Khemirish. A description of the language in the novel 'Ett öga rött' by Jonas Hassen Khemiri] (BA thesis). Göteborg: Institutionen för svenska språket, Göteborgs universitet.
Gårding, E. (1974) Den efterhängsna prosodin [The persistent prosody]. In U. Teleman and T.G. Hultman (eds) *Språket i bruk* (pp. 50–71). Lund: Gleerups.
Hagen, J.E. (1992) Feilinvertering, overinvertering og underinvertering [Wrong inversion, over-inversion and under-inversion]. *NOA. Norsk som andrespråk* 15, 27–38.
Haglund, C. (2005) Social interaction and identification among adolescents in multilingual suburban Sweden: A study of institutional order and sociocultural change. PhD thesis, Stockholm University.
Haglund, C. (2007a) Ethnicity at work in peer-group interactions at school. In M. Martin-Jones, A.M. de Meíja and N. Hornberger (eds) *Encyclopedia of Language and Education*, Vol. 3: *Discourse and Education* (2nd edn, pp. 171–184). Heidelberg: Springer.

Haglund, C. (2007b) Flerspråkighet, institutionell ordning och sociokulturell förändring i det senmoderna Sverige [Multilingualism, institutional order and socio-cultural change in late modern Sweden]. *Nordand* 2/2007, 7–23.

Haglund, C. (2008) Linguistic diversity, institutional order and sociocultural change: Discourses and practices among teachers in Sweden. In G. Budach, J. Erfurt, and M. Kunkel (eds) *Écoles Plurilingues – Multilingual Schools: Konzepte, Institutionen und Akteure. Internationale Perspektiven* (pp. 147–168). Frankfurt am Main: Peter Lang.

Haglund, C. (in press) Multilingualism in young adulthood transitions: A theory and research review. In K. Hyltenstam (ed.) *High-level Proficiency in Second Language Use*. Berlin: Mouton de Gruyter.

Hall, S. (1990) Cultural identity and diaspora. In J. Rutherford (ed.) *Identity, Community, Culture, Difference* (pp. 222–237). London: Lawrence & Wishart.

Hammarlund, A. (1990) Från gudstjänarnas berg til folkets hus. In O. Ronström (ed.) *Musik och Kultur* (pp. 65–98). Lund: Studentlitteratur.

Hammarberg, B. (2007) Nyare utvecklingar inom forskningen om svenska som andraspråk [New developments in research on Swedish as a second language]. In *Nordand*, 1, 43–61.

Hansen, G.F. and Pharao, N. (2005) Prosodic aspects of the Copenhagen multi-ethnolect. In G. Bruce and M. Horne (eds) *Nordic Prosody*, Proceedings of the IXth Conference, Lund 2004, 87–96.

Hansson, P. (2003) Prosodic phrasing in spontaneous Swedish. Travaux de l'institut de linguistique de Lund 43. PhD thesis, Lund: Department of Linguistics, Lund University.

Hansson, P. and Svensson, G. (2004) Listening for "Rosengård Swedish". In P. Branderud and H. Traunmüller (eds) *Proceedings FONETIK 2004* (pp. 24–27). Department of Linguistics, Stockholm University.

Harnæs, L.A. (2001) Reaksjoner på utenlandsk aksent i norsk [Reactions towards Norwegian with a foreign accent]. In *NOA. Norsk som andrespråk*, 23, 79–112.

Hart, J.'t., Collier, R. and Cohen, A. (1990) *A Perceptual Study of Intonation. An Experimental Phonetic Approach to Speech Melody*. Cambridge: Cambridge University Press.

Hasund, I.K. (2003) The discourse markers "like" in English and "liksom" in Norwegian teenage language. A corpus-based, cross-linguistic study. PhD thesis, University of Bergen.

Heine, B. (1997) *Cognitive Foundations of Grammar*. New York/Oxford: Oxford University Press.

Heldner, M. and Strangert, E. (2001) Temporal effects on focus in Swedish. *Journal of Phonetics* 29, 329–361.

Heller, M. (1994), *Crosswords. Language, Education and Ethnicity in French Ontario*. Berlin: Mouton de Gruyter.

Heller, M. (1999) *Linguistic Minorities and Modernity. A Sociolinguistic Ethnography*. London: Longman.

Heller, M. (2007) Bilingualism as ideology and practice. In M. Heller (ed.) *Bilingualism: A Social Approach* (pp. 1–24). London: Palgrave Macmillan.

Hewitt, R. (1992) Language, youth and the destabilisation of ethnicity. In C. Palmgren, K. Lövgren, G. Bolin (eds) *Ethnicity in Youth Culture* (pp. 27–42). Stockholm: Stockholm University.

Himmelmann, N.P. (1996) Demonstratives in narrative discourse: A taxonomy of universal uses. In B. Fox (ed.) *Studies in Anaphora* (pp. 205–254). Amsterdam/Philadelphia: John Benjamins Publishing Co.

Hincks, R. (2003) Pronouncing the academic word list: Features of L2 student presentations. In M.J. Solé, D. Recasens and J. Romero (eds) *Proceedings of the 15th*

International Congress of Phonetic Sciences, Barcelona 3–9 August 2003 (pp. 1545–1548). Barcelona: Universitat Autònoma de Barcelona.
Hogg, M. A. and Abrams, D. (1988) *Social Identifications. A Social Psychology of Intergroup Relations and Group Processes.* London: Routledge.
Holmen, A. and Lund, K. (eds) (1999) *Studier i dansk som andetsprog* [Studies in Danish as a second language]. Copenhagen: Akademisk Forlag.
Holmen, A., Glahn E. and Ruus, H. (eds) (2003) *Veje til dansk* [Ways to Danish]. Copenhagen: Akademisk Forlag.
Huss, L. (1991) Simultan tvåspråkighet i svensk-finsk kontext [Simultaneous bilingualism in a Swedish-Finnish context]. PhD thesis, Uppsala University.
Hutters, B. and Bay, A. (2006) Danske indskolingsbørns udtale af /s/ med særligt henblik på læsp. [The pronounciation of /s/ in Danish early primary school children with a special focus on lisp]. *Dansk Audiologopædi* 1, 16–28.
Hyltenstam, K. (1977) Implicational patterns in interlanguage syntax variation. *Language Learning* 27 (2), 383–411.
Hyltenstam, K. (1978) Progress in immigrant Swedish syntax: A variability analysis. PhD thesis, Lund University.
Håkansson, G. (1992) Variation och rigiditet i ordföljdsmönster [Variation and rigidity in word order patterns]. In M. Axelsson and Å. Viberg (eds) *Nordens Språk som Andraspråk* (pp. 314–324). Stockholm: Stockholm University.
Håkansson, G. (2004) Utveckling och variation i svenska som andraspråk enligt processbarhetsteorin [Development and variation in Swedish as a second language according to the Processability Theory]. In K. Hyltenstam and I. Lindberg (eds) *Svenska som Andraspråk: I Forskning, Undervisning och Samhälle* (pp. 153–169). Lund: Studentlitteratur.
Håkansson, G. and Nettelbladt, U. (1993) Developmental sequences in L1 (normal and impaired) and L2 acquisition of Swedish syntax. *International Journal of Applied Linguistics* 3 (2), 131–157.
Hårstad, S. (2008) Kva skjer i dag? [What happens today?]. In A. Dalen, J-R. Hagland, S. Hårstad, H. Rydving and O. Stemshaug (eds) *Trøndersk språkhistorie: språkforhold i ein region* (pp. 399–424). Trondheim: Tapir.
Hårstad, S. (in press) Performing 'Dangerousness' linguistically: The case of the 'Bad Norwegian' on the streets of Trondheim. In J.N. Jørgensen (ed.) *"Love Ya Hate Ya". Studies in Youth Language and Youth Identities.* Cambridge: Cambridge Scholars Press.
Ims, I. (in progress) Adolescents in multiethnic Oslo – Language practices and perceptions. PhD thesis, University of Oslo.
Jahani, C. (1999) Språkbruk och språkattityder bland iranska invandrare i Sverige [Language use and language attitudes among Iranian immigrants in Sweden]. In R. Boström Andersson (ed.) *Ordets makt och tankens frihet* (pp. 219–227). Uppsala: Uppsala University.
Jaspers, J. (2007) In the name of science?: On identifying an ethnolect in an Antwerp secondary school. *Working Papers in Urban Language and Literacies*, Paper 42. King's College. On WWW at http://www.kcl.ac.uk/content/1/c6/04/20/06/paper42.pdf Accessed 02.04.10.
Jaspers, J. (2008) Problematizing ethnolects: Naming linguistic practices in an Antwerp secondary school. *International Journal of Bilingualism* 12 (1 & 2), 85–103.
Jernsletten, N. (1993) Sami language communities and the conflict between Sami and Norwegian. In E.H. Jahr (ed.) *Language Conflict and Language Planning* (pp. 115–132). Berlin: Mouton de Gruyter.
Johannessen, J.B. (2008) Oslospråket i tall [The Oslo language in numbers]. In J.B. Johannessen and K. Hagen (eds) *Språk i Oslo. Ny forskning omkring talespråk* (pp. 235–242). Oslo: Novus.

Johannessen, J.B. and Hagen, K. (eds) (2008) *Språk i Oslo. Ny forskning omkring talespråk* [Language in Oslo. New research on spoken language]. Oslo: Novus.

Johansen, H. (2007) Ja takk, begge deler: en undersøkelse av variasjonsmønstre i anvendelse av invertert ordstilling i norske mellomspråktekster [Both, please: A study of variation patterns in the use of inverted word order in Norwegian interlanguage texts]. MA thesis, University of Bergen.

Johansson, F.A. (1973) Immigrant Swedish Phonology. Travaux de l'institut de Lund. Publiés par Bertil Malmberg et Kerstin Hadding IX. PhD thesis. Lund: CWK Gleerup.

Jonsson, R. (2007) Blatte betyder kompis. Om maskulinitet och språk i en högstadieskola [Blatte means friend. On masculinity and language in a high school] PhD thesis, Stockholm: Ordfront.

Jørgensen, J.N. (1993) Children's code switching in group conversations. In *European Science Foundation Network on Code-Switching and Language Contact Code-Switching Summer School* (pp. 165–181). Pavia, 9–12 September 1992. Paris: European Science Foundation.

Jørgensen, J.N. (1998) Children's acquisition of code-switching for power wielding. In P. Auer (ed.) *Code-Switching in Conversation* (pp. 237–261). London: Routledge.

Jørgensen, J.N. (2003) Bilingualism in the Køge Project. *International Journal of Bilingualism* 7 (4), 333–352.

Jørgensen, J.N. (2004) Languaging and languagers. In C.B. Dabelsteen and J.N. Jørgensen (eds) *Language and Language Practices: Copenhagen Studies in Bilingualism* (Vol. 36, pp. 5–22). Faculty of Humanities, University of Copenhagen.

Jørgensen, J.N. (forthcoming) Languaging. Nine years of poly-lingual development of young Turkish-Danish grade school students. Doctor's thesis. Copenhagen: Danish School of Education, University of Aarhus.

Jørgensen J.N., Holmen, A., Gimbel, J. and Nørgaard, I. (1991) From Köy to Køge. A longitudinal study of the bilingual development of Turkish immigrant children in Danish schools. *Language & Education* 4 (3), 215–217.

Jørgensen, J.N. and Møller, J. (2008) Poly-lingual languaging in peer group interaction. *Nordand* 3 (2), 39–56.

Jørgensen, J.N., Møller, J., Quist, P. and Holmen, A. (1998) Introduktion til Køgeprojektet [Introduction to the Køge Project]. In J. Møller, P. Quist, A. Holmen and J.N. Jørgensen (eds) *Tosproget udvikling. Køgeserien bind K4. Københavnerstudier i tosprogethed* (pp. 5–19). København: Danmarks Lærerhøjskole.

Kahlin, L. (2008) Sociala kategoriseringar i samspel: hur kön, etnicitet och generation konstitueras i ungdomars samtal [Social categorisation in interaction: How gender, ethnicity and generation is constituted in conversations among youth]. PhD thesis, Stockholm University.

Kallmeyer, W. and Keim, I. (2003) Linguistic variation and the construction of social identity in a German-Turkish setting. A case study of an immigrant youth group in Mannheim, Germany. In J. Androutsopoulos and A. Georgakopoulou (eds) *Discourse Constructions of Youth Identities* (pp. 29–46). Amsterdam: John Benjamins.

Källström, R. (2003) Ett språkligt genombrott? [A linguistic breakthrough?] In H. Landqvist, S-G. Malmgren, K. Norén, L. Rogström and B. Wallgren Hemlin (eds) *Texten framför allt. Festskrift till Aina Lundqvist på 65-årsdagen den 11 september 2003* (pp. 94–102). Göteborg: Institutionen för svenska språket, Göteborgs universitet.

Källström, R. (2005) Litterärt språk på tvärs: Något om språket hos Leiva Wenger och Hassen Khemiri. [Literary language crosswise: On language in Leiva Wenger and Hassen Khemiri]. In B. De Geer and A. Malmbjer (eds) *Språk på Tvärs. Rapport från ASLA:s Höstsymposium Södertörn, 11–12 November 2004.* (ASLA:s skriftserie 18) (pp. 147–158). Uppsala: ASLA.

Källström, R. (2006) "Flygande blattesvenska" – recensenter om språket i Ett öga rött ['Flying 'Blatte' Swedish' – literary critics on the language in 'Ett öga rött']. In P. Ledin, L. Lind Palicki, C. Melin, G. Nilsson, K. Wirdenäs and H. Åbrink (eds) *Svenskans Beskrivning 28* (pp. 125–135). Örebro: Örebro University.

Källström, R. (2008) Vilhelm Moberg och amerikasvenskan [Vilhelm Moberg and American Swedish]. In K. Jóhannesson, H. Landqvist, A. Lundqvist, L. Rogström, E. Sköldberg and B. Wallgren Hemlin (eds) *Nog ordat? Festskrift till Sven-Göran Malmgren* (pp. 225–232). Göteborg: Meijerbergs arkiv för svensk ordforskning.

Källström, R. (forthcoming) 'Flying Blatte Swedish' – reviewers' treatment of language in the novel Ett öga rött. In R. Källström and I. Lindberg (eds) (forthcoming) *Language and Language Use among Adolescents in Multilingual Urban Settings* [preliminary title]. ROSA (Rapporter om svenska som andraspråk). Gothenborg: Institutet för svenska som andraspråk, Göteborgs universitet.

Källström, R. and Lindberg, I. (eds) (forthcoming) *Language and Language Use among Adolescents in Multilingual Urban Settings* [preliminary title]. ROSA (Rapporter om svenska som andraspråk). Gothenburg: Institutet för svenska som andraspråk, Göteborgs universitet.

Khemiri, J.H. (2003) *Ett öga rött [An eye red]*. Stockholm: Månpocket.

Knudsen, J.S. (2006 (2004)) Those That Fly Without Wings: Music and Dance in a Chilean Immigrant Community. PhD thesis. Oslo: Unipub.

Knudsen, J.S. (2008) Glatte Gater – musikkproduksjon i et urbant ungdomsmiljø [Slippery streets – music production in an urban youth environment]. In M. Krogh and B. Stougaard (eds) *Hiphop i Skandinavien.* Aarhus: Aarhus Universitetsforlag.

Kotsinas, U-B. (1982) Svenska svårt. Några invandrares svenska talspråk [Swedish difficult. Some immigrants' spoken language]. PhD thesis, Stockholm University.

Kotsinas, U-B. (1985) Invandrarsvenska och språkförändringar [Immigrant Swedish and language change]. In S. Allén, L-G. Andersson, J. Löfström, K. Nordenstam and B. Ralph (eds) *Svenskans beskrivning 15* (pp. 276–290). Gothenburg: Gothenburg University.

Kotsinas, U-B. (1988a) Rinkebysvenska – en dialekt? [Rinkeby-Swedish – a dialect?] In P. Linell, V. Adelswärd, T. Nilsson and P.A. Petersson (eds) *Svenskans beskrivning 16* (pp. 264–278). Linköping: Linköping University.

Kotsinas, U-B. (1988b) Immigrant children's Swedish – A new variety? *Journal of Multilingual and Multicultural Development* 9, 129–141.

Kotsinas, U-B. (1989) Stockholmsspråk genom 100 år [The language of Stockholm over 100 years]. *Tijdschrift voor Skandinavistiek* 12/10, 14–37.

Kotsinas, U-B. (1990) Svensk, invandrarsvensk eller invandrare. Om bedömningar av "främmande" drag i svenskt talspråk [Swede, immigrant Swede or immigrant. About judgements of "foreign" features in spoken Swedish]. In G. Tingbjörn (ed.) *Andra symposiet om svenska som andraspråk i Göteborg 1989* (pp. 244–273). Stockholm: Scriptor.

Kotsinas, U-B. (1994) *Ungdomsspråk* [Youth Language]. Uppsala: Hallgren & Fallgren.

Kotsinas, U-B. (1996) Rinkebysvenska – ett ungdomsspråk [Rinkeby Swedish – a language of the youth]. In Å. Daun and B. Klein (eds) *Alla Vi Svenskar* (pp. 29–45). Stockholm: Nordiska museet och Skansens årsbok, Fataburen.
Kotsinas, U-B. (1998) Language contact in Rinkeby, an immigrant suburb. In J. Androutsopoulous and A. Scholz (eds) *Jugensprache Langue de Jeunes Youth Language* (pp. 125–148). Frankfurt am Main: Peter Lang.
Kotsinas, U-B. (2000) Pidginization, creolization and creoloids in Stockholm, Sweden. In B.-L. Gunnarsson, S. Hellberg and K. Svartholm (eds) *Kontakt, variation och förändring – studier i Stockholmsspråk. Ett urval uppsatser av Ulla-Britt Kotsinas* (pp. 160–190). Stockholm: Almqvist & Wiksell International.
Kotsinas, U-B. (2002) Engelska ord i nordisk slang [English words in Nordic slang]. In E.-M. Drange, U.-B. Kotsinas and A.-B. Stenström (eds) *Jallaspråk. Slanguage og andre ungdomsspråk i Norden* (pp. 37–61). Kristiansand: Høyskoleforlaget.
Kotsinas, U-B. and Doggelito, D. (2004) *Förortsslang [Suburban Slang]*. Stockholm: Nordstedts Akademiska Förlag.
Kristiansen, T. (1991a) Sprogholdninger hos folkeskolelærere, unge mennesker og personalechefer på Næstevedegnen [Language attitudes among school teachers, adolescents and H. R. managers around Næstved]. *Danske Folkemål* 33, 51–62.
Kristiansen, T. (1991b) Sproglige normidealer på Næstvedegnen. Kvantitative sprogholdningsundersøgelser [Linguistic norm ideals in Næstved. Quantitative studies of language attitudes]. PhD thesis, University of Copenhagen.
Kristiansen, T. (1997) Language attitudes in a Danish cinema. In N. Coupland and Jaworski, A. (eds) *Sociolinguistics. A Reader and Coursebook* (pp. 291–305). Basingstoke: Palgrave.
Kristiansen, T. (1999) Unge sprogholdninger i Næstved 89 og 98 [Young language attitudes in Næstved 89 and 98]. *Danske folkemål* 41, 139–162.
Kristiansen, G. (2006) Towards a usage-based cognitive phonology. *International Journal of English Studies* 6 (2), 107–140.
Kristiansen, T. (2006) Social meaning and subjective processes: A presentation of theories and methods from the Næstved studies. Paper presented at *Approaches to the Study of Folk Linguistics, Sociolinguistic Awareness and Language Attitudes*. Centre for Reseach on Bilingualism, Stockholm University, 7 March, 2006.
Kristiansen, T. (2009) The macro-level social meanings of late modern Danish accents. *Acta Linguistica Hafniensia* 41, 167–192.
Kristiansen, T., Garrett, P. and Coupland, N. (2005) Introducing subjectivities in language variation and change. *Acta Linguistica Hafniensia* 37, 9–36.
Kulbrandstad, L.A. (1997) *Språkportretter. Studier av tolv minoritetselevers språkbruksmønstre, språkholdninger og språkferdigheter [Language portraits. Studies of patterns of language use, attitudes and competences among twelve minority students]*. Vallset: Oplandske Bokforlag.
Kulbrandstad, L.A. (2002) Omtale av innvandreres måte å snakke norsk på. En studie av et avismateriale fra Internett [Public comments on immigrants' ways of speaking. A study of newspaper material from the internet]. In *Forskning i nordiske sprog som andet- og fremmedsprog. Rapport fra konference i Reykjavík 23.-25. maj 2001* (pp. 383–398). Reykjavík: Háskóli Íslands Háskólaútgáfan.
Kulbrandstad, L.A. (2004) "Kebabnorsk", "perkerdansk" og "gebrokken" – ord om innvandreres mate å snakke majoritetsspråket på ['Kebab-Norwegian', 'Perker-Danish' and 'broken' – words describing immigrants' way of speaking the majority language]. In H. Sandøy, E. Brunstad, J.E. Hagen and K. Tenfjord (eds) *Den fleirspråklege utfordringa* (pp. 108–130). Oslo: Novus.
Kulbrandstad, L.A. (2006a) "Det va jo norsk da, men det va'kje norsk" Ungdommer møter andrespråksfaget norsk ["It was Norwegian, but it wasn't Norwegian"

Young people meet the subject L2-Norwegian]. In H. Sandøy and K. Tenfjord (eds) *Den nye norsken? Nokre peilepunkt under globaliseringa* (pp. 99–123). Oslo: Novus forlag.

Kulbrandstad, L.A. (2006b) Språklig oppmerksomhet og metaspråk [Linguistic attention and meta-language]. Paper presented at *Noran 2006, Den andre forskerkonferansen i norsk som andrespråk*. University of Oslo, November 18th–17th, 2006.

Kulk, F., Odé, C. and Woidich, M. (2003) The intonation of colloquial Damascene Arabic: A pilot study. In *Proceedings 25* (pp. 15–20). Institute of Phonetic Sciences, University of Amsterdam.

Kyst B. (2004) *Trykgruppens toner i århusiansk regionalsprog [Stress group intonation in Aarhusian]*, Unpublished thesis, University of Århus. On WWW at www.bodilkyst.dk Accessed 02.04.10.

Kyst, B. and Henrichsen, P.J. (2005) Synthetic regional Danish. Manuscript from *NODALIDA 2005, the 15th Nordic Conference of Computational Linguistics*, University of Joensuu, 20–21 May 2005. Online document: www.bodilkyst.dt (Accessed: 2010-04-02).

Labov, W. (1972) *Sociolinguistic Patterns*. Philadelphia: University of Pennsylvania Press.

Labov, W. (2001) *Principles of Linguistic Change. Social Factors*. Oxford: Blackwell Publishers.

Labov, W. (2006) *The Social Stratification of English in New York City* (2nd edn). Cambridge: Cambridge University Press.

Ladefoged, P. and Maddieson, I. (1996) *The Sounds of the World's Languages*. Cornwall: Blackwell Publishers.

Lainio, J. (1989) Spoken Finnish in urban Sweden. PhD thesis, Uppsala University.

Lambert, W.E., Hodgson, R., Gardner, R.C. and Fillenbaum, S. (1960) Evaluational reactions to spoken language. *Journal of Abnormal and Social Psychology* 60, 44–51.

Lambert, W.E., Hodgson, R.C., Gardner, R.C. and Fillenbaum, S. (1972) Evaluational reactions to spoken languages. In A.S. Dil (ed.) *Language, Psychology and Culture. Essays by Wallace E. Lambert* (pp. 80–96). CA: Stanford University Press.

Lane, P.M.J. (2006) A tale of two towns: A comparative study of language and culture contact. PhD thesis, Oslo: Unipub.

Lanza, E. (1992) Can bilingual two-year-olds code-switch? *Journal of Child Language* 19, 633–658.

Lanza, E. and Svendsen, B.A. (2007) Tell me who your friends are and I might be able to tell you what language(s) you speak: Social network analysis, multilingualism, and identity. *International Journal of Bilingualism* 11/3, 275–300.

Larsen, A.B. (1907) *Kristiania bymål. Vulgærsproget med henblik på den utvungne dagligtale [Kristiania city language. The vulgar language with an eye to the natural everyday speech]*. Kristiania, Norway: Cammermeyer.

Lecomte, B. (2008) De slutter med "kebabnorsk [-They stop speaking "Kebab Norwegian"]". *Nettavisen*. On WWW at http://pub.tv2.no/nettavisen/innenriks/ioslo/article1610041.ece Accessed 18.02.08.

Leiva Wenger, A. (2001) *Till vår ära [In our honor]*. Stockholm: Bonniers.

Le Page, R.B. (1977) Processes of pidginization and creolization. In A. Valdman (ed.) *Pidgin and Creole Linguistics* (pp. 222–255). Bloomington: University of Indiana Press.

Le Page, R.B. (1994) The notion of "linguistic system" revisited. *International Journal of the Sociology of Language* 109, 109–120.

Le Page, R.B. and Tabouret-Keller, A. (1985) *Acts of Identity. Creole-Based Approaches to Language and Ethnicity*. Cambridge: Cambridge University Press.

Lie, S. (2008) Veldig sånn festejente [Very such party girl]. In J.B. Johannessen and K. Hagen (eds) *Språk i Oslo. Ny forskning omkring talespråk* (pp. 78–95). Oslo: Novus.
Lindblad, P. (1992) *Rösten [The Voice]*. Lund: Studentlitteratur.
Lindblom, B. (1978) Final lengthening in speech and music. In E. Gårding, G. Bruce and R. Bannert (eds) *Nordic Prosody: Papers from a Symposium* (pp. 85–101). Malmö: Department of Linguistics and Phonetics, Lund University.
Lindström, E. (2000) Some uses of demonstratives in spoken Swedish. In S. Botley and A.M. McEnery (eds) *Corpus-based and Computational Approaches to Discourse Anaphora* (pp. 107–128). Amsterdam/Philadelphia: John Benjamins Publishing Co.
Lindström, A. (2004) English and other foreign linguistic elements in spoken Swedish. Studies of productive processes and their modelling using finite-state tools. PhD thesis, Linköping: Department of Computer and Information Science, Linköping University.
Linell, P. (1998) *Approaching Dialogue. Talk, Interaction and Contexts in Dialogical Perspectives*. Amsterdam: John Benjamins.
Linell, P. (2001) Dynamics of discourse or stability of structure: Sociolinguistics and the legacy from linguistics. In N. Coupland, S. Sarangi and C.N. Chandlin (eds) *Sociolinguistics and Social Theory* (pp. 107–126). Harlow: Pearson.
Lundberg, D., Malm, K. and Ronström, O. (2003) *Music Media Multiculture – Changing Musicscapes*. Stockholm: Svenskt Visarkiv.
Madsen, L.M. (2008a) Figthers and outsiders: Linguistic practices, social identities, and social relationships among urban youth in a martial arts club. PhD dissertation, University of Copenhagen.
Madsen, L.M. (2008b) Un Deux Trois? Speak English!: Young Taekwondo-fighters' identity construction through linguistic competition. *International Journal of Multilingualism* 5 (3), 197–216.
Maegaard, M. (1998) Sprogvalg i gruppesamtaler [Language choice in group conversations]. In J. Møller, P. Quist, A. Holmen and J.N. Jørgensen (eds) *Tosproget udvikling. Køgeserien bind K4. Københavnerstudier i tosprogethed* (pp. 21–40). København: Danmarks Lærerhøjskole.
Maegaard, M. (2001) 'Jeg er da stolt af at jeg er sønderjyde – altså sådan forholdsvis' – om sprogbrug og sprogholdninger hos sønderjyske unge ["I'm proud I'm from Southern Jutland – well, relatively"]. On language use and language attitudes among Southern Jutlandic youth]. *Danske Talesprog* 2, 77–167.
Maegaard, M. (2005) Language attitudes, norms and gender. A presentation of the method and results from a language attitude study. In T. Kristiansen, P. Garret and N. Coupland (eds) *Acta Linguistica Hafniensia* (pp. 55–80). København: C. A. Reitzels Forlag.
Maegaard, M. (2007) *Udtalevariation og -forandring i københavnsk: En etnografisk undersøgelse af sprogbrug, sociale kategorier og social praksis blandt unge på en københavnsk folkeskole [Phonetic variation and change in Copenhagen: An ethnographic study of language use, social categories and social practice among young people in a Copenhagen school]. Danske Talesprog 8.* København: C.A. Reitzels Forlag.
Maegaard, M. (2009) Den kvalitative sprogholdningsmetode – mellem ideologi og praksis [The qualitative language attitudes method – between ideology and practice]. In A. Gudiksen, H. Hovmark, P. Quist, J. Scheuer and I. Sletten (eds) *Dialektforskning i 100 år* (pp. 171–96). Copenhagen: Department of Scandinavian Research, University of Copenhagen.
Major, R.C. (2001) *Foreign Accent: The Ontogeny and Phylogeny of Second Language Phonology*. New Jersey: Lawrence Erlbaum Associates.

Makoni, S. and Pennycook, A. (2006) Disinventing and reconstituting languages. In S. Makoni and A. Pennycook (eds) *Disinventing and Reconstituting Languages* (pp. 1–41). Clevedon: Multilingual Matters.

McLaughlin, B. (1978) *Second-language Acquisition in Childhood*. New Jersey: Lawrence

McLaughlin, B. (1987) *Theories of Second-Language Learning*. London: Arnold.

Milani, T. (2007a) Voices of authority in conflict: The making of the expert in a language debate in Sweden. *Linguistics and Education* 18, 99–120.

Milani, T.M. (2007b) Debating Swedish: Language politics and ideology in contemporary Sweden. PhD thesis, Stockholm: Stockholm University, Centre for Research on Bilingualism.

Mitchell, T. (2001) *Global Noise: Rap and Hip-Hop Outside the USA*. Middletown, CT: Wesleyan University Press.

Mitchell, T. (2004) Doin' damage in my native language: the use of 'resistance vernaculars' in hip hop in Europe and Aotearoa/New Zealand. In S. Whiteley, A. Bennett and S. Hawkins (eds) *Music, Space and Place : Popular Music and Cultural Identity* (pp. 124–146). Aldershot: Ashgate.

Modern Loanwords in the Nordic Countries. On WWW at http://moderne-importord. info/ Accessed 10.01.10.

Møller, J.S. (2008a) Polylingual performance among Turkish-Danes in late-modern Copenhagen. *International Journal of Multilingualism* 5 (3), 217–236.

Møller, J.S. (2008b) Polylingual behavior in different life stages. In V. Lytra and J.N. Jørgensen (eds) *Multilingualism and Identities across Contexts. Cross-Disciplinary Perspectives on Turkish-Speaking Youth in Europe* (Vol. 45, pp. 44–59). Copenhagen Studies of Bilingualism, University of Copenhagen.

Møller, J.S. (2009) Stereotyping categorisations of speech styles among linguistic minority Danes in Køge. In M. Maegaard, F. Gregersen, P. Quist and J.N. Jørgensen (eds) *Language Attitudes, Standardization and Language Change* (pp. 231–254). Oslo: Novus Forlag.

Møller, J.S. and Jørgensen, J.N. (2008) Poly-lingual languaging in group interaction. *Nordand* 3 (2), 39–56.

Møller, J., Quist, P.H. and Jørgensen, J.N. (eds) (1998) *Tosproget udvikling [Bilingual development]*. Køgeserien bind K4. Københavnerstudier i tosprogethed. København: Danmarks Lærerhøjskole.

Mæhlum, B. and Røyneland, U. (2009) Dialektparadiset Norge – en sannhet med modifikasjoner [The dialect paradise Norway – a truism with modifications]. In H. Hovmark, I. Sletten and A. Gudiksen (eds) *I mund og bog - 25 artikler om sprog tilegnet Inge Lise Pedersen på 70-årsdagen d. 5. juni 2009* (pp. 219–231). Afdeling for Dialektforskning og Nordisk Forskningsinsitut, Unversity of Copenhagen.

Nesse, A. (2008) *Bydialekt, riksmål og identitet: sett fra Bodø [City dialect, standard language and identity: Perspectives from Bodø]*. Oslo: Novus.

Niedzielski, N. and Preston, D.R. (2003) *Folk Linguistics*. Berlin: Mouton de Gruyter.

Nielsen, B.J. (1998) Talesprogsvariationen i Århus – en sociolingvistisk redegørelse og en sammenligning med sproget i Odder. [Language variation in Aarhus – a sociolinguistic account and a comparison with the language in Odder] *Danske Folkemål* 40, 51–78.

Nielsen, B.J. and Nyberg, M. (1988) Talesprogsvariationen i Odder kommune. En foreløbig rapport [Language variation in Odder. A preliminary report.]. *Danske Folkemål* 30, 31–87.

Nielsen, B.J. and Nyberg, M. (1989) Talesprogsvariationen i Odder kommune. En foreløbig rapport II [Language variation in Odder. A preliminary report II]. *Danske Folkemål* 31, 119–153.

Nielsen, B.J. and Nyberg, M. (1992) Talesprogsvariationen i Odder Kommune. I. Lokalsprog og rigsmål i sociolingvistisk belysning [Language variation in Odder. Local dialect and standard Danish, a sociolinguistic examination]. *Danske Folkemål* 34, 45–201.

Nielsen, B.J. and Nyberg, M. (1993) Talesprogsvariationen i Odder kommune. II. Yngre og ældre rigsmålsformer i sociolingvistisk belysning [Language variation in Odder. II. New and older standard Danish language forms, a sociolinguistic examination]. *Danske Folkemål* 35, 249–348.

Nistov, I. (1991) Morsmål og mellomspråk. Ei longitudinell undersøking av trekk i norske mellomspråkstekstar skrivne av fire tyrkiske elevar [Mother tongue and inter language. A longitudinal study of interlanguage texts written by four Turkish students]. *NOA. Norsk som andrespråk* 13, 1–212.

Nistov, I. and Opsahl, T. (2009) Plutselig du vinner fem tusen...Manglande inversjon i norsken til Oslo-ungdom i fleirspråklege miljø [Suddenly you win five thousand. The lack of inversion in the speech of adolescents in multilingual settings in Oslo]. Paper presented at *Den 9.konference om Nordens sprog som andetsprog*. 11th–13th June 2009. Helsingør.

Nordberg, B. (1984) Om ungdomars samtalsstil. Några preliminära iakttagelser [Young people's conversational style. Some preliminary observations]. *Nysvenska Studier* 64, 5–27.

Norwegian Language Council (2009) On WWW at http://www.sprakrad.no/ Toppmeny/Aktuelt/Haldningsundersoking-om-sprakbruk-i-NRK/. Accessed 07.01.10.

Norwegian Spoken Language Corpus. On WWW at http://hf.uio.no/tekstlab/ Accessed 10.06.10.

Nortier, J. (2001) "Fawaka, what's up?" Language use among adolescents in monoethnic and ethnically mixed groups. In A. Hvenekilde and J. Nortier (eds) *Meetings at the Crossroads. Studies of Multilingualism and Multiculturalism in Oslo and Utrecht* (pp. 61–72). Oslo: Novus.

Opsahl, C.P. (2000) Blant mikrofonriddere og plateryttere. Selvpresentasjon i norsk hip hop [Among microphone knights and record riders. Self presentation in Norwegian hip-hop]. *Kirke og Kultur* [*Culture and Church*] 105 (3), 195–207.

Opsahl, T. (2009a) Wolla I swear this is typical for the conversational style of adolescents in multiethnic areas in Oslo. In F. Gregersen and U. Røyneland (eds) *Special Issue of Nordic Journal of Linguistics. Sociolinguistics* 32–2, 221–244.

Opsahl, T. (2009b) Genusmarkering og sånn i norsk i multietniske ungdomsmiljøer i Oslo [Gender and such in Norwegian spoken among youth in multiethnic settings in Oslo]. In "Egentlig alle kan bidra!" - en samling sosiolingvistiske studier av strukturelle trekk ved norsk i multietniske ungdomsmiljøer i Oslo. PhD thesis, University of Oslo.

Opsahl, T. (2009c) Enkelt og tøft: Non-V2 i deklarativsetninger med topikaliserte elementer hos ungdommer i multietniske miljøer i Oslo [Easy and cool: Non-V2 in declarative sentences with topicalised elements among youth in multiethnic settings in Oslo]. In "Egentlig alle kan bidra!" – en samling sosiolingvistiske studier av strukturelle trekk ved norsk i multietniske ungdomsmiljøer i Oslo. PhD thesis, University of Oslo.

Opsahl, T. and Røyneland, U. (2008) Hiphop and the formation of a Norwegian multiethnolectal speech style. Paper presented at *Jugendsprache: The Fifth International Conference on Youth Language* (pp. 27–29). March 2008, University of Copenhagen.

Opsahl, T., Røyneland, U. and Svendsen, B.A. (2008) "Syns du jallanorsk er lættis, eller?" – om taggen [lang = X] i NoTa-Oslo-korpuset ["Jalla-Norwegian is a riot, innit?" On the tag [lang = X] in the NoTa-Oslo corpus]. In J.B. Johannessen and

K. Hagen (eds) *Språk i Oslo. Ny forskning omkring talespråk* (pp. 29–41). Oslo: Novus.
Öqvist, J. (1997) Jamen förr i tiden så va re ju mera sär "å vicken vacker hatt du har". Om partikeln 'sär's funktioner i samtal [Well in the past then it was more like "oh what a beautiful hat you have." On the particle 'sär's' functions in conversations] Thesis, Institutionen för Lingvistik, Stockholms Universitet.
Oslo Municipality (2009) On WWW at http://www.oslo.kommune.no. Accessed 24.03.09
Østby, A. (2005) *Kebabnorsk ordbok [Kebab-Norwegian Dictionary]*. Oslo: Gyldendal.
Otterup, T. (2005) "Jag känner mej begåvad bara": om flerspråkighet och identitetskonstruktion i ett multietniskt förortsområde ['It's Simply a Gift': Multilingualism and Identity Formation among Young People in a Multiethnic Urban Area]. PhD thesis, University of Gothenburg.
Papazian, E. (1997) Dialektdød i Numedal? Om språkutviklinga i Nore og Uvdal [Dialect death in Numedal? On language change in Nore and Uvdal]. *Maal og Minne* 2, 161–190.
Park, H-S. (2000) Korean-Swedish code-switching: Theoretical models and linguistic reality. PhD thesis, Uppsala University.
Pavlenko, A. and Blackledge, A. (2004a) Introduction: New theoretical approaches to the study of negotiation of identities in multilingual contexts. In A. Pavlenko and A. Blackledge (eds) *Negotiation of Identities in Multilingual Contexts* (pp. 1–33). Clevedon: Multilingual Matters.
Pavlenko, A. and Blackledge, A. (eds) (2004b) *Negotiation of Identities in Multilingual Contexts*. Clevedon: Multilingual Matters.
Pedersen, I.L. (2003) Traditional dialects of Danish and the de-dialectisation 1900–2000. *International Journal of the Sociology of Language* 159, 9–28.
Pharao, N. and Hansen, G.F. (2005) Prosodiske træk i et- og tosprogede unges københavnsk [Prosodic features in the speech of mono- and bilingual Copenhagen youths]. *Danske Talesprog* 6/2005, 1–50.
Philipsson, A. (2007) Interrogative Clauses and Verb Morphology in L2 Swedish. Theoretical Interpretations of Grammatical Development and Effects of Different Elicitation Techniques. PhD thesis. Stockholm: Centre for Research on Bilingualism.
Piller, I. and Takahashi, K. (2006) A passion for English: Desire and the language market. In A. Pavlenko (ed.) *Bilingual Minds: Emotional Experience, Expression and Representation* (pp. 59–83). Clevedon: Multilingual Matters.
Podesva, R. (2007) Phonation type as a stylistic variable: The use of falsetto in constructing a persona. *Journal of Sociolinguistics* 11 (4), 478–504.
Potter, R.A. (1995) *Spectacular Vernaculars: Hip-hop and the Politics of Postmodernism*. Albany, NY: State University of New York Press.
Pratt, M.L. (1987) Linguistic utopias. In N. Fabb, D. Attridge, A. Durant and C. McCabe (eds) *The Linguistics of Writing* (pp. 48–66). Manchester: Manchester University Press.
Prentice, J. (2010) Påraksak. Om idiomatiska, figurativa och konventionaliserade flerordsuttryck bland ungdomar i flerspråkiga miljöer [Word combinations and conventionalized expressions among adolescent language users in multilingual environments]. PhD thesis, University of Gothenburg.
Preston, D. (1996) Whaddayaknow? The modes of folk linguistic awareness. *Language Awareness* 5 (1), 40–75.
Preston, D. (2010) Variation in language regard. In E. Zeigler, P. Gilles and J. Scharloth (eds) *Variatio delectat:Empirische Evidenzen und theoretische Passungen sprachlicher Variation* (für Klaus J. Mattheier zum 65. Geburtstag.) Frankfurt am Main: Peter Lang.

Prince, E.F. (1992) The ZPG letter: Subjects, definiteness, and information-status. In W.C. Mann and S.A. Thompson (eds) *Discourse Description: Diverse Linguistic Analyses of a Fund-Raising Text* (pp. 295–325). Amsterdam/Philadelphia: John Benjamins Publishing Co.

Pripp, O. (2002) Mediabilder och levd erfarenhet. In I. Ramberg and O. Pripp (eds) *Fittja, världen och vardagen [Media picture and lived experience]* (pp. 41–72). Tumba: Mångkulturellt centrum.

Quist, P. (2000) Ny københavnsk 'multietnolekt'. Om sprogbrug blandt unge i sprogligt og kulturelt heterogene miljøer [New Copenhagen 'multiethnolect'. On language use among youth in linguistically and culturally heterogeneous environments]. *Danske Talesprog* 1, 143–212.

Quist, P. (2003) Et flydende sprogsamfund? Sociolingvistikkens 'sprogsamfund' historisk og teoretisk [A fluid speech community? The concept of 'speech community' in sociolinguistics historically and theoretically]. *Danske Talesprog* 4, 37–58.

Quist, P. (2005) Stilistiske Praksisser i Storbyens Heterogene Skole. En etnografisk og sociolingvistisk undersøgelse af sproglig variation [Stylistic practices in the urban, heterogeneous high school. An ethnographic and sociolinguistic study]. PhD thesis, Copenhagen: Department of Scandinavian Research/Dialectology, Copenhagen University.

Quist, P. (2008) Sociolinguistic approaches to multiethnolect: Language variety and stylistic practice. *International Journal of Bilingualism* 12 (1 & 2), 43–61.

Quist, P. (forthcoming) *Stilistisk praksis. Unge og sprog i den senmoderne storby [Stylistic Practice. Youth and language in the late modern city]*. Copenhagen: Museum Tusculanum.

Quist, P. and Jørgensen, J.N. (2007) Crossing – negotiating social boundaries. In P. Auer and L. Wei (eds) *Handbook of Multilingualism and Multilingual Communication* (pp. 371–389). Berlin: Mouton de Gruyter.

Rampton, B. (1995a) *Crossing: Language and Ethnicity Among Adolescents*. London: Longman.

Rampton, B. (1995b) Language crossing and the problematisation of ethnicity and socialisation. *Pragmatics* 5 (4), 485–513.

Rampton, B. (1998) Speech community. In J. Verscheren, J-O. Östman, J. Blommaert and C. Bulcaen (eds) *Handbook of Pragmatics*. Amsterdam/Philadelphia: John Benjamins.

Rampton, B. (2006a) *Language in Late Modernity. Interaction in an Urban School*. Cambridge: Cambridge University Press.

Rampton, B. (2006b) *Crossing: Language and Ethnicity among Adolescents* (2nd edn). Manchester: St Jerome Press.

Rampton, B. (2009) Ritual more than performance in crossing and stylisation. *Language in Society* 38 (2), 149–176.

Roberts, C. and Street, B. (1997) Spoken and written language. In F. Coulmas (ed.) *The Handbook of Sociolinguistics* (pp. 168–186). Oxford: Blackwell.

Romaine, S. and Lange, D. (1991) The use of like as a marker of reported speech and thought: A case of grammaticalization in progress. *American Speech* 66 (3), 227–279.

Røyneland, U. (2009) Dialects in Norway – catching up with the rest of Europe? In D. Britain and R. Vandekerckhove (eds) *Are Dialects in Europe Dying? Special Issue of the International Journal of the Sociology of Language* 196/197, 7–30.

Røyneland, U. (in prep.) Phonological characteristics associated with the Norwegian speech of adolescents in multilingual and multicultural communities of practice in Oslo. A subproject in UPUS/Oslo.

Røynesdal, H.H. (2007) Diversitet og aksept. Språkpraksis og språkhaldningar blant sju ungdomar på Holmlia [Diversity and Acceptance. Language practices and language attitudes among seven young people at Holmlia]. Master's thesis, University of Bergen.
Runfors, A. (2003) *Mångfald, motsägelser och marginaliseringar: en studie av hur invandrarskap formas i skolan*. Stockholm: Prisma.
Sandberg, S. (2005) Stereotypiens dilemma, iscenesettelser av etnisitet på "gata" [The dilemma of stereotypes. Self-directed acts of ethnicity in the 'street']. *Tidsskrift for ungdomsforskning* 5 (2), 27–46.
Sandberg, S. (2009) A narrative search for respect. *Deviant Behavior* 30, 487–510.
Sandberg, S. and Pedersen, W. (2006) *Gatekapital [Street Capital]*. Oslo: Universitetsforlaget.
Sandøy, H. (2006) Nordiske språkkulturar i møte med globaliseringa [Scandinavian language cultures meeting globalisation]. In H. Sandøy and K. Tenfjord (eds) *Den nye norsken? Nokre peilepunkt under globaliseringa* (pp. 73–98). Oslo: Novus forlag.
Sebba, M. and Wootton, T. (1998) We, they and identity: Sequential versus identity-related explanation in code-switching. In P. Auer (ed.) *Code-Switching in Conversation. Language, Interaction and Identity* (pp. 262–286). London: Routledge.
Seim, I.M.H. (2007) Identitet og etnisitet i samtale: En analyse av innhold og struktur i en samtale mellom to ungdommer i et flerkulturelt miljø i Oslo [Identity and ethnicity in conversation: An analysis of content and structure in a conversation between two teenagers in a multicultural environment in Oslo]. MA thesis, University of Oslo.
Sickinghe, A-V. (2005) Getting across: A trilingual five-year-old's language socialisation through repair. MA thesis, University of Oslo.
Sjögren, A. (2001) Den lilla röda stugan i Fittja. Institutionell svenskhet som uteslutande mekanism [The little red room in Fittja. Institutional Swedishness as an expelling mechanism]. In B. Blehr (ed.) *Kritisk etnologi. Artiklar till Åke Daun* (pp. 136–162). Stockholm: Prisma.
Skaaden, H. (1998) In short supply of language. Signs of first language attrition in the speech of adult migrants. PhD thesis, Oslo: Unipub.
Solheim, R. (2009) Dialect development in a melting pot: The formation of a new culture and a new dialect in the industrial town of Høyanger. *Nordic Journal of Linguistics. Sociolinguistics* 32–2, 191–206.
Sollid, H. (2005) *Språkdannelse og -stabilisering i møtet mellom norsk og kvensk [Language development and stabilisation in the encounter between Norwegian and Kven]*. Oslo: Novus.
Sollid, H. (2008) Autentisitet på nordnorsk [Authenticity in Northern Norwegian]. *Målbryting* 9, 69–91.
Sollid, H. and Eide, K M. (2007) Om verbplassering og så-konstruksjonen i to språkmøter [On verb placement and så-constructions in two language contact settings]. In *NOA. Norsk som andrespråk* 2, 5–32.
Solomon, T. (2005) "Living underground is tough": Authenticity and locality in the hip-hop community in Istanbul, Turkey. *Popular Music* 24 (1), 1–20.
Spindler, G. and Spindler, L. (1971) *Dreamers without Power: The Menomini Indians*. New York: Holt, Rinehart and Winston.
Statistics Denmark (2009) On WWW at http://www.dst.dk/. Accessed 20.02.09.
Statistics Norway (2010) On WWW at http://www.ssb.no/english/. Accessed 04.01.10.
Statistics Sweden (2009) On WWW at http://www.ssd.scb.se/databaser/makro/ Accessed 25.12.09.
Stroud, C. (2004) Rinkeby Swedish and semilingualism in language ideological debates: A Bourdieuean perspective. *Journal of Sociolinguistics* 8 (2), 196–214.

Stroud, C. and Wingstedt, M. (1989) Språklig chauvinism? [*Linguistic chauvinism?*] *Invandrare och Minoriteter* 4–5, 5–8.
Svendsen, B.A. (2004) Språkvalg, flerspråklige ferdigheter og språklig sosialisering hos norsk-filippinske barn i Oslo [Language choice, multilingual competences and linguistic socialization among Norwegian-Filipino children in Oslo]. PhD thesis, Oslo: Unipub.
Svendsen, B.A. (2006) Flerspråklig identitet [Multilingual identity]. *Nordand* 1, 33–55.
Svendsen, B.A. (2009) Flerspråklighet i teori og praksis [Multilingualism in theory and practice]. In R. Hvistendahl (ed.) *Flerspråklighet i skolen* (pp. 28–59). Oslo: Universitetsforlaget.
Svendsen, B.A. and Røyneland, U. (2008) Multiethnolectal facts and functions in Oslo, Norway. *International Journal of Bilingualism* 12 (1 & 2), 63–83.
Svenska Akademiens Grammatik [The Swedish Academy Grammar] (SAG) (1999) Stockholm: Norstedts ordbok.
Svensson, G. (2007) Funktion och betydelse hos duvet i två gymnasistgrupper i Malmö [Function and meaning of 'duvet' (you know) in two groups of adolescents in upper secondary school]. In L. Ekberg (ed.) *Språket hos dungomdar i en flerspråkig miljö i Malmö* (pp. 78–119). Nordlund 27. Lund: Lund University.
Svensson, G. (2009) Diskurspartiklar hos ungdomar i mångspråkiga miljöer i Malmö [Discourse particles among adolescents in multilingual contexts in Malmö]. PhD thesis, Lund: Department of Scandinavian Languages, Lund University.
Tajfel, H. (1981) *Human Groups and Social Categories*. Cambridge: Cambridge University Press.
Tannen, D. (1984) *Conversational Style: Analyzing Talk among Friends*. Norwood, NJ: Ablex Publishing Corporation.
Teleman, U., Hellberg, S. and Andersson, E. (1999) *Svenska Akademiens grammatik* [The Grammar of Swedish Academy]. Stockholm: Norstedts Ordbok.
Thornton, S. (1995) *Club Cultures: Music, Media and Subcultural Capital*. Cambridge: Polity Press.
Tingsell, S. (2007) Reflexivt och personligt pronomen: anaforisk syftning hos ungdomar i flerspråkiga storstadsmiljöer [Reflexive and personal pronoun: anaphoric aiming among youth in multilingual cities]. PhD thesis, University of Gothenburg.
Trosterud, T. (2001) Genustilordning i norsk er regelstyrt [Gender assignment is governed by rules]. *Norsk lingvistisk tidsskrift* 19 (1), 29–57.
Trudgill, P. (1974) *The Social Differentiation of English in Norwich*. Cambridge: Cambridge University Press.
Trudgill, P. (1986) *Dialects in Contact*. Oxford: Blackwell.
Turker, E. (2000) Turkish-Norwegian codeswitching. Evidence from intermediate and second generation Turkish immigrants in Norway. PhD thesis, Oslo: Unipub.
Underhill, R. (1988) Like is, like, focus. *American Speech* 63 (3), 234–246.
UPUS. Developmental processes in urban linguistic contexts in Norway. On WWW at http://www.hf.uio.no/iln/forskning/forskningsprosjekter/upus/english/. Accessed 10.01.10.
Utrzén, A. (in prep.) Concepts and expressions of politeness in Swedish among young people in multilingual urban settings [preliminary title]. PhD thesis, University of Gothenburg.
Wagner, J. (1999) Faglig identitet og faglig udvikling i dansk som andetsprog [Scientific identity and development in Danish as a second language]. In A. Holmen and K. Lund (eds) *Studier i dansk som andetsprog* (pp. 167–197). Copenhagen: Akademisk Forlag.

Wenger, E. (1998) *Communities of Practice*. Cambridge: Cambridge University Press.
Werndin, M. (in prep.) Skilda attityder, diskurser och utrymmen för identitetsförhandlingar i tre skolor i Stockholm [Differences in attitudes, discourses and spaces of identity negotiation in three schools in Stockholm] [preliminary title]. PhD thesis, Stockholm University.
Western, K. (1978) *A-endinger i Oslo-mål [A-endings in Oslo dialect]*. Skrifter fra Talemålsundersøkelsen i Oslo (TAUS) 5, Universitetet i Oslo: Institutt for nordisk språk og litteratur.
Wiese, H. (2006) "Ich mach dich Messer" – Grammatische Produktivität in Kiezdeutsch. *Linguistische Berichte* 207, 245–273.
Wiese, H. (2009) Grammatical innovation in multiethnic urban Europe: New linguistic practices among adolescents. *Lingua* 119, 782–806.
Wiggen, G. (1990) Oslo bymål [Oslo urban dialect]. In E.H. Jahr (ed.) *Den store dialektboka* (pp. 179–184). Oslo: Novus.
Zahn, C.J. and Hopper, R. (1985) Measuring language attitudes: The speech evaluation instrument. *Journal of Language and Social Psychology* 4 (2), 113–123.

Index

Aarhus adolescent language, 210–212, 221t–222t
allophone, 71
alternative grammar, 160
attitude, 198
– scales, 181f
– as spoken by immigrants and children, 3–4
– studies, 180, 207, 208
– toward speakers and ways of speaking, 180–181
authority register, 140

backbeat, 167
bilingual children, 6–7
bilingual development, 1
blattedebatten, 186
blattesvenska, 186–187
Borta i tankar (Wenger), 142, 145, 147–149, 154
– styling and stylization, 152–153

City School, 199–204
– style clusters, 191, 192t–193t
classical language attitude studies, 208
clause initial nonsubjects. See XSV
code-alternation, 129–130
code switching, 7, 163–164
Copenhagen adolescents
– community of practice, 190, 198, 199, 204
– linguistic practice and stereotypes, 189–206
– phonetic variation, 193–197
– social categories and practice, 190–193
– social identity, 198, 199
– speakers perceptions, 197–199
– verbal guise study, 199–204
Copenhagen multiethnolect prosody, 79–95
– average vowel durations for two structures comparison, 90f
– current investigation preliminaries, 80–81
– expected *vs.* observed quantity, 91t
– fundamental frequency, 91–93
– perceived vowel quantity, 90–91
– phonologically short and long vowels duration, 87–90
– phonological units phonetic properties, 85–86
– recording process and segmentation, 85

– recordings preliminary recordings, 83–84
– rhythm, 80, 94
– short unstressed stressed vowels, 86
– subjects, 82, 84f
– test design and implementation, 81–86
– test words, 82, 83t
– token distributions, 88f
Copenhagen Steak House
– data analyses, 130–131
– discussion, 140–141
– identity work in interaction and enregisterment, 128–130
– linguistic features, 135–140
– microscope, 135–136
– polylingual interaction, 131–135
– polylingualism concept, 127–138
– polylingualism exploring linguistic practices, 127–141
– register formations displays and uptakes, 135–140
cultural model of action, 129, 140, 141

deception, 151
Denmark language and ethnicity among adolescents, 207–224
– Aarhus adolescent language, 210–212
– Aarhus boys looks and speech, 221t
– Aarhus girls looks and speech, 221t, 222t
– Christian recognition, 214f, 217f
– conclusions, 224
– identification, 221–224
– local speech forms, 213t
– Maja recognition, 214f, 217f
– methodology, 208–210
– minority background boys looks and speech, 222t
– minority background girls looks and speech, 223t
– multiethnic speech forms, 213t
– Orhan recognition, 214f, 215f
– preliminary conclusions, 220
– respondents, 210t
– Saad recognition, 214f, 216f
– Samira recognition, 214f, 218f
– Trine recognition, 214f, 219f
– voice pseudonym, 213t
– voice recognition, 214f
– voices, 212–214, 213t
– voices recognition, 214–220

Denmark sociolinguistic study
- Køge Project, 6–8
- multilingualism and dialectology multiethnolect, 8–9
- social and stylistic practices, 9–10
- sociolect, 8
- youth and multilingual practices, 6–11
dialect diversity, 16
dialect levels, 14
discourse
- function, 18, 22, 28
- identity, 140
- marker, 17, 23, 24, 131, 212
- particle, 5, 15, 144
- referent, 18, 25–28, 62, 63

early bilingual development, 1
Elixir (Wenger), 142
- inversion, 145–146
- monolingual Swedish background, 149–150
- noninversion, 145–146
- stylization, 151, 154
enregisterment, 127–130
ethnicity. *See also* Denmark language and ethnicity among adolescents; multiethnolect
- adolescent awareness, 104
- community and adolescents, 223
- important parameter, 222
- intersecting with geography, 208
- intersecting with linguistic variation, 102, 106, 210
- negotiations of identities, 101
- neighborhoods, 99
- nonstandard variants, 195t
- stereotypes, 189
- within streets, 120, 121
ethnographic study, 9
Ett öga rött (Khemiri), 142
- deception, 151–152
- monolingual Swedish background, 149–150
- noninversion, 146–147, 151–152

F0 contour, 76f
- range, 75f
F0 tracings
- stress group pattern, 92f
Finnish, 3–4
- imitated, 106
- research focus, 1
focus sample, 33–36, 34
foreign accent
- adolescents speaking Swedish, 65–67
- attitude towards, viii, 16, 178
- detecting, 183
foreign-born persons
- Gothenburg, Malmö, Stockholm, and Sweden, 2t

gangster discourse, 159
gender, 190
- agreement, 62–63
- Eastern *vs.* Western systems, 59–60
- mixture, 60–61
- nonstandard variants, 195t
- Oslo, Norway, 59–63
- stereotypes, 189
genus simplification, 164
grammaticalization, 27, 29
- and functions in discourse, 63

hip-hop. *See also* Oslo, Norway, hip-hop street language
- admiration, 168–169
- cultural resistance movement, 157
- gangster discourse, 163
- improvisation, 169
- major language, 158, 168, 169
- minor language, 158
- rhythmic beats, 167
- Signifyin(g) similarity and difference, 162
- verbal strategies, 158
hip-hop vernacular, 157–158

identity, 114–117, 132–133. *See also* Swedish suburban transnational identifications
- discourse, 140
- linguistic diversity, 141
- linguistic features, 141
- multilingual young people, 4
- registers, 141
- semiotic potential, 128
immigrants, 12, 224
- attitude, 3–4
- children, 6–7
- children's language shift, 1
- multiethnolect, 68
- music, 162
indefinite article
- feminine, 60
intelligibility, 157

kebabnorsk, 161
Kebab Norwegian, 111, 122–125, 160
Khemiri, Jonas Hassen, 142, 146–147, 151–152
Køge Project, 6–8, 11

language. *See also* Copenhagen adolescents, linguistic practice and stereotypes; Stockholm, Sweden, studying listener perceptions
- attitudes, 16, 170, 172, 174, 180, 198, 207, 208
- crossing, 165
- internal variables, 40
- maintenance, 1, 3, 13
- mixing, 128

– recognition, 170–188, 189–202, 207–224
– shift, 1, 15
– social relations, 129
– use, 1–8, 13–14, 17, 28, 45, 111, 144–145, 153–155, 193
– variations, 13, 170–187, 189, 207, 211, 212
languagers, 128
lexical level, 13
lexical loans, 53
linguistic behavior
– *vs.* speech reflections, 52
linguistic diversity, 141
linguistic features
– enregistering on level of interaction, 141
– everyday interactions, 129
literary use of multiethnic youth language noninversion in Swedish fiction, 142–155
– analysis, 149–154
– Halim's language, 146
– inversion and noninversion in standard Swedish and learner language, 143–144
– inversion as stylization and deception, 150–153
– language use and literature stylization, 153–154
– literary realism, 150, 152
– literary texts noninversion, 145–149
– noninversion in language use of young people from multilingual areas, 144–145
– performance, 143, 150–152
loan words, 13, 14
– gender, 60

M1. *See* Minoritet1 (M1)
Malmö, Sweden extended uses of 'Sån' (Such)
– among adolescents, 17–30
– informants and data, 19–20
– meaning and use of 'Sån' as determiner, 25–28
– polyfunctional 'Sån', 20–25
– 'Sån' construed without indefinite article, 26t
Minoritet1 (M1), 158–159
– ambiguous character, 163
– hybrid language variety, 160
– lyrics, 162
– underground environment, 159–160
Multiethnic Youth Language, 17–28, 49–61, 111–124, 142, 148, 153. *See also* Oslo, Norway, multiethnic youth language
– defined, 155
multiethnolect, 210–211. *See also* Swedish multiethnolect pronunciation
– expected *vs.* observed quantity, 91t
– immigrant background, 68
– listeners' share, 69f
– subphonemic salient contrast, 71

multiethnolect prosody, 79–95
multilingual urban contexts, 67. *See also* Norway linguistic practices in multilingual urban contexts
– adolescents' language practices, 13
multilingual young people
– identity development, 4

navigating, 185
noninversion. *See* literary use of multiethnic youth language noninversion in Swedish fiction
North School, 200
Norway linguistic practices in multilingual urban contexts, 12–16
– UPUS Project, 14–16
Norwegian 2 (Norsk 2), 161

oral language
– sociolinguistic and interactional socio-pragmatic perspective, 13
Oslo, Norway, hip-hop street language, 156–169
– difference and ambiguity, 162–164
– Language and Music connections, 165–168
– lyrics street language features, 164–165
– Minoritet1, 158–159
– mistake becomes a take, 168–169
– rap game, 157–158
– street language, 159–160
– vernacular, 157–158, 161–162
Oslo, Norway, multiethnic youth language, 111–126
– accompanying verbal excitement, 121
– community feeling, 120
– data and participants, 111
– East-Enders *vs.* West-Enders, 116–121
– east-west dichotomy, 120
– identity, 114–115, 116–117
– in-group phenomenon, 116
– Kebab Norwegian and bad Norwegian link, 122–125
– labelling by public and young people, 121–122
– language name, 124f
– linguistic features, 112
– minority's language, 119–120
– multiethnolectal style, 113
– optional linguistic practice, 114
– peer conversations, 113
– purpose, 114–115
– research questions, 111–112
– socioeconomic differences, 118–119
– *vs.* South-Eastern Norwegian, 114f
– speaking Wollah to create posh West End, 115–119
– togetherness, 119
– toughness and aggressiveness, 120–121

Oslo, Norway structural aspects of Norwegian language
- background, 49
- characteristics in previous readings, 50
- characteristics in recorded speech data, 53–63
- data, 51
- different speech situations, 52
- findings, 52–53
- grammatical gender, 59–63
- informants, 51, 51t
- spoken among adolescents in multilingual settings, 49–64
- study design, 51–52
- V2 constraint violations, 53–59
- words emphasis, 52–53
othering, 128–129, 134

pan-immigrant, 224
peer conversation, 14, 128
perception, 170–186, 189–204, 207–224
- experiment, 19–20
phonetic variation
- Copenhagen adolescents, 193–197
- nonstandard variants, 194t
polylingualism, 7–8, 127. *See also* Copenhagen Steak House, polylingualism exploring linguistic practices
prosody, 52, 70–71, 76, 176. *See also* Copenhagen multiethnolect prosody; Swedish multiethnolect pronunciation
- rap, 165
- South-East Norwegian, 166

rap. *See also* Oslo, Norway, hip-hop street language, rap game
- lyrics and social group, 164
resistance vernacular, 157
rinkebysvenska phenomenon, 50, 170, 197
Rinkeby Swedish, 182t, 197. *See also* Stockholm, Sweden, studying listener perceptions
- defined, 171
- obituary notice, 186f
Rosengård Swedish, 17, 19, 20, 29, 65, 71, 171, 185

'Sån'. *See also* Malmö, Sweden extended uses of 'Sån' (Such)
- comparative pronoun, 27
- comparative use, 20–21
- deictical use, 21
- demonstrative use, 21
- descriptive meaning, 28
- determiner, 17, 18, 20–22, 25–28
- discourse marker, 23–24
- focusing, 18, 22, 23
- investigative use, 29

- recognitional function, 22
- *vs.* såhär, 24–25
segmented wave form, 73f, 74f
semantic differential scales, 180
sequential microanalysis, 127
Signifyin(g), 158, 161–162
slang, 13, 14
social attractiveness, 209
social categorization, 128–129, 190
social meaning
- global patterns of variation, 189
- microanalyses, 189
social practice, 190, 191
- category, 195–196
- Copenhagen adolescents, 190–193
- linguistic variation, 195, 197
social relations
- language, 129
sociolinguistic awareness, 170. *See also* Copenhagen adolescents, linguistic practice and stereotypes
- among adolescents, 207
- and attitudes, 180
- differences, 172
speakers
- attitude toward, 198
- perceptions, 197–199
- profile evaluation, 201t
speech
- model labeling, 160
- personality, 208
- speakers' background, 69t
- styles, 209
status, 209
stereotypes, 189, 198–199. *See also* Copenhagen adolescents
- ethnicity, 189
- gender, 189
- questionnaires, 200
stigmatizing label, 111
Stockholm, Sweden, studying listener perceptions, 170–188
- all listeners' guesses on residence, 177f
- attitudes toward speakers, 180–181
- awareness, 172
- factor analysis of attitude scales, 181f
- labeling ways of speaking, 181–184, 182t, 183t
- language variation Rinkeby Swedish, 170–188
- lexicon, 176
- listeners' guesses on origination and length of residence, 179f
- macro level reflections public discourse and labeling, 185–187
- navigating in linguistic space of young Stockholm, 184–185
- prosody, 176
- results, 174–178

- schools, 178
- sociolect, 170, 188n
- sociolinguistic, 170, 172, 180
- Stockholm subway map with participating schools, 173f
- study design, 172–174
- verbal guise, 172
- ways of speaking, 180–181
street language, 160, 161
- concentration, 164
stress correlate duration, 74
style clusters
- City School, 191, 192t–193t
- nonstandard variants, 196t
style group, 193
stylization, 9–10, 127, 130, 150–151, 152–153
subconscious attitude, 198
subject verb order. *See* Oslo, Norway structural aspects of Norwegian language; Swedish subject-verb order variation; XSV
Swedish
- attitude as spoken by immigrants and children, 3–4
- foreign-sounding varieties, 3
- as second language, 3, 32, 34
- used by immigrants and children, 3
Swedish Multiethnic Youth Language, 142
Swedish multiethnolect pronunciation, 65–78
- affricate, 71–72
- allophone, 72
- auditory and acoustic analyses, 68
- context sensitivity, 69–70
- delimitation of variety and selection of speakers, 66–68
- delimiting variety, 68–69
- method, 66–69
- multiethnolect and speakers' background, 68–69
- results and discussion, 69–77
- segmentals, 70–72
- suprasegmentals, 72–77
Swedish multiethnolect suprasegmentals
- intonational patterns, 74–77
- temporal patterns, 73–74
Swedish research on language, 1–5
- multilingual urban settings, 1–5
- sociolinguistic research in multilingual communities, 3–4
- substudies, 5
- SUF project, 4–5
Swedish subject verb order variation
- literary use, 145–149
Swedish subject-verb order variation, 31–48
- analysis procedure, 34–35
- different background variables importance, 40–43
- focus sample, 36t

- large sample, 33
- large sample results distribution, 36t
- linguistic context importance, 37–40
- participants and data, 33–34
- subject-verb inversion after topic placeholder, 39–40
- XSV as linguistic strategy, 43–47
- XSV relatively infrequent use, 35–37
- in young people in multilingual urban areas, 31–48
Swedish suburban transnational identifications, 96–110
- among adolescents, 96–110
- culture, 97
- dominant societal discourse, 98–100
- education, 99
- ethnographic fieldwork, 97–98
- globalisation, 97, 101, 107, 108
- identification preference monitoring, 109
- identity negotiations, 100
- interactive positionings, 104–109
- interactive space, 108
- Internet, 107–109
- linguistic play, 107
- media, music, and movies, 99, 101
- nationality and tradition, 101
- negative media picture, 105–106
- peer group, 104–107
- power, 97, 98, 99, 105
- reflective positionings, 100–104
- social interaction, 101–104
- stigmatization, 105
- transnationalism, 97, 101, 102
- youth identity, 97
switching, 185
syntactic characterization, 53

telegram style, 167
tonal contour
- multiethnolect *vs.* Copenhagen, 92f
two-syllable words
- trochaic pronunciation, 165

underground imagery, 158–159
underground urban culture, 164

variety, xv, 171
V2 constraint violations, 31–32, 53–59
- background and assumptions, 53–54
- linguistic context role, 58
- literary use, 145–149
- parental background, 58
- speaker types, 55–57
- XSV distribution in two speech situations, 54–55
verbal guise method, 198–199
- City School, 199–204
- matched guise, 172
- social class, 173

verbal performance mode, 162
voice pseudonym, 213t

Wenger, Alejandro Leiva, 142, 145–149, 151–154
Wollah. *See* Oslo, Norway, multiethnic youth language
word order. *See also* XSV
– deviations, 50
– noninverted, 202–203
– nonstandard Rashid9, 202
– pattern, 143–144
– standard Norwegian, 168
– V2 rule, 167
– X-clauses, 35
– XSV, 54
– XVS, 53, 167

X-clauses, 35–38, 40
– subject inversions, 38
XSV, 32–33
– after clause-initial subordinate clause, 39
– contestation act, 46–47
– contexts and occurrences, 56t
– contexts in interview data *vs.* peer conversation data, 59
– distribution in two speech situations, 54–55
– high-involvement style, 43–45
– learner phenomenon, 41–42
– linguistic strategy, 45–46
– as linguistic strategy, 43–47
– number of available contexts, 54t
– relatively infrequent use, 35–37
– retellings, 40–41

For Product Safety Concerns and Information please contact our EU Authorised Representative:

Easy Access System Europe

Mustamäe tee 50

10621 Tallinn

Estonia

gpsr.requests@easproject.com

www.ingramcontent.com/pod-product-compliance
Lightning Source LLC
Chambersburg PA
CBHW070557300426
44113CB00010B/1284